HENRY JAMES, OSCAR WILDE AND AESTHETIC CULTURE

EDINBURGH STUDIES IN TRANSATLANTIC LITERATURES
Series Editors: Susan Manning & Andrew Taylor

With the end of the Cold War and the burgeoning of a global culture, the premises upon which Area Studies were based have come into question. Starting from the assumption that the study of American literatures can no longer operate on a nation-based or exceptionalist paradigm, the books in this new series work within a comparative framework to interrogate place-based identities and monocular visions. The authors attempt instead to develop new paradigms for literary criticism in historical and contemporary contexts of exchange, circulation and transformation. Edinburgh Studies in Transatlantic Literatures seeks uniquely to further the critical, theoretical and ideational work of the developing field of transatlantic literary studies.

Titles in the series include:

Henry James, Oscar Wilde and Aesthetic Culture
Michèle Mendelssohn

Ethnicity and Cultural Authority: From Arnold to Du Bois
Daniel G. Williams

HENRY JAMES, OSCAR WILDE AND AESTHETIC CULTURE

◆ ◆ ◆

MICHÈLE MENDELSSOHN

EDINBURGH UNIVERSITY PRESS

Edinburgh University Press Ltd
22 George Square, Edinburgh

Typeset in 11/13 Adobe Sabon by
Servis Filmsetting Ltd, Manchester and
printed and bound in Great Britain by
Antony Rowe Ltd, Chippenham, Wilts

A CIP record for this book is available from the British Library

ISBN 978 0 7486 2385 3 (hardback)

CONTENTS

ACKNOWLEDGEMENTS

At Cambridge University, where I began this book, at Harvard and Boston University, where I wrote most of it, and at Edinburgh University, where I finished it, I encountered a number of close readers who deserve special thanks for their counsel and encouragement. First among these is Adrian Poole, who saw this project through its earliest phase with a great deal of care and consideration. John Picker and others kindly acted as intellectual good shepherds during my extended research period in the 'other Cambridge' under the auspices of the Canada-US Fulbright Foundation. At Boston University, I was blessed to encounter Christopher Ricks and Frances Whistler, who proved to be rigorous and sympathetic readers. My colleagues at Edinburgh have also enriched my thinking; for this I would especially like to thank Susan Manning, Andy Taylor and Jonathan Wild. I am particularly grateful to Andy, who tirelessly read through several draft chapters, and whose judicious critiques helped me shape this book. Many thanks also to Sonja Nikkila, who assisted me with the notes and bibliography.

At different stages in this project, I had the benefit of conversations or correspondence that substantially enriched my work. For this I would like to thank Mary Warner Blanchard, Dennis Denisoff, Sarah Emsley, Charlotte Gere, Phillip Horne, Patrick Leary and the members of the VICTORIA-listserv, Leonee Ormond, Leah Price, Bernard Prusak, Peter Raby, David C. Rose, John Stauffer, John Stokes, Emma Sutton, Pam Thurschwell and Peter Walker. Caroline Dakers was instrumental in helping me obtain images of Clouds House.

For permission to reproduce material I would like to thank: the National Library of Scotland; the British Library; the Rare Book, Manuscript and Special Collections Library at Duke University; the Houghton Library at Harvard University; the William Andrews Clark Memorial Library at UCLA; the Rauner Special Collections Library at Dartmouth College; the Rare Books and Special Collections Division at McGill University; the New York State Library; Bay James; Lord Max Egremont; Mrs Helen Brandon-Jones. Every effort has been made to trace current copyright and permission holders, and I apologise in advance for any unintentional omission of those whom I have been unable to find.

For their support of my research, I would like to thank: the Social Sciences and Humanities Research Council of Canada; King's College, Cambridge; the Cambridge Commonwealth Trust; the Overseas Research Students' Award Scheme (Committee of Vice Chancellors and Principals of the Universities of the United Kingdom); the Allen, Meek and Read Scholarship, Cambridge University; the Canada-US Fulbright Foundation.

My personal debts are many. I am grateful to all my friends for their patience and encouragement, and especially to Anne Vial and Errollyn Wallen. Long ago and an ocean away, I was privileged to find myself in classes taught by Judy Adamson and Antoinette Taddeo. I learned from them both far more than I can begin to say here.

My greatest debt is to my family – Joe, Monique and Maxine. Their love, affirmation and sense of humour sustained me during these last years, and long before. I dedicate this book to them.

LIST OF ABBREVIATIONS

Full details of all works cited are given in the bibliography. The following abbreviations of frequently cited works are used within the text and throughout the endnotes:

Works by Oscar Wilde

LW	*The Complete Letters of Oscar Wilde*, ed. Merlin Holland and Rupert Hart-Davis. London: Fourth Estate, 2000.
PW	*The Importance of Being Earnest and Other Plays*, ed. Peter Raby. Oxford: Oxford UP, 1995.
RW	*Aristotle at Afternoon Tea: The Rare Oscar Wilde*, ed. John Wyse Jackson. London: Fourth Estate, 1991.
SJW	*Selected Journalism*, ed. Anya Clayworth. Oxford: Oxford UP, 2004.
W	*Collins Complete Works of Oscar Wilde*. Glasgow: HarperCollins, 1999.

Works by Henry James

CS1	*Complete Stories, 1864–1874*, ed. Jean Strouse, vol. 1. New York: Library of America, 1999.
CS2	*Complete Stories, 1874–1884*, ed. William Vance, vol. 2. New York: Library of America, 1999.

CS3   *Complete Stories, 1884–1891*, ed. Edward Said, vol. 3. New York: Library of America, 1999.

CS4   *Complete Stories, 1892–1898*, ed. John Hollander, David Bromwich and Denis Donoghue, vol. 4. New York: Library of America, 1996.

CS5   *Complete Stories, 1898–1910*, ed. John Hollander, David Bromwich and Denis Donoghue, vol. 5. New York: Library of America, 1996.

L1, 2, 3, 4   *Letters, 1843–1875*, ed. Leon Edel, vol. 1. Cambridge, MA: Harvard UP, 1974.

Letters, 1875–1883, ed. Leon Edel, vol. 2. Cambridge, MA: Harvard UP, 1975.

Letters, 1883–1895, ed. Leon Edel, vol. 3. Cambridge, MA: Harvard UP, 1980.

Letters, 1895–1916, ed. Leon Edel, vol. 4. Cambridge, MA: Harvard UP, 1984.

LC1   *Literary Criticism: Essays on Literature, American Writers, English Writers*, ed. Leon Edel and Mark Wilson, vol. 1. New York: Library of America, 1984.

LC2   *Literary Criticism: French Writers, Other European Writers, the Prefaces to the New York Edition*, ed. Leon Edel and Mark Wilson, vol. 2. New York: Library of America, 1984.

LL   *Henry James: A Life in Letters*, ed. Philip Horne. London: Allen Lane, 1999.

N1   *Novels, 1871–1880: Watch and Ward, Roderick Hudson, The American, The Europeans, Confidence*, ed. William T. Stafford, vol. 1. New York: Library of America, 1983.

N2   *Novels, 1881–1886: Washington Square, The Portrait of a Lady, The Bostonians*, ed. William T. Stafford, vol. 2. New York: Library of America, 1985.

N3   *Novels, 1886–1890: The Princess Casamassima, The Reverberator, The Tragic Muse*, ed. Daniel

Mark Fogel, vol. 3. New York: Library of America, 1989.

N4   *Novels, 1896–1899: The Other House, The Spoils of Poynton, What Maisie Knew, The Awkward Age*, ed. Myra Jehlen, vol. 4. New York: Library of America, 2003.

Notebooks   *The Complete Notebooks of Henry James*, ed. Leon Edel and Lyall H. Powers. Oxford: Oxford UP, 1987.

Plays   *The Complete Plays of Henry James*, ed. Leon Edel. London: Rupert Hart-Davis, 1949.

Works by Other Authors

Edel *1, 2, 3, 4, 5*   Edel, Leon. *Henry James*, 5 vols. Philadelphia: J. B. Lippincott, 1953–72.

Whistler   Whistler, James McNeill. *The Gentle Art of Making Enemies*, introduction by Alfred Werner. New York: Dover, 1967.

LIST OF FIGURES

We were too far apart to call to each other, but there was a moment at which, at shorter range, some challenge between us, breaking the hush, would have been the right result of our straight mutual stare.

'The Turn of the Screw' (CS4 654)

This in fact I have ever found rather terribly the point – that the figures in any picture, the agents in any drama, are interesting only in proportion as they feel their respective situations; since the consciousness, on their part, of the complication exhibited forms for us their link of connexion with it. But there are degrees of feeling – the muffled, the faint, the just sufficient, the barely intelligent, as we may say; and the acute, the intense, the complete, in a word – the power to be finely aware and richly responsible. It is those moved in this latter fashion who 'get most' out of all that happens to them and who in so doing enable us, as readers of their record, as participators by a fond attention, also to get most. *Their being finely aware – as Hamlet and Lear, say, are finely aware – makes absolutely the intensity of their adventure, gives the maximum of sense to what befalls them.*

Preface to The Princess Casamassima (LC2 1088, emphasis added)

INTRODUCTION

What did it mean 'to be truly aesthetic'? In 1882, J. N. Piercy's of Binghamton, NY would have had us believe that 'being aesthetic' meant buying ice cream and confections at their store (Figure Intro.1, overleaf). If we look more closely at their advertisement, we might also conclude that in the nineteenth century 'being aesthetic' entailed wearing velvet knee breeches, having a predilection for lilies and sunflowers and, most importantly, being Oscar Wilde. What would the citizens of Binghamton have found appealing about Wilde, a young man with exactly one volume of poetry and one play to his name? And what would Wilde, the self-proclaimed apostle of Aestheticism, have found to attract him in rural New York State? Situated nearly 200 miles northwest of Manhattan, at the junction of the Susquehanna and Chenango rivers, late nineteenth-century Binghamton was known for its furniture, wagon and cigar manufacturing[1] – realities that seem far removed from Wilde's world as we now think of it. It is, indeed, difficult to imagine what Americans would have found to interest them in the Irish author of a long poem beginning 'this English Thames is holier far than Rome' (W 786). Yet J. N. Piercy's choice of Wilde as the poster boy for their sweets was a brilliant marketing ploy for it reflected the mania of the time, a fascination with aesthetic culture that gripped Americans from Binghamton to San Francisco, and from Dubuque to Savannah.

Although Americans were aware of Aestheticism before Wilde's highly publicised 1882 lecture tour of the United States and Canada, Wilde became a convenient and controversial symbol of what aesthetic culture entailed. In fact, J. N. Piercy's advertisement is only one

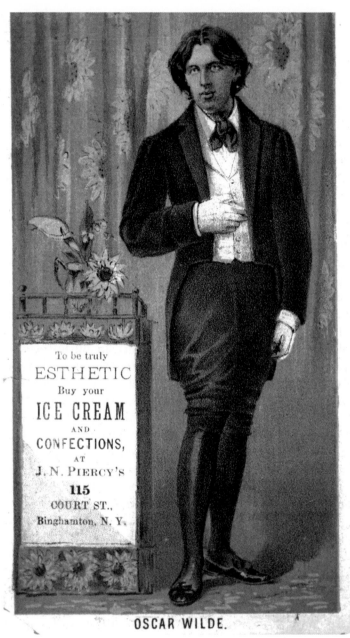

Intro. 1 *'To be truly esthetic buy your ice cream and confections at J. N. Piercy's, 115 Court St., Binghamton, N. Y.', 1882.*
This advertisement closely reproduces the photographic portrait Napoleon Sarony made of Wilde in New York in 1882. (Courtesy of the William Andrews Clark Memorial Library.)

of the scores of trade cards distributed that year that used Wilde to endorse products ranging from hosiery and corsets to stoves and sewing machines.[2] Wilde neither personally endorsed these products, nor received a fee for the use of his image, yet the cards insidiously implied that he was part of this commercial enterprise and that consumerism was an integral part of being 'truly aesthetic'. This image of Aestheticism is difficult to reconcile with the commonplace view of English aesthetes as part of a cultural and artistic elite. In *The Aesthetic Movement in England* (1882), one of the very first studies of the phenomenon of aesthetic culture, Walter Hamilton wrote that the aesthetes were generally thought to be part of 'aristocratic circles'[3] and to belong to the cultural 'Upper Crust' – a claim that does not accord with J. N. Piercy's aesthetic scream for ice cream. English Aestheticism undoubtedly had its commercial side, but it was also intimately and prominently linked to exclusive centres of art and culture, such as London's Grosvenor Gallery, to which Hamilton dedicated an entire chapter. Heralded as the 'Temple of Aestheticism'[4] and 'the Palace of the Aesthetes', the Grosvenor was *the* place to see aesthetic art and people. The gallery's opening celebrations were a veritable who's who of the Anglo-American elite; they included Wilde, Henry James, the Prince of Wales, Mr and Mrs Gladstone, John Ruskin, James Abbott McNeill Whistler, and John Millais.[5]

It was at the Grosvenor's opening in 1877 that James and Wilde almost certainly met for the first time. Although there is no extant record of this meeting, we can imagine that Wilde, decked out in a spectacular cello-shaped coat custom-made for the occasion, would have attracted James's attention, though perhaps not his admiration.[6] Wilde was then a talkative Oxford undergraduate with a passion for Aestheticism and delft, but no serious accomplishments to his name. James, who had recently taken up residence in London, had by then published tales, travel essays and two novels. Wilde and James, aged twenty-three and thirty-four respectively, were both in attendance in their capacity as art critics. It was a measure of their differences that James reviewed the exhibition for the *Nation*, an American magazine with more influence than circulation, while Wilde published his review in the *Dublin University Magazine*. Wilde subsequently sent his review to Walter Pater, whose *Studies in the History of the Renaissance* (1873) was often mooted as a breviary to Aestheticism. Pater responded by inviting Wilde to call on him and, in later years, Wilde described *The Renaissance* as 'that book which has had such a strange influence over my life' (*LW* 735). For his part, James saw the book in an English bookseller's window the year it was published. He disingenuously claimed Pater's study 'treats of several things I know nothing about' (*L1* 391) even as he admitted that he was 'inflamed to think of buying it' – an allusion to the book's well-known concluding encouragement 'to burn always'[7] and maintain the 'flame-like'[8] element of life.

Wilde immortalised the Grosvenor's social and artistic significance in *The Picture of Dorian Gray* (1890), where the first words we hear from the irrepressible aesthete Lord Henry Wotton are that 'the Grosvenor is really the only place' (*W* 18). How could 'the only place' for aesthetic culture be the Grosvenor when Aestheticism had visibly found a footing in an ice cream store in Binghamton, New York? How did an incongruous pair such as James and Wilde participate in shaping Anglo-American Aestheticism, a movement James would commemorate as 'a queer high-flavoured fruit from overseas' (*LC2* 908)?[9] Which version of Wilde – the Grosvenor Gallery art critic or the silk-stockinged lecturer – was truly aesthetic, and which was pathetic sham? Why did 'being aesthetic' become, after 1895, almost a code for 'being homosexual?'[10] How did Wilde, who was perceived by at least one observant nineteenth-century American woman as being of 'undecided'[11] sexuality become 'honoured as a proto-martyr to freedom'[12] by the twentieth century and, in our own time, 'a poster boy for gay liberation'?[13] Was aesthetic sense a vehicle for the social integration of same-sex desires, as Susan Sontag has argued in 'Notes on Camp'?[14] In other words, was aesthetic interior decoration – synonymous in the nineteenth century with 'dadoes, Japanese fans, and peacocks' feathers'[15] – a forerunner of television shows like *Queer Eye for the Straight Guy*? If these questions point up the ambiguities inherent in English and American aesthetic culture, then they hint at the purpose of this book, which is to analyse the conflicting energies that animated what was indubitably one of the most exciting artistic enterprises of the late nineteenth century.

This book tells the story of James's and Wilde's intricate, decades-long relationship and how it shaped transatlantic aesthetic relations. What the book hopes to show is that their relationship allegorises nineteenth-century American and British Aestheticism. *Henry James, Oscar Wilde and Aesthetic Culture* is a parable about two cultures in conflict that stridently externalised their concerns about one another and themselves while quietly internalising each others' values in print, exercising their ideas so that they could strengthen their respective cultures.

Given the paradoxical dynamics outlined above, we are now in a better position to understand what it meant to 'be aesthetic'. Throughout this book Aestheticism will be used to refer to the literary and artistic movement that flourished in Britain and America between 1870 and 1900 and that advanced art for art's sake in opposition to the utilitarian doctrine of moral or practical usefulness. 'Aesthetic culture' will be used to indicate a catholic conception of Aestheticism. In the following pages, the discussion will alternate between these two related expressions, and appropriate capitalization will help the reader distinguish between the two and their application.

Aestheticism was an *argument* about art and culture. According to Wilde, its chief characteristics were to increase appreciation for 'beautiful workmanship' (*RW* 197), to recognise 'the primary importance of the sensuous element in art', and to liberate art from ethical considerations by embracing 'art for art's sake'. In a 1904 essay on Gabriele D'Annunzio, James retrospectively defined Aestheticism as a 'spectacle' (*LC2* 908) and a 'bulwark against ugliness' (935) whose activating principle was 'not easily formulated, but which we may conveniently speak of as that of beauty at any price, beauty appealing alike to the senses and the mind' (908). There could be 'no esthetic [*sic*] beauty' (940) where there was 'no process, no complexity, no suspense'; in short, where art was not intertwined with life. 'Zoological sociability' (939), 'erotic exercise' (937), 'the play closely studied and frankly represented, of the sexual relation' (936) could not be the object of 'detached pictures' (942) but needed to be connected through art to the scope of human experience.

Understood in a historically-contingent sense, Aestheticism stands for a short-lived but heady period of cultural innovation that is often also referred to as the Aesthetic Movement and, occasionally, the Aesthetic School.[16] In order to avoid misconstruing Aestheticism, I should enter a caveat here. Unlike most 'Movements', the aesthetes were not a clique or band pursuing a common goal, but a heterogeneous aggregate of loosely connected people whose accumulated efforts moulded the culture of the day. As E. H. Mikhail succinctly puts it, 'the so-called Movement was in the air, never in committee' and there is some doubt whether the figures we now label aesthetes – James, Morris, Ruskin, Pater, Swinburne, and Whistler among them – would consent to this appellation if they had a say in the matter.[17] What this study hopes to show is that these artists were not invested in Aestheticism despite their divergent views but *because* of them, which is to say that Aestheticism's strength resides in its elegant flexibility, in its ability to encompass oppositions without claiming to reconcile them.

I hope that the foregoing has given the reader a sense of the dramatis personae that will inform this book's critical performance, and I would now like to fill in the social setting that was the backdrop for Wilde's and James's first meeting in 1877. It needs to be said that, despite their differences, the two authors moved in similar and even overlapping social circles. There is no better illustration of these intersections than the Grosvenor's opening, which brought together some of the greatest shapers of late nineteenth-century arts and culture, as even an incomplete list of exhibitors and guests suggests. Edward Burne-Jones was among the artists whose work was exhibited, and whom Wilde and James both praised in their reviews.[18] Also in attendance were Walter Crane (who later illustrated Wilde's *The Happy Prince and Other Tales*); Johnston Forbes-Robertson (for whom James would write *Summersoft*, and to whose brothers Wilde would send *Salomé* and *An Ideal Husband*, among others); the Grosvenor's founders, Lady and Sir Coutts Lindsay (who would provide the germs for 'The Wheel of Time' and *The Spoils of Poynton*);[19] Gustave Moreau (whose painting *L'Apparition* prompted Wilde's *Salomé*); G. F. Watts (who exhibited a portrait of Madeline Wyndham (Figure 5.7), a leading member of a select social group well acquainted with James and Wilde); James McNeill Whistler (the *Nocturne in Blue and Gold* he exhibited belonged to Mrs Wyndham; he was friendly with both Wilde and James). Whistler's soon-to-be enemy, John Ruskin, was also in attendance.[20] *Punch* magazine, which was prone to exaggerate for comic effect, provided a surprisingly accurate account of the Gallery's opening:

> The Grosvenor! the view that's called private,
> Yet all the world seems to be there . . .
> The haunt of the very aesthetic,
> Here come the supremely intense.[21]

The Latent and the Patent or,
Who is the Agent and Who is the Patient?

In Chapter 1 I will discuss in greater detail James's and Wilde's first documented meeting, in 1882. But for now I want to turn the spotlight on a number of figures whose views inform this book: the scholars and critics who have devoted their energies to James, Wilde and Aestheticism. The James-Wilde relationship has been on the critical radar for decades now, yet it often seems to flare up in the same circumstances, and to elicit similar responses. Two misconceptions about the pair are pervasive: first, that Wilde had very little interest in James; second, that James's reaction to Wilde was essentially motivated by sexual fear or panic; in other words, James could only respond to Wilde *qua* homosexual. With regard to the first view, there have been few critics willing to engage seriously with the idea that James influenced Wilde. Foremost among them is Jonathan Freedman, who devotes a chapter of his magisterial study *Professions of Taste: Henry James, British Aestheticism, and Commodity Culture* to analysing the pair's 'quarrels of affinity'[22] in order to show how James absorbed Wilde and eventually 'blaze[d] the trail that leads from British aestheticism to Anglo-American modernism.' That Freedman's is virtually the only voice that has spoken on the subject of James's influence on Wilde says a lot about the implicit critical consensus on the issue. Indeed, criticism seems to operate under the mistaken impression that the relationship was a one-way street: that James did not influence Wilde, or did not do so in any significant way.[23] This is a remarkable assumption, not least because Wilde is so well known for being a supreme anthologiser or, to put it less euphemistically, the century's most famous plagiarist, as I will discuss in Chapters 2 and 3. It defies logic that Wilde would have refrained from borrowing from James (whom we know he read closely), while he freely availed himself of the wisdom of Morris, Swinburne, Whistler, Shakespeare, Sidney, Donne and others.[24]

Moreover, the implicit critical consensus on Wilde's relation to James defies what we know of the complicated ways in which influence works. Indeed, the art historian Michael Baxandall has shrewdly observed that the idea of influence (which applies equally to the visual as well as the literary arts) is premised on a misdirected grammatical bias about 'who is the agent and who is the patient',[25] and who acts upon whom:

> If one says that X influenced Y it does seem that one is saying that X did something to Y rather than that Y did something to X. But in the consideration of good pictures and painters the second is always the more lively reality . . . If we think of Y rather than X as the agent, the vocabulary is much richer and more attractively diversified: draw on, resort to,

avail oneself of, appropriate from, have recourse to, adapt, misunder-
stand, refer to, pick up, take on, engage with, react to, quote, differenti-
ate oneself from, assimilate oneself to, assimilate, align oneself with,
copy, address, paraphrase, absorb, make a variation on, revive, continue,
remodel, ape, emulate, travesty, parody . . . Most of these relations just
cannot be stated the other way around – in terms of X acting on Y rather
than Y acting on X.[26]

I have quoted this long passage because it evokes the many and mul-
tifarious ways in which Wilde and James influenced each other, and
it illustrates this book's axiomatic belief that their relationship was
indeed a two-way street.

The second misconception about the Wilde-James relationship –
that its keynote is panic and loathing – has principally gained acceptance as a result of the influential work of Richard Ellmann, Eve
Kosofsky Sedgwick and Hugh Stevens. Ellmann's 1983 essay 'Henry
James Among the Aesthetes' and his 1987 biography of Wilde suggested that James's reaction to Aestheticism (and thus to Pater and
Wilde as well) was fashioned largely out of sexual fear and homo-
phobia. According to Ellmann, when James read Pater's *Studies in
the History of the Renaissance*, he 'took alarm, he heard the incrim-
inating footfalls . . . he wished to describe himself neither as aesthetic
nor homosexual.'[27] Ellmann believes that James's reaction to Wilde
was similar, and that James perceived Wilde primarily as a sexual
threat:

We must imagine Henry James revolted by Wilde's kneebreeches, con-
temptuous of the self-advertising and pointless nomadism, and nervous
about the sensuality. He informed Mrs Adams [who had called Wilde
'a noodle'] that she was right. ' "Hosscar" Wilde is a fatuous fool,
tenth-rate cad,' 'an unclean beast.' The images are so steamy as to
suggest that James saw in Wilde a threat. For the tolerance of deviation,
or ignorance of it, were alike in jeopardy because of Wilde's flouting
and flaunting. *James's homosexuality was latent, Wilde's was patent. It
was as if James, foreseeing scandal, separated himself from this menace
in motley.*[28]

Jonathan Freedman, Joseph Litvak and Richard A. Kaye approvingly
cite versions of Ellmann's James-Wilde sexual dualism. Still, it cannot
be said that James and Wilde 'perfectly exemplified . . . the latent and
the blatant',[29] nor is it Ellmann who has most forcefully shaped our

common conception of James and Wilde. Alert readers will have noticed that Ellmann's analysis – with its talk of menace, incrimination, deviation, latent and patent homosexuality – is just a footfall away from 'homosexual panic', Sedgwick's powerful theoretical articulation of the phenomenon that will be familiar to readers as 'the most private, psychologized form in which . . . western men experience their vulnerability to the social pressure of homophobic blackmail.'[30] Since her first iteration of the concept in 1985, Sedgwick's theoretical mapping has proved valuable to a large number of scholars who have used it to extend the boundaries of James studies.[31] Although Sedgwick has not discussed James's and Wilde's relationship, she has written about both authors separately and has persuasively argued that James is 'an emboldening figure for a literary discussion of male homosexual panic.'[32] While there is certainly a cogency to speaking about historically freighted sexual anxieties, reducing the exquisite and elaborate patternings of same-sex desire in James's and Wilde's lives and art to Sedgwick's pithy formulation does little to accurately elucidate them. Through its persistent privileging of the secret and its preference for reading silences, this theory turns a deaf ear to the vocal expressions of complicity and sympathy in James and Wilde. For these reasons and more, it would be equally misguided to read James's response to Wilde solely in terms of what Hugh Stevens's *Henry James and Sexuality* calls 'homosexual self-loathing':[33] the phenomenon of 'queers who hate other queers for the particular reason that they are queer.' Such a line of argumentation – which Stevens explains further as 'the discreet loathes the blatant'[34] – essentially updates Ellmann's old chestnut about the covert homosexual rejecting the overt – 'when they come to the beautiful boy, Wilde is all atremble, James all aslant.'[35]

There are good reasons for resisting the all-encompassing energies of the simplifying summations proffered by Ellmann, Sedgwick and Stevens: first, because they imply that Wilde and James could only engage with each other as homosexuals, and that their every interaction was dominated (whether implicitly or explicitly) by a form of same-sex desire, a notion as absurd as it is reductive. As I will show in Chapter 4 in particular, the identity-formation processes in James's and Wilde's plays purposefully and consistently enshrine sexuality within a range of characteristics constitutive of modern selfhood. One of the key images in this book's understanding of selfhood is that of weaving; so, to pick out this one thread and call it the figure in the carpet is to claim that the intricate tapestry of modern selfhood is woven of a single strand, which, as everyone knows, is not the case. In other words: we are more than the sum of our (private) parts. The second reason for a cautious appreciation of these useful theories is quite simply that panic and loathing were not the keynotes of the James-Wilde relationship, as this book will demonstrate. Through a reading of works, letters and conversations in which the authors refer to each other, the book reveals that the themes were puerility, esteem, contempt, admiration, frustration, jealousy, mockery, sympathy, flirtation, fascination, *Schadenfreude*, concern and care.

Despite my reservations about theories such as Ellmann's, Sedgwick's and Stevens's it will be evident in the following chapters that they have informed my work both directly and indirectly. However, this study's outcome also challenges substantially the sufficiency of 'homosexual panic' and 'homosexual self-loathing' descriptors for James's and Wilde's relationship. If we insist on truth in labelling, we cannot unreservedly apply either Sedgwick's or Stevens's theories to the James-Wilde relationship. By the same token, it would be valuable for criticism to reconsider its tendency to apply 'homosexual panic' as a panacea for the explication of difficult relationships. Appealing as it is, it is not a sort of cure-all for social, sexual and emotional complexity. Instead, we should begin to study in earnest the ways in which same-sex associations may be shaped by a very wide range of feelings, many of which are not negative. In Chapter 6, I will illustrate this by examining James's simultaneously flirtatious and sympathetic response to Wilde. James's responses to other homosexual men also suggest that a rich terrain lies before us if we are willing to look beyond the fairly limited horizons of homosexual panic. Consider, for instance, James's responses to other homosexual men. He wrote affectionately and often to Howard Sturgis, a socialite and author who began his homoerotic novel *Tim: A Story of School Life* (1891) with the epigraph 'thy love to me was wonderful, passing the love of women.'[36] More than once, James told Sturgis 'I repeat, almost to indiscretion, that I could live with you.'[37] The letters overflow with playful, humorous and erotic allusions – phrases such as 'my queer tale (or tail)',[38] 'our so happy little congress of two',[39] are characteristic – as well as exaggerated demonstrations of affection such as in James's letter of 1912: 'You have the art of writing letters which make those who already adore you to the verge of dementia slide over the dizzy edge & fairly sit raving their passion.'[40]

Consider also James's letters to Robert Ross, Wilde's literary executor – a Canadian who had attended King's College, Cambridge, openly declared his homosexuality to his family, and lived abroad. Ross and Wilde both told friends that Ross had been Wilde's first lover.[41] In 1912, James warmly wrote to Ross about a banquet 'favouring our friends',[42] and he empathised two years later when Ross entered into a vicious legal battle with Lord Alfred Douglas, Wilde's former lover. In his letters, James showed how deeply moved he was by what he referred to as Ross's 'tragically demoralized state'[43] and Douglas's 'hellish machinations'. He insisted that it was a 'scandal' that the 'authorities' were '*listening* to a man with A.[lfred] D.[ouglas]'s history', since Douglas had incited Wilde to enter into the trial that eventually destroyed him. 'What a state of things when the "authorities" are open to influence from a man with D.'s infamous history! . . . What a torture, truly, is the faculty of pity,'[44] James wrote, demonstrating his sympathy as well as just how much he knew about the private history behind Wilde's public downfall. These playful, empathetic letters bear witness to James's ability to associate with homosexual men in a carefree and open manner. They give the lie to the notion of a perpetually homosexually panicked James and, most importantly, they also invite us to think beyond panic, and towards pleasure.

When it comes to Jamesian sexuality, criticism operates under a logical fallacy. Its willingness to read James's fiction as rife with sophisticated and diverse sexual styles[45] James's been accompanied by a proportional unwillingness to read James's response to Wilde and his works as anything other than negative. In fact, the terms most often marshalled to describe James's sexuality are 'panicked', 'anxiety',[46] 'haunted',[47] and 'frozen'.[48] This does not amount to negative capability, which he is so often taken to epitomise, but to negativity and incapacity. Of course there is some truth to these negative readings of Jamesian sexuality, and yet they do not accurately represent the range of feelings that animated James's response to Wilde. There is another curious effect at work in the critical assessment of the intersection between the author's work and his private life. Indeed, criticism's readiness to grant James knowledge of the negative aspects of desire has been matched by an equal and opposite urge to deny him knowledge of desire's more positive features. By this logic, James becomes a supreme connoisseur of pain who knows virtually nothing of pleasure. One reason for this disparity in criticism is the notorious uncertainty surrounding the specificity of James's sexual preference and identification. Sedgwick has accurately captured the (unhappy?) blank which is Jamesian sexuality in saying that, 'James had – well, exactly that which we now all know that we know not.'[49] Still another reason for the discrepancy in criticism is queer theory's understandable investment in investigating and recovering negative experiences as identity-constituting moments. To this end, concepts such as shame,[50] embarrassment,[51] the unsaid, and the unspeakable have gainfully been recuperated. These critical emphases have resulted in a conspicuous aversion to imagining pleasure in James.[52] If we assign his texts knowledge of all the pain, surely we cannot deny them a share of the pleasure? Whether we know what 'James had' or not, can we imagine that he at least enjoyed some of it, whatever it was? Must we cast James's fictions east of Eden without granting them the lingering taste of the apple? Can we envisage the idea of James admiring, flirting and being sympathetic to a 'posing Somdomite [*sic*]',[53] as Wilde was once called? The following chapters will reveal some the patently positive emotions attendant upon this relationship, along with its ambivalences and rivalries. As well, they will parse the multifaceted nature of James's response to Wilde and demonstrate the connection between negative and positive experiences as identity-constituting moments.

Henry James, Oscar Wilde and Aesthetic Culture reveals the literary relationship between Wilde and James and the aesthetic matrix in which it developed. I use the word 'relationship' with purpose: the works James and Wilde published between the late 1870s and early 1900s reveal a sustained and reciprocal engagement with each other. Although their association was often ambivalent, Wilde and James shared much: social circles and friends; Irish-Protestant backgrounds; comparable sexual proclivities; a deep attraction to Aestheticism, Catholicism and the theatre; concern for commodity, visual and material culture; and a lifelong fascination with psychology. How can we define the James-Wilde relationship? Perhaps one of the reasons for criticism's inability to think beyond fear and loathing is because the relationship is so difficult to encapsulate. Taken individually, neither anxiety, nor influence, nor even Bloomian anxiety of influence begins to do justice to the marvellous complexity that characterises this intense and sustained association. James's and Wilde's relationship sits between two stools. They were not friends but certainly more than acquaintances; they were not enemies but definitely rivals. They were neither collaborators nor colleagues, yet they conspired (separately) to alter both British and American literary and artistic culture. They borrowed each others' tropes and themes. And they were as fascinated with each other as they were disdainful of each other. There is no single label that encompasses a relationship so rich, although 'long-term intellectual flirtation' would be as valid (and incomplete) as those discussed above. This phrase might stand for the highly charged middle-ground between the two different types of flirtation Freud defines as the 'American flirtation, in which it is understood from the first that nothing is to happen, as contrasted with a Continental love-affair in which both partners must constantly bear its serious consequences in mind.'[54] Even as I offer this illustrative metaphor, I realise that it is incommensurate, yet it is useful because it suggests a new way of thinking of this particular case of personal, artistic and cultural influence.

Aestheticism as Crisis

Aestheticism emerged at a uniquely fortuitous moment in British and American history, when fact and fiction, mimesis and artifice became part of a continuum that affected every aspect of literature and culture. What Erik Erikson said of national identity – that its uniqueness derives from the ways in which 'opposite potentialities'[55] are juxtaposed rather than allowed to 'disintegrate into mere contradiction' – can also be said of Wilde, James and their relations to their respective cultures. A number of recent studies of British and American Aestheticism have demonstrated that both versions responded to late nineteenth-century realignments in gender and class, and that Aestheticism itself was an agent of social reform.[56] Often disdainful of materialism and commercialism, British Aestheticism was largely the story of aspirational culture among the middle and upper classes. By contrast, American Aestheticism held a much wider appeal and was proposed in a more popular, smilingly consumerist form. This is the version illustrated by J. N. Piercy's soft sell for their aesthetic ice cream. The reasons for American Aestheticism's ability to span classes and gender are numerous. Industrialisation, professionalisation, urbanisation and repeated depressions created the need for new cultural developments that would cater to all segments of society and increase quality of life among several classes.[57] To a country traumatised by the Civil War and Reconstruction, Aestheticism offered an attractive prospect: art and beauty for all meant new vistas of social possibility.

While Aestheticism responded to English and American cultural needs, it also brought to the fore underlying cultural incongruities. The conflict between the labouring classes and the upper classes,

between the sexual threat of the New Woman and the sexually indeterminate dandy, between longing for the vanishing natural world
and the allure of artifice, between craving for authenticity and fulfilment through ersatz – all these amalgamated into a powerful impulse
towards implosion. The discernible tension between these violent
instabilities and the dream of permanent peace was a situation which,
following Wallace Stevens, can be described as 'a violent order and a
violent disorder'.[58] This explains why late in life James wearily
observed that Aestheticism had 'brought with it no repose' (*LC2* 908)
and that it had always generated a slightly *unheimlich* effect that
never allowed one 'to feel at home with *it*'. The Anglo-American aesthete was, in short, a consummate connoisseur of chaos.

I want to explain briefly the idea of order that informs this book.
The stopping-off points in the book's trajectory will be determined by
the individual sites of contestation and transformation in James's and
Wilde's works, as well as in aesthetic culture. Following a historical
and thematic trajectory, this study will take us from the late 1870s to
the early 1900s and chart the cultural anxieties that defined Anglo-
American Aestheticism, from crises of nationality and authenticity, to
sexuality and identity crises, as well as social and moral crises. Since
this book's argument is that Aestheticism finds its strength in the con-
tinual ruptures it generates – in its arguments, antagonisms and
dialectics – and that James's and Wilde's relationship is an exemplary
instance of this type of highly productive interaction, it would therefore be counterproductive to write Aestheticism into an order that
would, by the same token, flout the presence of the radical ruptures
within this culture. This study does not, therefore, write aesthetic
culture into a consistent and ameliorative movement, nor does it
inscribe Aestheticism into a teleological narrative of cultural progression and literary development in which James is always the Master *in
spe* and Wilde a potential post-modernist. Aestheticism makes a
virtue of tension and, so doing, defies the notion of persistent progress
that dictates that any one setback will, in time, propel us twice as far
(were this strictly true, Wilde's imprisonment would have set him up
for life). What my account of the relation between James and Wilde
offers readers instead is a new way of configuring Aestheticism as a
permeable, elastic transatlantic movement that finds its creative force
in its antagonisms.

The tension between British and American culture is the most
important aspect of transatlantic Aestheticism, and it is with this issue
that the first chapter begins to analyse the politics underlying James's

early stories of Americans abroad and Wilde's 1882 North American lecture tour. It reveals that James was deeply involved in the formulation and advancement of transatlantic Aestheticism and that he knowingly explored the movement's more popular and commercial incarnations. By examining James's early depictions of aesthetes in light of Wilde's self-presentation and George Du Maurier's illustrations for *Punch* and *Washington Square*, this chapter shows that James developed, codified and catalogued aesthetic modes of being long before Wilde entered on the scene. It also reveals James's vigorous efforts to write an American narrative of Aestheticism's origins, and to create *ex post facto* a vibrant American prehistory for the ideas that imbued British Aestheticism.

Chapters 2 and 3 focus on the anxiety of authenticity that emerged in conjunction with Aestheticism's reformation in the late 1880s. When Wilde, the aesthetic *poseur* of the early 1880s, sought to transform himself into a serious artist and a professional man of letters, he did so by appropriating and transforming works by Henry James and James McNeill Whistler. These chapters argue that the publication of Wilde's criticism marks a turning point in Aestheticism's creative mode because *Intentions* and *The Picture of Dorian Gray* legitimated a mode of creativity premised on plagiarism and appropriation. Wilde's vigorous rejection and absorption of Whistler and James demonstrates that he reinvented himself and Aestheticism by successfully challenging assumptions about artistic legitimacy.

In the fourth chapter, the book turns its attention to the identity and sexuality crises of 1895. The close of the nineteenth century saw the articulation of a discourse of male homosexuality because of the public dramatisation Wilde's trial entailed, and this new idiom of transgressive selfhood is latent in James's *Guy Domville* and Wilde's *The Importance of Being Earnest*. The century's sexual turning point is thus closely intertwined with another crisis in aesthetic culture, as Wilde's trial forever changed the way the movement would be perceived. These plays expose the personal cost of transgression against normative masculinity and, I argue, their historical context also inscribes this concern into a larger project, namely Wilde's and James's attempts to represent the effect of transgressive desires and behaviours on identity.[59]

The fifth chapter concentrates on the social rupture caused by Wilde's trial. It argues that the events of 1895 ripped apart the fabric of aesthetic social culture and that this is manifest in contemporary interior decoration as well as in *The Spoils of Poynton*. The novel not only reflects James's uneasiness about the Wilde trials and their implications but, more compellingly, his sense that the aesthetics of interior decoration embodied in the notion of the 'House Beautiful' was richly expressive of (and thoroughly caught up in) the crisis of sexual ideology that emerged from the trials.

The final chapter is an end and a beginning, for it marks the demise of Aestheticism and the beginning of James's decadent turn. Starting from a close analysis of the language of puerility and animality that pervades James's and Wilde's interaction, the chapter charts the manner in which, post-1895, both authors recuperate this idiom to describe an innocent and erotic child of power that radically undermines Aestheticism's moral stance. 'The Turn of the Screw' and *De Profundis* replicate and interrogate the unmitigated state of moral crisis that resulted from Wilde's trial. In this final crisis, both narratives radically reassess Aestheticism's central tenets, particularly its uncoupling of the aesthetic and the moral.

This entire study is framed by much larger questions of how Aestheticism was able to span differences as considerable as those between James and Wilde, America and Britain, authenticity and fakery, conventionality and eccentricity, morality and immorality. The ability to maintain these tensions makes transatlantic Aestheticism a bridge over troubled waters in every sense.

NOTES

1. http://www.cityofbinghamton.com/history.asp.
2. Merlin Holland, *The Wilde Album* (London: Fourth Estate, 1997) 92. See also Stein, Roger B., 'Artifact as Ideology: The Aesthetic Movement in Its American Cultural Context', in *In Pursuit of Beauty: Americans and the Aesthetic Movement*, ed. Doreen Bolger Burke (New York: Rizzoli, 1986) 23–51.
3. Walter Hamilton, *The Aesthetic Movement in England*, 3rd edn. (Folcroft, PA: Folcroft Library Editions, 1973) 93.
4. Colleen Denney, *At the Temple of Art: The Grosvenor Gallery, 1877–1890* (London: Associated UP, 2000) 67, 32.
5. Ibid. 59.
6. Richard Ellmann, *Oscar Wilde* (London: Hamish Hamilton, 1987) 75.
7. Walter Pater, *The Renaissance*, ed. Adam Phillips (New York: Oxford UP, 1986) 152.
8. Ibid. 150.
9. On the French and German origins of Anglo-American Aestheticism, see Gene H. Bell-Villada, *Art for Art's Sake and Literary Life* (Lincoln:

U of Nebraska P, 1996); Leon Chai, *Aestheticism: The Religion of Art in Post-Romantic Literature* (New York: Columbia UP, 1990); David Weir, *Decadence and the Making of Modernism* (Amherst: U of Massachusetts P, 1995).

10. In his biography of Wilde, Ellmann claims that the term 'aesthete,' in context, is 'almost a euphemism for homosexual' (*Oscar Wilde* 80). I will have much more to say about this question in Chapters 1, 4, and 6.

11. Marian Adams, *The Letters of Mrs Henry Adams, 1865–1883*, ed. Ward Thoron (Boston: Little, Brown, & Co., 1936) 342.

12. Edmund Gosse uses this phrase in a 1908 letter to Robert Ross (Evan Charteris (ed.), *The Life and Letters of Edmund Gosse* (London: Heinemann, 1931) 313).

13. Shelton Waldrep, 'The Uses and Misuses of Oscar Wilde', *Victorian Afterlife: Postmodern Culture Rewrites the Nineteenth Century*, eds. John Kucich and Dianne F. Sadoff (Minneapolis: U of Minnesota P, 2000) 51.

14. Susan Sontag, *Against Interpretation and Other Essays* (New York: Farrar, Straus & Giroux, 1966) 290.

15. Christopher Millard [Stuart Mason], *Oscar Wilde and the Aesthetic Movement* (Dublin: Townley Searle, 1920) 1.

16. David Weir advocates for the use of the expression 'aesthetic school' over 'aesthetic movement', explaining that 'movement' implies something much more organised than Aestheticism ever was, while 'a school implies a small group of individuals who share common interests and look to one person as master and leader' (Weir, *Decadence*, 60). While I agree with Weir, the prevalence of the expression 'Aesthetic Movement' makes it unavoidable in a discussion of aesthetic culture; I have therefore used School and Movement interchangeably throughout.

17. E. H. Mikhail, *Oscar Wilde: Interviews and Recollections*, 2 vols (London: Macmillan, 1979) 1: 41–2 n. 1.

18. Oscar Wilde, 'The Grosvenor Gallery,' *Dublin University Magazine* July 1877, 122; Henry James, *The Painter's Eye: Notes and Essays on the Pictorial Arts*, ed. John L. Sweeney (London: Rupert Hart-Davis, 1956) 144–5.

19. *Notebooks* 69, 121. I discuss this relationship in Chapter 5.

20. The significance of the Grosvenor's opening was amplified when, later that year, Ruskin accused Whistler of 'asking two hundred guineas for flinging a pot of paint in the public's face' (Whistler, *The Gentle Art*, 1). The libel trial that ensued became one of the century's most famous artistic legal battles.

21. 'The Grosvenor Gallery: A Lay of the Private View', *Punch* 14 May 1881, 218.

22. Jonathan Freedman, *Professions of Taste: Henry James, British Aestheticism, and Commodity Culture* (Stanford: Stanford UP, 1990) 171, 201.

23. There are only two other critics who have considered James's influence on Wilde more than in passing. They are Richard Ellmann (in 'Henry James Among the Aesthetes', in *Henry James and Homo-Erotic Desire*, ed. John R. Bradley (New York: St Martin's, 1999)) and Rodney Shewan, who observes parallels between Wilde's 'The Canterville Ghost' and *The Portrait of a Lady*, as well as between Wilde's 'The Model Millionaire' and James's 'The Real Thing' (Shewan, *Oscar Wilde: Art and Egotism* (London: Macmillan, 1977) 25–6, 32). In Chapter 3, I address in greater detail the way in which Wilde's professional and creative transformation was powerfully shaped by his response to James.

24. Ellmann, 'Henry James Among the Aesthetes', 37.

25. Michael Baxandall, *Patterns of Intention: On the Historical Explanation of Pictures* (New Haven, CT: Yale UP, 1985) 58.

26. Ibid. 59.

27. Ellmann, 'Henry James Among the Aesthetes', 27.

28. Ellmann, *Oscar Wilde*, 170–1, emphasis added. Freedman concurs with Ellmann and claims that 'the aestheticized homoeroticism James shared with Pater was affronted by Wilde's extravagant sexuality and threatened by his social disgrace' (Freedman, *Professions*, 172–3).

29. Freedman, *Professions*, 171. See also Richard A. Kaye, *The Flirt's Tragedy: Desire Without End in Victorian and Edwardian Fiction* (Charlottesville: U of Virginia P, 2002) 178; Joseph Litvak, *Caught in the Act: Theatricality in the Nineteenth-Century English Novel* (Berkeley: U of California P, 1992) 271 n. 2. Alan Sinfield takes issue with Ellmann's claim and counters that it mistakenly suggests that Wilde's contemporaries had the same conceptual framework as we now do (Sinfield, *The Wilde Century* (New York: Columbia UP, 1994) 5–6, 91, 97). Wendy Graham also contests Ellmann's assertion with a view to suggesting that James was more sexually aware than has been thought (Graham, *Henry James's Thwarted Love* (Stanford, CA: Stanford UP, 1999) 11, 25–6).

30. Eve Kosofsky Sedgwick, *Between Men: English Literature and Male Homosocial Desire* (New York: Columbia UP, 1985) 89; *Epistemology of the Closet* (Berkeley: U of California P, 1990) 185.

31. See, among others, Kaye, *Flirt's Tragedy*, 179–80; Ronald Knowles, ' "The Hideous Obscure": "The Turn of the Screw" and Oscar Wilde', in *The Turn of the Screw and What Maisie Knew*, ed. Neill Cornwell and Maggie Malone (Basingstoke: Macmillan, 1998); Nicola Nixon, 'The "Reading Gaol" of Henry James's "In the Cage" ', *ELH* 66.1 (1999); Kevin Ohi, *Innocence and Rapture* (New York: Palgrave, 2005)

123–54; John Carlos Rowe, *The Other Henry James* (Durham, NC: Duke UP, 1998) 26–7, 101–4, 140–1; Eric Savoy, ' "In the Cage" and the Queer Effects of Gay History', *Novel* 28.3 (1995); Michael Trask, 'Getting into It with James: Substitution and Erotic Reversal in *The Awkward Age*', *American Literature* 69 (1997).

32. Sedgwick, *Epistemology*, 195.

33. Hugh Stevens, *Henry James and Sexuality* (New York: Cambridge UP, 1998) 131.

34. Ibid. 141.

35. Ellmann, *Oscar Wilde*, 77.

36. Quoted in Henry James, *Dearly Beloved Friends: Henry James's Letters to Younger Men*, ed. Susan E. Gunter and Steven H. Jobe (Ann Arbor, MI: U of Michigan P, 2001) 118.

37. Ibid. 115.

38. Ibid. 139.

39. Ibid. 125.

40. Ibid. 161. For a discussion of James's response to other men (some of whom were gay), including Paul Zhukovski, Count Robert de Montesquiou-Fezensac, and J.A. Symonds, see Stevens, Henry James, 131–2. On James's relationships with Hendrik Andersen, Jocelyn Persse and Hugh Walpole, see James, *Dearly*, 125.

41. Ellmann, *Oscar Wilde*, 261.

42. Henry James, letter to Robert Ross, 6 August 1912, ts, Leon Edel Papers, Rare Books and Special Collections Division, McGill University.

43. James, *Dearly*, 225–6.

44. Rayburn S. Moore (ed.), *Selected Letters of Henry James to Edmund Gosse, 1882–1915: A Literary Friendship* (Baton Rouge: Louisiana State UP, 1988) 296. For James's other comments about and to Ross, see James, *Dearly* 233, and Henry James, letter to Robert Ross, 18 April 1913, ts, Leon Edel Papers, McGill University.

45. One typical example is Stevens's description of 'the interplay of machismo and sadomasochism' in *The Golden Bowl* (*Henry James*, 58).

46. Litvak, *Caught in The Act*, 236.

47. See, for instance, John Fletcher, 'The Haunted Closet: Henry James's Queer Spectrality', *Textual Practice* 14.1 (2000); Christopher Lane, 'Framing Fears, Reading Designs: The Homosexual Art of Painting in James, Wilde and Beerbohm', *ELH* 61.4 (1994); Neil Matheson, 'Talking Horrors: Henry James, Euphemism, and the Specter of Wilde,' *American Literature* 71.4 (1999); Colm Tóibín, 'Love in a Dark Time', *London Review of Books* (19 April 2001). Stevens notes that James's 'specular and spectral moments' are often suffused with homoerotic tensions that instance what he, following the lead of Terry Castle's *The Apparitional Lesbian*, calls 'queer spectrality' (132–3). For an example of one of James's positive figurations of haunting (haunting-as-empathy),

see his letter about Robert Ross of 29 January 1914 (Rayburn S. Moore (ed.), *Selected Letters of Henry James to Edmund Gosse, 1882–1915*, 296.

48. Colm Tóibín, *Love in a Dark Time: Gay Lives from Wilde to Almodovar* (London: Picador, 2002) 34.

49. Sedgwick, *Epistemology*, 196. I should mention that Sheldon Novick's biography, *Henry James: the Young Master*, suggests there is a body of evidence that proves 'James was gay . . . for nearly everyone from Leon Edel onwards . . . now admits this to be true' (quoted in Lane, 'Jamesian Inscrutability', *Henry James Review* 20.3 (1999): 246). Lane discusses the critical response to Novick and calls his suggestion 'historically anachronistic for any Victorian subject . . . specious and irresponsible.'

50. Shame, Sedgwick explains, 'floods into being as a moment, a disruptive moment, in a circuit of identity-constituting identificatory communica- tion . . . But in interrupting identification, shame, too, makes identity' (*Touching Feeling: Affect, Pedagogy, Performativity* (Durham, NC: Duke UP, 2004) 36). I discuss shame in Chapter 4.

51. See 'Making a Scene: Henry James's Theater of Embarassment,' in Litvak, *Caught in The Act*, 195–234.

52. See, for example, Ellmann, 'Henry James Among the Aesthetes', 26. Notable exceptions to this trend are Tessa Hadley, *Henry James and the Imagination of Pleasure* (Cambridge: Cambridge UP, 2002); Eric Haralson, *Henry James and Queer Modernity* (Cambridge: Cambridge UP, 2003).

53. Ellmann, *Oscar Wilde*, 412.

54. Sigmund Freud, 'Thoughts for the Times on War and Death', in *The Standard Edition of the Complete Psychological Works of Sigmund Freud*, ed. James Strachey, vol. 14 (London: Hogarth, 1953) 290.

55. Erik H. Erikson, *Childhood and Society* (New York: Norton, 1963) 285.

56. See, for instance, Regenia Gagnier, *Idylls of the Marketplace* (Stanford, CA: Stanford UP, 1986); Diana Maltz, *British Aestheticism and the Urban Working Classes, 1870–1900* (Basingstoke: Palgrave, 2006); Talia Schaffer, *The Forgotten Female Aesthetes* (Charlottesville: U of Virginia P, 2000).

57. Mary Warner Blanchard, *Oscar Wilde's America: Counterculture in the Gilded Age* (New Haven, CT: Yale UP, 1998) 4.

58. My formulation here is indebted to Miles Orvell, who has brilliantly described the social and intellectual tensions in turn-of-the-century American culture and how the period saw a significant change 'from a culture in which the arts of imitation and illusion were valorized to a culture in which the notion of authenticity became of primary value' (Orvell, *The Real Thing: Imitation and Authenticity in American Culture, 1880–1940* (Chapel Hill: U of North Carolina P, 1989) xv,

xvii). Likewise, Lionel Trilling notes that the credence once given to
material and social establishment, to moral certainties, and to one's
ability to attain happiness, gave way in the later half of the nineteenth
century to a wilful repudiation of this norm which persists to this day
(Trilling, *Sincerity and Authenticity* (Cambridge, MA: Harvard UP,
1972) 40–1).

59. In his insightful examination of *Guy Domville*'s relation to eighteenth-
century Catholic riots, Fred Bernard reminds us that James favoured
broad interpretations, going so far as to claim that a study of the 'history
of religious intolerance . . . is, I really believe, the history of humanity'
(James quoted in Fred V. Bernard, 'Portents of Violence: Jamesian
Realism in *Guy Domville*,' *Henry James Review* 17.1 (1996), 86).

CHAPTER 1

'I HAVE ASKED HENRY JAMES NOT TO BRING HIS FRIEND OSCAR WILDE': *DAISY MILLER*, *WASHINGTON SQUARE* AND THE POLITICS OF TRANSATLANTIC AESTHETICISM

At a Whistler exhibition, the mischievous painter brought the *Punch* caricaturist George Du Maurier face to face with the twenty-six-year-old Oscar Wilde, who was widely assumed to be the model for Du Maurier's enormously popular aesthetes, Postlethwaite and Maudle. 'Which one of you two invented the other, eh?'[1] Whistler asked, relishing the incisiveness of his facetious inquiry. Whistler's chicken-and-egg question encapsulated the public's curiosity about the enigmatic origins of *Punch*'s popular images of aesthetes by implying that Wilde and Du Maurier had created each other. Whistler was probably right to think that Du Maurier's caricatures of aesthetes had contributed as much to his own success as to Wilde's. Heralded as the real Postlethwaite and Maudle of Du Maurier's lampoons, Wilde's phenomenal artistic and social pretensions provided the material for Du Maurier's popular tongue-in-cheek tributes. Attempting to evade this connection, Du Maurier denied that Postlethwaite was a caricature of Wilde and, in later years, claimed the character was founded on the whole aesthetic school.[2] For his part, Wilde saw the association as an opportunity and unabashedly told the *New York Daily Tribune*:

> As to Du Maurier's characters, I suppose that I am the original of *Mautle* [*sic*], the poet. *Postlethwaite*, the artist, has no original, but is a combination of the peculiarities of a number of my friends. As an artist, my attitude toward all this is that a true artist who believes in his art and his mission must necessarily be altogether insensible to praise or blame.

If he is not a mere sham, he cannot be disturbed by any caricature or exaggeration.[3]

This was a characteristic display of media savvy from a young man who already knew the truth that Lord Henry would reveal years later in *The Picture of Dorian Gray*: 'there is only one thing in the world worse than being talked about, and that is not being talked about' (W 18–19).[4] In an 1883 article for the *Century Magazine*, James confessed his fondness for the *Punch* caricatures of aesthetes, and credited Du Maurier with having 'invented Maudle and Postlethwaite'.[5] 'These remarkable people have had a great success in America,' James observed, 'and have contributed not a little to the curiosity felt in that country on the subject of the English Renascence.'

Americans' fascination with Aestheticism ensured that Du Maurier's caricatural incarnations were in great demand in the United States in the late 1870s and early 1880s. Spurred by their success, a number of London playwrights had burlesqued Aestheticism's 'a-Postlethwaites'[6] in *The Grasshopper*, *Where's the Cat?*, and *The Colonel*.[7] However, it was Gilbert and Sullivan's *Patience, or Bunthorne's Bride* that achieved the greatest popularity, with a run in London as well as New York. Inspired by Du Maurier's *Punch* caricatures, the operetta simplified the Aesthetic Movement to a type and a recognisable figure, an alliance that significantly helped Wilde's rise to fame.[8] The plot centres on Patience, a village milkmaid who must choose between two suitors: a 'fleshly poet' named Bunthorne (who was supposed to remind audiences of Wilde), and an 'idyllic poet' named Grosvenor. In the end, Patience prefers Grosvenor – who has, in the interim, agreed to renounce poetry and become a 'commonplace young man' – while Bunthorne settles for a lily as his life companion. In 1881, Richard D'Oyly Carte, the operetta's New York producer, hit on the idea of allowing Americans the opportunity to see the real-life version of Gilbert and Sullivan's singing and dancing aesthetes (W 123).[9] D'Oyly Carte approached Wilde, who quickly consented to become the star of a lecture tour designed as a thinly-veiled publicity stunt for the American tour of Gilbert and Sullivan's operetta. Wilde was scheduled to appear in each city just before *Patience* opened there, and he agreed to be presented as an artist, aesthete and a figure of English society.[10]

By the beginning of 1882, Bunthorne, Maudle and Postlethwaite were not the only ones who had made it to American shores by wanly warbling and gently garbling excerpts from Pater's

Renaissance. From his lecture podium, Wilde, too, urged Americans to 'burn always with one of the passions of this fiery-coloured world' (*RW* 26) in his lectures on 'The English Renaissance of Art' and interior decoration. In his earliest lecture, Wilde used the parodies of Du Maurier and Gilbert and Sullivan to bolster his own aesthetic views:

> You have listened to *Patience* for a hundred nights and have listened to me for only one. You have heard, I think, a few of you, of two flowers connected with the aesthetic movement in England, and said (I assure you, erroneously) to be the food of some aesthetic young men [a reference to Du Maurier's 'An Aesthetic Midday Meal' (Figure 1.1)]. Well, let me tell you the reason we love the lily and the sunflower, in spite of what Mr Gilbert may tell you, is not for any vegetable fashion at all [a reference to *Patience*'s recurring lyric about aesthetes having 'a sentimental passion of a vegetable fashion'].[11] It is because these two lovely flowers are in England the most perfect models of design, the most naturally adapted for decorative art . . . We spend our days looking for the secret of life. Well, the secret of life is art.[12]

Wilde had managed to make a silk purse from a sow's ear by turning aesthetic lampoons to his own ends. His brilliant deployment of aesthetic parodies to reinforce the movement's earnest message confirmed him to some as a man of more substance than Du Maurier's two-dimensional portrayals. However, others were more sceptical of Wilde's manoeuvres, and not a little suspicious of the manner in which he was displayed as an example of fine English society. These doubts were given weight by *Patience*. The operetta's most important moment, for our purposes, comes in the middle of act one, when Bunthorne, thinking he is alone, delivers a solo that reveals him as a fraud. He lets his aesthetic mask drop and melodramatically confesses that his manner is nothing more than a refined social ruse:

> Am I alone,
>   And unobserved? I am!
> Then let me own
>   I'm an aesthetic sham! . . .
> This cynic smile
>   Is but a wile
>   Of guile! . . .

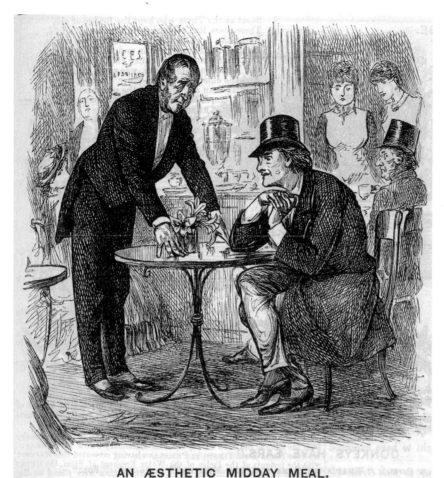

AN ÆSTHETIC MIDDAY MEAL.

At the Luncheon hour, Jellaby Postlethwaite enters a Pastrycook's and calls for a glass of Water, into which he puts a freshly-cut Lily, and loses himself in contemplation thereof.

Waiter. "Shall I bring you anything else, Sir?"
Jellaby Postlethwaite. "Thanks, no! I have all I require, and shall soon have done!"

1.1 Du Maurier's caricature of Wilde lent credence to the widespread belief that aesthetes literally lived on lilies. (George Du Maurier, 'An Aesthetic Midday Meal', *Punch* 17 July 1880, 23. Courtesy of the Trustees of the National Library of Scotland.)

> Let me confess!
> A languid love for Lilies does *not* blight me!
> Lank limbs and haggard cheeks do *not* delight me!
> I do *not* care for dirty greens
> By any means . . .

> In short, my mediaevalism's affection,
> Born of a morbid love of admiration!

If you're anxious for to shine in the high aesthetic line as a man of
  culture rare,
You must get up all the germs of the transcendental terms, and plant
  them everywhere.
You must lie upon the daisies and discourse in novel phrases of your
  complicated state of mind,
The meaning doesn't matter if it's only idle chatter of a transcendental
  kind.
>   And every one will say,
>   As you walk your mystic way,
'If this young man expresses himself in terms too deep for *me*,
Why, what a very singularly deep young man this deep young man
  must be!'
' . . . Why, what a very cultivated kind of youth this kind of youth
  must be!'[13]

Coalescing connoisseurship with social manoeuvring, Bunthorne underscores the degree to which aesthetic discernment could be useful in violating social standards and hierarchies. This reductive image of the aesthete was unflattering to Wilde, but this was of little consequence to him for he saw this, too, as another occasion for self-promotion, an opportunity to make his name and his gospel of Aestheticism more widely known. 'There is nothing that shows Mr Wilde in his true light so completely as his great appreciation for Bunthorne,' *The Nation* observed. 'It never occurred to any reformer before Mr Wilde that it would be a good thing to encourage parody and satire as a means of keeping the ball going . . . It was left to Mr Wilde to discover the commercial value of ridicule.'[14] Although James would not have called himself a reformer, he had already discovered that parody could enhance his profit margin. As this chapter will show, James's early stories and *Washington Square* articulated a cogent American narrative of Aestheticism through parody and social criticism prior to Wilde's 'discovery' of America.

It was in this Anglo-American atmosphere of Aestheticism and parody that Wilde and James met. While we can assume that they had encountered each other before, given the intersections between their social circles in England, no evidence of such meetings remains. Thus the first recorded interaction between this transatlantic pair was not in the English capital, where they both lived, but in the American capital, which they were both visiting. Whereas Wilde had been interviewed in the press almost as soon as he arrived in the United States, James escaped the press by coming through Canada and telling friends he had 'stole[n] into the country, as it were, by the back-door' (L2 361).[15] Intent on travelling incognito, James took the extra precaution of adopting 'Harry Heliotrope'[16] for his alias, a floral moniker fit for an aesthete. On 15 January 1882, James spent the evening with the George Maxwell Robesons, who were sponsoring Wilde during his visit to Washington and had elicited a good deal of controversy because of their hospitality.

Wilde and James met on 22 January, at a reception held in the Washington home of Judge Edward G. Loring.[17] The next day, James wrote to the Boston socialite and art collector Isabella Stewart Gardner that he had found at the Lorings' not the *sortie de bal* Gardner said she had flung down there 'like a bunch of hyacinths', but the musky flower of Aestheticism itself, 'the repulsive and fatuous Oscar Wilde' (L2 372). James was 'happy to say, no one was looking at' Wilde that evening, but he nevertheless determined that he should like to have a private view of him. He called on Wilde at his hotel on 24 January and, hoping to turn the conversation to an aspect of mutual interest, told Wilde that he was homesick for London. Wilde briskly rebuffed this opener: 'Really! You care for *places*? The *world* is my home.'[18] His next stop, he told James, was '*Boston*; there I have a letter to the dearest friend of my dearest friend – Charles Norton from Burne Jones.' James, too, was headed for Boston and was friendly with Norton, but Wilde's brashness precluded a third meeting. Wilde later told the press that 'no living English novelist can be named with Henry James and Howells',[19] the two American novelists he admired most of all. Under the watchful gaze of a newspaper reporter, he went into a bookstore to replenish his supply of novels by Howells and James.[20]

Such belated reverence did nothing to change James's initial impressions of Wilde. He reported to Marian Adams that Wilde was 'a fatuous fool, a tenth-rate cad'.[21] Oddly enough, James does not mention this second Washington visit in any of his letters.[22] Richard Ellmann suggests that this encounter negatively impacted James's opinion of Aestheticism because 'to this expert in deracination no quality more impugned the value of aestheticism than its rootlessness'.[23] James may have been frustrated, but his declaration that

Wilde was 'repulsive'[24] to him is misleading. The fact that he met Wilde a second time, and in relative secrecy, proves that he was nevertheless intrigued by him. James's repeated use of the word 'fatuous' in relation to Wilde reveals his ambivalence. On the one hand, he thought Wilde was a fool. On the other, he was also fascinatingly attractive. Like a fatuous fire, Wilde enticed James only to elude him. Rather than being 'nervous about [Wilde's] sensuality',[25] as Ellmann has claimed, James was intrigued by Wilde and wanted to sound him out. He would do the same with J. A. Symonds when he wrote to him that 'it seemed to me that the victims of a common passion should sometimes exchange a look' (*L3* 30). Wilde's rebuff crushed James's friendly feelings for him and, in subsequent years, James would publicly dissociate himself from him. James's disenchantment would not have registered so strongly had he not fully invested himself in his meeting with a man who seemed to promise so much but, in the end, was as hard to pin down as a will-o'-the-wisp.

Marian and Henry Adams, with whom James was staying in Washington, declined to receive the guests of an evening at the popular Bachelor's Club because they included the Robesons and Wilde.[26] Marian Adams thought Wilde was a sham and a fool, and zealously avoided him, describing her escape as a *'tour de force'*.[27] She commented on the suspect society James was keeping by quoting the parable of the good Samaritan: 'And a certain man came down to? from? [*sic*] Jerusalem and fell among thieves . . . and they sprang up and choked him.'[28] James was aware of the Adamses' disdain for this type of society but also knew that they were not uninterested in it. 'The Adamses consider it very bad,' he told E. L. Godkin, 'though I notice that they are eagerly anxious to hear what I have seen and heard at places which they decline to frequent. After I had been to Mrs Robeson's they mobbed me for revelations' (*LL* 135). Marian Adams warned James that she would not receive Wilde, whom she took to be James's comrade. 'I have asked Henry James *not* to bring his friend Oscar Wilde when he comes; I must keep out thieves and noodles or else take down my sign and go West',[29] she wrote. What did she mean by calling James and Wilde 'friends'? She may have assumed that they had met in London, or that their shared artistic interests would have made them sympathetic to each other, and it is likely that her allusion was intended to encapsulate both these sentiments. Yet she and her husband had known James for over a decade and had many friends in common, including artistic sympathisers such as Isabella Stewart

Gardner, William Dean Howells, Charles Eliot Norton and John Singer Sargent. The Adamses knew James well enough to know who his true friends were. The biting wit in Marian's allusion to 'friendship' indicates that she intended it as a *double-entendre* laden with innuendo about mutual benevolence, intimacy and shared secrets. The significance of Adams's observation is heightened by the fact that she doubted Wilde's sexuality long before such suspicions became commonplace. In a letter, she offhandedly referred to Wilde's homosexuality by saying 'the sexes of my nouns are as undecided as that of Oscar Wilde'.[30] In calling James a friend of Wilde, Adams alluded to and identified James's sexuality with Wilde's. For his part, James denied his friendship with Wilde well into the 1890s, when he excused himself from signing a petition for Wilde's release from prison because 'the document would only exist as a manifesto of personal loyalty to Oscar by his friends, of which he was never one' (*LW* 643 n. 1), as Jonathan Sturges told the petition's proposer.

Separately, Wilde and James continued on to Boston in January 1882. After arriving in the city on 28 January, Wilde lectured on 'The English Renaissance' at Boston Music Hall on 31 January. James had planned to tour various parts of the United States and to spend April in Boston, but soon after his encounter with Wilde he received news that his mother was ill, and she died on 29 January. James arrived in Cambridge (Boston's academic suburb) on the day of Wilde's lecture. Mary James's funeral took place the next day (*LL* 136).

'I am sure that you have in your head lots of aesthetic novelettes'

Wilde had arrived in the United States with nothing to declare but his genius. To Americans, however, Aestheticism was hardly a revelation. Manifesting a protectionist tendency, *The Nation* declared after his arrival: 'Mr Wilde is an essentially foreign product, and can hardly succeed in this country. What he has to say is not new, and his extravagance is not extravagant enough to amuse the average American audience.'[31] As numerous social historians and literary scholars have shown, Americans had already founded aesthetic societies, been to Europe in order to enrich their understanding, and devoured proselytising books preaching aesthetic approaches to interior decoration.[32] The catalyst for the widespread popularity of the Aesthetic Movement in America was the Philadelphia Centennial Exposition of 1876, which exposed Americans to art objects from a variety of nations and periods.[33] Followed by a proliferation of publications related to art, the Exposition also generated enthusiasm for art collecting. Aestheticism affected American conceptions of nature, religion, ideology and womanhood by suggesting a spiritual, material and social alternative which answered to the needs of the post-Civil War era and adapted to the country's urban and industrial change.[34] The Apostle of Aestheticism was preaching to the converted.

Though James avoided Wilde during the rest of his American visit, James's fiction continued to embrace aesthetic figures. Wilde's reception in the United States presented a rich conjunction between the values of Aestheticism, American culture and social hierarchies – a nexus that James had already explored in stories such as 'A Bundle of Letters' (*The Parisian*, 18 December 1879), 'An International Episode' (*Cornhill Magazine*, December 1878–January 1879), 'The Pension Beaurepas' (*Atlantic Monthly*, April 1879), and novels such as *Washington Square* (*Cornhill Magazine*, June–November 1880, illustrated by Du Maurier; *Harper's New Monthly Magazine*, July–December 1880, no illustrations) and *The Portrait of a Lady* (*Macmillan's Magazine*, October 1880–December 1881). James's 1882 encounter with Wilde thus represents an important moment in James's narrative exploration of the aesthete, for in his meeting with Wilde, James was confronted with the incarnation of many of the aesthetic values he had been scrutinising in his fiction and observing through the prism of Du Maurier's *Punch* caricatures, of which he was a devoted student. During the same years that James had been developing the aesthete in his art, Wilde had been developing it in his life and this positioned him as a fellow player on the international aesthetic scene. Though Wilde was often ridiculed during his American tour, he also represented the actualisation of a number of the aesthetic characteristics James had emphasised in his fiction. While James was happy that no one was looking at Wilde when he went to the Lorings', he was also concerned that Wilde looked too much like the transatlantic aesthetes James was already portraying. The publication history of James's stories of British and American aesthetes speaks volumes about James's cosmopolitan, transnational scope, and the standing he had already achieved in this niche market by the early 1880s.

As early as *Roderick Hudson* (1875) and *The Europeans* (1878), James's fiction had a thoroughgoing concern with the dandy and the *flâneur*.[35] However, in 1879–84, the height of the craze for depictions of aesthetic young men, these images focused for James, becoming sharp renditions of characters that could be recognised as aesthetes analogous to those one might find on the stage or in the pages of *Punch*. James's early interest in these figures has of course not gone undetected, though the majority of criticism has focused on unpacking the aesthetic dynamics in 'The Author of Beltraffio' (1884) and *The Portrait of a Lady* and has left James's other early stories largely unexplored.[36] These neglected stories richly repay study, however, for they reveal James's thoroughgoing interest in popular forms of transatlantic Aestheticism quite distinct from the elite articulations he is (somewhat unjustly) known for. Although Wilde had bragged to James that the world was his home, James's aesthetes had already taken up residence in French publications (*The Parisian*), American magazines (*Atlantic Monthly* and *Harper's New Monthly Magazine*), and British periodicals (*Macmillan's Magazine* and *Cornhill Magazine*).

By 1882, James was already deeply invested in the transatlantic aesthetic culture Wilde now claimed to represent to James's countrymen and -women. In *Professions of Taste*, Jonathan Freedman persuasively argues that 'James formulated his conception of the novelist as an elite artist'[37] out of his encounter with Wilde and the tradition of British Aestheticism, and that this cultural moment was crucial to James eventually achieving 'his final monumentalization as the elite novelist par excellence – the internationally acclaimed but rarely read master of the art of fiction'.[38] This line of argument traces a convincing teleological narrative of cultural progression that emphatically confirms some of scholarship's dearest beliefs about James's career, and while my own work is certainly indebted to Freedman's erudite and influential study, there is much to be gained by reading James's Aestheticism synchronically rather than diachronically. Such an approach – which is the one this chapter privileges – reveals another picture of the Jamesian artist, one involved at the grass roots of transatlantic Aestheticism from its germination to its first flowering, and one not afraid of getting his hands dirty, so to speak, by exploring Aestheticism's more popular and commercial incarnations.

By examining James's early aesthetes in light of Wilde's American tour and George Du Maurier's illustrations for *Punch* and *Washington Square* (1880), this chapter argues that James developed, codified and catalogued aesthetic modes of being long before Wilde entered upon the scene. This is important for three reasons: first, because the robust American tenor James gave his aesthetes suggests James's role in the formation of an American Aestheticism. Second, the temporal dislocation in many of James's aesthetic narratives – *Roderick Hudson*, *The Europeans*, and *Washington Square* are all set prior to the flowering of British Aestheticism in the 1870s – demonstrates James's spirited endeavour to constitute a distinctly American narrative of Aestheticism's origins. By giving evidence of a vibrant American prehistory for the ideas that imbued British Aestheticism, James challenged contemporary British Aestheticism's implicit claims of originality. James's narratives imagine an American genealogy for the ideas that Wilde would soon trumpet as British. James's *ex post facto* articulation of a national artistic ideology radically revises Aestheticism's chronology and nationality. By relocating Aestheticism in this manner, James pursued an artistic policy not far removed from Manifest Destiny, the justification for the United States's territorial expansion that was pervasive during James's youth in the 1840s and 1850s. If the rhetoric of Manifest Destiny could justify the American policy of geographical imperialism, then James's narratives also worked hard to rationalise American intellectual and artistic imperialism. The embedded narrative of American literary history in James's early stories served as a legitimating document that would endow Americans with ancestral intellectual rights, and thereby legitimate the American annexation of British Aestheticism's intellectual and artistic territories. Fictional literary history served to verify artistic progress.

The third reason why James's early classification of aesthetic modes is significant is that it ultimately led him to be perceived as the American arm of Aestheticism. In particular, the Jamesian aesthete's ability to manipulate social distinctions to his own (often economic) ends was a feature that would eventually become central to James's proprietary conception of the American aesthete, a vision that would boldly come into focus in *Washington Square*. Although Leonée Ormond considers Du Maurier's illustrations for *Washington Square* 'sadly uninteresting',[39] Du Maurier's iconography suggests that in drawing the characters for James's story, he was also drawing heavily on his *Punch* caricatures. Dennis Denisoff has shown that Du Maurier was thoroughly invested in defining aesthetic cultural values despite his 'antagonism towards what he viewed as the dandy-aesthetes' vulgar self-advertisement'.[40] Regenia Gagnier asserts that the aesthete 'cannot be divorced from advertising, consumerist culture' and that it was partly because the aesthete was so adaptable that he could infiltrate society with minimal repression and thus challenge social hierarchies.[41] Aestheticism was only possible 'in a society with social mobility, economic security, and waning sincerity',[42] which is the society in which James set *Washington Square*, his purely American tale of society, refinement and finance. The novel's want of an overtly aesthetic theme therefore seems not so much 'a digression from certain established Jamesianisms',[43] as the occasion for the formulation of a distinctly American prehistory for Aestheticism.

The term 'aesthete' came into usage in Britain in the late 1870s as a means of describing the adherents of the new Aesthetic Movement, as well as a more general category of men and women interested in form and appearances.[44] Linda Hughes notes that the term always carries with it the implication of a 'commitment to . . . cultural authority (in the form of taste)'.[45] In the mid- and late nineteenth century, the aesthete might be assumed to subscribe to Pater's idea of 'art for art's sake', and to the cleavage between art and social reform advocated in the preface to Théophile Gautier's *Mademoiselle de Maupin* (1835). The aesthete was unafraid to shock the middle class with his taste for medievalism, Pre-Raphaelite art, Japonism and Swinburne's poetry.[46] According to Wilde's bibliographer, Stuart Mason, the aesthete's trappings rapidly became stereotyped and subsumed under those represented in the pages of *Punch*:

> The male members of this school, if we may believe the late George Du Maurier and his imitators, wore sad superfluous collars and had 'lank limbs and haggard cheeks'; its female adherents clad themselves in garments of sage-green, and decorated their drawing-rooms with dadoes, Japanese fans, and peacocks' feathers. Both sexes indulged in writing poetry, which was described as 'a mixture of Swinburne and water'; and all had the reputation of living on lilies and of trying to live up to their blue china.[47]

As a result of the aesthete's popularity, his characteristics were simplified even further. Doing away with specificity, James described him in an 1883 article for the *Century Magazine* as a smooth-tongued devotee of 'the lovely and the precious, living in goodly houses and walking in gracious garments'.[48] This chronology suggests that James contributed substantially to the cultural definition of the aesthete by expanding it to include Anglo-American versions as well as significantly enlarging the characteristics that came to be associated with the type. One of the hallmarks of the Jamesian aesthete, for instance, is that his emphasis on form threatens the distinction between objects and people, since he views both in the same superficial terms. For instance, in *Daisy Miller* (*Cornhill Magazine*, June–July 1878), James's Europeanised American proto-aesthete, Winterbourne, conducts an analysis of Daisy's beauty so detailed that he reduces her to her parts, rather than the sum of them:

> Winterbourne had not seen for a long time anything prettier than his fair countrywoman's various features – her complexion, her nose, her ears, her teeth. He had a great relish for feminine beauty; he was addicted to observing and analyzing it; and as regards this young lady's face he made several observations. (CS2 243)

More often than not, as John Landau observes, 'the Jamesian aesthete is only concerned with his own specific, and generally self-interested, conception of the beautiful'.[49]

In the late 1870s, *Daisy Miller* made Henry James a household name. Instantly pirated, the novel's authorised edition sold 20,000 copies in a few weeks.[50] Between 1878 and 1884 James achieved the greatest social and financial success of his career on both sides of the ocean. His literary income more than doubled, and a torrent of invitations allowed him to dine out no less 107 times during the winter of 1879.[51] Despite his success, he worried about financial matters, complaining to his brother William: 'My reputation in England seems ludicrously larger than any cash payments that I have yet received for it' (*LL* 108). In order to stretch *Daisy Miller*'s popularity and pay-off, James reworked it for the stage, arranged a private printing and a reading at the St James's Theatre.[52] Though the play was not performed, his golden girl proved her mettle, earning him £1200 for her dramatic debut in *The Atlantic Monthly* magazine.[53] In order to further popularise the transatlantic aesthete, James repeated the same *modus operandi* that he had used with *Daisy Miller*. He had positioned his narrative of the American woman abroad at the intersection of two fashionable literary modes of the 1870s – travel writing and polite fiction.[54] As a result, the story captured a wider, unisex audience. James sought to repeat his success by coupling his American girl with the increasingly popular aesthete. By locating his work within this fashionable sphere, James would concurrently build upon his reputation as a popular chronicler of the international scene and benefit from the vogue for depictions of aesthetes. In order to do so, he first appropriated the aesthetic theme by casting it in the American mould, and then partnered this new transatlantic aesthete with his trademark American girl. James thus situated himself within an established parodic tradition (derived in part from *Punch* and Gilbert and Sullivan), but subverted the standard by making his characters distinctly American. This was the subject in which he put his hope for success; it was, he later said, the 'solution where, with the help of Heaven, I hope to find many others in work to come, viz., in the idea of the Europeanized American' (*Notebooks* 42).

In an 1881 letter to Robert Louis Stevenson (who had slurred James as 'a mere club fizzle'),[55] the British editor W. E. Henley defended James and explained, 'he is passing through a certain stage of development, & not yet himself'.[56] Henley already had a strong sense of what James could become and how he could improve Aestheticism and American literature. He put this to James with characteristic candour in 1882, while James was in the United States: 'I am sure that you have in your head lots of aesthetic novelettes . . . stories about art & artists . . . Confess that you have; & promise me the first offer of one of them . . . If you don't I shall think you not half the cosmopolitan you would have us believe.'[57] Henley's attempt to flatter James into contributing to his *Magazine of Art* was unsuccessful but Henley had divined exactly how James would achieve his own success. Henley's letter vividly underscored the need for a differentiated, American version of Aestheticism, one distinguishable from naturalism and 'Zolaism, Wagnerism, Whistlerism',[58] artistic movements that Henley roundly disparaged as 'aesthetic syphilis'. Henley's words confirmed to James that transatlantic-themed 'aesthetic novelettes' and 'stories about art & artists' would allow him to cater to Americans' yearning to read about themselves and about Britain and thereby grant James the popular and financial success he craved. Britain retained a high level of cultural magnetism for Americans, who were attracted and repelled by Britain in equal measure but rarely remained indifferent. Henley told James that, as an editor, he could not afford to ignore the American market, and needed to find an author who could fulfil the desires of this transatlantically-minded readership.

> What you say about the incompatibility of the two nations is pretty right. But I'm not my own master. I've a sale of over 20,000 (another reason why you should write for me); & a great part of it is American. Consequently I am in demand to cater for Columbia, happy land, & to do as much for the home of the brave & land of the free as I possibly can . . . if your people buy me at all, they buy me because I tell them not about themselves, but about the art of England – such as it is. But my

orders are imperative; & I must obey them. If therefore, you know of any American who can write well & graphically about his own country, I shall be grateful for his name & address . . . I hope that you are well in health & active in mind, & deep in a new Mrs Prettyman [i.e. Mrs Penniman in *Washington Square*].[59]

Though James's response to Henley is not extant, James's works testify to the fact that he was already responding to the market Henley described.

(En)gendering the Transatlantic Aesthete

It is worth pausing here, before getting into the particularities of the Jamesian aesthete, to explain the significance of the American girl in this equation and to explain further how she functioned as a model for the literary and financial success James hoped to achieve through his treatment of the aesthete. *Daisy Miller* hit a nerve with the American public. The story described a well-known (but until then unnamed) social phenomenon of epidemic proportions: a daughter of the New World blithely and undiscerningly hazarding her fortunes in the Old one. 'Daisy Miller-ism' soon became common parlance or, as one reviewer put it, 'the *sobriquet* in European journalism of the American woman of the period'.[60] William King Richardson, an American studying at Oxford, was startled by 'the prominence of the "Daisy Miller" style of Americans' and, in *The Rise of Silas Lapham* (1884), William Dean Howells wrote of redeeming American women from 'the national reproach of Daisy Millerism'.[61] The far-reaching influence of the American woman can also be detected in *The Picture of Dorian Gray*'s allusion, almost a decade later, to the power exerted by the Daisy Miller type. In Wilde's novel, a Duchess worries about the glut of American girls abroad and the English fashion for marrying them and says, 'I wish to goodness [America] never had been discovered at all! . . . Really, our girls have no chance nowadays. It is most unfair' (W 38). An equally anxious Englishman concludes, 'Why can't these American women stay in their own country?' (39). Controversial and timely, *Daisy Miller* was, to some, a delightful piece of social observation and, to others, a libel on American womanhood. *Daisy Miller* earned James the title of 'inventor, beyond question, of the international American girl'.[62] Howells commended James for having 'recognized and portrayed the innocently adventuring, unconsciously periculant American maiden' and depicted her in a 'flattering if a little mocking' manner. Having 'invented' the international American girl, James would reinvent the aesthete by poking fun at his American incarnation.

To extend his American girl's pay-potential, James created literary siblings for her: 'An International Episode', 'Pandora' (New York *Sun* 1 & 8 June 1884), 'A Bundle of Letters', 'The Point of View' (*Century Magazine* December 1882), 'The Pension Beaurepas', *Washington Square* and *The Portrait of a Lady* were also stories about male and female innocents abroad and, occasionally, at home.[63] Expressly written as a counterpart to *Daisy Miller*, 'An International Episode' is the story of Bessie Alden, a nubile Bostonian who captivates an English lord she meets at Newport but spurns his affections during her subsequent visit to England. Cultivated and serious, Bessie hails from the American city where 'girls, it was propounded, were more like English young ladies' (CS2 370), but she is not immune to unladylike cravings, such as her desire to scour London's side-streets unchaperoned. Unlike Daisy Miller, Bessie is tremendously well read and, as a result, her experience of England is mediated through her reading. She is a thoroughly informed tourist and wants to see the people and places she has read about in Thackeray, Eliot, *The Morning Post* and *Punch* (349). Like James, whose childhood devotion to *Punch* made the magazine's images 'as real to him as the furniture of his own home',[64] Bessie perceives most of her own experiences through a literary filter. For great numbers of Americans, *Punch* was *the* periodical through which they gained the most discriminating insights into contemporary British culture. 'In the United States,' M. H. Spielmann explains in his history of the magazine, 'to Mr Du Maurier many people have looked almost exclusively, not only for English fashions in male and female attire, and the *dernière mode* in social etiquette, but for the truest reflections of English life and character.'[65] By associating his American girl with *Punch*, James represented a recognisable reality, a class of Anglophile Americans keenly attuned to socio-cultural and artistic developments. To Bessie, Hyde Park seems familiar because its 'humors had been made familiar to . . . [her] by the pictures in *Punch*' (CS2 370) just as James fondly remembers his joy at his first real-life encounter with the artistic London snobs he had seen in the magazine. 'We were taken in due course to Europe, and we met him [the "little London snob"] on a steam-boat on the Lake of Geneva',[66] James remembers. This encounter may have provided the germ for Daisy Miller's boat ride with Winterbourne to the Castle of Chillon by Lake Geneva, as well as the Atlantic crossing that is the opening scene of Miranda Hope's letter in 'The Point of View'.

When James set out to write 'Pandora,' he conceived a transatlantic setting in which he would place a ' "self-made girl" . . . a rival to D[aisy] M[iller]' (*Notebooks* 24). James had sold the story to a New York newspaper '*à prix d'or*' and hoped that such a mainstream venue would garner him 'the enjoyment of a popularity' that would allow him to ask a higher fee for subsequent serials (*L3* 25). The tale self-consciously refers to Daisy Millerism by describing Pandora as one of 'the new type. It has only come up lately. They have had articles about it in the papers' (*CS2* 846). Much of the story revolves around the difficulty in placing Pandora within the social scale, a frequent concern in depictions of American girls of the time. Baffled by her familiar manner, one character is relieved to find a 'Tauchnitz novel by an American author' (819) that explains Pandora's behaviour. This scene is a clever *mise-en-abyme* since the novel in question is none other than *Daisy Miller*, which had been published by the Leipzig-based publisher in 1879 (ironically, in the 'Collection of *British* Authors' series).[67] Pandora's performance amplifies Daisy's indifference to codes of behaviour. The American girl's unwitting violation of mores allows her to penetrate social spheres that would otherwise remain closed to her, while marginalising her because of her actions. James had also used this approach with his transatlantic aesthete.

In 'A Bundle of Letters' and 'The Point of View' James paired his American girl with the American aesthete for the first time. These complementary stories are both written in epistolary form, and include Louis Leverett, a Bostonian aesthete who writes from Paris in the first story and from Boston in the second. 'A Bundle of Letters' is entirely set in Europe, whereas 'The Point of View' is set in New York, Newport, Boston and Washington. In 'The Point of View', James reinforced the connection between the transatlantic aesthete and the American girl by engineering a shipboard encounter between Leverett and Aurora Church, a penny-wise American girl who had been the focus of 'The Pension Beaurepas', a story James had published three years before in *Atlantic Monthly*. Although 'The Point of View' was first published in the *Century Magazine* of December 1882, James included a note next to Aurora's name 'referring [the reader] to a little tale entitled "The Pension Beaurepas" ',[68] a strong hint that he intended his aesthetic story to be read as ancillary to his tale of an American girl abroad.

Leverett's type is partly drawn from *Punch* and the popular caricatures produced to sate the public fascination with the aesthete. He looks and sounds the part: he has the Jack Spratt physique typical of aesthetes, and he appropriates the aesthetic byword 'intense', as does Bunthorne, *Patience*'s 'most intense young man'.[69] To Miranda Hope (a Daisy Miller-type from Bangor, Maine), Leverett 'looks pretty sick' despite his 'beautiful ideas' (CS2 502). To Violet Ray, a smug New Yorker with a well-trained eye, Leverett is unmistakably 'an aesthetic young man, who talks about its being "a real Corot day" ' (494), an affectation that was also ascribed to James, who talked about a woman's frescoed face as being a Michelangelo ceiling.[70] Leverett's letters have a vague Paterian perfume mixed with the robust aroma Emersonian self-reliance: he proclaims that 'the great thing is to *live*, you know – to feel, to be conscious of one's possibilities; not to pass through life mechanically and insensibly, like a letter through the post-office' (CS2 495). James repeats this prescription in *The Art of Fiction* – 'Try to be one of the people on whom nothing is lost' (LC1 53) – and again in *The Ambassadors*, when Strether tells Little Bilham to 'Live all you can; it's a mistake not to'.[71] Lord Henry Wotton similarly tells Dorian Gray to 'Live the wonderful life that is in you! Let nothing be lost upon you. Be always searching for new sensations' (W 31), and Gabriel Nash, in *The Tragic Muse* (1890), anticipates Wilde with his proclamation that 'We must feel everything, everything we can. We are here for that' (N3 722). Sounding like Thoreau's introduction to *Walden*, Leverett aims 'to turn aside into more unfrequented ways; to plunge beneath the surface and see what I should discover' (CS2 495). Both a frontiersman and a Casanova, he is 'looking out for experiences, for sensations . . . for adventures.' He exalts originality and does not 'want any second-hand, spurious sensations; . . . [but] the knowledge that leaves a trace – that leaves strange scars and stains and reveries behind it' (495–6). Paradoxically, Leverett's pursuit of first-hand experience has led him 'along the dusty, beaten track' where he has not encountered 'those opportunities that we hear about and read about – the things that happen to people in novels and biographies'. This ostensible lack of opportunity has more to do with Leverett's own shortcomings and cowardliness than anything else. We know that he has a disease of the liver that may be jaundice, but he is also yellow and lily-livered (502). He is disappointed that the last time he was in Europe he missed the opportunity to visit Gautier, 'the great apostle of beauty' who has since passed away (496). At the time, he was travelling with an unpardonably unaesthetic family who made him feel so ashamed of his 'artistic temperament' that he was unable to go. Accusing the family of reducing everything 'to the question of right and wrong', Leverett says that their moralism prohibited him from appreciating life and art. Leverett's censorious appraisal of the family echoes Gautier's advocacy of *l'art pour l'art* and, more specifically, it matches James's appraisal of Ruskin in the late 1870s. As well, it foreshadows Wilde's 1882 introduction to Rennell Rodd's poems, 'L'envoi', in which he criticised Ruskin and said aesthetes were '*jeunes guerriers du drapeau romantique*, as Gautier would have called us'.[72] 'The many young men in England who are seeking along with me to continue to perfect the English Renaissance . . . have made a departure from the teaching of Mr Ruskin – a departure definite and different and decisive' based on the 'recognition of the primary importance of the sensuous element in art, this love of art for art's sake'.[73]

Though Leverett professes art for art's sake as his religion, he hardly knows the names of the saints he patronizes. He admits that he revels in his *naiveté* since 'that is the great thing – to be free, to be frank, to be naif. Doesn't Matthew Arnold say that somewhere – or is it Swinburne, or Pater?' (CS2 496). Dr Rudolf Staub (a German scientist whose surname evokes his preference for 'dusty', time-honoured tradition) censures Leverett's Aestheticism along lines that prefigure the scathing chapter Max Nordau would devote to 'Decadents and Aesthetes' in *Degeneration* (1895). Aestheticism is, according to Staub,

> an illustration of the period of culture in which the faculty of appreciation has obtained such a preponderance over that of production that the latter sinks into a kind of rank sterility, and the mental condition becomes analogous to that of a malarious bog. (516)

It is not just the mental faculties that have begun to atrophy, there are physical signs of degeneration, too, in American aesthetes. 'The American types here are not, I am sorry to say, so interesting as they might be,' Leverett explains to his Bostonian friend Harvard Tremont. 'We are *thin*, my dear Harvard; we are pale, we are sharp. There is something meagre about us; our line is wanting in roundness, our composition in richness' (498). Leverett might as well be describing the American people as line drawings or *Punch* aesthetes. The supreme irony in Leverett's disaffected description of the American physique resides in the fact that the skeletal image he attributes to them was, in fact, one of the aesthetes' most commonly remarked features – from Bunthorne's ecstasy over 'a pallid and thin young man'[74] to the American heroine of Lucy Lillie's *Prudence: A Story of Aesthetic London* who declares that the pictures at the Grosvenor Gallery 'look so hungry' she wishes she 'could give all the poor people Mr Burne-Jones and those other gentlemen paint a good dinner'.[75] The 1884 *Health Exhibition Literature* reported that 'in the aesthetic woman delicacy has passed into sickliness and emaciation'.[76] A thorough Anglophile, Leverett much prefers the pretty English girl, Evelyn Vane, whose aesthetic 'sage-green robe' drapes over her pre-Raphaelitic figure. Contrasting the 'cold, slim, sexless' American girls whose 'physique is not generous, not abundant', Evelyn is 'much a woman' because she is 'simpler, softer, rounder, richer than the young [American] girls' (CS2 499).

Leverett believes his Aestheticism is such an integral part of his identity that it supersedes his nationality. 'My temperament is not at all American' (498), he declares, underscoring the manner in which the aesthete's cosmopolitanism defies national tags. There is a great advantage in cosmopolitanism because, he claims, it allows one to shift points of view, collect impressions and 'enter into strange, exotic ways of looking at life' (497). Turning to study 'the American temperament', he considers Miranda Hope and Violet Ray and concludes that they think they are very different from one another but 'are both specimens of the emancipated young American girl – practical, positive, passionless, subtle, and knowing' (498). But the American girls are not the only ones to regard each other with intense suspicion. In 'The Point of View', James triangulates Aurora Church with two contrasting types of American manhood: Louis Leverett and Marcellus Cockerel, a proud young lawyer from Philadelphia who lives up to his surname. Like their female counterparts Miranda Hope and Violet Ray in 'A Bundle of Letters', these men 'hate each other awfully' (523). To Cockerel, Leverett is an affected, dyspeptic 'little ass'. Cockerel was modelled on Marian Adams, whom James visited in Washington in 1882, during which time she and her husband strenuously avoided all social gatherings where they might encounter the man she referred to as 'the ridiculous, "Hosscar" Wilde'.[77] In the transition from fact to fiction, James changed the gender valence from female to male; the ease with which he effected this transition between Marian and Leverett suggests the fluidity associated with the aesthete. The American compulsion to assess who best represents their national type proves mystifying to Staub, who notes that they 'look with the greatest mistrust and aversion upon each other; and each has repeatedly taken me apart and assured me, secretly, that he or she only is the real, the genuine, the typical American' (CS2 517). Worried that the others misrepresent the United States, each American vies for the chance to define national identity on his or her own terms, a rivalry that puzzles Staub – 'a type that has lost itself before it has been fixed – what can you look for from this?' he wonders.

In December 1882, at the conclusion of his tour, Wilde sailed back to England and Louis Leverett sailed home to Boston and into the pages of *Century Magazine*. Two and a half years had passed between his first appearance in 'A Bundle of Letters' and his reappearance in 'The Point of View', and in the interim James and Wilde had had their ill-starred encounter. James commemorated this meeting by having Leverett speak words evocative of those James had addressed to Wilde: 'I have been so long away that I have dropped out of my place in this little Boston world, and the shallow tides of New England life have closed over it.' Leverett said, 'I am a stranger here, and I find it hard to believe that I ever was a native' (548). James's encounter with Wilde afforded him a further opportunity to distinguish his Aestheticism from Wilde's, to imbue his international American aesthete with a homesickness all his own. This charged pose of alienation would become a significant motif in *The Portrait of a Lady*. James's friends recognised this depiction of alienated transatlantic aesthetes as autobiographical, 'a cry from the heart'.[78] There is undoubtedly a strong autobiographical element to these stories. In 'The Point of View', Gustave Lejaune, a French Academician visiting Washington, illustrates James's ability to mock himself. Lejaune observes that Americans have a James-like author who fancies himself a chronicler of the international scene.

> They have a novelist with pretensions to literature, who writes about the chase for the husband and the adventures of the rich Americans in our corrupt old Europe, where their primaeval candour puts the Europeans to shame. *C'est proprement écrit*; but it's terribly pale. (CS2 553)

James takes this exercise in humorous self-deprecation a step further when Lejaune rattles off a litany of lacunae such as 'no salons, no society, no conversation' and 'no architecture . . . no art, no literature, no theatre' (552–3). This was a direct response to the critics who had chastised James for his enumeration of America's shortcomings in his long 1879 essay, *Hawthorne* (*LC1* 351–2).[79] In *The Portrait of a Lady*, James transferred this negative enumeration to the aesthete by having Isabel find pleasure in Osmond's deficiencies – 'no property, no title, no honours, no houses, nor lands, nor position, nor reputation, nor brilliant belongings of any sort. It is the total absence of these things that pleases me' (*N2* 549–50). Isabel is, of course, utterly misguided about Osmond, who is a crude collector of people, objects and experiences. In Wilde's 'The Canterville Ghost' (1887), little American Virginia Otis cannot grasp why the English ghost does not want to emigrate to America. ' "I suppose because we have no ruins and no curiosities," she says. "No ruins! No curiosities!" answers the ghost, "you have your navy and your manners" (W 197).[80] A variation on this joke reappears in *A Woman of No Importance* (W 482). Wilde was aware of James's enumeration as early as 1882, when he told his Washington hostess "You have no ruins, no natural curiosities, in this country."[81] She smartly replied, "No, but our ruins will come soon enough, and we *import* our curiosities." '

Leverett symbolises the tensions between James and Wilde and the manner in which they hinge on the aesthete's claims to nationality and authenticity. James's satirical take on Leverett's philosophy augurs his reaction to Wilde, whose version of Aestheticism James would view in the same critical light. Leverett has all the trappings of a real aesthete, but that is James's trap and his ploy reveals the distinction between style and substance, between the 'real thing' and its counterfeit. By the same token, the preoccupation with authenticity and legitimacy in 'A Bundle of Letters' and 'The Point of View' resonates with James's and Wilde's encounters in this period and the social anxieties surrounding them. The aesthete and the American girl exacerbate this situation by violating of the tacit social order and norms of conduct. This anxiety about national types and characteristics also suggests the fault-lines along which *Washington Square* – which pits a traditionalist against an artistic, cosmopolitan idler – would rupture the conventional conception of the American as a unified type. The concern about 'the real, the genuine, the typical American' (*CS2* 517) in James's aesthetic stories mirrors the early controversy surrounding his unsympathetic representation of his female compatriots in *Daisy Miller* and the stories that followed. As well, it suggests the increasingly fraught nature of the public's perception of James's nationality and sexuality in this period. The reproach of Daisy Millerism, Leverett's anti-Americanism, and *Hawthorne*'s roll-call of the country's delinquencies did little to endear James to Americans. Rather, it encouraged

Americans to conflate him with his characters. Though his stories exposed societal failings, they reflected back on him. John Hay, a mutual friend of Howells and James, wrote that James was 'catching it for his "Point of View"' from 'Howling Patriots' who believed that one of the characters (who says that American children are hysterical, and women's voices higher than their manners) was James himself.[82] Similarly, the *Dial* thought Isabel Archer was 'only Mr James in domino. If popular opinion be not at fault, Osmond is the sort of man to attract a female James'.[83]

The late 1870s and early 1880s saw the publication of an abundance of aesthetic satires. While some sought to ridicule the entire movement, others singled out Wilde. A number of the West End aesthetic burlesques produced between December 1877 and February 1881 specifically caricatured Wilde: he was Bunthorne in *Patience*, Percival Gay in *Where's the Cat?* and Lambert Streyke in *The Colonel*.[84] Walter Hamilton observes that Lambert Streyke's part is that of a 'paltry swindler, who, shamming Aesthetic tastes, imposes upon a number of rather silly ladies and is finally exposed by the Colonel',[85] and that when Wilde's *Poems* first appeared, the review in *Punch* explicitly connected the two saying, 'Mr Lambert Streyke . . . published a book of poems for the benefit of his followers and his own; Mr Oscar Wilde has followed this example.'[86]

Satires of Wilde were definitely more prominent, but the many satires of James are not to be overlooked. From its inception in 1883, the New York-based *Life* magazine made it its purpose to poke fun at James and aesthetic culture. In the inaugural issue, published on 4 January 1883, *Life* bade 'farewell to '82! Year of blended gloom and glee, of foreign stars and sillies, of Oscars and lilies',[87] and by its second issue it greeted readers with a mock discussion of the morals of James's writing. Making fun of James became a mainstay of the magazine. It regularly printed parodies of James's articles written in mock-Jamesian style (such as a spoof of James's *Century* article on Du Maurier and *Punch*);[88] it ruminated at length and often about James's nationality – one symptomatic suggestion: 'James was probably an Italian Jew (a race notoriously mystic and subjective)';[89] it opined that reading James and enjoying Du Maurier's caricatures would make a man a snob;[90] and it related how, out of concern to find 'a new sensation for his jaded palate'[91] and add to his income, James had begun a second career as a highwayman. Even James's acquaintances satirised him and his version of Aestheticism. Among them was Violet Paget, who wrote under the pseudonym Vernon Lee.

Lee ostentatiously dedicated her first novel, *Miss Brown* (1884), to James and included in her book a Wildean character named Postlethwaite. James told Lee he was frightened by her invocation, and politely explained that he was 'really not *de taille* to carry' (*L3* 50) the honour. Privately, he admitted that he thought the reverse: it was Lee's 'very bad' book that was not really *de taille* to carry the honour of his name. 'I may whisper in your ear that as it is her first attempt at a novel, so it is to be hoped it may be her last,' he told T. S. Perry (61). 'It is very bad . . . and (to me at least) painfully disagreeable in tone . . . It is violently satirical, but the satire is strangely without delicacy or fineness.'

Lucy Lillie's *Prudence: A Story of Aesthetic London* was an even more indelicate tribute to James. This heavy-handed rewrite of *The Portrait of a Lady* closely imitated James's novel and was serialised in *Harper's New Monthly Magazine* from February to April 1882 before being published, with illustrations by Du Maurier, later the same year.[92] Lillie's story culminated with her heroine – Prudence Marlitt of Ponkamak, Maine – seeing the errors of her aesthetic ways and choosing Jonas Fielding (a sensible Caspar Goodwood type), while Barley Simmonson (the Gilbert Osmond figure) was made to abscond to Algiers, much to the heroine's relief. Far from deploying James's subtle moral scheme, Lillie repeatedly reminds her reader of the perils of Aestheticism with clumsy propositions such as 'the evil of this aesthetic movement is that it tortures every sentiment either with analysis or sensuousness. The honest fibre of the thing is lost.'[93] We can be certain that Du Maurier saw the parallel between this story and James's because he made Lillie's version of Osmond look exactly like the moustachioed, monocle-wearing painter Whistler, another public aesthete who was commonly mooted as a source for Du Maurier's *Punch* caricatures (Figure 1.2). Just a year earlier, Du Maurier had depicted *Washington Square*'s shady hero, Morris Townsend, as Wilde, who was during those days often seen with Whistler in London society.

The charge of anti-Americanism levelled against James was quickly conjoined with accusations of effeminacy, a characterisation that conspired to unite James and Wilde in the collective consciousness. Fictional characters inspired by James reinforced the public perception of him as an effeminate dandy, separate but equal to Wilde's type. Lee's short story 'Lady Tal' (1892) contrasts Jamesian and Wildean types as 'the well turned out, subdued, Parisian-American aesthete talking with an English accent about modern

"MR. FIELDING, WHAT DO YOU THINK OF THESE PICTURES? THIS IS ART."

1.2 Lucy Lillie's *Prudence: A Story of Aesthetic London* was a heavy-handed rewrite of *The Portrait of a Lady*, illustrated by Du Maurier. Lillie's Isabel Archer figure, Prudence Marlitt, is seated at the centre and flanked by two moustachioed men resembling Whistler on her left and a standing figure resembling Wilde on her right. (George Du Maurier, 'Mr. Fielding, what do you think of these pictures? This is art', in *Prudence: A Story of Aesthetic London*. New York: Harper & Brothers, 1882, 109. Courtesy of the Trustees of the National Library of Scotland.)

pictures and ladies' dresses; and the awkward, enthusiastic English aesthete who considered Ruskin a ranter and creaked over the marble floors with dusty seven-mile boots.'[94] The story satirises James as the womanish, cosmopolitan American, Jervase Marion. 'A kind of Henry James, of a lesser magnitude', a 'dainty but frugal bachelor',[95] Marion's name is pronounced '*Mary Anne*, with unfailing relish of the joke'.[96] Marion has a flat in Westminster, across from St James's Park, an area of London that was part of the 'homosocial circuit'.[97] James did not see the comedy in Lee's 'flagrant and markedly "saucy"' story, which made his sexuality more obvious than he liked (*L3* 402). The term 'Mary-Ann' had become part of homosexual subculture by the first decade of the eighteenth century, when it was adopted as a euphemism for (often cross-dressed) male prostitutes who had sex with men.[98] The porno-graphic novel *Sins of the Cities of the Plain, or Confessions of a Mary-Ann* (1881) casually reports that the ' "Mary-Ann's" [*sic*] of London' are often 'seen sauntering in the neighbourhood of Regent Street, or the Haymarket'.[99] The term became slang for effeminate or dandified men who were assumed to be homosexual, which is the sense which Lee's story plays on. Almost as soon as Wilde arrived in America, he was described as a 'Charlotte-Ann',[100] a double-valenced moniker that identified him as a charlatan but had the same implications of effeminacy as the 'Mary-Ann'. For Americans, the period of cultural expansion and experimentation encouraged by the Aesthetic Movement was rapidly brought to a halt in 1895. Wilde's trial, the revival of a masculine ethos Theodore Roosevelt's rise and the imperialist projects of the late 1890s suddenly made Aestheticism irrelevant.[101]As part of his patriotic programme, Roosevelt connected James's lack of Americanness with effeminacy 'verging on total emasculation' by calling him sensitive and 'under-sized'.[102] In 1884, Roosevelt gave a highly disparaging speech to the Brooklyn Young Republican Club in which the *New York Times* claimed he had said that James 'bore the same relation to other lit-erary men that a poodle did to other dogs. The poodle had his hair combed and was somewhat ornamental, but never useful.'[103] In 1915, Roosevelt compared Henry and William James and found the former lacking all-American virility and drive:

> [Henry] cannot play a man's part among men, and so goes where he will be sheltered from the winds that harden stouter souls. This *emigré* may write graceful and pretty verses, essays, novels; but he will never do work to compare with that of his brother, who is strong enough to stand on his own feet, and do his work as an American.[104]

As Andrew Taylor explains, William's pragmatism was promoted as an American, manly philosophy, whereas Henry's work was regarded as soft and un-American. A similar distinction underlies William's commentary on Henry's work: from the outset he criticised Henry's stories for their 'want of blood'[105] and their inclination to be 'trifling'. Following James's change of citizenship, in 1915, the *Times* criticised Jamesian cosmopolitanism for being conducive to 'a flaccid habit of mind' which 'disqualif[ied] a man from doing good work in the world'.[106]

Wilde in the United States

Perhaps the most remarkable feature of the transatlantic aesthete is the lengths to which James goes to fix him as a Bostonian: 'A Bundle of Letters' and 'The Point of View' painstakingly call attention to the fact that Louis Leverett is a Bostonian aesthete, not an English one. Leverett proudly tells his fellow *pensionnaires* that 'there is an immense number of Americans exactly resembling him, and that the city of Boston, indeed, is almost exclusively composed of them' (*CS2* 515). In the late 1870s and early 1880s, Boston was known for its flourishing aesthetic culture, but it was also known for its intellectualism and worldly Puritanism, as Wilde attested when he called it 'the paradise of prigs' (*RW* 36). The American girl's enthusiastic questions about Boston lead Leverett to the conclusion that she feels about Boston 'as a good Mahommedan feels toward Mecca, and regards it as a kind of focus of light for the whole human race' (*CS2* 498). Despite this focus on Boston, Leverett believes that Aestheticism will conquer the world for 'a great aesthetic renascence is at hand, and that a great light will be kindled in England, for all the world to see' (499). Leverett does not yearn for Pater's *Renaissance* but for 'the revival of taste, of the sense of beauty, in England'. In short, he seems to point towards Wilde's 1882 lecture on 'The English Renaissance of Art'.

As a lecturer in America, Wilde was fundamentally theatrical and dependent on the largesse of an audience who often professed to disdain him. Most members of Wilde's audience thought of him as an aesthetic creation, not as an artist in his own right, and that most critics judged him on these terms. *Patience* and *Punch* implicitly claimed Wilde as their words and images made flesh. Despite unfavourable incidents and feeble reviews, Americans were generally charitable to Wilde. In considering Wilde's American reception, we must remember how scant his literary accomplishments were at this time, a reality that caused one American reviewer to comment that Wilde's 'only distinction is that he has written a volume of very mediocre verse and that he makes himself something very like a buffoon for notoriety and money'.[107]

Boston's reaction to Wilde illustrates the degree to which the American public ran hot and cold. The city that billed itself 'the Athens of America' was less than enthusiastic about the author of 'Charmides', a poem about 'a Grecian lad' who made love to a statue of Athena. Home to an affluent population that had richly profited from speculation in railroads, manufacturing, banking and other business, Boston billed itself the most intellectual of American cities. Though Wilde was rebuked on a few occasions – in reviews by Thomas Wentworth Higginson and by the publicised seclusion of the T. W. Aldrichs – these petty displays were not the measure of the city's reception.[108] The extent of Wilde's success in Boston is better understood by the degree to which he penetrated to the inner sancta of its Brahmin circles. Wilde met Harriet Beecher Stowe's brother, Henry Ward Beecher, Julian Hawthorne (whom both James and Wilde had met in England),[109] Oliver Wendell Holmes,[110] Isabella Stewart Gardner, Francis Marion Crawford, Henry Wadsworth Longfellow, George Lewis (whom James had known since 1879), Norman Forbes-Robertson and Julia Ward Howe. Many of these people were James's longstanding friends, and he called on a number of them while Wilde was in the country.

Wilde's greatest champions in the Boston area were the writer and social activist Julia Ward Howe, and her brother Sam Ward, an internationally celebrated *bon vivant*. James had breakfasted with Ward and Charles Eliot Norton in 1869, during his first adult trip abroad, before going to visit William Morris. It was now Wilde's turn to be received by Sam Ward, 'The King of the Lobby', who justified the lavish dinners he offered congressmen by explaining that 'the way to a man's "aye" is through his stomach'.[111] Ward welcomed Wilde with a poem titled 'The Aesthetic' in the New York *World*, and an invitation to dinner addressed to 'My dear Charmides'.[112] *Frank Leslie's Illustrated Newspaper* ran a drawing of the pair at the beach featuring Wilde in a bathing suit.[113] Ward had already met Wilde a few years earlier, on a visit to Lord Ronald Sutherland Gower's cottage, to which Wilde had brought the young poet Rennell Rodd from Oxford.[114] Commenting on Wilde's American reception, Ward deplored the fact that this 'sincere fellow' was caught 'in a false position, having been imported as a speculation by D'Oyly Carte to revive the flagging public interest in "Patience"' and condemned to be treated by the American crowds 'like a Barnum Jumbo' wherever he went.[115] Wilde was delighted to dine with Howe's family and spend the night at her house in Newport, complimenting her by saying that 'when you are present, the air is cosmopolitan and the room seems to be full of brilliant people' (*LW* 176). Howe held a Sunday luncheon for Wilde, which Isabella Stewart Gardner and a dozen or so others attended.[116] Inspired by her aesthetic visitor, Howe even wrote her own version of *Patience*.[117] Howe's daughter, Maude Howe Elliott, records that the 'most sensational incident' of 1882 was without a doubt 'the advent of the Apostle of Aestheticism, Oscar Wilde, already a familiar figure from Du Maurier's caricatures of him as Postlethwaite in *Punch* and by Gilbert and Sullivan's character of Bunthorne in *Patience*.'[118] The fact that Wilde made Boston his summer base, from approximately 16 July to 8 August, and again from 17 August to 25 September, is a measure of the degree of acceptance he gained there.

We can assume that talk turned to Wilde during James's April 1882 visit to Julia Ward Howe.[119] Howe's warm reception of Wilde in Boston provides a stark contrast to Marian Adams's coolness in Washington. Their divergent responses are representative of the ways in which the American public reacted to Wilde. Howe risked her reputation by associating with Wilde, enduring an attack by Higginson in the pages of the *Woman's Journal*. Higginson thought it unseemly that she should receive Wilde, Howe fought back in a letter to the *Boston Transcript*, and the *Nation* publicised the debate by publishing an article on Wilde's social treatment. Howe argued that Wilde deserved 'a fair hearing' and that it was unchristian 'to cut off even an offensive member of society from its best influences and most humanizing resources'.[120] The *Nation* summarised the debate with mock seriousness:

> This is a new view of the relation which society ought to adopt toward the aesthete; and that it should exist at all, accounts in a measure for the increasing seriousness of the discussion about him in New England. The suggestion that the author of *Charmides* may be made pure and good by cordial and kindly intercourse with the ladies of Boston, will probably make the young man and his manager weep for joy.[121]

Marian Adams was amused to read this. She considered Howe's attitude to 'that vulgar cad Oscar Wilde'[122] ludicrous: 'that Julia Howe should reform sinners by suppers and flattery is charming on the same principle that her moral brother Sam Ward gave him a feast in New York from which he is said to have been carried home drunk.' Adams's and Howe's differing responses to Wilde, and Adams's disdain for Howe's defiance of social codes, mirror the behaviour of James's American girls who gossiped about each other and the aesthetic Louis Leverett.

Washington Square

Washington Square is a tale of romance and finance. The story turns on the fate of an American heiress whose father prevents her from marrying the penniless lounger she loves. Though the absence of explicit references to Aestheticism as well as the novel's pre-Civil War setting seems to distinguish it from the European-American fictions James was rapidly turning into his speciality, the novel actually recuperates and extends the characteristics of the transatlantic aesthete in a number of significant and surprising ways, not least through Du Maurier's illustrations for the novel and the dramatisation of the problem of taste in an American context.

Washington Square was a double first for James: it was the first of his novels to be illustrated, and with it he achieved serialisation on both sides of the Atlantic. Du Maurier's twelve illustrations for *Washington Square* first appeared in Britain in *Cornhill Magazine* from June to November 1880 and were then reproduced in the American book edition published by Harper and Brothers in December 1880. As a result, the images were seen by both British and American readers.[123] This is highly significant because Du Maurier's illustrations unmistakeably portray the indolent beau, Morris Townsend, as Oscar Wilde. This put greater emphasis on the narrative's exploration of social currency (especially in relation to taste and money), a theme that had rapidly become one of the cultural keynotes of Anglo-American Aestheticism. By situating *Washington Square* in 1850s New York and including Aesthetic types current in the late 1870s and early 1880s, James was effectively rewriting literary and cultural history and providing an explicitly American genealogy for Aestheticism's concern with discernment and money. Giving his readers a thirty-year perspective on the novel's events and setting them in the United States allowed *Washington Square*'s readers to see American, rather than British society, as the antecedent for many of the concerns that animated Aestheticism. Noting the affinity between contemporary New York and *Washington Square*'s mid-century society, one reviewer noted that the novel's characters 'are no strangers to metropolitan residents today'.[124] With *Washington Square*, James developed further his explicitly American aesthetic genealogy for the characters and characteristics Wilde and his ilk claimed to have invented.

Du Maurier's illustrations for *Washington Square* accentuate the continuities between Townsend, Wilde and Jamesian aesthetes. When informed that his work would be illustrated, James was concerned that images were inappropriate for the 'purely American' (*LL* 119) tale he had carefully 'constructed in crude defiance of the illustrator'.[125] Yet he found comfort, and even pleasure, in the prospect of being associated with *Punch*'s most successful satirist of the Aesthetic Movement. James described Du Maurier's commission as a 'happy accident' that instantly reassured him because his confidence 'had been fed by all the happy years of [Du Maurier's] work on *Punch*'. Du Maurier's interest in the American girl suited him to the project, as did the closeness of his method to James's. Du Maurier's *Punch* caricatures had not only taken aim at the aesthetes, but at the American girl, whom Du Maurier considered a sort of liberated, ill-mannered, vernacular of her English counterpart.[126] Like Daisy Miller and her sisters, Du Maurier's enchantingly gauche American young women had a thoroughly touristic interest in England, cared little for transcendental subtleties, and dreamed of marrying a lord. Du Maurier's interrelated drawings, like James's own interrelated stories, sketched 'a general satiric picture of the social life of his time and country', and James called Du Maurier 'a wonderfully copious and veracious historian of his age and his civilization'[127] – words often ascribed to James himself. They are, moreover, oddly evocative of those that adorn his gravestone in Cambridge Cemetery: 'Henry James, O. M. Novelist, citizen of two countries, interpreter of his generation on both sides of the sea.'

So close were their artistic affinities that James likened his sense of Du Maurier to a 'language' in which he had acquired fluency, confessing that their idiom was so fused that it was a struggle to consider Du Maurier with any degree of exteriority.[128] Du Maurier's visual style had helped James define the way in which he wrote about aesthetes because, James affirmed,

> no one has rendered like Du Maurier the ridiculous little people who crop up in the interstices of that huge and complicated London world . . . We have no such finished types as these in America . . . the snob, the cad, the prig, the duffer, – Du Maurier has given us a thousand times the portrait of such specialities. No one has done the 'duffer' so well . . . None of his duffers have been so good as his aesthetic duffers.[129]

With Du Maurier's illustrations for the novel, *Washington Square* became a vehicle for James's vision of the idle, manipulative proto-aesthete.

Washington Square is a novel about varieties of Americans and it thus problematised the social stratification that Aestheticism exacerbated despite the movement's avowedly democratic ambitions. 'I am helped by a habit I have of dividing people into classes, into types,' Dr Sloper tells Townsend's sister. 'I may easily be mistaken about your brother as an individual, but his type is written on his whole person' (N2 75). The markers of Townsend's type, we learn, are hedonism, laziness, and the ability to attract devoted female followers eager to ensure the satisfaction of his every whim. Likewise, the Punch aesthete was often girdled by female admirers of his beauty and artistic nature (Figure 1.3). These female aesthetes were often older than their male counterparts and were willing to marry for poverty (not despite it) because they considered simplicity noble, a sentiment illustrated by Mariana Bilderbogie's engagement to poor Peter Pilcox in 'Aesthetic Love in a Cottage' (Figure 1.4). Townsend is a version of the artistic, indolent types James portrayed in Roderick Hudson. Barnaby Striker, the practical lawyer who calls their work ethic into question is a precursor for Dr Sloper, whose reproving relationship to Townsend mirrors the one between Striker and Hudson. Catherine Sloper's innocence, determination and unconventionality inscribe her into the catalogue of womanhood James was elaborating in this period. Catherine is an ugly duckling in a sisterhood that includes Daisy Miller, Bessie Alden, Isabel Archer, Miranda Hope and Violet Ray.

Townsend is a proto-aesthete; Louis Leverett, Du Maurier's Postlethwaite and Maudle, Bunthorne and Wilde are his cognates. Townsend's interest in Catherine is expressed in terms that coalesce the financial and the aesthetic, for he has more taste than funds, and her situation is the reverse. James insinuates this theme early on, describing Catherine's unfortunate choice of evening wear as a garish 'red satin gown trimmed with gold fringe' (N2 14). The gilt edging, with its evident economic symbolism, frames a picture of femininity that even Catherine's father finds distasteful. It is in this dress that the broad-backed Catherine is placed alongside her newly-engaged cousin, 'a pretty little person of seventeen, with a very small figure and a very big sash, to the elegance of whose manners matrimony had nothing to add' (18). This is the scene, in chapter four, in which Catherine is presented to Townsend, the man who promises to give her, if nothing else, the refinement she lacks. He takes her for what she is – a young woman who looks like she has 80,000 dollars a year – and during the carriage ride home,

THE MUTUAL ADMIRATIONISTS.

(*Fragments overheard by Grigsby and the Colonel at one of Prigsby's Afternoon Teas.*)

Young Maudle (to Mrs. Lyon Hunter and her Daughters). "IN THE SUPREMEST POETRY, SHAKSPEARE'S, FOR INSTANCE, OR POSTLE-THWAITE'S, OR SHELLEY'S, ONE ALWAYS FEELS THAT, &c., &c., &c."

Young Postlethwaite (to the three Miss Bilderbogies). "THE GREATEST PAINTERS OF ALL, SUCH AS VELASQUEZ, OR MAUDLE, OR EVEN TITIAN, INVARIABLY SUGGEST TO ONE, &c., &c., &c."

1.3 (*Fragments overheard by Grigsby and the Colonel at one of Prigsby's Afternoon Teas.*)

Young Maudle (to Mrs. Lyon Hunter and her Daughters). '*In the Supremest Poetry, Shakespeare's, for instance, or Postlethwaite's, or Shelley's, one always feels that, &c., &c., &c.*'

Young Postlethwaite (to the three Miss Bilderbogies). '*The greatest painters of all, such as Velasquez, or Maudle, or even Titian, invariably suggest to one, &c., &c., &c.*'

Young Maudle, in the background at left, closely resembles Wilde. *Punch* aesthetes, such as Young Postlethwaite in the foreground at right, were often depicted as being surrounded by female admirers. (George Du Maurier, 'The Mutual Admirationists', *Punch* 22 May 1880, 234. Courtesy of the Trustees of the National Library of Scotland.)

Catherine's aunt explains, in a roundabout manner, that she has been speaking to Townsend to see if he would like to take Catherine.

> 'The devotion was not to me,' said Mrs Penniman. 'It was to Catherine; he talked to me of her.'

ÆSTHETIC LOVE IN A COTTAGE.

Miss Bilderbogie. "YES, DEAREST JOCONDA! I AM GOING TO MARRY YOUNG PETER PILCOX! WE SHALL BE VERY, VERY POOR! INDEED HOW WE ARE GOING TO *LIVE*, I CANNOT TELL!"

Mrs. Cimabue Brown. "OH, MY BEAUTIFUL MARIANA, HOW *NOBLE* OF YOU BOTH! NEVER MIND *HOW*, BUT *WHERE* ARE YOU GOING TO LIVE?"

Miss Bilderbogie. "OH, IN DEAR OLD KENSINGTON, I SUPPOSE—EVERYTHING IS SO CHEAP THERE, YOU KNOW!—PEACOCK FEATHERS ONLY A *PENNY A-PIECE!*"

1.4 Punch's female aesthetes were usually older than their male counterparts and were willing to marry for high-minded reasons. (George Du Maurier, 'Aesthetic Love in a Cottage', *Punch* 19 February 1881, 78. Courtesy of the Trustees of the National Library of Scotland.)

> Catherine had been listening with all her ears. 'Oh, Aunt Penniman!' she
>   exclaimed faintly.
> 'He is very handsome; he is very clever; he expressed himself with a great
>   deal – a great deal of felicity,' her aunt went on.
> 'He is in love with this regal creature, then?' the Doctor inquired humor-
>   ously.
> 'Oh, father,' cried the girl, still more faintly, devoutly thankful the car-
>   riage was dark.
> 'I don't know that; but he admired her dress.' . . .
> 'You see,' said her father, 'he thinks you have 80,000 a year.' (N2 23)

We know, of course, that Townsend does not admire Catherine's dress any more than her father thinks her a 'regal creature'. But James's counterpointing of love, aesthetic taste and money tells us everything we need to know about what Townsend really thinks he will acquire if he marries Catherine.

In my discussion of James's early stories, I considered how James presented the aesthete as a socially unclassifiable, artistic, duplicitous, cosmopolitan young man. The years in which *Washington Square* were written and published represent a critical moment in the history of Aestheticism when idleness, social indeterminacy and mercenariness were rapidly becoming affiliated to the aesthetic type. This conglomerate of attributes would be cemented with Wilde's 1882 North American lecture tour, because Wilde was almost universally seen as the personification of these characteristics.

The anecdote for *Washington Square* was suggested to James by the actress Fanny Kemble, who was a friend of William Morris as well as of James. James's choice of Morris Townsend as the name of his hero hints at this connection, as well as at his personal valuation of William Morris, whom James once described as 'a boisterous, boyish, British man of action and practical faculty, launched indeed by his imagination, but really floundering and romping and roaring through the arts, both literary and plastic, very much as a bull through a chinashop' (*L4* 123). James had been introduced to Morris by Charles Eliot Norton in 1869, on the same day he met Sam Ward. In an excited letter to his sister Alice, the twenty-six year-old James described the afternoon and evening he had spent with William Morris and described him as a marginal artistic type similar to Morris Townsend. 'Morris lives on the same premises as his shop, in Queen's Square, Bloomsbury, an antiquated ex-fashionable region . . . with a hoary effigy of Queen Anne in the middle . . . Everything he has and does is superb and beautiful' (*L1* 93). Despite the positive impression Morris created, James concluded that 'there was something very quaint and remote from our actual life, it seemed to me in the whole scene' (94). This association may have been an impetus for James's decision to shift his novel back in time and to make Morris Townsend's geographical and social dislocation one of *Washington Square*'s primary themes.

Townsend's name emphasises his displacement by underscoring the fact that he does not belong in Washington Square, the then-fashionable centre of New York.[130] In addition, Townsend's utter disregard for social codes marks him as an intruder.[131] Though he freely admits to Catherine on first meeting her that he is 'a great stranger in New York' (*N2* 20), there is a *louche* edge to him, which is further sharpened by his admission that he has 'been knocking about the world, and living in far-away lands'. His behaviour indicates that he is not a part of this social set, and thus incongruity is exacerbated by the foreign airs he has acquired during his vague travels abroad. He has seen all the major actors, visited the best theatres in London and Paris, but he does not know anyone in New York (27). Though 'he's very sociable, and he wants to know every one,' the problem is that the society which he would like to enter knows very little about him, except for 'a vague story that he has been "wild"' (35). Like Louis Leverett, Townsend 'is artistic – tremendously artistic' (131) and out of his element. James called Aestheticism 'a queer high-flavoured fruit from overseas' (*LC2* 908), and his artistic young men partake of this vaguely threatening foreign association. James ably played on the ambiguous menace of 'a foreign manner' (*N3* 1208) through characters such as Louis Leverett and, later, Mark Ambient and Gabriel Nash. James had rehearsed this predicament in 'The Point of View', where Aurora Church's mother worries about her daughter's relationship with Louis Leverett because 'he offers absolutely no guarantees' (*CS2* 532). Leverett has lived abroad a great deal which gives Mrs Church 'no means whatever of ascertaining his pecuniary situation'. During James's 1905 lecture tour of America, he played on the perceived 'foreignness' of Aestheticism's most famous exponent by calling Wilde a foreigner and trickster, 'one of those Irish adventurers who had something of the Roman character – able but false' (Edel 5: 278). James's behaviour here can be read as an instance of his well-documented practice of occasionally kowtowing to the cultural chauvinisms of his time.

Townsend has lived abroad and developed 'a kind of system, a theory' (*N2* 36), and he has come back to America to begin life in earnest. Sounding like Louis Leverett and prefiguring Lambert Strether, Townsend tells Catherine that he always tried to experience things first-hand because, 'to see for yourself – that was the great thing; he always tried to see for himself' (33). Like the aesthete whose predilections are incomprehensible to those who are not part of his clique, Townsend's system and tastes seem perverse to Dr Sloper. What counts for him is that Townsend is 'not a commonplace young man' (39), which is why his daughter must give him up. As Grosvenor and Bunthorne put it in *Patience*, the opposite of 'a matter-of-fact young man'[132] is 'an ultra-poetical, super-aesthetical, out-of-the-way young man!' The problem, for Dr Sloper, is that Townsend and his tastes 'belong to the wrong category' (N2 63), just as Bunthorne admits that Aestheticism is 'but good taste misplaced'.[133] The aesthete's exaltation of taste is an expression of his power, a means of awing a gullible audience or seducing innocents.[134] Through his mysterious preferences, he gains the advancement and financial success unavailable to him by birth or social status.

Like the *Punch* caricatures of young men who eschew the professions, Townsend has plenty of leisure, and he revels in his indolence. He has expensive tastes, and he indulges them at the expense of others, taking advantage of Dr Sloper's absence to turn the house into 'a club with a single member' (N2 122). The danger of idleness registers fully here as its dependence on parasitism and duplicity is made clear: Townsend makes others pay for his indolence by working himself into their good graces. The man without a profession represented an equally perilous prospect (or lack thereof). This threat is palpable in Du Maurier's 'Maudle on the Choice of a Profession' (Figure 1.5), where existing beautifully is occupation enough for the Wilde-looking aesthete. Likewise, in *The Tragic Muse*, when Gabriel Nash is asked if he is an aesthete, he responds that he has no profession because 'merely to be is such a métier; to live is such an art; to feel is such a career!' (N3 724). Parasitism and deception are common themes in representations of the aesthete. James makes Louis Leverett 'sensitive to the charm of fatigue, of duplicity' (CS2 497) and, when unobserved, *Patience*'s Bunthorne admits he is a 'sham'.[135] *Punch* compares Wilde to 'a shallow swindler' who 'may be Aesthetic, but is not original',[136] and Francis C. Burnand's popular aesthetic burlesque, *The Colonel* (1881), includes an aesthete-swindler whose preposterous conversation and manners were said to be representative of Wilde's foibles.[137] Morris's courting of Catherine anticipates this mercenary attitude, as well as Wilde's assault on America.

The visual similarities between Du Maurier's version of Townsend, *Punch*'s 'aesthetic duffers' and Wilde resonate with James's text for *Washington Square*. Moreover, Townsend's attitude foreshadows Wilde's attitude during his lecture tour. Americans were aware of the commercial implications of Wilde's visit and knowingly dubbed him an 'a$$-thete' and an 'ass-thete' (Figure 1.6).[138] Archibald Forbes, a British war correspondent who was lecturing in America at the same time as Wilde, threatened Wilde with 'the knowledge I have, and

MAUDLE ON THE CHOICE OF A PROFESSION.

Maudle. "How CONSUMMATELY LOVELY YOUR SON IS, MRS. BROWN!"

Mrs. Brown (a Philistine from the country). "WHAT? HE'S A NICE, MANLY BOY, IF YOU MEAN THAT, MR. MAUDLE. HE HAS JUST LEFT SCHOOL, YOU KNOW, AND WISHES TO BE AN ARTIST."

Maudle. "WHY SHOULD HE BE AN ARTIST?"

Mrs. Brown. "WELL, HE MUST BE SOMETHING!"

Maudle. "WHY SHOULD HE BE ANYTHING? WHY NOT LET HIM REMAIN FOR EVER CONTENT TO EXIST BEAUTIFULLY?"

[*Mrs. Brown determines that at all events her Son shall not study Art under Maudle.*

1.5 Maudle. *'How consummately lovely your son is, Mrs. Brown!'*

Mrs. Brown (a Philistine from the country). *'What? He's a nice, manly boy, if you mean that, Mr. Maudle. He has just left school, you know and wishes to be an artist.'*

Maudle. *'Why should he be an artist?'*

Mrs. Brown. *'Well, he must be something!'*

Maudle. *'Why should he be anything? Why not let him remain for ever content to exist beautifully?'*

Mrs. Brown determines that at all events her son shall not study Art under Maudle. (George Du Maurier, 'Maudle on the Choice of a Profession', *Punch* 12 February 1881, 62. Courtesy of the Trustees of the National Library of Scotland.)

1.6 *D'oily Cod (aside) – 'Have Patience with Oscar and I'll manage the rest.'*

During Wilde's American lecture tour, D'Oyly Carte (centre) scheduled Wilde's lectures on Aestheticism to take place just before *Patience* would open in various American cities. Americans were aware of the commercial implications of Wilde's visit and knowingly dubbed him an 'a$$-thete'. This contemporary cartoon makes explicit the widespread connection between Wilde and Bunthorne, the sham aesthete. (Detail from 'Aestheticism as Oscar Understands It', *The Daily Graphic: An Illustrated Evening Newspaper* [New York] 11 January 1882, 1. Courtesy of the New York State Library.)

which you know I have, of the utterly mercenary aim of your visit to America'.[139] This was a feeble menace since the objective of Wilde's tour could easily be divined from its sponsorship by Richard D'Oyly Carte. For James, too, Wilde and wealth were part of the same semantic field. Though money was deemed nearly unmentionable in genteel society, financial concerns are a leitmotiv in James's relation to Wilde, a theme to which James would return again and again over the years, referring euphemistically to Wilde's 'success' (but often omitting to modify his noun with the implicit adjective: financial). When James eschewed propriety, he overcompensated by gossiping, as in 1895 when he wrote that 'with his two roaring successes [*An Ideal Husband* and *The Importance of Being Earnest*] running now at once [Wilde] must be raking in the profits.'[140]

Townsend has many of the qualities associated with the aesthete, and one more: he is a clever talker, a quality for which Wilde was famous.[141] Townsend's talk is all sparkle and wit against the dim backdrop of Catherine's silence, and his scintillating oral performance does much to endear him to her. When they first meet, she is grateful for his informality (despite the fact that it is inappropriate, which she does not seem to notice), because his loquaciousness relieves her of the need to talk, so that she can lean back and admire his handsome figure (*N2* 19). 'Catherine had never heard any one – especially any young man – talk just like that. It was the way a young man might talk in a novel; or, better still, in a play, on the stage, close before the footlights' (20). Townsend's hope is that his silver tongue will earn him gold, and this is what makes his behaviour with Catherine a performance worthy of an actor. The objective of his clever talk is to sway her to marry him and share her fortune, in other words, to develop such as strong taste for him that she will put her money where his mouth is. James's narrative closely twines economics and discernment and the novel reaches its first climax when Dr Sloper abruptly attempts to rupture this narrative thread by confronting Townsend in chapter twelve:

> 'Did you really expect I would say I was delighted, and throw my daughter into your arms?'
>
> 'Oh no; I had an idea you didn't like me.'
>
> 'What gave you the idea?'
>
> 'The fact that I am poor.'
>
> 'That has a harsh sound,' said the Doctor, 'but it is about the truth – speaking of you strictly as a son-in-law. Your absence of means, of a profession, of visible resources or prospects, places you in a category from which it would be imprudent for me to select a husband for my daughter . . .'
>
> ' . . . you mean, I am mercenary – I only want your daughter's money.'
>
> 'I don't say that. I am not obliged to say it; and to say it, save under stress of compulsion, would be very bad taste.' (63)

Dr Sloper rejects Townsend in order to uphold his personal standard of taste. 'Bad taste' is a compact emblem for everything Townsend symbolises to Dr Sloper, and his lack of money is just another indicator of Townsend's objectionableness. Bill Brown is right that Townsend's devotion to Catherine is motivated by his 'hope of securing her father's things for himself'[142] and that Townsend's taste is 'expressed through acquisitive eyes that motivate the descriptions of the Doctor's house, extending and intensifying his every glance.' Yet Townsend has also been sounding out Catherine's tastes, as in chapter six when his interview with her takes 'a practical turn, and he asked a number of questions about herself – what were her tastes – if she liked this and that' (N2 32).[143] When Dr Sloper offers to take Catherine to Europe in the hope that she will develop good taste, Catherine counters with a proposition that displeases Dr Sloper so much that he growls, 'that idea is in very bad taste . . . did you get it from Mr Townsend?' (117). Yet Dr Sloper's European proposition is certainly more crass and financially-driven than anything he could attribute to Townsend. 'I have done a mighty good thing . . . in taking you abroad,' Dr Sloper tells Catherine. 'Your value is twice as great, with all the knowledge and taste that you have acquired. A year ago, you were perhaps a little limited – a little rustic; but now you have seen everything, and appreciated everything, and you will be a most entertaining companion' (127).

Washington Square dramatises the moral ugliness of Dr Sloper and Townsend, and it is equally unstinting in its depiction of aesthetic ugliness. 'The reason Catherine has received so little attention,' her aunt explains, 'is that she seems to all the young men to be older than themselves. She is so large, and she dresses – so richly. They are rather afraid of her, I think; she looks as if she had been married already' (36). At every turn, James's narrative assures us that Catherine is not pretty, clever or quick, and that she is a glutton (10). Given the precision of these disparaging observations, Du Maurier's complete disregard for them in his illustration of Catherine proves jarring for even the most superficial of readers. The pretty, wasp-waisted Catherine in his illustrations looks nothing like the large, 'absolutely unattractive' (36) young woman James describes in the novel (Figures 1.8, 1.11). James's unromanticised rendition was an extreme version of his earlier unsympathetic portrayals of American girls and aesthetes. By making Catherine unattractive, James emphasised his agreement with Du Maurier's satirical vision and their shared ability to make ugliness a successful subject. In 'Du Maurier and London Society', James commended Du Maurier for seeing 'ugliness wonderfully well when he has a strong motive for looking for it, as witness so many of the figures in his crusade against the "aesthetic" movement.'[144] Why wouldn't Du

Maurier have readers see Catherine's ugliness? It is likely that he had a stronger motive to look for it in Townsend and Mrs Penniman, since they shared so many of the features of the aesthetic men and women he had done in *Punch*. In 'Du Maurier and London Society', James wondered

> who could be uglier than Maudle and Postlethwaite, and all the other apparitions from 'passionate Brompton'? Who could have more bulging foreheads, more protuberant eyes, more retreating jaws, more sloping shoulders, more objectionable hair, more of the signs generally of personal debility? (54–5)

The answer, in *Washington Square*, was Townsend and Mrs Penniman, the two characters most markedly drawn from the pages of *Punch*.

Physically, Du Maurier's Townsend is the exact counterpart of Wilde and *Punch*'s aesthetes. His posture – a stoop that gives the body a marked S- or C-shape – imitates that of Du Maurier's aesthetes, such as Postlethwaite and Maudle in 'Affiliating an Aesthete', a caricature that was published at the same time as the first instalment of *Washington Square* (Figures 1.7, 1.8). The aesthete's slouch may have been reinterpreted as a stereotypical homosexual pose due to its association with Wilde and its effeminate implications.[145] The shape of Townsend's face and his floppy hair also emulate those of the aesthetes, and Wilde's hair was much remarked on during his time in the United States (Figures 1.9, 1.10).[146] 'The Mutual Admirationists' (Figure 1.3) shows a long-haired young Maudle in the upper left wholeheartedly recommending the poetry of Postlethwaite to Mrs Lyon Hunter, while young Postlethwaite sincerely recommends Maudle's paintings to the three Misses Bilderbogie.

Young Maudle's exceptionally erect carriage is the same as Morris's in Du Maurier's illustration for chapter 20 (Figure 1.11). As a result of Townsend's powers of persuasion, Catherine agrees to marry him and he, realising all of a sudden what this involves, looks down at his 'prize' and then, steeling himself, looks up 'rather vaguely, with parted lips and lifted eyebrows' (N2 108) – a complex mixture of emotions that Du Maurier's drawing portrays eloquently. Townsend's broad chest is also reminiscent of aesthetes' physiques, such as Prigsby in 'Nincompoopiana' (Figure 1.12), who also sports Wilde's characteristic long hair, top hat and long coat.

AFFILIATING AN ÆSTHETE.

Pilcox, a promising young Pharmaceutical Chemist, has modelled from memory an Heroic Group, in which Mrs. Cimabue Brown is represented as the Muse of this Century, crowning Postlethwaite and Maudle as the Twin Gods of its Poetry and Art.

Postlethwaite. "No loftiah Theme has evah employed the Sculptah's chisel!"
Maudle. "Distinctly so. Only work on in this reverent spirit, Mr. Pilcox, and you will achieve the Truly Great!"
Mrs. Cimabue Brown. "Nay, you have achieved it! Oh, my young Friend, do you not know that you are a Heaven-born Genius!"   *Poor Pilcox.* "I do!"   [*Gives up his pestle and mortar, and becomes a hopeless Nincompoop for life.*

1.7 The posture of aesthetes was a cross between a stoop and a swoon that gave the body a marked S- or C-shape. (George Du Maurier, 'Affiliating an Aesthete', *Punch* 19 June 1880, 14. Courtesy of the Trustees of the National Library of Scotland.)

In terms of dress, the younger Townsend depicted at the start of chapter twenty-five (Figure 1.9), probably shares the same tailor as Postlethwaite and Maudle in 'Affiliating an Aesthete' (Figure 1.7). The older Townsend who visits Catherine in the novel's final chapter has a face that, according to James's text and Du Maurier's caption, is 'very different from his old – from his young – face' (Figure 1.13), but it is very similar to the faces of the bearded art connoisseurs in 'Artistic Amenities' (Figure 1.14). Townsend also seems to have borrowed their long coats and top hats. Du Maurier's depiction of the older version of Townsend is echoed in his drawing of Postlethwaite in 'Postlethwaite on Refraction' (Figure 1.10), where the aesthete refuses an invitation to join a swimming party by saying, 'I never bathe. I always see myself so dreadfully foreshortened in the water.' During Wilde's American tour, Postlethwaite's reply was quoted in

1.8 From left: Townsend, Marian Almond, and Catherine Sloper. In the scene of Catherine's first meeting with Townsend, his physique and posture suggest that of aesthetes. Catherine's economic value is highlighted by her gown, which is far more elaborate than Marian Almond's. (George Du Maurier, 'Marian Almond came up to Catherine in company with a tall young man', *Washington Square*. New York: Harper and Brothers, 1881, frontispiece. Courtesy of the Trustees of the National Library of Scotland.)

1.9 Townsend's face, hair, dress and demeanour mirror the aesthetic persona Wilde affected while in the United States. (George Du Maurier, illustration for chapter 25, *Washington Square*, 183. Courtesy of the Trustees of the National Library of Scotland.)

POSTLETHWAITE ON "REFRACTION."

Grigsby. "Hullo, my Jellaby, *you* here! Come and take a dip in the Briny, old Man. I'm sure you look as if you *wanted* it!"

Postlethwaite. "Thanks, no. I never bathe. I always see myself so dreadfully foreshortened in the Water, you know!"

1.10 Grigsby. *'Hullo, my Jellaby, you here! Come and take a dip in the briny, old man. I'm sure you look as if you wanted it!'*
Postlethwaite. *'Thanks, no. I never bathe. I always see myself so dreadfully fore-shortened in the water, you know!'*

Du Maurier's depiction of the aesthete, Postlethwaite, at right, bears a strong resemblance to his illustrations of Townsend as an old man. (George Du Maurier, 'Postlethwaite on Refraction', *Punch* 15 January 1881, 14. Courtesy of the Trustees of the National Library of Scotland.)

"MY DEAR GOOD GIRL!" HE EXCLAIMED, LOOKING DOWN AT HIS PRIZE.
AND THEN HE LOOKED UP AGAIN, RATHER VAGUELY.

1.11 This illustration captures the complex mixture of emotions elicited by Catherine's agreement to marry Townsend, whose face was clearly modelled on Wilde's. (George Du Maurier, ' "My dear good girl!" he exclaimed, looking down at his prize. And then he looked up again, rather vaguely', *Washington Square*,154. Courtesy of the Trustees of the National Library of Scotland.)

NINCOMPOOPIANA.

(*A Test.*)

The Squire. "I BELIEVE IT'S A BOTTICELLI."
Prigsby. "OH, NO! PARDON ME! IT IS *NOT* A BOTTICELLI. BEFORE A
BOTTICELLI I AM MUTE!"   [*The Squire wishes it was.*

1.12 The Squire. '*I believe it is a Botticelli.*'
Prigsby. '*Oh no! Pardon me! It is not a Botticelli. Before a Botticelli I am mute!*'
                              [The Squire wishes it was.

A recognisable caricature of Wilde masquerading as the aesthete 'Prigsby' (George
Du Maurier, 'Nincompoopiana', *Punch's Almanac for 1881* 31 December 1881, 318.
Courtesy of the Trustees of the National Library of Scotland.)

IT WAS VERY DIFFERENT FROM HIS OLD—FROM HIS YOUNG—FACE.

1.13 Townsend has the stooped physique of aesthetes and closely resembles *Punch*'s bearded art connoisseurs. (George Du Maurier, 'It was very different from his old – from his young – face', *Washington Square*, 262. Courtesy of the Trustees of the National Library of Scotland.)

ARTISTIC AMENITIES.

Bellamy Brown (pictor ignotus) on a Picture by Rigby Robinson. "QUITE A POEM!
DISTINCTLY PRECIOUS, BLESSED, SUBTILE, SIGNIFICANT, AND SUPREME!"

*Jordan Jones (to whom a Picture by R. Robinson is as a red rag to a bull, as B. B.
knows).* "WHY, HANG IT, MAN, THE DRAWING'S VILE, THE COLOUR BEASTLY,
THE COMPOSITION IDIOTIC, AND THE SUBJECT ABSURD!"

Bellamy Brown. "AH, *ALL* WORKS OF THE *HIGHEST* GENIUS HAVE FAULTS OF
THAT DESCRIPTION!"

Jordan Jones. "HAVE THEY? I'M GLAD TO HEAR IT, THEN, FOR THERE'S
A CHANCE FOR *YOU*, OLD MAN!"

1.14 In order to develop his illustration for the older version of Townsend, Du
Maurier probably returned to the art connoisseurs he had depicted in *Punch*. (George
Du Maurier, 'Artistic Amenities', *Punch* 26 July 1879, 14. Courtesy of the Trustees
of the National Library of Scotland.)

American newspapers as a statement made by Wilde.[147] Du Maurier's illustration of Townsend taking his ease in Dr Sloper's home heads chapter twenty-five (Figure 1.9). It faithfully renders James's description of Townsend's visits to the Sloper home where

> he had his chair – a very easy one at the fireside in the back parlour . . . and he used to smoke cigars in the Doctor's study . . . as a young man of luxurious tastes and scant resources, he found the house a perfect castle of indolence. It became for him a club with a single member. (*N2* 122)

In Du Maurier's illustration (Figure 1.9), Townsend is unmistakeably Wilde and the resemblance between this portrait and the photographic portraits Napoleon Sarony made of Wilde in New York in 1882 is uncanny (Figure 1.15). Moreover, the pose, setting and dress in this illustration recuperate the iconography of 'A Consideration' (Figure 1.16), which Du Maurier had published in *Punch* only a few months earlier. In that cartoon, a lackadaisical son rebuffs his father's suggestion of a parliamentary career with a flick of his cigarette-wielding hand.[148]

In James' narrative, Townsend, the proto-aesthete, finds a willing accomplice in Catherine's eccentric aunt, Lavinia Penniman. Her intellectual life is wholly based on extrapolations from romances and she is disappointed when reality fails to live up to her fancy. She is fond of imagining Catherine visiting Townsend to tearfully reproach him, but she feels 'a sort of aesthetic disappointment' (*N2* 159) when the visit lacks 'the harmonious accompaniments of darkness and storm'. James's satire of Mrs Penniman emphasises his own critique of the Aesthetic Movement as a whole: she shows no concern for decency or morality and only values superficial beauty and romantic quality. She is unwilling to acknowledge the inappropriateness of her relationship with Townsend, and delights in her tawdry trysts with him. Her ignorance of manners and standard criteria of taste resembles Du Maurier's rendering of aesthetes' opinions on art, particularly their propensity to rhapsodise about objectionable artistic objects, such as a painting by the barbaric-sounding Fra Porcinello Barbaragianno, which Du Maurier's anti-aesthetes declare to have a vile subject and colour, a total lack of perspective and naturalness – while the aesthete falls into ecstasies over it.[149]

Mrs Penniman's obstinately romantic perspective on the decidedly un-romantic relationship between Catherine and Townsend also abstracts from the reality of their rapport. Du Maurier's illustrations

1.15 During Wilde's lecture tour, Napoleon Sarony made a number of photographic portraits which became current in advertising of the day. (Courtesy of the William Andrews Clark Memorial Library.)

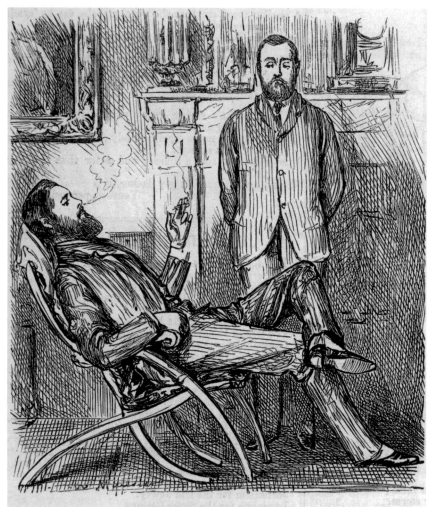

A CONSIDERATION.

Sir Charles. "I SHOULD LIKE OF ALL THINGS TO SEE YOU IN PARLIAMENT, CHARLEY."

Son and Heir. "WELL, SIR, I DON'T MIND ; I BELIEVE IT'S A VERY GOOD SORT OF PLACE ; AND THEN IT'S SO HANDY TO THE AQUARIUM."

1.16 This early *Punch* caricature foreshadows the lackadaisical pose Townsend strikes in Du Maurier's illustration for chapter 25 of *Washington Square*. (George Du Maurier, 'A Consideration', *Punch* 13 September 1879, 110. Courtesy of the Trustees of the National Library of Scotland.)

66   PUNCH, OR THE LONDON CHARIVARI.   [FEBRUARY 14, 1880.

NINCOMPOOPIANA.—THE MUTUAL ADMIRATION SOCIETY.

Our Gallant Colonel (who is not a Member thereof, to Mrs. Cimabue Brown, who is). "AND WHO'S THIS YOUNG HERO THEY'RE ALL SWARMING OVER NOW!"

Mrs. Cimabue Brown. "JELLABY POSTLETHWAITE, THE GREAT POET, YOU KNOW, WHO SAT FOR MAUDLE'S 'DEAD NARCISSUS'! HE HAS JUST DEDICATED HIS *LATTER-DAY SAPPHICS* TO ME. *Is not he BEAUTIFUL!*"

Our Gallant Colonel. "WHY, WHAT'S THERE *BEAUTIFUL* ABOUT HIM!"

Mrs. Cimabue Brown. "OH, LOOK AT HIS GRAND HEAD AND POETIC FACE, WITH THOSE FLOWERLIKE EYES, AND THAT EXQUISITE SAD SMILE! LOOK AT HIS SLENDER WILLOWY FRAME, AS YIELDING AND FRAGILE AS A WOMAN'S! THAT'S YOUNG MAUDLE, STANDING JUST BEHIND HIM—THE GREAT PAINTER, YOU KNOW. HE HAS JUST PAINTED ME AS 'HÉLOÏSE,' AND MY HUSBAND AS 'ABÉLARD.' *Is not he DIVINE!*"

N.B.—Postlethwaite and Maudle are quite unknown to fame.   [*The Colonel hooks it.*

1.17 The slender, cyphotic older woman aesthete was the usual accomplice of young male aesthetes. (George Du Maurier, 'Nincompoopiana – the Mutual Admiration Society', *Punch* 14 February 1880, 66. Courtesy of the Trustees of the National Library of Scotland.)

of Lavinia Penniman portray her in exactly the same manner as the standard accomplice of his young male aesthetes: the slender, cyphotic older woman aesthete (Figure 1.17). The illustrations for *Washington Square* assimilate Townsend and Mrs Penniman's relationship to the prevalent affiliation between young male and older female aesthetes in *Punch*, which was premised on the intense admiration of the latter for her junior counterpart. Lavinia's idolisation of Townsend is encapsulated in Du Maurier's illustration for chapter seven, where she drapes herself across the piano while he is playing (Figure 1.18). Du Maurier's image is loyal to James's text, which describes Mrs Penniman as the most attentive and inspired of Townsend's listeners. 'Mrs Penniman declared that his manner of

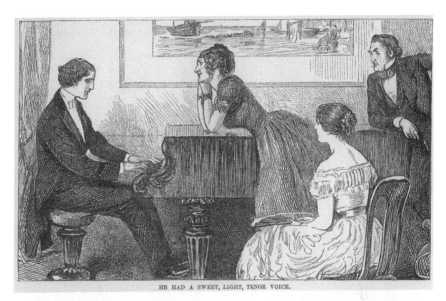

HE HAD A SWEET, LIGHT, TENOR VOICE.

1.18 Du Maurier's illustration for chapter 7 is loyal to James's text, which describes Mrs Penniman (leaning on the piano) as the most attentive of Townsend's listeners. (George Du Maurier, 'He had a sweet, light tenor voice', *Washington Square*, 57. Courtesy of the Trustees of the National Library of Scotland.)

singing was "most artistic" ' (N2 40), but Du Maurier's image ably conveys that there is more to Mrs Penniman's fascination than just her aesthetic appreciation for Townsend's 'sweet, light tenor voice'. Mrs Penniman thinks of herself as Catherine's advocate in matters of the heart – a self-image that gives her a great deal of vicarious pleasure and satisfies 'her sense of the picturesque only a shade less strongly than the idea of a clandestine marriage' (159). Desiccated and plain, Mrs Penniman prefigures the lady aesthetes in 'Aesthetic Love in a Cottage' (Figure 1.4), and her absurd notions of romance also parallel theirs. Just as Mrs Penniman does not let reality stop her from dreaming up idyllic scenarios for Catherine and Townsend, so these aesthetic women regard marrying a poor man as a 'beautiful' occasion. Their worn faces and the draping of their clothes resembles Du Maurier's depiction of Mrs Penniman's expression in chapter twenty-five, where she tries on the cashmere shawl Catherine has brought her from Europe (Figure 1.19).

The caricatures of aesthetes Du Maurier produced after having illustrated *Washington Square* reveal that the characters in James's 'purely American' (LL 119) tale had influenced the British aesthetes

"I SHALL REGARD IT ONLY AS A LOAN," SHE SAID.

1.19 Mrs Penniman's face and figure closely resemble those of female aesthetes. (George Du Maurier, ' "I shall regard it only as a loan," she said,' *Washington Square*, 188. Courtesy of the Trustees of the National Library of Scotland.)

DISTINGUISHED AMATEURS—THE WAY TO PLEASE THEM.

Miss Lavinia Sopely (to the Hon. Fitz-Lavender Belairs, who, at her urgent request, has just been explaining how, in spite of his tender years, he has come to be— in her estimation at least, the greatest Painter, Poet, and Musician of his time). "OH, MORE, MORE, MORE ABOUT YOURSELF !"

I.20 Lavinia Sopely, one of *Punch*'s fawning aesthetic women, bears a striking resemblance to Mrs Penniman (*née* Lavinia Sloper). (George Du Maurier, 'Distinguished Amateurs – The Way to Please Them', *Punch* 11 June 1881, 267. Courtesy of the Trustees of the National Library of Scotland.)

who paraded through the pages of *Punch*. *Née* Lavinia Sloper, Mrs Penniman could be the twin of Du Maurier's Lavinia Sopely, the fawning aesthetic woman in 'Distinguished Amateurs – The Way to Please Them' who urges the younger Fitz-Lavender Belairs to explain how 'in spite of his tender years, he has come to be – in her estimation at least, the greatest Painter, Poet and Musician of his time' (Figure 1.20).[150] Though Du Maurier's cartoon appeared a few months after the publication of James's illustrated serial of *Washington Square*, it indicates the intense resonance Du Maurier perceived between James's story and his own visual tales of aesthetes, and it suggests that Du Maurier was willing to incorporate American perspectives into his satiric vision of the aesthete.

British and American reviewers failed to see the various ways in which *Washington Square* provided an American pre-history for the transatlantic aesthete James had depicted in his earlier tales. Reviewers noted the incongruity between Du Maurier's illustrations and James's tale, and observed that their Englishness jarred with the ostensible Americanness of James's story. 'Not only do they fail to illustrate,' the Chicago *Tribune* wrote, 'but they are not at all in harmony with the book, being as thoroughly English in construction and design as the latter is un-English and American in locale and detail'.[151] The *Dial* agreed that the illustrations were 'of a style which is more common in English than in American novels'.[152]

With the publication of *Washington Square*, an important shift in the public perception of James also occurred, and critics began to single out James as the American aesthete *par excellence*. American reviews generally played up similarities between James and Townsend, stressing their witty talk and foreign points of view. The Chicago *Tribune* judged James as Dr Sloper judged Townsend: 'Mr James is not one of our favourite authors. He is too supercilious, too dilettante, talks too much and says too little.' *Scribner's Monthly* remarked that in the novel James's 'view of New York City . . . is more like that of a foreigner, who has lived a good portion of his life in America, than that of a person American-born'.[153]

The New York *Herald* found Du Maurier's illustrations 'disappointing',[154] and described James as 'a cynical dandy lying back in his easy chair . . . knocking the ashes from a cigar' – the very pose Townsend affected in the illustration to chapter twenty-five, one of the illustrations where he most resembles Wilde (Figure 1.9). To some, including Marian Adams, James seemed to represent an American version of Wilde. The meaning of this perception, and its impact on James's career, comes into dramatic focus when we consider the negative buzz surrounding Wilde's 1882 lecture tour. Though James had been pleased to be associated with *Punch*, he did not intend to become a punch bag at which Americans critical of Aestheticism could take aim – and he himself was highly critical of the movement, as I have suggested. James had already witnessed the mixture of contempt and curiosity that attended Wilde's visit and was eager to avert the accusation of being a 'thief' or a 'noodle'.[155] *Pace* Mrs Adams, James did not want to be considered one of Wilde's 'friends'. He distanced himself from him by developing the aesthetic type further, and extending his domain to the transatlantic aesthete whom, James hoped, was well beyond Wilde's reach.

NOTES

1. Leonée Ormond, *George Du Maurier* (Pittsburgh: U of Pittsburgh P, 1969) 468. Du Maurier wished he had responded, 'We have both invented you'. Instead, he included this witticism in the original text of *Trilby* (Ellmann, *Oscar Wilde*, 136). Vincent O'Sullivan gives another account of the encounter with *Wilde* answering Whistler: 'We have both discovered you' (*Aspects of Wilde* (London: Constable, 1936) 159). Du Maurier's 'Frustrated Social Ambition' imitates this scene with the caption 'Collapse of Postlethwaite, Maudle and Mrs Cimabue Brown, on reading in a widely-circulated contemporary journal that they only exist in *Mr Punch's* vivid imagination. They had fondly flattered themselves that universal fame was theirs at last' ('Frustrated Social Ambition,' *Punch* 21 May 1881, 229; reproduced in Denney, *At the Temple of Art*, 92).

2. Du Maurier's initial claim has been largely disregarded because the visual similarity is more convincing than his denial. In 1894 he told the *Pall Mall Gazette* that 'Postlethwaite was said to be Mr Oscar Wilde, but the character was founded not on one person at all, but a whole school' (Ormond, *George du Maurier*, 253).

3. E. H. Mikhail, *Oscar Wilde: Interviews and Recollections*, 2 vols (London: Routledge, 1970) 1: 40.

4. Gagnier gives Wilde and the culture of publicity extensive and insightful consideration in *Idylls*. Richard Salmon situates James's fictional practice within this context in *Henry James and the Culture of Publicity* (Cambridge: Cambridge UP, 1997).

5. Henry James, 'Du Maurier and London Society', *Century Illustrated Monthly Magazine* (May 1883) 63.

6. E. H. Mikhail, *Oscar Wilde: An Annotated Bibliography of Criticism* (Totowa, NJ: Rowman and Littlefield, 1978) 25.

7. Ellmann, *Oscar Wilde*, 128–9
8. O'Sullivan, *Aspects of Wilde*, 157.
9. Ellmann, *Oscar Wilde*, 144.
10. Ibid. 145
11. William Gilbert and Arthur Sullivan, 'Patience', in *The Annotated Gilbert and Sullivan*, ed. Ian Bradley, vol. 2 (Harmondsworth: Penguin, 1984) 149.
12. Quoted in Ellmann, *Oscar Wilde*, 158.
13. Gilbert and Sullivan, *Patience*, 147–9.
14. *The Nation*, 12 January 1882, quoted in Robert Harborough Sherard, *The Life of Oscar Wilde* (New York: Mitchell Kennerley, 1906) 431–2.
15. See also Adams, *Letters*, 327; Ernest Samuels, *Henry Adams: The Middle Years* (Cambridge, MA: Harvard UP, 1958) 168.
16. Henry James, letter to T. S. Perry, microfilm, unpublished, 7 January [1882], Duke University.
17. Loring's daughter, Harriet, wrote in February 1882 that the most prominent feature of the season 'has been the lions that have roared for us – first we had Mr Henry James Jr . . . Very well meaning but slow minded . . . Then we had Oscar. He is the most gruesome object I ever saw, but he was very amusing. Full of Irish keenness and humor.' Quoted in George Monteiro, 'A Contemporary View of Henry James and Oscar Wilde, 1882', *American Literature* 35.4 (1964), 530.
18. Adams, *Letters*, 338.
19. Lloyd Lewis and Henry Justin Smith, *Oscar Wilde Discovers America, 1882* (New York: Harcourt, Brace, 1936) 355, 108.
20. Ibid. 189.
21. Adams, *Letters*, 339.
22. Ibid. 338. The only record remaining is Adams's letter to her father, in which she relates a few snatches of James's conversation with Wilde. None of James's letters written between 24 and 26 January is extant. On 23 January, James wrote a (still unpublished) letter to his close friend Sir John Forbes Clark in which he did not mention Wilde.
23. Ellmann, *Oscar Wilde*, 170.
24. Henry James, *Selected Letters*, ed. Leon Edel (Cambridge, MA: Harvard UP, 1987) 179.
25. Ellmann, *Oscar Wilde*, 171.
26. Adams, *Letters*, 328–9.
27. Ibid. 328. Adams generally preferred 'moral quarantine' over visits from unvouched-for visitors; she also avoided Sarah Bernhardt, Adelina Patti, Emma Albani and Lillie Langtry (Samuels, *Henry Adams*, 165).
28. Adams, *Letters*, 329.
29. Ibid. 328.
30. Ibid. 342.

31. *The Nation*, 12 January 1882, quoted in Sherard, *Life*, 432.

32. Blanchard, *Oscar Wilde's America*, 3. Jonathan Freedman, 'An Aestheticism of Our Own: American Writers and the Aesthetic Movement', in *In Pursuit of Beauty: Americans and the Aesthetic Movement*, ed. Doreen Bolger Burke (New York: Rizzoli, 1986); Roger B. Stein, 'Artifact as Ideology: The Aesthetic Movement in Its American Cultural Context', in *In Pursuit of Beauty*, ed. Burke, 23–51.

33. Burke (ed.), *In Pursuit of Beauty*.

34. Stein, 'Artifact as Ideology', 23.

35. Since *Roderick Hudson* (1875) precedes the beginning of the James-Wilde relationship by some years, I do not discuss it here, though I have explored the novel's homosexual and aesthetic aspects elsewhere ('Homosociality and the Aesthetic in Henry James's *Roderick Hudson*', *Nineteenth-Century Literature* 57.4 (2003)). In *The Europeans*, Eugenia functions as a female dandy who tries to exert her foreign, 'peculiar influences' (*N1* 917) on high-minded New Englanders. I am grateful to Andy Taylor for pointing out this valuable connection.

36. There exists a substantial body of excellent work on Aestheticism in 'The Author of Beltraffio' and *The Portrait of a Lady* and this is one of the reasons I have chosen not to treat these two works at length here. See Freedman, *Professions*; Haralson, *Henry James and Queer Modernity*; J. T. Laird, 'Cracks in Precious Objects: Aestheticism and Humanity in *The Portrait of a Lady*', *American Literature* 52.4 (1981); Leland Monk, 'A Terrible Beauty Is Born: Henry James, Aestheticism, and Homosexual Panic,' *Bodies of Writing, Bodies in Performance*, special issue of *Genders* 23 (1996); Kevin Ohi, 'The Author of "Beltraffio": The Exquisite Boy and Henry James's Equivocal Aestheticism', *ELH* 72.3 (2005); Sara Stambaugh, 'The Aesthetic Movement and *The Portrait of a Lady*', *Nineteenth-Century Fiction* 30.4 (1976).

37. Freedman, *Professions*, 170.

38. Ibid. 82.

39. Ormond, *George du Maurier*, 392.

40. Dennis Denisoff, *Aestheticism and Sexual Parody, 1840–1940* (Cambridge: Cambridge UP, 2001) 83.

41. Gagnier, *Idylls*, 51, 73, 76.

42. Ibid. 14.

43. Millicent Bell, 'From *Washington Square* to *The Spoils of Poynton*: Jamesian Metamorphosis', in *Henry James: The Shorter Fiction: Reassessments*, ed. N. H. Reeve (Basingstoke: Macmillan, 1997) 96.

44. On women aesthetes' contributions to the movement, particularly its social side, see Maltz, *British Aestheticism*; Kathy Alexis Psomiades,

Beauty's Body: Femininity and Representation in British Aestheticism (Stanford: Stanford UP, 1997); Schaffer, *The Forgotten Female Aesthetes*; Schaffer and Psomiades, *Women and British Aestheticism* (Charlottesville: U of Virginia P, 1999).

45. Linda Hughes, 'A Female Aesthete at the Helm: *Sylvia's Journal* and "Graham R. Tomson," 1893–1894', *Victorian Periodicals Review* 29.2 (1996) 173.

46. Karl Beckson (ed.), *Aesthetes and Decadents of the 1890s: An Anthology of British Poetry and Prose* (Chicago: Academy, 1981) xxi–xliv.

47. Millard, *Oscar Wilde*, 1.

48. James, 'Du Maurier and London Society', 63.

49. John Landau, *'A Thing Divided': Representation in the Late Novels of Henry James* (Madison, NJ: Fairleigh Dickinson UP, 1996) 28.

50. Richard A. Hocks, *Henry James: A Study of the Short Fiction* (Boston: Twayne, 1990) 2.

51. Michael Anesko, *'Friction with the Market': Henry James and the Profession of Authorship* (New York: Oxford UP, 1986) 176–7; Fred Kaplan, *Henry James: The Imagination of Genius* (New York: William Morrow, 1992) 180.

52. Kaplan, *Henry James: The Imagination of Genius*, 249.

53. Ibid. 251.

54. Sarah A. Wadsworth, 'Innocence Abroad: Henry James and the Re-Inventions of the American Woman Abroad', *Henry James Review* 22.2 (2001), 108.

55. William Ernest Henley, *The Selected Letters of W. E. Henley*, ed. Damian Atkinson (Aldershot: Ashgate, 2000) 61 n. 5.

56. Ibid. 60.

57. Ibid. 105.

58. Ibid. 106.

59. Ibid. 105–6.

60. Roger Gard (ed.), *Henry James: the Critical Heritage* (London: Routledge, 1968) 61.

61. William King Richardson, letter to Roland Lincoln, ts, 18 July 1880, bMS Am 2006, Houghton Library, Harvard University. William Dean Howells, *The Rise of Silas Lapham* (Boston: Houghton, Mifflin, 1884) 27.

62. William Dean Howells, 'Introduction', *Daisy Miller*, by Henry James (New York: Harper & Brothers, 1906) ix.

63. Of these, two were illustrated: *Washington Square* and 'An International Episode' (by Harry McVickar in 1892). In 1882, McVickar illustrated Davison Dalziel's weak imitation of Gilbert and Sullivan's *Patience*, which was set in an American railroad department (*A Parody on Patience (Respectfully Dedicated to the Conductors of the Chicago & Alton Railroad)* (New York: Wemple & Co., 1882). In

1883, McVickar began illustrating the newly founded *Life* magazine, an American periodical with a distinctly anti-English and anti-Jamesian slant. This, however, did not prevent him from illustrating *Daisy Miller* and 'An International Episode' for *Harper's* in 1892.

64. James, 'Du Maurier and London Society', 49.

65. M. H. Spielmann, *The History of 'Punch'* (London: Cassell & Co., 1895) 506.

66. James, 'Du Maurier and London Society', 50.

67. Leon Edel and Dan H. Laurence, *A Bibliography of Henry James*, 3rd edn. (New Castle, DE: Oak Knoll, 1999) 384.

68. James, 'The Point of View', *Century Magazine* December 1882, 248.

69. Gilbert and Sullivan, 'Patience', 199.

70. Adams, *Letters*, 328.

71. Henry James, *The Ambassadors*, ed. S. P. Rosenbaum, 1909 edn. (New York: Norton, 1964) 132. See also Freedman, *Professions*, 168–9.

72. Rennell Rodd, *Rose-Leaf and Apple-Leaf: L'envoi* (Philadephia: Stoddart, 1882) 7.

73. Ibid. 7, 10.

74. Gilbert and Sullivan, 'Patience', 201.

75. Lucy Lillie, *Prudence: A Story of Aesthetic London* (New York: Harper & Brothers, 1882) 113.

76. *The Health Exhibition Literature*, vol. 1 (London: W. Clowes & Sons, 1884) 161. In 1869, James appreciatively described Jane Burden, William Morris's wife, as 'a tall lean woman in a long dress of some dead purple stuff . . . a thin pale face, a pair of strange sad, deep, dark Swinburnish eyes' (*L1* 93).

77. Samuels, *Henry Adams*, 169; Adams, *Letters* 328–9. Marian Adams and her friends recognised the caricature and thought it accurate.

78. Samuels, *Henry Adams*, 169.

79. James's enumeration included 'no great Universities nor public schools – no Oxford, nor Eton, nor Harrow; no literature, no novels, no museums, no pictures, no political society . . . ' (*LC1* 352). This infamous list is actually an echo of Hawthorne's own description of America as a country 'where there is no shadow, no antiquity, no mystery, no picturesque and gloomy wrong' (Nathaniel Hawthorne, *The Marble Faun*, Everyman's Library (London: J. M. Dent, 1995) 4.

80. The names in Wilde's story may be taken from James's 'Lady Barbarina' (1884), which includes characters called Lord and Lady Canterville.

81. Lewis and Smith, *Oscar Wilde*, 89.

82. Gard, *Henry James*, 139.

83. Ibid. 111.

84. James Albery, 'Where's the Cat?', *The Dramatic Works of James Albery*, ed. Wyndham Albery, vol. 2 (London: Peter Davies, 1939); Lionel Lambourne, *The Aesthetic Movement* (London: Phaidon, 1996) 118–21.

85. Hamilton, *Aesthetic Movement*, 103.

86. Quoted in Hamilton, *Aesthetic Movement*, 102. The similarity between the name of *The Colonel*'s aesthetic character, Lambert Streyke, and James's aesthetic hero, Lambert Strether, is a subject that merits further inquiry.

87. 'The Macaulayflower Papers', *Life* 4 January 1883, 8. On the history and social currency of the magazine, see Martha Banta, *Barbaric Intercourse: Caricature and the Culture of Conduct, 1841–1936* (Chicago: U of Chicago P, 2003) and 'From "Harry Jim" to "St. James" in *Life Magazine* (1883–1916): Twitting the Author; Prompting the Public', *Henry James Review* 14 (1993) 237–56.

88. 'Du Maurier (Condensed from a Review by H-nry J-mes, Jr, in the last "Century"', *Life* 3 May 1883, 209. See also 'Bookishness', *Life* 8 March 1883, 128.

89. 'The Macaulayflower Papers', *Life* 11 January 1883, 16. See also 'Born So', *Life*, 3 May 1883, 213.

90. 'A Code for Anglomaniacs', *Life* 26 April 1883, 201.

91. 'American Appreciation (From the *London Saturday Review*)', *Life*, 7 June 1883, 272.

92. Colleen Denney suggests that there are similarities between Lillie's *Prudence* and Vernon Lee's *Miss Brown*, published two years later (At the Temple of Art, 110).

93. Lillie, *Prudence*, 165.

94. Vernon Lee (Violet Paget), *Vanitas: Polite Stories*, Lovell's International Series (New York: Lovell, Coryell & Co., 1892) 9. On James's reaction to the story, see Adeline Tintner, *Henry James's Legacy: The Afterlife of His Figure and Fiction* (Baton Rouge: Louisiana State UP, 1998) 17–19. See also Graham, *Henry James's Thwarted Love*, 23–5.

95. Lee, *Vanitas*, 12.

96. Ibid. 70.

97. Matt Cook, *London and the Culture of Homosexuality, 1885–1914* (Cambridge: Cambridge UP, 2003) 31.

98. Alan Bray, *Homosexuality in Renaissance England* (London: Gay Men's Press, 1982) 82, 133 n. 5. See also Rictor Norton, *Mother Clap's Molly House: The Gay Subculture in England 1700–1830* (London: Gay Men's Press, 1992). During the Euston libel case of 1890, Jack Saul stated in his deposition that he was a 'professional Maryanne' (quoted in Jeffrey Weeks, 'Inverts, Perverts, and Mary-Annes: Male Prostitution and the Regulation of Homosexuality in England in the Nineteenth and Early

Twentieth Centuries', in *Hidden from History: Reclaiming the Gay and Lesbian Past*, ed. Martin Duberman, (New York: Meridian, 1989) 207.

99. *The Sins of the Cities of the Plain, or Confessions of a Mary-Ann*, (New York: Masquerade, 1881) 8.

100. Quoted in Blanchard, *Oscar Wilde's America*, 12.

101. Ibid. xii.

102. Andrew Taylor, *Henry James and the Father Question* (Cambridge: Cambridge UP, 2002) 3.

103. Quoted in Taylor, *Henry James*, 2.

104. Theodore Roosevelt, *American Ideals: And Other Essays, Social and Political* (New York: Putnam, 1897) 24–5, quoted in Taylor, *Henry James*, 3.

105. F. W. Dupee, *Henry James* (New York: Doubleday, 1956) 69.

106. Taylor, *Henry James*, 3.

107. Quoted in Lewis and Smith, *Oscar Wilde*, 119.

108. Ibid. 115.

109. Michael Anesko, *'Friction with the Market': Henry James and the Profession of Authorship* (New York: Oxford UP, 1986) 76; Lewis and Smith, *Oscar Wilde*, 377.

110. Wilde was invited to a party at Holmes's on 28 January and went to a meeting of the Saturday Club with him.

111. Quoted in Ronald J. Hrebenar, *Interest Group Politics in America* (London: M. E. Sharpe, 1997) 106.

112. Samuel Ward, letter to Oscar Wilde, ms, 9 January 1882, William Andrews Clark Memorial Library.

113. 'A Scene at Long Beach', *Frank Leslie's Illustrated Newspaper* 1882. The image is reproduced in Maude Howe Elliott, *Uncle Sam Ward and His Circle* (New York: Macmillan, 1938) 606.

114. Lately Thomas, *Sam Ward: 'King of the Lobby'* (Boston: Houghton, Mifflin Co., 1965) 404.

115. Elliott, *Uncle*, 608.

116. Ibid. 605.

117. Ibid 605. Maude Howe Elliott's comic operetta was titled 'Lord Buncombe's Daughter' and the music for it was composed by Timothy Adamowski. The piece was rehearsed but never produced although Elliott Howe's article describing the rehearsal was widely quoted in the press (Elliott, *Uncle*, 629).

118. Ibid. 602.

119. Julia Ward Howe met with James regularly when he was in the United States. James escorted her around London in 1877; she may have been the model for Louisa Brash in 'The Beldonald Holbein'. James gave her a copy of *The Europeans* (Maude Howe Elliott, *This Was My Newport* (Cambridge, MA: A. Marshall Jones, 1944) 86).

120. *Boston Transcript* 16 February 1882, quoted in Adams, *Letters*, 352.

121. The *Nation* 23 February 1882, quoted in Adams, *Letters*, 352.

122. Adams, *Letters*, 352.

123. *Washington Square* was one of only three book editions of James's fictions to be illustrated, besides the New York Edition. The other illustrated versions were Harper's American limited edition of *Daisy Miller*, 'An International Episode' and *Julia Bride*; see Bogardus, *Pictures and Texts*, 67; Edel and Laurence, *Bibliography* 40, 141.

124. Kevin J. Hayes (ed.), *Henry James: The Contemporary Reviews* (Cambridge UP, 1996) 102. The narrator tells us that Dr Sloper's house was built 'forty years ago' (N2 15), in 1835.

125. Henry James, 'George Du Maurier', *Harper's New Monthly Magazine* September 1897, 595.

126. Spielmann, *History*, 511.

127. Henry James, *Picture and Text* (New York: Harper & Brothers, 1893) 36. James might have written this without thinking of the self-reflexive nature of his compliment, but critics quickly seized on it as an instance of his arrogance. *Life* ran a satirical version of James's article in which he was made to say that Du Maurier was 'by an inborn and British power [. . .] constrained to be a matchless agent in his way, as I [James] am in mine.' ('Du Maurier. Condensed from a Review by H-nry J-mes, Jr., in the last "Century" ', *Life* 3 May 1883, 209)

128. James, *Picture and Text*, 33.

129. James, 'Du Maurier and London Society', 55.

130. John Lucas, 'Washington Square', *The Air of Reality: New Essays on Henry James*, ed. John Goode (London: Methuen, 1972) 41.

131. Ibid. 41.

132. Gilbert and Sullivan, 'Patience', 201.

133. Ibid. 147.

134. Freedman, *Professions*, 148–9.

135. Gilbert and Sullivan, 'Patience' 147.

136. Hamilton, *Aesthetic Movement*, 103.

137. Gilbert and Sullivan, 'Patience', 124.

138. Lewis and Smith, *Oscar Wilde*, 155. This is also evident in the trade cards of the time, particularly those produced by E. B. Duval. See Sandra Siegel, 'Caricature, Wilde, "Cartomania" ', *The Center and Clark Newsletter* 32; and, for a consideration of the racial politics behind some depictions of Wilde, see Curtis Marez, 'The Other Addict: Reflections on Colonialism and Oscar Wilde's Opium Smoke Screen', *ELH* 64.1 (1997).

139. Archibald Forbes, letter to Oscar Wilde, ms, 26 January 1882. William Andrews Clark Memorial Library.

140. William James, *The Correspondence of William James*, ed. Ignas K. Skrupskelis and Elizabeth M. Berkeley, 10 vols (Charlottesville: U of Virginia P, 1993) 2: 349.

141. Shelley Salamesky compares James's and Wilde's oral abilities in 'Henry James, Oscar Wilde and "Fin-de-Siècle Talk": A Brief Reading', *Henry James Review* 20.3 (1999). Millicent Bell perceptively notes Townsend's 'gift for false eloquence' in 'From *Washington Square* to *The Spoils of Poynton*: Jamesian Metamorphosis.' 'William R. Veeder gives careful consideration to the parallels between Townsend's and Sloper's rhetoric in *Henry James: The Lessons of the Master: Popular Fiction and Personal Style in the Nineteenth Century* (Chicago: U of Chicago P, 1975) 187–205.

142. Bill Brown, *A Sense of Things: The Object Matter of American Literature* (Chicago: U of Chicago P, 2003) 152.

143. Note also Townsend's disappointment at Catherine's lack of interest in Europe which was of great interest to American aesthetes (*N2* 119).

144. James, 'Du Maurier and London Society', 54–5.

145. Joseph Bristow and Alan Sinfield have cogently argued that the correlation between effeminacy and homosexuality was not established in the public imagination until after the Wilde trials (Joseph Bristow, *Effeminate England: Homoerotic Writing after 1885* (Buckingham: Open UP, 1995) 2; Sinfield, *The Wilde Century*, 4). This connection has been been taken up by Lisa Hamilton ('Oscar Wilde, New Women, and the Rhetoric of Effeminacy', in *Wilde Writings: Contextual Conditions*, ed. Joseph Bristow (Toronto: U of Toronto P, 2003) and Dennis Denisoff (*Aestheticism and Sexual Parody*), among others. A 1905 cartoon in the New York press depicted James as an imitation of Holman Hunt's *Lady of Shalott*, entangled in his own language (Adeline Tintner reproduces the image in *Henry James's Legacy*, 72). In the cartoon, James affects the aesthete's wilting pose, which by this date inescapably entwines the caricature with implications of effeminacy and homosexuality. In his Preface to *Roderick Hudson* (1907), James implicitly compared his artistic plight to Tennyson's cursed Lady of Shalott, who fearfully 'weaveth steadily', just as James was 'a young embroider of the canvas of life . . . work[ing] in terror, fairly, of the vast expanse of that surface' (*LC2* 1041). This may shed light on the final line of *Washington Square*, where Catherine takes up 'her morsel of fancy-work . . . for life, as it were' (*N2* 189).

146. See Lewis and Smith, *Oscar Wilde*, 317.

147. Ibid. 19, 21.

148. Wilde was often depicted smoking in the late 1880s and early 1890s and famously held a lit cigarette during his curtain speech for *Lady Windermere's Fan* in 1892. On the sexual politics of Wilde's smoking, see Bristow, *Effeminate England*, 26–32.

149. This is the subject of 'Modern Aesthetics' by George Du Maurier, *Punch* 10 February 1877, 77.

150. An aesthetic young man named Milkington Sopley also made several appearances in Du Maurier's caricatures of the period. In 'Nincompoopiana', he looks like Whistler and is designated as 'a follower of Postlethwaites's' (*Punch* 27 November 1880, 243). See also 'Fleur des Alpes; or Postlethwaite's Last Love', *Punch* 25 December 1880, 293–4.
151. Hayes, *Henry James*, 102.
152. Ibid. 103.
153. Ibid. 110.
154. Ibid. 101.
155. Adams, *Letters*, 328.

CHAPTER 2

THE GENTLE ART OF MAKING ENEMIES AND OF REMAKING AESTHETICISM

Wilde: 'I wish I had said that, Whistler'
Whistler: 'You will, Oscar, you will'[1]

Widely perceived to be an aesthete-for-hire or, in Max Beerbohm's words, 'a sandwich board for *Patience*',[2] Wilde's purpose in the late 1880s and early 1890s was to shed this image and develop his own aesthetic ideals. One of the ways he did this was quite literally by putting things between boards. During these prolific years, Wilde published *The Happy Prince and Other Tales* (1888), *The Picture of Dorian Gray* (1890), *Intentions* (1891), *Lord Arthur Savile's Crime and Other Stories* (1891), and *A House of Pomegranates* (1891). He lectured on dress, interior decoration and his 'Personal Impressions of America'; he became a regular contributor to the *Pall Mall Gazette*; he edited a magazine that he rechristened the *Woman's World*. As a result, Wilde transformed himself into a real artist and a professional man of letters.[3] He also reinvented Aestheticism in the process, as this chapter reveals. This metamorphosis was due in no small part to his clashes with the painter James McNeill Whistler, as well as with James. Wilde's systematic assimilation and reformulation of their views suggests that plagiarism and appropriation were integral to Aestheticism's evolution.

In the first chapter we saw how, between 1879 and 1884, James's international novels integrated sharp renditions of aesthetic types who rehearsed and rebutted some of Wilde's most salient traits; in doing so, James had created an American prehistory for Aestheticism. While James was busy writing the past, Wilde had his eye on the future. This chapter and the next tell the story of how

Wilde redeveloped Aestheticism through a programmatic assault on the two artists he considered his greatest personal and artistic threats, Whistler and James. Due to the intricate nature of Wilde's relationship to Whistler and James, I write about his engagement with each in two separate chapters, but the ways in which these two chapters build upon one another should become clear as the reader progresses. They lead the way to the James-Wilde meeting of the minds detailed in Chapter 4, when both entered the theatre with the view of staging recognisably modern identities. Examined through the lens of Wilde's evolving artistic philosophy, *Intentions* and *The Picture of Dorian Gray* unequivocally testify to his intention to remodel Aestheticism and to make it over in his own image. The aesthetic views propounded in *Intentions*' four critical essays – 'The Truth of Masks', 'The Critic as Artist', 'Pen, Pencil and Poison', and 'The Decay of Lying' – are far more radical and wide-reaching than is suggested by the widespread critical opinion that they are simply 'Wilde's response to Whistler'.[4]

The title of this chapter alludes to *The Gentle Art of Making Enemies*, Whistler's collection of critical barbs and venomous epistolary exchanges with Wilde. Published in 1890, *The Gentle Art* constellates aesthetic debates analogous to those drawn out in the pages of *The Picture of Dorian Gray* and *The Tragic Muse*, both of which were published the same year. The collection lived up to its title; it confirmed former friends as foes, and previous artistic allies as entrenched antagonists. As a literary and an intellectual model, *The Gentle Art* hints at the very rivalries that were central to the shift in Aestheticism during this period and it provides a suggestive centre around which to cluster the adversarial dynamics that lead to Aestheticism's reinvention. The landmark lecture Whistler had delivered in 1885 – known as his 'Ten O'Clock' – was included in *The Gentle Art*. Although Linda Merrill claims that 'the "Ten O'Clock" lecture was the aesthetic movement's epilogue',[5] Whistler's talk-cum-sermon was actually the catalyst for Aestheticism's reformation, instigating a new beginning which would ultimately lead to Wilde's move to the forefront of the movement's leadership in the early 1890s. As this chapter will show, the 'Ten O'Clock' lecture and *The Gentle Art* were literary sparks that ignited a blistering artistic debate, and led to a bonfire that would ultimately consume Whistler's vanity and force him to yield to Wilde.

In his Oxford days, Wilde had told friends his 'two great gods' (*LW* 39) were 'Money and Ambition', and he never seems to have dismissed these idols as false. With the publication of *Intentions* and *The Picture of Dorian Gray* he came a step closer to both. Yet professional and commercial success was not an end in itself but the means to challenging the sufficiency of the versions of Aestheticism prevalent in contemporary culture. Whistler's cautionary assessment of Wilde as a 'thick heeled' Apollo, a 'meddler [who] beckons the vengeance of the Gods' (Whistler 152–3) efficiently conveys Wilde's talent for provoking self-important taste-makers of the day. Though Wilde was eager to shed his reputation as an amateur, advocating plagiarism was hardly the best way to achieve this. Wilde's vigorous and consistent positioning contra Whistler evinces his desire to challenge the legitimacy and validity of Whistler's claims, as well as his intention to position himself at the hub of Aestheticism. This aggressive stance suggests that Wilde was not only attracted to professionalisation's promise of respectability and a stable income,[6] but to the idea of defending a communal aesthetic terrain. By entrenching himself opposite Whistler and efficiently campaigning against him, Wilde would ultimately succeed in establishing a legitimate place for himself in Aestheticism's vanguard. After all, they stood on opposite ends of a professional continuum: the older Whistler in the fading days of his tenure as art's *enfant terrible*, the younger Wilde attempting to gain a foothold on the artistic ladder. Wilde was concerned with profit as much as he was concerned with becoming Aestheticism's prophet.

In 'The Critic as Artist' Wilde declared that 'to arrive at what one really believes, one must speak through lips different from one's own' (W 1143). Those who accepted his artistic credo he called 'the elect'. Wilde became a literary giant in his own right by standing on Whistler and James's shoulders: by assimilating their views and casting them in his own mould, he refashioned himself as a professional author and the prime exponent of Aestheticism in the early 1890s. This is why, in his prefatory remarks to *The Picture of Dorian Gray*, he would declare that the artist, like the critic, 'is he who can translate into another manner or a new material his impression of beautiful things' (17). In his own way, Wilde actualised Whistler's opinion that the writer's art resided in mere 'translation from canvas to paper' (Whistler 147). In order to become an artist and critic, Wilde had translated his impressions of Whistler and James's aesthetic beliefs into new material.

In assessing Wilde's ambitions it is vital that we keep in mind the professional and artistic ends he hoped to achieve. Josephine Guy and Ian Small have shown that Wilde strongly desired economic and cultural success and that he was highly attentive to issues of readership and commercialisation.[7] But neither his commercial success nor his attention to issues of marketability should obscure his cultural significance in advancing a version of Aestheticism that could survive the criticisms of it prevalent in the early 1880s. Out of his encounter with James and Whistler, Wilde devised a new aesthetic doctrine and legitimated his claim to Aestheticism's leadership. Within this framework, Wilde's professional concerns become clearer: Wilde's growth as an author and respectable man of letters is inextricably linked to the process of remaking Aestheticism. The conflicts that arose out of his attempts to reinvent Aestheticism enabled him to formulate provocative answers to the questions of plagiarism, originality and creativity. By modifying the rules of artistic and personal engagement, Wilde succeeded in generating an artistic ethos that would propel him to the forefront of a revitalised and reformed Aestheticism.

The paradox inherent in Wilde's accomplishment is suggested by the fact that, by the early 1890s, he was being heralded as both an 'all-pervading plagiarist' (Whistler 236) and as one of the most 'original and stimulating'[8] writers on art in the last twenty years. The story of Wilde's reformation of Aestheticism moves in two quite opposite directions since, on the one hand, it was highly successful and, on the other, it was marked by bitter controversies that threatened it with implosion.

My position modifies the two prevalent assessments of Wilde's plagiarism in this period. The first, championed by Harold Bloom and Patricia Clements, suggests that Wilde 'lacked strength to overcome his anxiety of influence'[9] but was anxious to be original and therefore suppressed his sources. According to this view, Wilde's poetry 'becomes an embarrassment to read, directly one recognizes that every lustre it exhibits is reflected from *The Rime of the Ancient Mariner . . .* [it] anthologizes the whole of English High Romanticism.'[10] The second position – which has found advocates in Lawrence Danson, Josephine M. Guy and Ian Small, and Richard Allen Cave, among others – considers Wilde the creator of 'an originality founded on the already made, a newness that flaunts belatedness'[11] because 'what he borrowed he intended to make wholly his own'.[12] Wilde is not just 'ostentatiously, and most entertainingly, derivative',[13] and we need to be careful not to confuse his derivativeness with professional naiveté and amateurishness. My argument steers a middle course between these two positions in order to challenge the view that, for Wilde, 'influence is a reason for celebration not a cause of anxiety',[14] and to suggest that there is a discernible and deliberate pattern in Wilde's creative process.

The Gentle Art marks an important shift in Aestheticism's creative mode by questioning and drastically undermining the movement's dominant mode of artistic interaction. A certain amount of overt and covert borrowing had been part of Aestheticism from the start. This license to take one's ideas where one found them, with little regard for the niceties of attribution, fostered a sense of freedom and shared intellectual property which E. H. Mikhail describes as the sentiment that 'the so-called Movement was in the air, never in committee'.[15] For the most part, this informal agreement went unchallenged, and so Aestheticism grew up side by side with parodies and borrowings.

Pastiche, parody, mimicry and imitation shaped Aestheticism in the late 1870s and early 1880s. Its reputation as a movement both popular and exclusive is due in no small part to the interplay between artistic forms that it consistently encouraged in this period. At home in the pages of *Punch* as well as in the halls of the Grosvenor Gallery, early Aestheticism was strengthened by the variety of genres it contained. In *Patience*, Gilbert and Sullivan's aesthete had crooned that to 'shine in the high aesthetic line' one needed only to 'get up all the germs of the transcendental terms, and plant them ev'rywhere'.[16] Now Whistler challenged those who cultivated the seeds of others' ideas, or claimed for their own the flowers they had transplanted from the communal aesthetic patch to their private ones. What most viewed as Aestheticism's commensalism Whistler considered parasitism and, as a result, he endorsed the parcelling out of what had, until then, been a sort of public intellectual property.[17] Until the mid-1880s, interplay might be said to have been the watchword of this most flexible of movements. The rules of the game were irrevocably altered by Whistler's 'shrill shrieks of 'Plagiarism'' (*LW* 419), as Wilde termed the painter's denunciations in a pointed letter to the editor of *Truth*. By dint of decrying every appropriation and parody, by denouncing mimicry and imitation, Whistler effectively called for Aestheticism's strongest creative mode to be curtailed. The implications of Whistler's actions were far-reaching and, if put into practice, would have imposed serious limitations on the way others' ideas could be used and, consequently, torn Aestheticism away from the practices that had nurtured it.

Whistler might never have been provoked to deliver his 'Ten O'Clock' lecture were it not for his sense that 'Wilde was poaching dangerously upon his own intellectual preserve',[18] as Stanley Weintraub puts it. This delineation of intellectual and artistic property marks a turn in Aestheticism's creative mode. The Whistler-Wilde originality controversy is intertwined with questions of authority, territoriality and artistic ascendancy. Though Whistler claimed to want to protect his intellectual property, it is unmistakable that there was much more at stake in his protracted public quarrel with Wilde. It was not just the moral high ground, but the aesthetic landscape itself, that was up for grabs.

Whistler's crusade against Wilde's plagiarism was an attempt to claim the title of 'originator', and to appropriate for himself alone the power of the authentic. This debate heralds the late nineteenth-century tension between imitation and authenticity. That Wilde eventually won out testifies to Anglo-American society's ability to be satisfied by 'a culture of the factitious', where hunger for authenticity is easily placated by 'ersatz facsimile'.[19] In the nineteenth century, sincerity became 'one of the most debased coins in the currency of the language',[20] but in Wilde's hands, this dross became gold. As Jonathan Dollimore has shown, in Wilde's 'transgressive aesthetic . . . insincerity, inauthenticity, and unnaturalness become the liberating attributes'[21] that enable him to reinvigorate Aestheticism. Wilde's Aestheticism brazenly transgresses (and therefore displaces) conventions about literary appropriation and creation, by resisting the commonplaces of intellectual honesty and artistic attribution. The question this chapter poses is whether the ambivalence it locates in Wilde's relations with Whistler and James marks a turn in the history of Anglo-American artistic life. The answer it proposes is that contradictions became, at a given moment in Aestheticism's career, a new mode of creation of which Wilde is the originator.

'Ten O'Clock': The War between the Brush and the Pen

The debate that led to Aestheticism's great schism began when Wilde met Whistler in 1879, and instantly took to him.[22] Whistler's influence shaped Wilde's views on art and led him to see with a painter's eye. Elizabeth and Joseph Pennell, Whistler's authorised biographers, sum up Wilde's progression as follows:

At Oxford Wilde had followed Ruskin . . . he had read with Pater, he had accepted the teaching of Morris and Burne-Jones, and their master, Rossetti. But Ruskin was impossible to follow, Pater was a recluse, Rossetti's health was broken, the prehistoric Fabians, Morris and Burne-Jones, were the foci of a little group of their own. When Wilde came to London Whistler was the focus of the world.[23]

Wilde recorded his admiration for the painter in early poems such as 'Impression du Matin', where Whistler's *Nocturne in Blue and Gold* is rendered ekphrastically as 'The Thames nocturne of blue and gold/Changed to a Harmony in grey' (W 862). From the mid-1880s onwards, the relationship soured, as Whistler became embittered about Wilde's borrowings. According to the painter William Rothenstein, both were *poseurs*, and Whistler soon developed a keen hostility towards the young man who acted and talked as Whistler himself painted.[24]

In 1885, eight years after Ruskin had accused Whistler of 'flinging a pot of paint in the public's face' (Whistler 1), Whistler decided more needed to be done to educate the 'Philistine' critics and public. Building on the remarkable racket created by his 1877–78 libel suit against Ruskin, Whistler again courted controversy. This time he did not want a Pyrrhic victory, but a personal and moral victory against Wilde and his plagiarism.

Given its title because of the atypical time at which it was delivered, Whistler's 'Ten O'Clock' lecture was a *succès de scandale*. In the lecture, as in society, Whistler relentlessly reminded Wilde of the two features of his public image he was most desperate to shed: associations with his American lecture tour and imputations of plagiarism. 'The Dilettante stalks abroad', Whistler warned, referring belatedly to Wilde's American lecture tour. 'The amateur is loosed. The voice of the aesthete is heard in the land, and catastrophe is upon us' (Whistler 152–4). The talk was delivered in London on 20 February 1885, at Cambridge on 24 March, and at Oxford on 30 April – the locales where Whistler lectured were not only those where opinions were made, but those in which Wilde had already done the rounds as a lecturer and socialite. It was here, Whistler no doubt thought, that Wilde's plagiarism might most effectively be denounced. As early as 1881, the Oxford Union rejected an inscribed copy of Wilde's *Poems* on the grounds that they were 'not by their putative father at all, but by a number of better-known and more deservedly reputed authors. They are in fact by William Shakespeare, by Philip Sidney, by John

Donne, by Lord Byron, by William Morris, by Algernon Swinburne, and by sixty more.'[25] Sneering at Wilde's 'House Beautiful' lectures, Whistler condemned him as a false prophet, who had 'brought the very name of the beautiful into disrepute' (Whistler 136). The lecture exacerbated the mounting antipathy between the pair. Wilde's review of it in the *Pall Mall Gazette* of 21 February 1885 confirmed the feeling as mutual. London was not big enough to accommodate two such ambitious aesthetes.

In the years following the lecture, relations between Wilde and Whistler grew increasingly strained and their private dispute about plagiarism turned into a public spectacle. Whistler published the lecture in 1888 in London and Paris, where it was translated by Mallarmé. Pens drawn, Wilde and Whistler clashed in the pages of *Truth*, each claiming to be the originator of the same ideas on art. Whistler claimed that he had assumed the role of benevolent master and 'crammed' his student, Wilde, so that he 'might not add deplorable failure to foolish appearance, in his anomalous position as art expounder' (*LW* 418–19). Whistler insisted he was a prophet who had been betrayed by one of his apostles: Wilde, he said, had gone forth as his 'St John' but without the humility befitting the role. Given the bitterness of his letters and the great care he took in writing them, Whistler might have identified Wilde with Judas, rather than John the Baptist (a prophet in his own right), or John the Evangelist (an author in his own right). Wilde responded by claiming both titles for himself; he would be an original, not 'a disciple' (420).

The main objectives of Whistler's 'Ten O'Clock' lecture were to attack moralism in art, representationality (the depiction of objects as they appear to the eye), art critics and writers (especially those whose process made use of the visual arts), and the principle of the sisterhood of the arts. Frederick Wedmore, a contemporary art writer, noted in the wake of the Whistler v. Ruskin libel suit that Whistler's campaign had not been 'so much against Mr Ruskin personally as against the rights or claims of criticism'.[26] In *The Gentle Art*, Whistler reminded his readers that his hostility towards writers and art critics had not diminished: 'the war, of which the opening skirmish was fought the other day in Westminster, is really one between the brush and the pen' (Whistler 25). The 'Ten O'Clock' lecture revived this debate and made Wilde, rather than Ruskin, the butt of his criticism.

The figure of Ruskin hovers in the wings of the 'Ten O'Clock' and occasionally takes centre stage as the unnamed 'Sage of the

Universities', 'exhorting – denouncing – directing', learned 'in all, save his subject' (149). Exploiting his erstwhile argument with Ruskin for maximum effect, Whistler played on old themes as a means of making himself appear the spokesman for new values in art. Whistler uses his lecture to break completely with the Renaissance convention that held the artist responsible for reproducing Nature; he argued instead that the artist was born to pick and choose from Nature since it 'contains the elements, in colour and form, of all pictures, as the keyboard contains the notes of all music' (142). Fidelity to Nature does not lie within the purview of the painter. 'To say to the painter, that Nature is to be taken as she is', Whistler avers, 'is to say to the player, that he may sit on the piano' (143). However, Whistler holds the writer to an altogether different standard. The writer, and the art critic in particular, must take Art as she is and must unquestioningly represent truth and fact. Rather than allowing the writer, like his brother of the brush, to gather and reinterpret his harmonies wherever he may find them, Whistler relegates him to the faithful reproduction of reality. Whistler forbids the writer to find poetry in paintings, 'invention in the intricacy of the *mise en scène,* and noble philosophy in some detail of philanthropy, courage, modesty or virtue, suggested to him by the occurrence' (147). Verboten, also, 'the accepted vocabulary of poetic symbolism' (148). What does this mean for literary Aestheticism? Whistler clearly erects a substantial obstacle to aesthetic writing, which relies on ekphrasis ('a verbal description of a visual representation')[27] as one of its most characteristic and recognisable features. To understand the extent to which Wilde and James were invested in this approach, it suffices to observe that their most successful titles – such as *The Picture of Dorian Gray* or *The Portrait of a Lady* – explicitly illustrate their interest in ekphrasis. Of course, this propensity to portray the visual arts verbally is not limited to Wilde and James; we need only look to Rossetti's *Sonnets for Pictures* or Pater's *Renaissance* to realise how generalised this tendency is.[28] Whistler's interdiction poses a serious challenge to writers and, as a result, begins to erode the sense of solidarity between literary and visual artists.

The concept of the sisterhood of the arts originates in antiquity, more specifically in Horace's *Ars Poetica,* which uses the expression *ut pictura poesis* (meaning, literally, 'as is painting so is poetry') to stress the complementarity of the arts.[29] In its early iterations, critics used *ut pictura poesis* to explain the poet's resemblance to the painter, his 'power to paint clear images of the external world in the mind's eye as a painter would record them on canvas'.[30] Historically, the maxim 'allowed the comparison between image and text to become a friendly rivalry. The mutual dependence and respect among the practitioners of the arts that developed out of a common culture, fostered competition among them.'[31] Though the tradition of *ut pictura poesis* was current in the eighteenth century, it had lain dormant for some time when Ruskin revived it in *Modern Painters*. There, he remarks:

> that infinite confusion has been introduced . . . by the careless and illogical custom of opposing painting to poetry, instead of regarding poetry as consisting in a noble use, whether of colours or words. Painting is properly to be opposed to *speaking* or *writing*, but not to *poetry*. Both painting and speaking are methods of expression. Poetry is the employment of either for the noblest purposes.[32]

Where Ruskin saw complementarity, Whistler considered such harmonious interplay an impossibility. The 'Ten O'Clock' refutes Ruskin's bid for harmony by setting up different criteria for painters and writers, and goes a step further by criticising Wilde's literary approach. The concept of *ut pictura poesis* facilitates the analogy I wish to draw between the painter and the writer, and between visual imagery and prose – ideas which make up Aestheticism's fabric and underpin its alteration in the late 1880s. As well, the predominance of this unifying concept indicates the degree to which Whistler's categorical assertions on the writer's role and method began to tear to pieces the material of what had, until then, been a communitarian movement informed by a modest sense of competition.

Whistler's aggressive positioning needs to be understood in its historical and personal contexts. In the Renaissance, painters, who had been denied the honours accorded to poetry, sought to arrogate some of poetry's prestige by deploying the maxim of *ut pictura poesis*.[33] As a result, advocates of painting declared its noble rank, and some, such as Leonardo da Vinci, went so far as to declare its pre-eminence over poetry.[34] It is tempting to read Whistler's lecture as an extension of this rhetorical and intellectual turning point and to see him as a self-proclaimed defender of painting's hard-won status, but to do so would be to underrate the egotistic element in his attack. Despite the lecture's defence of an altruistic, brotherly framework, its interest is to protect and advance Whistler's individual ambitions. The lecture therefore moves in a direction opposite to that of the previous debate. In Whistler's artistic alphabet, 'I' is capitalised at the expense of 'we' or, as Wilde aptly put it, 'Mr Whistler always spelt art, and we believe still spells it, with a capital "I" ' (*RW* 137). Since so much of the lecture centres on private retributions and personal point-making, it would be misguided to overemphasise Whistler's benevolence towards his fellow painters. Wilde is right to say that Whistler's 'gospel of art . . . usually took the form of an autobiography' (*RW* 137). We can see Whistler's bluster against writers for what it is, namely a fear that his 'mission', as he calls it, should be 'made a secondary one, even as a means is second to an end' (Whistler 147). By attacking the tradition of painting and poetry as sister arts, Whistler's battle is at once artistic and deeply personal.

Hard upon his critique of Ruskin and his sisterhood of the arts, Whistler's 'Ten O'Clock' directly confronted Wilde's democratising artistic beliefs. Whistler argued that setting store by the Shakespearean dictum that 'one touch of nature makes the whole world kin' condemns Wilde 'to remain without – to continue with the common' (151–2). Whistler's reference to *Troilus and Cressida* was apposite: in 1885, Wilde had published 'Shakespeare and Stage Costume' in *The Nineteenth Century*.[35] It is significant that the 'Ten O'Clock' lecture places Ruskin and Wilde, Whistler's old and new enemies, side by side: Whistler patently felt that Wilde now represented as much of a challenge to his authority, as Ruskin once had. Wilde caught scent of the approaching battle and organised a strategic response designed to annihilate his opponent. In 'The Decay of Lying' he deployed heavy artillery: in response to the terms of Whistler's attack, Wilde's essay proposes nothing less than 'a new Renaissance of Art' (*W* 1072) which rewrites *both* Shakespeare *and* Whistler by declaring that 'one touch of Nature may make the whole world kin, but two touches of Nature will destroy any work of Art' (1078).[36]

Whistler's diktat was a naked aggression against the rights and liberties of the author, and it was directed specifically at Wilde. The argument Whistler used to advance his attack on Wilde was the same one he had used in his offensive on Ruskin. This time, however, Whister wanted a different result. The point Whistler had tried to make by suing Ruskin for libel was essentially a moral one: Whistler v. Ruskin was instigated in order to rehabilitate Whistler's damaged reputation. By contrast, Whistler's motive for attacking Wilde hinged on a matter of intellectual property and artistic ownership. Whistler alleged that the writer was but a 'middleman in this matter of Art' (Whistler 146), who 'widen[ed] the gulf between the people and the painter' and therefore brought about 'the most complete misunderstanding'. He insisted that, for the writer,

> a picture is more or less a hieroglyph or symbol of a story . . . The work is considered absolutely from a literary point of view; indeed, from what other can he consider it? And in his essays he deals with it as with a novel – a history – or an anecdote. He fails entirely and most naturally to see its excellences, or demerits – artistic – and so degrades Art, by supposing it a method of bringing about a literary climax. (Whistler 146)

Whistler's equation of 'a novel – a history' sounds like the realism-inflected maxim James deploys in 'The Art of Fiction': 'as the picture is reality, so the novel is history' (*LC1* 46). Whistler applies an essentially realist paradigm to the literary arts, despite rejecting it outright for the visual arts. His aesthetic approach was premised on a double standard: the painter ought to be wholly unencumbered by any responsibility to reality, Nature, or 'human fact' (Whistler 138), but the writer must always be faithful to reality. According to this logic, the art critic must not reinterpret in words the work of art, but should render it exactly as it appears before him. In the hands of a writer who does not follow this formula, art becomes 'merely a means of perpetrating something further' (147). As a result, 'the work becomes his own'. Whistler situates the problem as one of artistic ownership and intellectual rights, the very same issue on which his personal relationship with Wilde founders. The concern is not with the writer's reinterpretation of the visual arts *per se*. Rather, Whistler's preoccupations cluster around artistic custody and, consequently, primacy. The artist who can legitimately claim a concept as his own also has a rightful claim to artistic ascendancy. A great deal of Whistler's lecture is concerned with asserting his originality as a means of buttressing his claim to pre-eminence, and his hyperbolical language, prophetic pronunciations and Biblical parallels trumpet his ambitions. The writer's very method – using a picture as 'a hieroglyph or symbol of a story' (146) – positions the visual artist as ancillary to the writer and suggests a return to a time when visual art was indeed considered the handmaiden to poetry. Whistler's concern stems from his perception of the writer's creative process as one of 'translation from canvas to paper' (147), which results in the writer's outright appropriation of the painter's ideas. Mobilising an idiom of possession, Whistler implies that the writer's creative process is not far removed from the plagiarist's. The writer, he says, need only 'transcribe the event' to feel as if it were he himself who had found the poetry in it. All the writer's results – from 'invention' to 'noble philosophy' – are derivative and 'suggested to him by the occurrence' in the visual arts.

For Whistler, giving free reign to literary imagination amounts to a licence to desecrate the visual arts. In *Degeneration*, Max Nordau takes a similar position by suggesting that:

> Poetical impressionism . . . is a complete misconception of the essence of imaginative work . . . Impressionism in literature is an example of that atavism which we have noticed as the most distinctive feature in the mental life of degenerates. It carries back the human mind to its brute-beginnings, and the artistic activity of its present high differentiation to an embryonic state; that state in which all the arts (which were later to emerge and diverge) lay side by side inchoate and inseparate.[37]

Whistler and Nordau's agreement extends to their assessment of Wilde's degenerate nature. Whistler invokes the language of disease to distinguish his self-sufficient ideas from Wilde's parasitic imitations: 'Shall this gaunt, ill-at-ease, distressed, abashed mixture of *mauvaise honte* and desperate assertion call itself artistic, and claim cousinship with the artist . . . No! – a thousand times no! Here are no connections of ours' (Whistler 152–3). Whistler's strident disavowal of a shared genealogy with Wilde is couched in degenerationist discourse that construes Wilde as a perversion of the more manly (because neither gaunt, nor abashed) artist. Whistler's description of Wilde's effeminacy and constitutional morbidity bears more resemblance to his own than to Wilde's fleshy physique. Wilde's Aestheticism is a perversion and a threat to femininity, and his followers are 'curious converts to a weird *culte*, in which all instinct for attractiveness – all freshness and sparkle – all woman's winsomeness – is to give way to a strange vocation for the unlovely' (152).

Both Whistler and Nordau agree that Wilde's eccentric dress transgresses conventional boundaries of gender and sexuality, and that his clothes complement his personal affectation. Wilde's clothes suggest 'the motley of many manners with the medley of the mummer's closet' (154) to Whistler, and 'buffoon mummery'[38] to Nordau. Whistler categorically rejects Wilde's style, saying 'Costume is not dress. And the wearers of wardrobes may not be doctors of taste!' (Whistler 154). Noting the scandalising ugliness of Wilde's 'new artistic style in dress',[39] Nordau diagnoses Wilde's physical and behavioural eccentricities as representative of the degeneration inherent in Aestheticism itself. Whistler's criticism in particular seems hypocritical given that Whistler was known for his dandyism, and that he bestowed such care on his appearance as a means of underlining distinctions between himself and other men.[40] His concern with Wilde's sartorial style elides this carefully constructed boundary and attests to the younger man's attempt to model himself on the elder. Wilde's clothes are as much a 'costume' as an actor's, a criticism that highlights his inauthenticity. Nordau's agreement with Whistler about Wilde registers as a challenge to Wilde's originality since both are explicit about the fact that the public has been misled by Wilde. According to Nordau, Wilde is not an 'innovator',[41] nor does he bring society any nearer to 'aesthetic satisfaction':

> When, therefore, an Oscar Wilde goes about in 'aesthetic costume' among gazing Philistines, . . . it is no indication of independence of character, but rather from a purely anti-socialistic, ego-maniacal recklessness and hysterical longing to make a sensation, justified by no exalted aim; nor is it from a strong desire for beauty, but from a malevolent mania for contradiction.

Nordau's concern about authenticity and originality registers on the same grounds as Whistler's, but Nordau goes a step further than Whistler: his concern is not so much that the public has been deceived in Wilde (though it has), but that Wilde's method ('a malevolent mania for contradiction') poses a threat to orthodox intellectual and artistic practice. So Wilde is again construed as a falling away from the norm, an artistic aberrance. Like Whistler, Nordau accuses Wilde of plagiarism. On the point of 'the influence of art on life', Nordau writes, 'Wilde does not refer to the fact, long ago established by me, that the reciprocal relation between the work of art and the public consists in this, that the former exercises suggestion and the latter submits to it'.[42] Nordau does little to support his case when he claims that the discussion of fogs in 'The Decay of Lying' stems from two chapters in his *Paradoxe*; as everyone knows, Wilde stole this passage from Whistler.[43]

The matter at issue, for both Whistler and Nordau, is the relation Wilde establishes between plagiarism, originality and opposition. Wilde's ability to make his own harmonies from disagreements with others threatens the normal order of things. In his resistance to the commonplaces of intellectual honesty and artistic attribution, Wilde represents much more than a sexual or stylistic threat to Nordau and Whistler. Wilde's unscrupulous artistic method poses a real problem for the future of art. And the problem is this: Wilde's compulsion and talent for creating novel impressions by appropriating and opposing others' ideas marks him as the author of an innovative method. But since this creative mode stands in an awkward relation to originality and authenticity, Wilde's theory is problematic. In suggesting and proving that it is possible for an artist to be derivative yet wholly original, Wilde's method contradicts the standard definitions by which art is valued. This problem – the juncture of originality and plagiarism, of creativity and imitation – becomes one of the major themes of his essays and the plot of *The Picture of Dorian Gray*.

Whistler's self-aggrandising prose reveals personal concerns as well as generalised apprehensions about the course of Aestheticism. Although he begins by declaring his intention to play 'the character of The Preacher' (Whistler 135) and 'cast forth false prophets' (136), his visionary gleam has fled by the lecture's end. It is almost as if Wordsworth's question – 'Where is it now the glory and the dream?' – hovers unexpressed behind Whistler's closing words, which are a plea for his audience's patience until the advent of an aesthetic messiah:

> We have then but to wait – until, with the mark of the Gods upon him, – there come among us again the chosen – who shall continue what has gone before. Satisfied that, even were he never to appear, the story of the beautiful is already complete – hewn in the marbles of the Parthenon – and broidered, with the birds, upon the fan of Hokusai – at the foot of Fusiyama. (159)

Two aspects of this unusually restrained conclusion are relevant to our analysis. First, we should note that Whistler excludes writing from his capsule 'story of the beautiful' in the arts. Second, he does not designate himself as 'the chosen – who shall continue what has gone before'. This concluding paragraph's melancholy tone is exacerbated by the temporal and geographical remoteness of Whistler's examples. Whistler's suggestion that our last, best hope for Aestheticism is located long ago and far away does little to instil confidence. As well, his suggestion that the aesthetic messiah may, in fact, never appear offers readers a rather pessimistic prospect. The remoteness, exoticism and surrendering tone of this passage have the disheartening finality of a fairy-tale gone wrong. By promising the past, Whistler finally pledges little to Aestheticism's present and nothing to its future.

In its review of *The Gentle Art*, the *Manchester Examiner* agreed that Whistler had taken his final bow. 'He has an artistic message to deliver, and he has proclaimed it both in paint and ink, but he knows, more sorrowfully than any man, that his message is not for this generation or the next'.[44] Whistler's final turn is unexpected since so much of the 'Ten O'Clock' is preoccupied with asserting Whistler's primacy, yet it is also expressive of the condition of Aestheticism in contemporary culture. In the literature of the day, uncertainties surrounding the future of Aestheticism hover as thick as one of Whistler's famous fogs. Images of death and decay are marshalled to describe a school on the wane. In *Women Must Weep*, Harald Williams suggests that aesthetes have made a 'fatal choice' and left 'behind what they ought to take' while 'exult[ing] in the basest blank or theft' (*RW* 167).[45] In William Larminie's poem 'London' (1892), art cannot save the polluted metropolis from its 'ugliness-ocean',[46] and even the city's 'roses aesthetic' have become 'pallid and bloomless as plants that have grown without the sun'. The flowers betoken evil and death 'such rather as grow in the gardens of Hades, with scents that are sweet for the mummy, and colours that dazzle the dead'. Whistler had begun by promising himself as 'the preacher', a guide through Aestheticism's crisis of faith, yet his vision had failed to evolve and offered but an unsatisfactory nostalgia. This crisis in 1880s Aestheticism has gone undetected by criticism, which has focused on the wistfulness, decay and fading excitement that plagued Aestheticism in the 1890s. Recognising that Aestheticism manifested signs of collapse and crisis in the mid-1880s entails realising that, in one form or another, *crisis is a constant*. 'Perennial decay', which criticism has come to associate with decadence and the fin-de-siècle,[47] finds its source in Aestheticism's upheavals and dilemmas.

What I want to flesh out in the following pages is the degree to which Aestheticism's reinvigoration in the 1880s is indebted to concurrent debates about Realism, and the relationship between painting and writing. As I will show, Aestheticism relies on a revision of Whistler's terms. This quality also describes the tendency that Whistler's 'Ten O'Clock' so unremittingly but futilely struggles against.[48]

The Review as Revision:
'Writing the thing over . . . my way, *. . . from within'*

The 'Ten O'Clock' lecture indicates a fork in the road for Aestheticism. One way leads to revision of its dominant methods of artistic interaction, and the other through territories unknown. Both paths beg the question *quo vadis?* Where does Aestheticism move from here? Wilde's response to Whistler (and James, as the next chapter explains) answers this question by offering a third way, a mode of Aestheticism based on revision and innovation, which offers a forward-looking backward glance that rises above Whistler's aesthetic nostalgia and stasis. The creative method Wilde developed was the fruit of his rivalry with Whistler and his struggle to surpass James in order to eventually claim for himself the title Howells had applied to James, that of 'a metaphysical genius working to aesthetic results'.[49]

Wilde attended the 'Ten O'Clock' lecture but would no longer be condescended to by 'the Preacher', as he made clear in two pointed reviews of Whistler's lecture. In 'Mr Whistler's "Ten O'Clock"' and 'The Relation of Dress to Art: A Note in Black and White on Mr Whistler's Lecture', Wilde uses the formal elements of the nineteenth-century review form in order to rewrite and refute Whistler.[50] Whereas contemporary reviews most often summarise and evaluate their subject, Wilde's returns the 'review' to its original meaning, namely as a revision with a view to correction and improvement. Rather than merely evaluating, Wilde is concerned to augment and enhance his subject. For Wilde, the review form becomes the occasion to reconsider and effectively rewrite another's work, a method of composition that is supported by Josephine Guy's analysis of the manuscript evidence for Wilde's self-plagiarism. As Guy has demonstrated, Wilde worked with several drafts at once, beginning 'with a rough first draft which included manuscript pages interleaved from other earlier works which he felt he could reuse', and discarding, revising and retaining as he went.[51] In writing his reviews, Wilde did what James told a friend he did when correcting his proofs: he 'read critically, constructively, *re*-constructively, writing the thing over . . . *my* way, & looking at it, so to speak, from within.'[52] The difference is that reviews do not invite revision and rewriting the way proofs do. Wilde's disregard for this fact explains why his reviews incorporate the standard elements of the review form – summary and judgment – but include a substantial corrective element, as if he were writing the thing over from within. More often than not, Wilde does not signal these emendations and incorpo-

rates them seamlessly into the rest of the review so that it becomes virtually impossible for the reader to distinguish his revisions from the
summary and judgment of conventional reviewery. As a result, the
ideas under review are incorporated into Wilde's own, and the review
effectively becomes a transcription, transformation and appropriation
of others' ideas. The review form, and the act of revision it entails, thus
becomes a prelude to Wilde's own creative process. In 'Mr Whistler's
"Ten O'Clock"', for example, Wilde paraphrases Whistler's ideas
about nature, alleges that they are derivative, and then appropriates
these ideas to his own ends in 'The Decay of Lying'. In his 'Ten
O'Clock' lecture, Whistler says:

> when the evening mist clothes the riverside with poetry, as with a veil,
> and the poor buildings lose themselves in the dim sky, and the tall chim-
> neys become campanili, and the warehouses are palaces in the night, and
> the whole city hangs in the heavens, and fairy-land is before us – . . .
> [Nature] sings her exquisite song to the artist alone, her son and her
> master. (Whistler 144)

Wilde's review paraphrases this and accuses Whistler of appropriation:

> Mr Whistler turned to nature . . . and then, in a passage of singular
> beauty, not unlike one that occurs in Corot's letters, spoke of the artistic
> value of dim dawns and dusks, when the mean facts of life are lost in
> exquisite and evanescent effects, when common things are touched with
> mystery and transfigured with beauty, when the warehouses become as
> palaces and the tall chimneys of the factory seem like campaniles in the
> silver air. (RW 48)

Finally, in 'The Decay of Lying' Wilde appropriates an emended
version of Whistler's concept, obliquely alludes to Whistler (as the
'master' of the Impressionists responsible for fogs), and uses this as
the basis for the assertion of his own aesthetic theory:

> Where, if not from the Impressionists, do we get those wonderful brown
> fogs that come creeping down our streets, blurring the gas-lamps and
> changing the houses into monstrous shadows? To whom, if not to them
> and their master, do we owe the lovely silver mists that brood over our
> river, and turn to faint forms of fading grace curved bridge and swaying
> barge? The extraordinary change that has taken place in the climate of
> London during the last ten years is entirely due to a particular school

of Art . . . Consider the matter from a scientific or metaphysical point of view, and you will find that I am right . . . At present, people see fogs, not because there are fogs, but because poets and painters have taught them the mysterious loveliness of such effects . . . Now, it must be admitted, fogs are carried to excess. They have become the mere mannerism of a clique, and the exaggerated realism of their method gives dull people bronchitis . . . And so, let us be humane, and invite Art to turn her wonderful eyes elsewhere. (W 1086)

After summarising Whistler's aesthetic accomplishments, Wilde subsumes them and ultimately discounts them in order to asserts his 'new aesthetics' (*RW* 1087). Unlike the uncertainties proffered by the conclusion of Whistler's 'Ten O'Clock', Wilde confidently suggests we follow him for 'you will find that I am right'. We know that one reader (at the very least) was swayed by Wilde's self-assured, tongue-in-cheek take on Whistler: Wilde's interpretation of Whistler's fog pleased James so much that he paraphrased it admiringly in a letter to their common friend, Elizabeth Robins, as 'London is all sad people and fogs. I don't know whether the fogs produce the sad people, or the sad people produce the fogs!' (Edel 4: 45)

It is not just the content of 'The Decay of Lying' that follows Wilde's principle of review-as-revision, but the essay itself also relies on the review form as its organising principle. Though critics have noted that the essay follows a dialogue form,[53] the fact that literary revision is the point of departure for this dialogue has escaped notice. The essay opens with Cyril (who has entered through an open window) inviting housebound Vivian to join him outside. 'You had better go back to your wearisome uncomfortable Nature, and leave me to correct my proofs', Vivian responds, 'my article is really a most salutary and valuable warning. If it is attended to, there may be a new Renaissance of Art' (W 1072). Cyril refuses to leave, Vivian succumbs to his questioning, puts aside his own article and a collaborative review ensues. Wilde's essay is not pure dialogue, it also incorporates long quotations from Vivian's essay, as well as commentaries, questions and entertaining if circuitous disquisitions. In other words, Vivian and Cyril perform Wilde's review-as-revision process – which relies on direct quotation, paraphrase, alteration and appropriation – in order to produce Wilde's essay. Though Wilde's and Vivian's essays seem to be one and the same – they are, after all, both titled 'The Decay of Lying' – they are quite different, as Wilde's essay has the benefit of incorporating Vivian's, reading it, and rewriting it from within. The essays' different subtitles – Wilde's is 'An Observation', whereas Vivian's is 'A Protest' – highlight Wilde's creative method of careful observation and commentary on another's protest, which is exactly the method Wilde follows in his reviews of Whistler's lecture. 'The Decay of Lying' is thus indebted to Whistler for its subject matter (as many have observed) and, crucially, in its technique. This was the approach Wilde honed through observation, reviews and revision. In writing that Wilde's method of review-as-revision is indebted to Whistler, I mean that it was generated through Wilde's encounter with him but that it is nevertheless wholly Wilde's own. This nuance is vital to understanding Wilde's reformation of Aestheticism since it quali-fies his approach as original and therefore legitimates his claim to the superintendency of a 'new Renaissance of Art' (W 1072).

The title of the publication in which Vivian's article is to be pub-lished, *The Retrospective Review*, points to the (re)visionary method that drives Vivian and Cyril's dialogue and forms the basis of Wilde's essay. Vivian's actions mirror Wilde's (as a reviewer and essay writer) on just about every level. It is crucial not only that Vivian begins by reading from his proofs – quoting himself *verbatim* and *viva voce* – but also that he is soon interrupted by Cyril, and eventually obliged to deliver extempore clarifications and reiterations of his initial impressions. These interruptions mimic those of the Wildean critic whose reviews are interventions in others' artistic domains.

But is this plagiarism? The essay's layering complicates this ques-tion. Is Vivian's tendency to plagiarism part of the character Wilde is portraying? When Vivian reads to Cyril from his own article and appropriates Whistler's words (as in the passage on fogs, quoted above), do we point the finger at Vivian, or at Wilde? And if we remember that Vivian and Cyril are actually having a conversation, are we really surprised that Vivian does not footnote Swinburne when he repeats his idea that the difference between Zola and Balzac is 'the difference between unimaginative realism and imaginative reality' (1076)? And are we willing to accuse Wilde of plagiarising from Vivian's essay? What is striking is the density of Wilde's web of allu-sions, and the uniformity of his method of appropriation. The Swinburne passage offers a case in point: Wilde takes it from *A Study of Shakespeare*, uses it in a review of 'Balzac in English', and reuses the review version in 'The Decay of Lying'. Wilde first uses a quota-tion in a review, then builds on this excerpt in an essay. This pattern underlies his approach to Whistler and James and is fundamental to his revision of Aestheticism. We can be fairly certain that Wilde always had a number of books open at his elbow while he wrote, yet this explanation does not account for his tendency to self-plagiarise and his propensity to return to his own texts. For Wilde writing is always a process of revision, by which I mean revision of his own writings as well as those of others. This tendency, which is habitually labelled wholesale 'plagiarism', is, I think, a more specific type of self-plagiarism whereby Wilde returns to his version of someone else's idea and reinterprets it. Time and time again, Wilde prefers to reuse his version of someone else's idea, rather than returning to the author's words and so, in the review-to-revision model I have been outlining, Wilde takes other authors' ideas at second- and sometimes third-hand. To call the resulting ideas derivative does not account for the fact that they become more refined, and more Wilde's own, with every reinterpretation. Every remove from the original purifies the thought by adding to it, and these successive accretions form the basis for something new.

Wilde returns to his own interpretations of Whistler or Swinburne because writing is a process of fine-tuning for him and he is interested in recasting ideas, not only appropriating them. When Wilde published 'The Decay of Lying' in *Intentions*, contemporary reviewers noted just that. 'Hardly any one has a better claim than Mr Wilde to be named as a contributor of something fresh, something original and stimulating, amongst the mass of matter about art that has been written during the last twenty years,' the *Athenaeum* declared.[54] Writing in *The Academy*, Richard Le Gallienne called Wilde a subtle thinker who embroidered upon others' ideas and was, therefore, 'a damascener of thought, [rather] than a forger of it'.[55] Le Gallienne elevated Wilde to the ranks of the few authors whose criticism he believed had produced 'exquisite things': Pater, Henley and James.[56] Arthur Symons, writing anonymously for *The Speaker*, praised 'The Decay of Lying' for containing 'an old doctrine, indeed, but a doctrine in which there is a great deal of sanity and a perfectly reasonable view of things'.[57] Ironically, while most reviewers were aware that the essays contained substantial borrowings, this did not deter them from declaring Wilde's aesthetic theory original. Though Whistler seethed over the success of the 'arch-impostor' and 'all-pervading plagiarist' (Whistler 236), critics agreed that Wilde had turned an aesthetic and professional corner. As Symons put it, 'after achieving a reputation by doing nothing, he is in a fair way to beat his own record by real achievements.'[58] Applauded for its value and originality, the aesthetic theory Wilde elaborated on the basis of his review-as-revision model realised Whistler's and Nordau's worst fears since Wilde's 'mania for contradiction' transcended Whistler's aesthetic nostalgia and stasis. According to the *Pall Mall Gazette*, Wilde's 'occasional detonation of an epigrammatic paradox served, like a fog-signal, to keep us awake and attent',[59] but it also serves to clear Whistler's aesthetic fog and awaken Aestheticism from its dogmatic slumbers. Most importantly, it justified Wilde's claim to Aesthetic leadership by giving an original and mature answer to the crucial question of mid-1880s Aestheticism, *quo vadis*.

Wilde's answer was also shaped by Pater, and the *Pall Mall Gazette* drew attention to the similarity by describing Wilde as a popular 'Pater-familias'. Building on the work of Richard Ellmann, Jesse Matz has convincingly argued that Pater's 'impression' marks his place in the beginning of literary modernity since it revolutionised British aesthetics.[60] Pater stands at the midway point between Matthew Arnold and Wilde. In the Preface to *The Renaissance*, Pater writes that 'in aesthetic criticism the first step towards seeing one's object as it really is, is to know one's own impression as it really is.'[61] This claim refutes Arnold's description of the aim of criticism as being to 'see the object as in itself it really is' and enables Wilde's assertion (in 'The Critic as Artist') that the critic's task is 'to see the object as in itself it really is *not*.'[62] Before arriving at his reinterpretation of Pater, Wilde had, as per his usual method, cited it without attribution in 'Pen, Pencil, and Poison', a review of the works of Thomas Griffiths Wainewright.[63] Much attention has been paid to Wilde's Paterian inheritance and my purpose here is neither to rehearse nor to dispute Wilde's intellectual debt.[64] Rather, my concern is to explain how Wilde's creative model builds on Pater's and partakes of a mode of aesthetic appreciation centring on impressions which elucidates Wilde's preference for self-plagiarism and multiply-derived plagiarism. This model, in turn, informs Wilde's engagement with James. In other words, it is Pater's critical ideal, not his critical ideas, that concerns us here. For if Wilde's creative model centres on review-as-revision, then this ideal is equally indebted to Pater's 'impressions' as an organising principle for his criticism.

In Pater's *Renaissance*, 'impressions' can signify two apparently antithetical ideas: a refined act of analysis and discernment, or a subject's superficial, preliminary response. In the Preface, realising one's impression is a stage in a multi-layered process of aesthetic apprehension. In the Conclusion, however, impressions are 'unstable, flickering, inconsistent, . . . [they] burn and are extinguished with our consciousness of them.'[65] The flame-like quality of this experience makes it both fleeting and intense, and leads Pater to announce, in the book's most famous passage, 'to burn always with this hard, gemlike flame, to maintain this ecstasy, is success in life.'[66] For Pater, 'the impression is a unit of subjective aesthetic response – single, substantial, and a mode of judgement' but the impression is also fleetingly inconsistent because it is in constant flux.[67]

Two models of aesthetic experience emerge from Pater's dual definition of the impression. The first is a stasis/flux paradigm of aesthetic experience, a scheme strikingly similar to Wilde's own mode of aesthetic criticism.[68] Indeed, Wilde's review-as-revision process relies on his impression being both fixed in time, vivisected and analysed to determine what it really is, but this impression is balanced by a fluid one that is constantly forming and reforming itself. This explains why, in converting his reviews into essays, Wilde always returns to his own paraphrases of other authors, rather than to the authors themselves, who bear no trace of his impression. The review-to-essay model thus allows Wilde to capture or freeze the aesthetic experience in time while acknowledging that his impressions of a subject will necessarily have changed since 'the secrets of life and death belong to those, and those only, whom the sequence of time affects, and who possess not merely the present but the future, and can rise or fall from a past of glory or of shame' (W 1124), as he put it in the 'The Critic As Artist'. Pater's definitions explain the productive instabilities at the core of Wilde's approach, for it is this principle of fluidity and exchange which makes him call the critic a creative 'interpreter' (1130) who can 'translate into another manner or a new material his impression of beautiful things' (17). As well, the personal element inherent in Pater's impression prefigures the critical subjectivity that Wilde celebrates in his criticism. Pater writes that our impressions are 'ringed round for each one of us by that thick wall of personality' and that every single impression 'is the impression of the individual in his isolation, each mind keeping as a solitary prisoner its own dream of a world. Analysis goes a step further still, and assures us that those impressions of the individual mind . . . are in perpetual flight.'[69] Building on this idea, Wilde writes: 'the highest Criticism, being the purest form of personal impression, is in its way more creative than creation, as it has least reference to any standard external to itself, and is, in fact, its own reason for existing' (W 1125). Pater's double definition of impression allows for subjectivity of the sort Wilde exploits by bringing his personal history to bear on his criticism, or lecturing on his 'Personal Impressions of America'.

This brings us to the second model of aesthetic experience that emerges from Pater's definition of the impression – the surface/depth paradigm – which complements and extends the first. Criticism tends to focus on Pater's deployment of the image of a 'hard, gem-like flame' to illustrate the play of the impression; however, Pater's deployment of fire's complementary natural element, water, also deserves notice. In the opening lines of the Conclusion, Pater instructs us to direct our attention to one of the more exquisite moments of our physical life, the moment 'of delicious recoil from the flood of water in summer heat'.[70] Pater extends the analogy of the swimmer's experience from the physical, external world to the 'inward world of thought and feeling, the whirlpool is still more rapid'.[71] The water's widening gyre symbolises our ever-expanding consciousness of the impression. Like the many currents which drive our physical lives, our consciousness is figured as an internal stream that appears placid but is, in actuality, subject to 'the race of the mid-stream, a drift of momentary acts of sight and passion and thought'. Though our experience seems to be buried 'under a flood of external objects', we retrieve it through 'reflexion'. The archaic spelling draws attention to reflexion's Latin root, *reflex*, which means a bending back, recess, or return. This underscores the importance of the inward turn. To extend Pater's water analogy, the impression is not reflected on the surface of the water, but *within* the water itself. It would be a mistake to read this passage as an encouragement to gaze at our reflection on the water, since this superficial narcissism would cancel the inward turn upon which the realisation of our impressions hinges. Through reflexion, Pater encourages us to turn our gaze inward, to the very depths of our consciousness instead of remaining on the surface of the self.

This inward turn offers a vision of 'unearthly liberation, but also of intimate terror', as Daniel Albright observes.[72] In a book review that Pater later incorporated into the Conclusion, he illustrates the perils of contemplation with the image of a stranded swimmer who has gone too far out and consequently risks losing himself. Such thoughts, Pater writes, 'bring the image of one washed out beyond the bar in a sea at ebb, losing even his personality, as the elements of which he is composed pass into new combinations. Struggling, as he must, to save himself, it is himself that he loses at every moment'.[73] In this formulation, Pater explicitly construes the individual's analysis of the impression as a self-dissolving process that involves 'that strange, perpetual weaving and unweaving of ourselves'.[74] Wilde understood the personal trepidation intrinsic in this process, and asserted that 'all art is at once surface and symbol. Those who go beneath the surface do so at their peril. Those who read the symbol do so at their peril' (*W* 17). Despite the apparent opposition between the superficial and the symbolic, Wilde's argument actually describes art as the result that emerges from the interplay between shallow and intense impressions. This line of reasoning overturns Whistler's claim that interpreting a painting as 'more or less a hieroglyph or symbol of a story' (Whistler 146) is deleterious to art. Following Pater, Wilde argues that the symbol, like the impression, augments the more it is analysed and derived.

The surface/depth paradigm explains another facet of Wilde's review-as-revision method, particularly his self-plagiarism. The self-conscious and self-centred nature of realising one's impressions accounts for Wilde's emphasis on the autobiographical element inherent in the creative process. 'A true artist', Wilde explains, 'reveals himself so perfectly in his work, that unless a biographer has something more valuable to give us than idle anecdotes and unmeaning tales, his labour is misspent and his industry misdirected' (*RW* 97). Against this dissolving self, Wilde defines art as the ultimate assertion of personality. The reason Wilde returns to his own reviews and paraphrases is that this revision *deepens* his initial impression. Building on Pater's water analogy, we can imagine the first, superficial impression as the expanding circular ripple we observe when we cast a stone into a pool of water. The subsequent, deeper impressions are those created by the stone as it sinks to the depths of the pool. Wilde's self-plagiarism partakes of this same surface/depth duality since the act of rewriting is, simultaneously, a return to the superficial impression, and an attempt to plumb the depths of this impression. Thus, returning to his earlier writings becomes the occasion to submerge himself anew in the impression, to plunge his consciousness into it again and expand the concentric ring of allusions created by the first impression. So, the process of revision is an opportunity to fathom the profundity beneath the first impression's shallow ripple.

Is there a relationship between literary impressions, Impressionist painting and Whistler? The association between Whistler and Impressionism is somewhat misleading since, unlike Impressionists such as Monet who sought to accurately portray the effects of light,

Whistler prefered to evoke moods and atmospheres.[75] As Alfred Werner notes, Whistler knew and associated with many of the Impressionists but he occupies a place apart from Impressionism proper. He neither adopted its specific technique of on-the-spot sketching, nor did he 'limit himself, as they did, to recording the ephemeral "impression" of a scene' (Whistler xi, xiii). Instead, he 'would let the impression be filtered through the fine screen of his retentive memory so that, in most cases, there was a long interval between observation and execution.' But Whistler complicates the relationship between literary and painterly impressions and, by extension, between the writer and the painter. Although Whistler makes impressions central to his painting, he denies his literary counterpart the right to develop his personal impressions of works of art. He believes the writer's attention to his own impressions of a painting might distract him from the painting itself and, as a result, he would impose a realist standard upon the writer. In his 'Ten O'Clock' lecture, he explains that if the writer's primary allegiance is to his impressions, rather than to the real painting that hangs before him, then the writer brings about 'the most complete misunderstanding' (146) of the painting. Whistler's theory poses a specific problem for the aesthetic writer, whose method, more often than not, relies on seeing through the arts. What becomes of a writer – such as Pater, Wilde or James – whose stock-in-trade is the emblematic use of art and the deployment of tropes from the visual arts? This problem makes Whistler a hinge-figure in the history of Aestheticism and his position vis-à-vis realism becomes a decisive element in Wilde's turn towards a new literary aesthetic indebted to James.

The Tragic Muse

James was not standing idly by while the Wilde-Whistler debate wore on. In 1890, shortly after he had finished writing *The Tragic Muse*, he shared with Edmund Gosse a piece of gossip,

> an anecdote I just heard of an answer made by the irrepressible Whistler to a lady who asked him (à propos of his late idiotic public squabble with Oscar Wilde,) why he couldn't 'let sleeping Oscars lie.' – 'Ah, he won't sleep & he *will* lie!'[76]

James had been alert to the debate between Wilde and Whistler from the first. He found it intriguing, alarming and endlessly fascinating.[77]

Five years before James completed *The Tragic Muse*, in 1885, the painter John Singer Sargent had asked him if he would act as a London guide to that 'the unique extrahuman' poet,[78] Robert de Montesquiou, and two other Frenchmen. James cheerfully obliged. James told Henrietta Reubell, a Parisian-American who was also friendly with Wilde, that he had gone out of his way to satisfy his visitors' 'yearning to see London aestheticism' (*L3* 93), going so far as to arrange a dinner at which Montesquiou could meet Whistler. By introducing Montesquiou and Whistler to each other, James offered his guest the opportunity to take in one of London Aestheticism's top attractions. James also appointed himself to the socially and artistically important role of American literary liaison between these incarnations of London-based American Aestheticism and French Aestheticism.[79] We should not underestimate the importance James would have placed on such an occasion, nor should we take too lightly James's choice of Whistler, a fellow American abroad, as representing 'London aestheticism'. Sargent's letter requesting that James make arrangements for the French visitors is the sole item of their correspondence that James retained before destroying the rest. While it is conceivable that a measure of patriotism informed James's choice of Whistler, we can be fairly certain that James's choice was a tactical one. He did not know Whistler particularly well and had been critical of his works, but he had followed the Whistler-Wilde debate closely enough to know that choosing Whistler as the representative of 'London aestheticism' was a move that would, at the very least, indicate his opposition to Wilde's version of Aestheticism.

This meeting foreshadows in a number of interesting ways James's treatment of the aesthete Gabriel Nash in *The Tragic Muse*, James's most patent effort to upstage Wilde and Whistler with his own response to Aestheticism. Most importantly, the figure of Nash allowed James to write himself into this tradition, and to outline how Aestheticism might appear were it given a Jamesian shading and set in Paris. In *The Tragic Muse*'s first chapter, the ambivalent artist-politician Nick Dormer and his sister wander about the Paris Salon, the French counterpart of the Royal Academy. In the second chapter, the Dormers encounter the aesthete Gabriel Nash girdled by a set of aesthetic-looking women. James's account of the scene ekprastically represents William Powell Frith's 1883 painting of the *Private View of the Royal Academy, 1881*, in which Wilde is encircled by a coterie of admiring, aesthetically dressed women, and George Du Maurier studies the group. In his memoirs, Frith explained that the painting's arrangement of 'a well-known apostle of the beautiful, with a herd of eager worshippers surrounding him' was intended as a historical record of 'the aesthetic craze', as well as a didactic illustration of 'the folly of listening to self-selected critics in matters of taste, whether in dress or art.'[80] Frith was not the first (or the last) to depict Wilde in this way. In the 1870s and early 1880s, Du Maurier repeatedly employed the same compositional structure – a Wilde-like aesthete surrounded by admiring women – in his *Punch* caricatures.[81] Frith's painting was so popular that a guard was necessary to control the throng of visitors who wanted to see it, and it was explicitly mimicked and adapted by *Punch* and the *World*, among others.[82] All these versions follow the same compositional structure by prominently placing Wilde in the foreground with one or several women. James's decision to have the reader encounter the novel's aesthete under the same conditions and compositional manner as Frith's famous picture attests to his interest in placing his account of Aestheticism within a historical continuum, to gently mock its adherents, and exploit the movement's ekphrastic tendencies.

As a character, Nash allowed James to insert himself into this visual aesthetic tradition, while also suggesting the manner in which it might be problematic. As D. J. Gordon and John Stokes rightly observe, 'hesitancy or confusion about identity hovers most crucially around the disturbing figure'[83] of Nash, who stands for Aestheticism's identity-crisis and represents the very confusion the movement was subject to in the late 1880s and early 1890s. Amid this vagueness, Nash's figure nevertheless comes into focus as a sharp and fairly true-to-life representation of what (or who) a James-Wilde fusion might look like, and what it might entail for Aestheticism. Though Nash's utterances are uncannily Wildean, James ornaments them with his own flourishes, such as Nash's use of French in his claim that, 'merely to be is such a *métier*; to live is such an art; to feel is such a career!' (*N3* 724). Physically, Nash does not recall the towering, floppy-haired Wilde but is, instead, 'fair and fat and of the middle stature; he had a round face and a short beard, and on his crown a mere reminiscence of hair, as the fact that he carried his hat in his hand permitted to be observed' (717). This is the very image of the balding, goateed James who, before embarking for America in 1881, warned that he looked 'fat and scant o' breath, and very middle-aged' (*L2* 360). Oscar Cargill has argued that Nash represents Wilde, while Lyall Powers has suggested James modelled Nash on himself. Gordon and Stokes think these are 'false trail[s]'[84] because 'this is not a novel about established or even real public identities'. Eric Haralson and Christopher Lane suggest that Nash's 'studiously cultivated ethereality'[85] implies an 'erasure of homosexual meaning'. Though Nash defies absolute identification, there is, however, a good deal in the novel that gestures towards particulars of James's and Wilde's shared experiences, and James's ruminations on them.

To return to the novel's second chapter: Nick Dormer realises in the Paris Salon 'that he had at last come to a crisis' (*N3* 716), a dilemma about whether to follow the path of duty which leads to the family business of politics, or the more alluring path of painting. As he ponders how to 'settle' himself, Gabriel Nash appears before him, not as the personification of his conundrum, but as someone who is unambiguously in a position to answer it. Dormer 'felt how it would help him to settle something. At the moment he made this reflection his eye fell upon a person who appeared – just in the first glimpse – to carry out the idea of help. He uttered a lively ejaculation . . . so pertinent, so relevant and congruous, was the other party to this encounter.' Nash himself is so attuned to Dormer's need that he offers without prompting, 'it was high time I should meet you – I see. I've an idea you need me' (*N3* 719). Dormer's hope-filled initial reaction to Nash mirrors the very optimism and promise James felt in the first moments of his ill-fated first meeting with Wilde in 1882. Though Wilde's ostentatious talk about the merits of deracination ('You care for *places*? The *world* is my home')[86] offended the cosmopolitan James, the novel transforms this rebuff into a moment of real Aesthetic comedy. Dormer's opening question to Nash is a patent attempt at rapprochement: 'Don't we both live in London, after all, and in the nineteenth century?' (*N3* 718). Nash's response conveys the humour of Wilde's affectation without its snub:

> 'Ah, my dear Dormer, excuse me: I don't live in the nineteenth century. *Jamais de la vie*!'
> 'Nor in London either?'
> 'Yes – when I'm not in Samarcand! But surely we've diverged since the old days. I adore what you burn; you burn what I adore.'

The passage highlights the degree to which James thought Wilde lived up to the movement's most caricatured tendencies, but James also hints at the distressing element in Nash's 'unclassified state' when he writes of the little cruelties of anonymity, like the fact that Dormer would not have known where to 'send him a doctor if he had heard he was ill' (1230).

The caricaturist Max Beerbohm, who was friendly with both James and Wilde, echoes James's concern for classification in a description of Wilde that could just as well be applied to Nash: 'So eclectic a creature is he, that there is in him a little of every time save that into which he was born, a little of every nation save that in which he lives.'[87] Even more surprising than James's allusion to his 1882 conversation with Wilde is that a version of it also appears, in truncated form, in *The Picture of Dorian Gray*, where Dorian is so enthralled by the actress Sybil Vane (perhaps a very pale relation of *The Tragic Muse*'s Miriam Rooth) that, he says, 'I forgot that I was in London, and in the nineteenth century' (W 65). We know that Wilde wrote his novel from September to December 1889, and that *The Tragic Muse* began to appear in the pages of the *Atlantic Monthly* a month later, in January 1889, so this is not a case of plagiarism but of mutual interest and coincidence.[88] This little-known quirk in literary history also testifies to another unfamiliar fact, namely the importance Wilde and James accorded to that ill-starred Washington meeting. Because their fictions indicate their recognition of this missed opportunity, it is tempting to imagine what Aestheticism might have become had this first encounter been more successful. Be this as it may, what we know with absolute certainty is that James and Wilde inhabited each other's imaginative worlds, as people and as artists, which is to say that they had a highly personalised professional relationship. What *The Tragic Muse* so ably conveys in Nash is the *impression* of Wilde and his artistic ideas, and the impression made on James himself. What we have in Nash is not a pale, objective rendition of a man we might (following Cargill) label 'Wilde', but the essence of the impression Wilde created for James, an impression at once highly personal and highly concentrated, the substrate of a repetitive analytical process. In other words, James's and Wilde's relationship intrinsically follows the model described by Pater's 'impression': their personal, literary and imagined dealings with each other are distinguished acts of analysis as well as superficial, preliminary and sometimes knee-jerk responses. Wilde's and James's ability to harness and exploit these dichotomous tendencies results in a relationship that is as productive as it is provocative. This explains why Nash notoriously flickers between presence and absence, like Pater's 'tremulous wisp constantly re-forming itself on the stream',[89] and ultimately ceases to exist. Dormer's portrait of Nash exemplifies the very dynamic between

James and Wilde, and formulates it in terms of an impressionist process of aesthetic and intellectual apprehension. Dormer's

> impression had been that Nash had a head quite fine enough to be a challenge, and that as he sat there, day by day, all sorts of pleasant and paintable things would come out in his face. This impression was not falsified, but the whole problem became more complicated. It struck our young man that he had never *seen* his subject before, and yet somehow this revelation was not produced by the sense of actually seeing it. What was revealed was the difficulty – what he saw was the indefinite and the elusive. (*N3* 1234)

As this passage skilfully conveys, the problem with trying to render impressions is that they always elude us, even when we think we have pinned them down or, in this case, painted them into a corner. When James revised the novel for the New York Edition, the last sentence of the excerpt quoted above became, 'What was revealed was the difficulty – what he saw was not the measurable mask but the ambiguous meaning.'[90] The addition of 'mask' underscores Nash's (and Wilde's) powers of performance and bolsters James's interpretation of them both as characters whose authentic selves are highly elusive because they flit between the 'measurable' and immeasurable 'ambiguous meaning'. Indeed, Dormer's conviction that his portrait of Nash is fading from the canvas, 'that the hand of time was rubbing it away little by little' (*N3* 1236), calls attention to the fluidity of impressions and the temporal contingencies to which they are always subject.

While James could gradually erase Nash from the painter's canvas, Wilde's presence within the aesthetic landscape became stronger as the 1880s drew to a close. By the time *The Tragic Muse* was published in 1890, Wilde had become a professional man of letters, as well as the most visible advocate of Anglo-American Aestheticism. Most importantly, he had become the author of a new artistic philosophy that had successfully painted Whistler out of the picture.

NOTES

1. Elizabeth Robins and Joseph Pennell, *The Life of James McNeill Whistler*, 5th edn. (Philadelphia: J. B. Lippincott, 1911) 226.
2. Quoted in Gilbert and Sullivan, 'Patience', 125.
3. It has been suggested by Wilde's contemporaries as well as by recent critics that Wilde 'strongly objected to being considered a professional

author' (O'Sullivan, *Aspects of Wilde*, 63) and that he considered professionalisation a 'diminution of personality' (Lawrence Danson, *The
Artist in His Criticism* (Oxford: Clarendon, 1997) 54). However, his
extraordinary productivity during this period challenges the sufficiency
of such an interpretation. Moreover, it seems clear from the degree of
specialism involved in his attacks on Whistler and James that Wilde was
fervently trying to become a professional man of letters, engaged in the
prominent intellectual and artistic debates of his day.

4. Danson, *Wilde's Intentions,* 26. See also Birgit Borelius, 'Oscar Wilde,
Whistler and Colours', *Scripta Minora* 3 (1966–7) 33; Aatos Ojala,
Aestheticism and Oscar Wilde (Helsinki: Finnish Academy of Sciences
and Letters, 1954) 112.

5. Linda Merrill, *A Pot of Paint: Aesthetics on Trial in Whistler v. Ruskin*
(Washington: Smithsonian Institute, 1992) 287.

6. On Wilde's professional ambitions and the degree to which he follows
a pattern for professionalisation exemplified by Pater and Arnold, see
Josephine M. Guy and Ian Small, *Oscar Wilde's Profession: Writing and
the Culture Industry in the Late Nineteenth Century* (Oxford: Oxford
UP, 2000) 50–91.

7. Guy and Small, *Oscar Wilde's Profession*, 261.

8. Karl Beckson (ed.), *Oscar Wilde: The Critical Heritage* (London:
Routledge, 1970) 93.

9. Harold Bloom, *The Anxiety of Influence: A Theory of Poetry*, 2nd edn.
(New York: Oxford UP, 1997) 6. Patricia Clements reiterates Bloom's
characterisation in her chapter on Wilde in *Baudelaire and the English
Tradition* (Princeton, NJ: Princeton UP, 1985) 140–83.

10. Bloom, *Anxiety*, 6.

11. Danson, *Wilde's Intentions*, 26.

12. Richard Allen Cave, 'Wilde's Plays: Some Lines of Influence', in *The
Cambridge Companion to Oscar Wilde*, ed. Peter Raby (Cambridge:
Cambridge UP, 1988) 235.

13. Clements, *Baudelaire*, 141.

14. Guy and Small, *Oscar Wilde's Profession*, 271.

15. Mikhail, *Oscar Wilde: Interviews*, 1: 41.

16. Gilbert and Sullivan, 'Patience', 149.

17. Paul Saint-Amour has suggested that Wilde's collectivism may have
been the outcome of his socialist leanings, as well as the oral culture in
which he was steeped ('Oscar Wilde: Orality, Literary Property, and
Crimes of Writing', *Nineteenth-Century Literature* 55.1 (2000) 61).

18. Stanley Weintraub, *Whistler: A Biography* (New York: Weybright &
Talley, 1974) 307.

19. Orvell, *The Real Thing*, xxiii. Alison Byerly suggests that Aestheticism
represents 'the erasure of the real', because 'the boundaries separating
different forms of art . . . are conflated in the works of Wilde and Pater'

(*Realism, Representation, and the Arts in Nineteenth-Century Literature* (Cambridge: Cambridge UP, 1997) 12).

20. Gagnier, *Idylls*, 14.

21. Jonathan Dollimore, *Sexual Dissidence: Augustine to Wilde, Freud to Foucault* (Oxford: Oxford UP, 1991) 14.

22. Wilde's post-1879 admiration for Whistler modified his earlier assessment, which he had published in a review titled 'The Grosvenor Gallery'. Whistler exhibited seven oils at the Grosvenor, including *Nocturne in Black and Gold: The Falling Rocket*, which was soon to be the object of Ruskin's famous attack. Noting that 'the most abused pictures in the whole Exhibition – [are] the "colour symphonies" of the "Great Dark Master", Mr Whistler', Wilde added dismissively that his pictures were 'certainly worth looking at for about as long as one looks at a real rocket, that is, for somewhat less than a quarter of a minute' ('The Grosvenor Gallery', *Dublin University Magazine* July 1877, 124). After his feud with Whistler, Wilde transformed this criticism into the tale of 'The Remarkable Rocket' (Anne Bruder, 'Constructing Artist and Critic between J. M. Whistler and Oscar Wilde: "In the Best Days of Art There Were No Art-Critics" ', *ELT* 47.2 (2004): 161–2).

23. E. R. Pennell and J. Pennell, *Whistler*, 225.

24. William Rothenstein, *Men and Memories: A History of the Arts 1872 to 1922, Being the Recollections of William Rothenstein* (Whitefish, MT: Kessinger, 2005) 85, 87, 92.

25. Quoted in Ellmann, *Oscar Wilde*, 146.

26. Quoted in Kate Flint, *The Victorians and the Visual Imagination* (Cambridge: Cambridge UP, 2000) 170–1.

27. W. J. T. Mitchell, 'Ekphrasis and the Other', *South Atlantic Quarterly* 91.3 (1992), 696.

28. On the evolution of ekphrasis in the nineteenth century, see Garrett Stewart, who also offers a persuasive reading of *The Picture of Dorian Gray* as unsettling 'precisely the formal delineations – between painting and writing – on which it would seem to depend' ('Reading Figures: The Legible Image of Victorian Textuality', in *Victorian Literature and the Victorian Visual Imagination*, ed. Carol T. Christ (Berkeley: U of California P, 1995) 347). On the relationship between ekphrasis and time, see Freedman, *Professions*, 19–24, 213–15.

29. There is some debate as to the origin and history of the expression. W. J. T. Mitchell contends that it was Simonides of Ceos who invented it. On the tradition of interart analogies, see Nell Irvin Painter, 'Ut Pictura Poesis; or the Sisterhood of the Verbal and Visual Arts', in *Writing Biography: Historians and Their Craft*, ed. Lloyd E. Ambrosius (Lincoln: U of Nebraska P, 2004); George P. Landow, 'Ruskin's Version of Ut Pictura Poesis', *Journal of Aesthetics and Art Criticism* 26 (1968); Rensselaer W. Lee, *Ut Pictura Poesis: The Humanistic Theory of*

Painting (New York: Norton, 1967); and the second chapter of Jesse Matz, *Literary Impressionism and Modernist Aesthetics* (Cambridge: Cambridge UP, 2001).

30. Lee, *Ut Pictura Poesis*, 4.
31. Amy Golahny, *Rembrandt's Reading: The Artist's Bookshelf of Ancient Poetry and History* (Amsterdam: Amsterdam UP, 2003) 46.
32. John Ruskin, *The Genius of John Ruskin: Selections from His Writings*, ed. John D. Rosenberg (Charlottesville: U of Virginia P, 1998) 52.
33. Lee, *Ut Pictura Poesis*, 6.
34. Ibid. 6.
35. The article was later retitled 'The Truth of Masks'.
36. In *An Ideal Husband*, Mrs Cheveley claims that a good platitude 'makes the whole world kin' (W 527).
37. Max Nordau, *Degeneration*, intro. George L. Mosse (Lincoln: U of Nebraska P, 1993) 485.
38. Nordau, *Degeneration* (1993) 319.
39. Ibid. 319. In a review of *Degeneration*, William James described Nordau as 'gloomily insane', and faulted him for taking Wilde seriously. William adduced as proof of Nordau's insanity his 'complete inability to see a joke (pages of heavy invective against Oscar Wilde's epigrams!)' (quoted in Sally Ledger and Roger Luckhurst (eds), *The Fin-De-Siècle: A Reader in Cultural History, c. 1880–1900* (Oxford: Oxford UP, 2000) 19).
40. Denys Sutton, *Nocturne: The Art of James McNeill Whistler* (Philadelphia: J. B. Lippincott, 1964) 14. Wilde was an advocate of dress reform, particularly for women, a fact that Whistler saw as further indication of the threat he posed to 'the fair daughters of the land' (Whistler 152). Wilde promoted rational dress for women in articles, lectures and as editor of the *Woman's World*. 'From a continuation of the Greek principles of beauty with the German principles of health will come, I feel certain, the costume of the future' (W 946), he wrote. See also Oscar Wilde, 'Woman's Dress', *Pall Mall Gazette* 14 October 1884 (rpt. in W 33). From October to April 1884, Wilde gave a series of lectures on dress entitled 'Dress', 'The Value of Art in Modern Life' and 'Beauty, Taste and Ugliness in Dress'. See Clair Hughes, *Henry James and the Art of Dress* (London: Palgrave, 2001); Joel H. Kaplan and Sheila Stowell, *Theatre and Fashion: Oscar Wilde to the Suffragettes* (Cambridge: Cambridge UP, 1994).
41. Nordau, *Degeneration* (1993), 319.
42. Ibid. 321.
43. I discuss this point in greater detail in the following section.
44. Quoted in Patricia De Monfort, 'The Gentle Art – An Artistic Autobiography?', *Whistler Review*, vol. 1 (1999) 38.
45. Wilde reviewed the collection of poems for the *Pall Mall Gazette* in 1888 (RW 166–73).

46. William Larminie, *Fand and Other Poems* (Dublin: Hodges, Figgis & Co., 1892) 49, 50.

47. Liz Constable et al., *Perennial Decay: On the Aesthetics and Politics of Decadence* (Philadelphia: U of Pennsylvania P, 1999) 11, 21.

48. John Robert Reed, *Decadent Style* (Athens, Ohio: Ohio UP, 1985) 14.

49. William Dean Howells, 'Henry James, Jr', *Century Illustrated Monthly Magazine* November 1882, 26.

50. The reviews were published in the *Pall Mall Gazette* on 21 and 28 February 1885.

51. Josephine M. Guy, 'Oscar Wilde's "Self-Plagiarism": Some New Manuscript Evidence', *Notes and Queries* 52.4 (2005) 485–8.

52. James, *Dearly*, 131.

53. See, among others, Julia Prewitt Brown, *Cosmopolitan Criticism: Oscar Wilde's Philosophy of Art* (Charlottesville: U of Virginia P, 1997) 69; Danson, *Wilde's Intentions*, 36–8.

54. Beckson, *Oscar Wilde: Critical Heritage*, 93.

55. Ibid. 99.

56. Ibid. 98.

57. Ibid. 95.

58. Ibid. 96.

59. Ibid. 91.

60. Matz, *Literary Impressionism*, 53.

61. Pater, *Renaissance* (1986), xxix.

62. Oscar Wilde, *The Artist as Critic: Critical Writings of Oscar Wilde*, ed. Richard Ellmann (Chicago: U of Chicago P, 1982) xi; see also Matz, *Literary Impressionism*, 53.

63. Wilde, *The Artist as Critic*, 326.

64. On Pater and Wilde, see Wendell V. Harris, 'Arnold, Pater, Wilde, and the Object as in Themselves They See It', *SEL* 11.4 (1971); Ellmann, 'Critic', xi–xv; John Paul Riquelme, 'Oscar Wilde's Aesthetic Gothic: Walter Pater, Dark Enlightenment, and *The Picture of Dorian Gray*', *Modern Fiction Studies* 46.3 (2000); Peter Rawlings, 'Pater, Wilde, and James: "The Reader's Share of the Task" ', *Studies in English Language & Literature*, 48 (1998).

65. Pater, *Renaissance* (1986), 151.

66. Ibid. 152.

67. Matz, *Literary Impressionism*, 56.

68. For a more general discussion of Aestheticism's 'rhetoric of atemporality' in relation to Paterian flux, see Freedman, *Professions*, 9–10, 14–19.

69. Pater, *Renaissance* (1986), 151.

70. Ibid. 150.

71. Ibid. 151.

72. Daniel Albright, *Quantum Poetics: Yeats, Pound, Eliot, and the Science of Modernism* (Cambridge: Cambridge UP, 1997) 63.

73. Walter Pater, *The Renaissance: Studies in Art and Poetry: The 1893 Text*, ed. Donald L. Hill (Berkeley: U of California P, 1980) 273. Pater's review of William Morris's poems was published in the *Westminster Review* (October 1868) and six of the last seven paragraphs of the piece were reprinted as the Conclusion to *The Renaissance*.

74. Pater, *Renaissance* (1986), 152.

75. On the general relationship between literary and visual impressionism, see Matz, *Literary Impressionism*, chapter one, 'Impressions of Modernity'. As Matz notes (48), Pater's use of 'impression' prefigures Impressionism since he used it five years before Monet's *Impression: Soleil Levant*.

76. Rayburn S. Moore (ed), *Selected Letters of Henry James to Edmund Gosse, 1882–1915: A Literary Friendship* (Baton Rouge: Louisiana State UP, 1988) 68.

77. Content to observe from his private box the jousting that was effectively a carve-up of Aestheticism, James did not comment publicly on the Whistler-Wilde squabble until several decades later when, during his 1905 lecture tour of America, he regaled the University Club of St Louis with some Whistler-Wilde stories (Edel 5: 278).

78. Edgar Munhall, *Whistler and Montesquiou: The Butterfly and the Bat* (Paris: Flammarion, 1995) 58.

79. The meeting was a success and Montesquiou, who had already served as a partial model for the hero of Huysmans's novel *A Rebours*, eventually modelled for Whistler. Work on *Arrangement in Black and Gold: Comte Robert de Montesquiou-Fezenzac* began in the spring of 1891, around the time *The Picture of Dorian Gray* was published in book form.

80. William Powell Frith, *My Autobiography and Reminiscences*, 2 vols (London: Richard Bentley & Son, 1887) 236.

81. See, for example, 'Modern Aesthetics' (*Punch* 10 February 1877), 'The Mutual Admirationists' (*Punch* 22 May 1880), and, most strikingly, 'Distinguished Amateurs – The Art-Critic' (*Punch* 13 March 1880), where the critic in question is undoubtedly Wilde.

82. Frith, *My Autobiography*, 262. Adaptations of Frith's image include: 'Staircase Scenes. – No. 1. The Private View, Royal Academy', *Punch* 30 April 1892, 215; 'The Private View', *World* Christmas Issue 1882.

83. D. J. Gordon and John Stokes, 'The Reference of *The Tragic Muse*', in *The Air of Reality: New Essays on James*, ed. John Goode (London: Methuen, 1972) 146. Kaye has recently claimed that *The Tragic Muse* and *The Picture of Dorian Gray* are 'self-consciously designed "homosexual novel[s]" of manners' (*The Flirt's Tragedy*, 18).

84. Gordon and Stokes, 'The Reference', 147. See also Oscar Cargill, 'Gabriel Nash – Somewhat Less Than Angel?', *Nineteenth-Century Fiction* 14.3 (1959); Cargill, 'Mr James's Aesthetic Mr Nash', *Nineteenth-Century Fiction* 12.3 (1957); Lyall H. Powers, 'James's The

Tragic Muse – Ave Atque Vale', in *Henry James: Modern Judgements*, ed. Tony Tanner (London: Macmillan, 1968); Powers, 'Mr James's Aesthetic Mr Nash–Again', *Nineteenth-Century Fiction* 13.4 (1959).

85. Haralson, *Henry James and Queer Modernity*, 58; Christopher Lane, *The Burdens of Intimacy: Psychoanalysis and Victorian Masculinity* (Chicago: U of Chicago P, 1999) 159.

86. Adams, *Letters*, 338.

87. Rupert Hart-Davis (ed.), *Letters to Reggie Turner* (London: Rupert Hart-Davis, 1964) 292.

88. On the dating of *The Picture of Dorian Gray*, see Oscar Wilde, *The Picture of Dorian Gray: The 1890 and 1891 Texts*, ed. Joseph Bristow (Oxford: Oxford UP, 2005) xxxiii.

89. Pater, *Renaissance* (1986), 151.

90. Henry James, *The Tragic Muse*, ed. Philip Horne (London: Penguin, 1995) 474.

CHAPTER 3

THE SCHOOL OF THE FUTURE AS WELL AS THE PRESENT:
WILDE'S IMPRESSIONS OF JAMES IN *INTENTIONS* AND *THE PICTURE OF DORIAN GRAY*

As we saw in Chapter 1, James's 1882 visit to the United States had been marked by the death of his mother. A year later, James was called back to wintry Cambridge, Massachusetts to bury his father. After the funeral, he stayed on as his father's executor and tried to keep busy. In the spring of 1883, he went to Washington, where he had met Wilde the year before. He visited Henry and Marian Adams again, but this time there was no worry, as there had been on James's previous visit, that he would 'bring his friend Oscar Wilde'[1] since Wilde had by then taken up residence in Paris.

From Washington, James wrote to the publisher James R. Osgood to describe his latest projects, many of which involved impressionism. There was a collection of travel writings he proposed to call 'Impressions of Art and Life' or 'Superficial Impressions', and a short story titled 'The Impressions of a Cousin'.[2] James's return to Washington brought still a third item to mind, 'an episode in the lives of a group of contemporary "aesthetes", the former American, the other "international" ' (*L2* 414). He detailed the prospective story as:

the history of an American aesthete (or possibly an English one), who conceives a violent admiration for a French aesthete (a contemporary novelist), and goes to Paris to make his acquaintance; where he finds that his Frenchman is so much more thoroughgoing a specimen of the day than himself, that he is appalled and returns to Philistinism. Or else (I haven't settled it) he is to discover that the Frenchman who is so Swinburnian in his writings, is a regular quiet *bourgeois* in his life; which operates upon the aesthete as a terrible disillusionment. I may add that there will be a woman in the case. *The idea of the thing is to show a contrast between the modern aesthete, who poses for artistic feelings, but is very hollow, and the real artist – who is immensely different'.* (emphasis added)

This story never materialised. Given James's fondness for transplanting American events to European locales, however, this outline vividly conjures a parable about an aesthetic *poseur* not unlike Wilde and a 'real artist' not unlike James. Even in skeletal form, the unwritten story reads as a thinly veiled allegory of aesthetic and personal authenticity. As for the 'woman in the case', she might well have been another fictionalisation of Marian Adams or, given James's propensity to alter the sexes of his characters, a male 'Mary-Ann' or a 'Charlotte-Ann'. James's unwritten story is not only a token of personal history, but a remarkable testament to the conflicting energies that animated Aestheticism. It proved extraordinarily prescient for it divined the issues on which Wilde's career, and the course of Aestheticism, hinged. As we saw in the previous chapter, from the mid-1880s to the early 1890s, Wilde transformed himself into a 'real artist' and reinvented Aestheticism in the process by developing an artistic method that was strongly informed by his debate with Whistler.

This chapter reveals that at the same time as Wilde was combatting Whistler, he was also energetically engaged with James. While Wilde's performance opposite James follows an antagonistic pattern similar to his interaction with Whistler, the vigour and single-mindedness with which he criticised James makes James a far more important influence on him than has been assumed. Wilde's critical response to James is a measure of the intensity of their mutual involvement. Far from being disinterested in James, Wilde's journalism and criticism indicate that the artistic ethos he developed in this period is as indebted to his response to James as it is to Whistler. It is not the case that Wilde was 'less overtly hostile to James'[3] than vice-versa, but rather that Wilde's criticism of James was always far more public and professionally directed than James's private and highly personal valuations. Jonathan Freedman has argued that the 'personal and professional warfare' between them culminated in James's formulation of his conception of the novelist as elite artist,[4] but the impact of this warfare on Wilde has been sorely underestimated.

In the following pages I will describe how, out of his rivalry with James, Wilde refined the terms of the aesthetic approach he had begun to forge out of his conflict with Whistler. In his essays and reviews, Wilde challenges James's legitimacy and, to this end, he consistently reads James either as a realist of the Howells variety, or as an American translation of French realism. He criticises James for his want of passion, disparages his analytic mode and what he refers to as his 'imperceptible "points of view"' (W 1074). Crucially, Wilde undervalues the degree to which he and James both adhere to a fictional interpretation of the impressionism Pater advocates in *The Renaissance*. In this respect, we might say that James's unwritten tale about the influence of 'a French aesthete (a contemporary novelist)' on 'an American aesthete (or possibly an English one)' proved prophetic yet again for it recognised the pivotal role played by impressions in defining the outcome of the encounter between our two aesthetes. By repeatedly refining and reforming his impression of James and Whistler, Wilde developed a stronger sense of his own artistic ethos and, by the time he came to write *The Picture of Dorian Gray* in the autumn of 1889, he had successfully defined an aesthetic approach that incorporated and aimed to supersede that of both James and Whistler.

'The Art of Fiction' and Paterian Impressions

Before turning to Wilde's impression of James, we need to consider two articles that defined James's artistic method in the 1880s and powerfully shaped Wilde's reading of James – 'Henry James, Jr' and 'The Art of Fiction'. In November 1882, when Wilde was still in the United States, an article appeared in the pages of the *Century Illustrated Monthly Magazine* that cannot have failed to attract Wilde's attention. William Dean Howells's 'Henry James, Jr' offered a sensitive synopsis of James's career, explicitly connected it to realism, and praised James by comparing him favourably to Dickens and Thackeray. Howells's lavish praise caused an uproar on both sides of the Atlantic and was said to be part of a campaign in a 'realism war'.[5] British critics were particularly irate that a fledgling American author should be ranked above recognised home-grown talents.[6] As a result of Howells's praise of James as 'a metaphysical genius working to aesthetic results',[7] British newspapers branded the pair 'mutual admirationists', a label usually associated with *Punch*'s self-loving aesthetes. Even Edmund Gosse, who was a friend to both James and Howells, could not restrain himself from composing a derisive quatrain in their honour:

Motto for the American Critic
Ho! the old school! Thackeray, Dickens!

Throw them out to feed the chickens.
Ho! the new school! James and –
Lay the flattery on with trowels.[8]

Howells's 'Henry James, Jr' situates James 'at the dividing ways of the novel and the romance'[9] and positions him as the leader of a 'new school' of realist fiction:

> The art of fiction has, in fact, become a finer art in our day than it was with Dickens and Thackeray. We could not suffer the confidential attitude of the latter now, nor the mannerism of the former, any more than we could endure the prolixity of Richardson or the coarseness of Fielding. These great men are of the past – they and their methods and interests; even Trollope and Reade are not of the present. The new school derives from Hawthorne and George Eliot rather than any others; but it studies human nature much more in its wonted aspects, and finds its ethical and dramatic examples in the operation of lighter but not really less vital motives. The moving accident is certainly not its trade; and it prefers to avoid all manner of dire catastrophes. *It is largely influenced by French fiction in form*; but it is the realism of Daudet rather than the realism of Zola that prevails with it, and it has a soul of its own which is above the business of recording the rather brutish pursuit of a woman by a man, which seems to be the chief end of the French novelist. *This school, which is so largely of the future as well as the present, finds its chief exemplar in Mr James*; it is he who is shaping and directing American fiction, at least.[10]

Combining French and English traditions and surpassing them both, James already has, Howells claims, 'a masterly hand'.[11] Yet Howells does more than declare James the prime exponent of a new school, he also declares him wholly original. 'A novelist he is not, after the old fashion, or after any fashion but his own', Howells writes before proudly noting that James is so popular that he has spawned imitators.

The three themes Howells unequivocally addresses in his article – James's realism, his vivid 'analytic tendency',[12] and his Francophilia – were the ones Wilde returned to again and again in his criticism of James. Howells assimilated James's fiction to an explicitly realist tradition and characterised James's style as a 'union of vivid expression and dispassionate analysis'[13] that favours 'artistic impartiality'.[14] Howells thus positioned James's fiction as an American improvement on French realism. There is an unmistakeably patriotic element to

Howells's claims which prefigures his famous iteration, four years later, of a national brand of realism concerned 'with the more smiling aspects of life, which are the more American'.[15] By stressing James's 'inveterate habit of French',[16] Howells encouraged the reader to consider James the acme of Franco-American realism as well as the leader of a new school. This is the label that stuck with Wilde, as we shall see.

To what extent is Howells's assimilation of James to the realist representative of James's literary allegiances at this time? In 'The Art of Fiction', which appeared two years after 'Henry James, Jr', James took it upon himself to respond (obliquely) to Howells and (directly) to the idea of realism in fiction. The essay is, prima facie, a reaction to Walter Besant's emphasis on reality and to Robert Louis Stevenson's ideality, an opposition which leads to a 'dialectical notion of "realism" ', as John Carlos Rowe has observed.[17] The opening paragraphs of 'The Art of Fiction' take pains to distance James from the claims of 'Henry James, Jr'. Seeking to make amends for Howells's most invidious Anglo-American comparison, James modestly writes that

> it would take much more courage than I possess to intimate that the form of the novel as Dickens and Thackeray (for instance) saw it had any taint of incompleteness. It was, however, *naïf* (if I may help myself out with another French word); and evidently if it be destined to suffer in any way for having lost its *naïveté* it has now an idea of making sure of the corresponding advantages. (*LC1* 44)

'The Art of Fiction' is not as meek as a cursory reading of this opening gambit might suggest. In fact, James mocks the terms of Howells's review. If his nod to Dickens and Thackeray tips his hand, his allusion to his own mania for Gallicisms gives away his game. The mock humility of his parenthetical comments underscores the confidence with which James plays at self-consciousness. And, later in the essay, James's not-so-modest inclusion (again, parenthetical) of the American novel within the English novel tradition also follows this model (63).

These tongue-in-cheek allusions aside, there is much in 'The Art of Fiction' that agrees with the realism of 'Henry James, Jr'. Not least is James's declaration that 'the only reason for the existence of a novel is that it does attempt to represent life' (46) and his assertion that the novelist must 'possess the sense of reality' (52). So far, so Howellsian. However, James's discussion of experience and repeated use of parentheses signals the limited appeal undiluted realism holds for him:

> If experience consists of impressions, it may be said that impressions *are* experience, just as (have we not seen it?) they are the very air we breathe . . . One can speak best from one's own taste, and I may therefore venture to say that the air of reality (solidity of specification) seems to me to be the supreme virtue of a novel. (53)

Though this passage is frequently cited to support of view that 'James is a "realist" ',[18] it actually draws quite substantially on literary impressionism of the sort Wilde was fruitfully exploring in his literary criticism. What is more, the collocation of experience, impressions and 'solidity of specification' echoes the terms of Pater's Conclusion to *The Renaissance*.[19]

According to Pater, experience fines itself down to impressions, and this distillation becomes possible when experience is stripped from its attendant materiality and language. Pater explains:

> At first sight experience seems to bury us under a flood of external objects, pressing upon us with a sharp and importunate reality, . . . but when reflexion begins to play upon those objects they are dissipated under its influence; the cohesive force seems suspended like some trick of magic; each object is loosed into a group of impressions – colour, odour, texture – in the mind of the observer.[20]

Consciousness consists in 'dwell[ing] in thought on this world, not of objects in the solidity with which language invests them, but of impressions, unstable, flickering, inconsistent'. James's 'solidity of specification' fines itself down to conveying the rarified *air* of reality, rather than reality itself. Like Pater, James invests his fiction with an air of reality that is, in fact, his *impression* of reality because it is always mediated through his particular consciousness.

James moves closer to Paterian impressionism abstraction by developing a parallel between objects mediated through consciousness and 'the look of things' (*LC1* 53). The novelist, like the painter, does not try to portray the things themselves but the impression these things create, that is, 'the look that conveys their meaning, to catch the colour, the relief, the expression, the surface, the substance of the human spectacle'. For the novelist to produce 'the illusion of life' he must recreate the multiple impressions on which the illusion depends, and marshal the superficial in aid of the essential. Here again James's smooth transition from the surface to the substance of the object rehearses the double-valence of Pater's impression, which always implies a dialectic between superficiality and depth. As Douglas Mao notes, James's fiction is crammed with 'solid objects, but since these objects come explicitly mediated through particular consciousness, the total effect of . . . [his] works (themselves insufficiently firm of outline) will be to undermine the solidity of the perceived world as surely as Pater's Heraclitean paroxysms undo our chances of capturing that which melts before us'.[21] Since the 'solidity of specifications' can be gleaned through impressions and inferred conclusions, the air of reality, for James, derives from 'the power to guess the unseen from the seen, to trace the implication of things, to judge the whole piece by the pattern' (*LC1* 53).

James strikes another characteristically Paterian chord when he describes experience as 'a kind of huge spider-web of the finest silken threads suspended in the chamber of consciousness and catching every air-borne particle in its tissue' (*LC1* 52).[22] This echoes Pater's 'design in a web, the actual threads of which pass out beyond it'[23] and strongly recalls one of *The Renaissance*'s most striking passages, the description of our impressions being responsible for 'that strange, perpetual, weaving and unweaving of ourselves'. This weaving makes James and Pater participants in a Penelopean process of self-realisation whereby the self is constantly being knit and unravelled. Directly we realise this, 'The Art of Fiction' comes into focus as an harmonious interlacing of two different threads: on the one hand, James calls for recognition of the web's specificity and particular design, while on the other hand he suggests that we go beyond it, to the end of our impression. James concludes the essay by bracketing realism's bid for representationality and impressionism's analytic turn. By applying this bivalent definition of the impression, James resolves that 'there is no impression of life, no manner of seeing it and feeling it, to which the plan of the novelist may not offer a place . . . try and catch the colour of life itself' (*LC1* 64–5).

'The Art of Fiction' successfully conjoins two divergent literary tendencies in late nineteenth-century art: the urge to represent life as it really is, and the desire to represent it as it seems to be or even, as Wilde puts it, as it is not (*RW* 129). James's unacknowledged deployment of Pater's impression bridges these troubled waters, not least through the complementary surface/depth and stasis/flux models it uses. In suggesting that Pater's paradigm offers a cohesive and harmonious vision of the aesthetic experience, I am intentionally deviating from criticism's tendency to examine Pater's impression in terms of its 'contradictions' and 'incompatible values'[24] in order to argue instead that the impression's essence resides in its ability to make change a constant. The impression unifies experience into a coherent, multi-faceted synthesis that encompasses the superficial and the profound, as well as the immutable and the ever-changing. For both Wilde and James, this synthetic interpretation forms a crucial element of their response to aesthetic debates of the late 1880s, as well as a way of reviving Aestheticism's flagging fortunes.

It is often noted that James's critical writings display a wide range of aesthetic positions that span from psychological realism to symbolist formalism.[25] Emphasis on the first position yields a picture of James determined to demonstrate that life makes art, whereas emphasis on the second produces a James bent on establishing the reverse, that art makes life. As Rowe observes, this second position comes close to

> turning James into a version of Vivian in Wilde's 'The Decay of Lying', whose view is that 'art takes life as part of her rough material, recreates it, and refashions it in fresh forms, is absolutely indifferent to fact, invents, imagines, dreams, and keeps between herself and reality the impenetrable barrier of beautiful style, of decorative or ideal treatment'.[26]

Even if we do not succumb to this second position, James's and Wilde's artistic visions are still quite similar and we should not fail to appreciate that this connection is partly the outcome of the impression James made on Wilde.

Wilde's position was the fruit of a decade-long artistic maturation process; in critical writings from the early 1880s to the early 1890s, he exhibited a range of aesthetic positions that are analogous to James's. Before the anti-realist fervour of 'The Decay of Lying' and 'The Critic As Artist', Wilde flirted with elements of the ideas he would later vehemently disavow in these same essays. Even in 'London Models', which was published at the same time as 'The Decay of Lying', Wilde acknowledges the artistic value for the 'artist sitting in his studio to be able to isolate "a little corner of life", as the French say, from disturbing surroundings' (RW 34), but in a move indebted to realism he encourages this same artist to return to life itself lest the studio's artificial isolation rob 'him of that broad acceptance of the general facts of life which is the very essence of art' (*RW* 34). This is a far cry from the uncompromising anti-realism of 'all bad art comes from returning to Life and Nature' (*W* 1091). When looked at chronologically and thematically, the aesthetic problems James and Wilde attempt to address during the 1880s seem quite similar, as is their reliance on the concept of impression.

Having suggested the manner in which Wilde's and James's aesthetic visions are both indebted to the Paterian impression, my argument has reached a turning-point which will determine the direction of the rest of this chapter. Rather than uniting James and Wilde, this resemblance drove them further apart. Just as similarities had led Whistler and Wilde's friendship to turn to antagonism and plagiarism, Wilde attempted to rise above his resemblances with James by attacking him and subtly imitating him. The productive tensions and harmonious interplay that made Pater's impression such a powerful trope for fiction, also bankrupted James's and Wilde's relationship. Through misinterpretation, hostile criticism, plagiarism and self-plagiarism, Wilde attempted to surpass James's aesthetic and assert himself as a dominant literary force.

As the following pages will explain, Wilde's critical assessments of James in the late 1880s are highly selective and, decisively for Wilde's own aesthetic, skewed by (mis)interpretations that are singularly advantageous for him. What is remarkable about this is *how* Wilde misconstrued James, and *why* Wilde insisted on seeing James as a realist. Wilde read James through 'The Art of Fiction'. But he seems to have preferred to retain James's claim that 'the novel is history' (*LC1* 46) and to ignore its complementary description of the novel as 'a personal, a direct impression of life' (50). Rather than seeing James through this harmonising pair of lenses, Wilde selected one and thus formed a rather distorted view. By monocling James, Wilde could only see him as a realist. The result was an aberrance in Wilde's habitually nuanced criticism. In his criticism from 1886 onwards, rather than being attentive to the subtleties of James's method (which would have exacerbated the parallels between them), Wilde briskly consigned James to the realist camp and returns to Howells's (by then outdated) 'Henry James, Jr' to shore up his view. It might be objected that Wilde generally omits James's name when he directly attacks his aesthetic theory. However, such an elision accords with Wilde's general tendency to drastically underplay the strength of his influences, as we have seen from his response to Whistler.

'The Realism of Paris filtered through the refining influence of Boston' or, James the Plagiarist?

It is well known that that the starting-point of Wilde's argument in 'The Decay of Lying' was Whistler's 'Ten O'Clock'.[27] The end-point of Wilde's essay, which was included in *Intentions*, is perhaps less well known. In the journalism and criticism that prefigured these essays, Wilde worked up an anti-realist philosophy of art by misinterpreting James and defining himself against him. Wilde's reaction to James mirrors his response to Whistler on the level of form and content. The structure of Wilde's response to James followed the same pattern of appropriation and reinterpretation as his response to Whistler: Wilde accused James of plagiarism in 'Balzac in English', then, in his literary notes for the *Woman's World*, he appropriated passages from Howells's 'Henry James, Jr' to describe James, and, finally, he reinterpreted his impression of Howells's article to declare himself superior to James in 'The Decay of Lying'. At every step, Wilde revised and rewrote his ideas about James, interpreting them to his own advantage. The grounds on which Wilde criticised James were substantially similar to those he focused on in his reviews of Whistler: realism and the relation of the painter to the writer formed a large part of his critique, just as they had been at the heart of his rebuttal of Whistler in his 'Mr Whistler's Ten O'Clock'. As a result, when he came to write 'The Decay of Lying', 'The Critic As Artist' and *The Picture of Dorian Gray*, he had developed an aesthetic doctrine that he marshalled to put an end to his antagonism with Whistler and James.

In 'Balzac in English', a review published in the *Pall Mall Gazette* of 13 September 1886, Wilde gently accused James of plagiarism:

> The two volumes that at present lie before us contain *César Birotteau*, that terrible tragedy of finance, and *L'Illustre Gaudissart*, the apotheosis of the commercial traveller, the *Duchesse de Langeais*, most marvellous of modern love stories, *Le Chef d'oeuvre Inconnu*, from which Mr Henry James took his *Madonna of the Future*, and that extraordinary romance *Une Passion dans le Désert*. (RW 164)

'The Madonna of the Future' (1873) centres on the misfortunes of Theobald, an American painter who defers the creation of his masterpiece so long that he ultimately dies, leaving behind nothing but 'a canvas that was a mere dead blank, cracked and discoloured by time'

(*CS1* 761). Wilde overstates his claim somewhat in saying that James 'took' his story from Balzac, since the subject of the failed painter of great promise was a staple of nineteenth-century literature. For one thing, James's tale pre-empts Wilde's accusation by having one character say that if one were to get into Theobald's 'studio, one would find something very like the picture in that tale of Balzac's – a mere mass of incoherent scratches and daubs, a jumble of dead paint!' (745).[28] Still, Wilde's claim has a kernel of truth to it. The editor W. E. Henley also noticed the similarity between James's tale and Balzac's but he put it to James more flatteringly than Wilde would have done:

> I am sure that you have in your head lots of aesthetic novelettes – such, for instance, as that one which you included in the 'Madame de Mauves' volumes [that is, *A Passionate Pilgrim*, which includes 'The Madonna of the Future']; stories about art & artists; improvements on the *Chef d'oeuvre Inconnu*.[29]

James's story is somewhat similar to Balzac's *Chef d'oeuvre Inconnu*, an 1838 tale of three painters, in which one, Frenhofer, exhibits a painting that has taken him years to complete. Though the picture does not represent Frenhofer's model at all, he is convinced he has created a masterpiece until his two artist friends tell him otherwise. When the terrible truth is revealed to him, he burns all his paintings and dies, just as Dorian Gray dies after destroying his own painting. There is a further parallel with Wilde's novel in Balzac's description of the painting's life-like reality. At first the painters only see 'colours in a jumbled heap, contained within a multitude of peculiar lines'[30] but on closer inspection,

> they could discern in a corner of the canvas the tip of a bare foot emerging from the chaos of colours, tints, and vague nuances, a sort of shapeless mist; but a delicious foot, a living foot! They stood awestruck with admiration before that fragment which had escaped from an unbelievable, slow, and progressive destruction. That foot appeared there like some Parian marble Venus rising up out of the ruins of a city that had been burned to the ground. 'There's a woman underneath all this!'[31]

Balzac's description melds indistinctness with sharp realism, and it conveys an impression that is at once superficial and profound. Like Dorian's portrait, Frenhofer's painting seems to come alive, to emerge from the illusions and myriad impressions with which the artist has imbued it. Frenhofer describes his painting as having such solidity of specification that, as he tells his colleagues, '*l'air y est si vrai*, que vous ne pouvez plus le distinguer de l'air qui nous environne' ('*the air in it is so real*, that you can't distinguish it from the air that surrounds us').[32] Balzac's story exemplifies (*avant la lettre*) the 'air of reality' that 'The Art of Fiction' encourages. Because Wilde thinks Balzac 'is no more a realist than Holbein was' (*W* 1077), Balzac escapes unscathed by the criticism of realists in 'The Decay of Lying' for 'not succeed[ing] in producing even that impression of reality at which they aim, and which is their only reason for existing. As a method, realism is a complete failure' (1080). James is the implicit target of this attack since Wilde's 'impression of reality' mimics the most familiar phrase in 'The Art of Fiction'.

In his Preface to the tale, James explained that 'The Madonna of the Future' was an early attempt 'to substitute the American romantic for the American real' (*LC2* 1204). James's tale straddles both genres and demonstrates the Pater-inspired imaginative realism which he would elaborate upon in 'The Art of Fiction'. When Theobald asks the narrator 'in a tone of most insinuating deference . . . for my "impressions"' (*CS1* 731), we hear strains of Pater's *Renaissance* (which James read shortly after his story was published).[33] However, they are not the harmonious keynotes we might expect. James's scare quotes around 'impressions' signpost his ironic use of the word, as Matz observes.[34] If Wilde read James's story closely enough to discern in it Balzac's influence, he could not have missed the tale's peculiar deployment of impressions. 'The Madonna of the Future' also undermines 'The Art of Fiction's idea of impression by using the word as shorthand for aesthetic pretentiousness and ineffectuality. 'I have taken notes, you know', Theobald says defensively to the cynical narrator, who suspects that the painter will never produce his masterpiece. 'I have got my grand fundamental impression. That's the great thing! But I have not actually had her as a model, posed and draped and lighted, before my easel' (*CS1* 752). Here, the term is not a reverential allusion to Pater's 'impression', but a mockery of it, an approach James had exploited in 'The Author of Beltraffio'.[35] 'A Bundle of Letters', another of James's aesthetic tales, rehearses a similarly scornful allusion to Aestheticism when the unconvincing aesthete declares, 'That is the great thing – to be free, to be frank, to be naif. Doesn't Matthew Arnold say that somewhere – or is it Swinburne, or Pater?' (*CS2* 469).

By making the failed painter a mouthpiece for Paterian impressions and, by extension, impressionism as a creative mode, James makes him speak for Aestheticism's most stale, sterile incarnation: the aesthetic *poseur*. Theobald's inability to make good on his promise to paint the Madonna makes him a fake, an impostor whose very appearance suggests simulation: 'he seemed picturesque, fantastic, slightly unreal . . . He might have passed for the genius of aesthetic hospitality – if the genius of aesthetic hospitality were not commonly some shabby little custode, flourishing a calico pocket-handkerchief and openly resentful of the divided franc' (*CS1* 731). The image of the aesthetic *poseur* was one from which Wilde urgently wanted to distance himself, and he may have projected himself into James's allegory of artistic failure. What we know for sure is that Wilde read the story as an iteration of James's realist stance, a position he wanted to define himself against. Wilde was looking to pin James down as a realist, and the story gave him several points on which to fix his critique. By reading him through 'The Madonna of the Future', 'Henry James, Jr', and the realist aspects of 'The Art of Fiction', Wilde arrived at a valid but partial interpretation of James's artistic philosophy that had the benefit of being completely different from Wilde's own. For a man with a mania for contradiction, this was a distinct advantage.

From the earliest reviews of James's work, critics detected that Balzac was among 'the writers by whose influence Mr James is most affected',[36] as the *Athenaeum* put it in 1879. Subsequent critics have agreed, some going so far as to say that Balzac was 'the chief influence on James from French or any other literature'.[37] We also know that Balzac, along with Flaubert, was among the French novelists Wilde most admired, and that despite being claimed as realist precursors, he assimilates them to his own anti-realist cause.[38] Though Wilde acknowledges that James exhibits characteristics similar to Balzac's and gives them the Paterian turn Wilde's artistic philosophy encourages, we would be wrong to look for logical consistency in Wilde's treatment of James. Indeed, as his mouthpiece, Vivian, warns in 'The Decay of Lying', 'Who wants to be consistent? The dullard and the doctrinaire, the tedious people who carry out their principles to the bitter end of action, to the *reductio ad absurdum* of practice. Not I. Like Emerson, I write over the door of my library the word "Whim" ' (*W* 1072). Wilde's misreading appears more flagrant in light of the fact that he praises Balzac for doing the self-same things he condemns in James. To Wilde, Balzac's fiction conveys 'imaginative reality' (1076) whereas James's fiction falls flat, because it does not imagine enough to succeed in 'making what is strange seem real' (*SJW* 116). Wilde consistently celebrates Balzac for his ability to mediate between realism and romance in order to convey an impression of his subject. Balzac's achievement, as Wilde put it in 'The Decay of Lying', was that 'he created life, he did not copy it' (*W* 1077). Wilde praises Balzac by quoting Baudelaire's belief that 'Balzac's characters . . . are gifted with the same ardour of life that animated himself. All his fictions are as deeply coloured as dreams', and by extending Baudelaire's idea of the 'colour' of Balzac's fiction by repeating it with a Paterian inflection. Using language infused with the gem-like tones of the Conclusion to *The Renaissance*, Wilde writes that Balzac's 'characters have a kind of fervent fiery-coloured existence'.

Wilde writes appreciatively that Balzac 'sees life from every point of view' (*SJW* 14), whereas James 'wastes upon mean motives and imperceptible "points of view" his neat literary style' (*W* 1074). In scare quotes here, 'points of view' is hardly the name for a laudable literary approach that is 'essentially universal', as Wilde deems it is in Balzac's fiction (*SJW* 14). 'Point of view' was James's hallmark, a feature of his writing which attracted critical notice from his earliest fictions and which he playfully mocked an eponymous early story. In 'Henry James, Jr', Howells noted that readers initially confused James's 'point of view with his private opinion'[39] – which is what Wilde does by reading the narrator's ironic use of 'impressions' in 'The Madonna of the Future' as consistent with James's personal views. In 'The Art of Fiction', James sees 'innumerable points of view' (*LC1* 61) and in his 1889 letter to the Deerfield Summer School he advises that 'any point of view is interesting that is a direct impression of life' (93), a position that elegantly brackets his own approach with a Pater-like realism. The point of view is the aspect of his art he consistently emphasises, refines and returns to over and over in his Prefaces. As Percy Lubbock stresses in *The Craft of Fiction*, James's point of view is fundamental to 'the whole intricate question of method, in the craft of fiction',[40] since it defines the narrator's relation to the story. The success of James's approach rests partly on his effective management of the point of view that governs his characters and, as a result, his fiction.

Wilde's accusation suggests that he regards James as someone with a creative mode similar to his own. It also instances his uneasiness at the growing proximity between their approaches. In an 1884 review of 'The Madonna of the Future', Julian Hawthorne, a friend of James and Wilde, unintentionally put his finger on the affinity between the two:

[James's early tales] as, for example, 'The Madonna of the Future', – while keeping near reality on one side, are on the other eminently fanciful and ideal. He seemed to feel the attraction of fairyland, but to lack resolution to swallow it whole; so instead of idealizing both persons and plot, as [Nathaniel] Hawthorne had ventured to do, he tried to persuade real persons to work out an ideal destiny.[41]

As the review suggests, the attempted reconciliation of romance and realism in 'The Madonna of the Future' reveals that James was working in the very direction Wilde was advocating in his criticism. The problem, for Wilde, was that James had not gone far enough. His criticism of 'The Turn of the Screw' echoes Hawthorne's judgement that James lacks the fortitude to 'swallow' fairyland. 'James is developing', Wilde said, 'but he will never arrive at passion, I fear' (*LW* 1118). In 'The Critic as Artist', he explains that 'to have a capacity for a passion and not to realise it, is to make oneself incomplete and limited' (*W* 1117). This perceived failure becomes the theme of Wilde's subsequent criticism of James, as does the problem of placing James in relation to realism and romance. In fact, Wilde's 'Literary Notes' and 'The Decay of Lying' make these concerns a matter of the future of literature.

Two months after the appearance of 'Balzac in English', Wilde wrote to the *Pall Mall Gazette*, asking, 'Have you any more books for me? I suppose Henry James's last novel is done?' (*LW* 289).[42] That Wilde eagerly sought the opportunity to 'do' James's fiction supports the argument that he was consciously choosing to review James as part of a wider creative process of review-as-revision. In October 1888, James was one of the members who supported Wilde's candidacy for the Savile Club. Wilde may have felt thankful for James's support, but his actions defy this sentiment. Instead of a slap on the back, Wilde's response seems more like a stab in the back.

In the January 1888 issue of *Woman's World*, Wilde devoted a long section of his usual column, 'Literary and Other Notes', to disparaging James's work, not deigning to mention the name of the novelist who had been heralded by Howells as the American leader of a 'new school'[43] of realism that far surpassed Dickens and Thackeray, that stood 'at the dividing ways of the novel and the romance', and that was 'largely influenced by French fiction in form'. If, to use Lawrence Danson's term, Balzac is 'the hero of Wilde's . . . anti-realist aesthetic',[44] then 'Literary and Other Notes' makes James the anti-hero of this aesthetic. Surveying 'the change and development of the art of novel-writing' in the nineteenth century, Wilde judges that France has 'had one great genius, Balzac, who invented the modern method of looking at life' (*SJW* 114). 'In England, we have had no schools worth speaking of' since Dickens is echoed only in newspapers and Thackeray's 'clever social satire[s] have found no echoes'. Trollope's point of view is provincial, and Meredith's style is, like Whistler's paintings, 'chaos illumined by brilliant flashes of lightning'.[45] Despite this rather pessimistic panorama, Wilde spies hope on the horizon, and declares:

> it is only fair to acknowledge that there are some signs of a school springing up amongst us. This school is not native, nor does it seek to reproduce any English master. It may be described as the result of the Realism of Paris filtered through the refining influence of Boston. Analysis, not action, is its aim; it has more psychology than passion, and it plays very cleverly upon one string and this is the commonplace. (*SJW* 115)

While this passage does not plagiarise directly from Howells's article, it summarises and pastiches it by incorporating the most distinctive elements of 'Henry James, Jr'. Though Wilde seems to be praising James in Howells's terms, he radically undercuts Howells's assessment. By using it as the basis for his subsequent attack, Wilde's intention is, in fact, not to celebrate James by borrowing Howells's words, but to criticise him in the very same terms. The pastiche is a springboard for parody and attack and, as such, it follows the form of Wilde's criticism of Whistler. By relying on paraphrase, alteration and appropriation, Wilde's review-as-revision process transforms and rebuts what are to Wilde the most threatening aspects of James's reputation. In Wilde's impressionistic reiteration of Howells and 'The Art of Fiction', James is not a great hope, but a great disappointment whose influence needs to be resisted. As laudatory as the passage quoted above may seem, Wilde stops short of expressing his support for this school and devotes the rest of the article to encouraging those novelists who oppose it. Indeed, his remark that 'as a reaction against this school, it is pleasant to come across a novel like Lady Augusta Noel's *Hithersea Mere*' unambiguously announces that the school he intends to side with is not that of James. What is arresting about this is not only that Wilde pastiches Howells's six-year-old article, but that he considers the literary debate to which it refers to be so current that he does not need to mention James by name for his readers to know who he is referring to. The debate's currency owes something to James's 1886 essay, 'William Dean Howells', in which James sought to distance himself from Howells and rehearsed the terms of 'Henry James, Jr' by echoing somewhat less enthusiastically Howells's flattering labelling of James as the chief exemplar of a new school. 'It would be absurd to speak of Mr Howells to-day in the encouraging tone that one would apply to a young writer who had given fine pledges, and one feels half guilty of that mistake if one makes a cheerful remark about his future' (*LC1* 506). James nevertheless concludes optimistically by wishing Howells a 'more and more fruitful' future.

Wilde not only compared his artistic philosophy to James's, he also measured his success against his. One of James's characteristics that repeatedly attracted Wilde's attention was his productivity. In 'Literary and Other Notes', Wilde describes James as 'an industrious Bostonian' (*SJW* 115) who 'would have made half a dozen novels . . . and have had enough left for a serial' had he been granted the same theme as Lady Augusta Noel.[46] By this time, Wilde had only published two books (and, significantly, no novels) to James's twenty-nine, and there is a hint of envy in Wilde's portrayal here. Being a professional author meant being highly productive, as Wilde must have realised. The novelist Francis Marion Crawford singled out Howells and James as 'the most distinctly professional novelists in America' because of their prolificacy, and the editor Horace Scudder described them as 'knights of labor' who never worked less than twenty-four hours a day.[47] Though Howells's and James's stamina never flags, according to Wilde their audience 'has grown weary of the Boston novelists' (*SJW* 80). In an 1886 review, James credited Howells with having 'become copious without detriment to his freshness' (*LC1* 502), and it was precisely this ability in James that must have mystified Wilde. Wilde reproached James his productivity while he idly reused the phraseology of 'Literary and Other Notes' to describe James's output in 'Some Literary Notes', where he wrote that 'a more economical writer would have made two novels and half a dozen psychological studies for publication in American magazines' (*SJW* 60) from the material.

Whereas Lady Augusta Noel's *Hithersea Mere* impresses Wilde by its 'delicacy and lightness of treatment' (115), James's fiction explains

too much, 'make[s] life too obviously rational', and cares too much
for 'vivisection'. In the 1870s and 1880s, reviewers often resorted to
the explicit surgical word 'vivisection' to describe James's analytical
style. After the X-ray was discovered in the 1890s, they used the new
word to describe his fiction and, as Kevin Hayes observes, these comments were 'merely an extension of the "mental microscope" and
"vivisection" metaphors applied to the fiction of James's middle
period'.[48] In his review of Whistler's 'Ten O'Clock' lecture, Wilde had
described the temperamental painter as being 'like a brilliant surgeon
lecturing to a class composed of subjects destined ultimately for dissection' (*RW* 48). Though Wilde's criticisms point towards his aversion to vivisection, he nevertheless uses the term to describe one of his
most memorable characters in *The Picture of Dorian Gray*. One of
Lord Henry Wotton's defining traits is a predisposition to the very
vivid analysis Wilde's essays condemn:

> He had been always enthralled by the methods of natural science, but the
> ordinary subject-matter of that science had seemed to him trivial and of
> no import. And so he had begun by vivisecting himself, as he had ended
> by vivisecting others. Human life – that appeared to him the one thing
> worth investigating . . . To note the curious hard logic of passion, and
> the emotional coloured life of the intellect – to observe where they met,
> and where they separated, at what point they were in unison, and at what
> point they were at discord – there was a delight in that! What matter
> what the cost was? One could never pay too high a price for any sensa-
> tion. (*W* 53)

The correspondence between Lord Henry's aesthetico-emotional vivisection and James's psychological realism suggests that Wilde saw the
perverse potential in what 'The Decay of Lying' termed the 'modern
novelist's' 'tedious *document humain*, his miserable little *coin de la
creation*, into which he peers with his microscope' (1073).[49] Wilde
had warmed to the idea of James's psychological realism but he could
only read it, and misread it, creatively. Wilde was, in fact, reading
James through Whistler's criticism of realism and representationality
in *The Gentle Art*. Wilde's 'tedious *document humain*' was an iteration of Whistler's attack on people who look 'not *at* a picture, but
through it, at some human fact' (Whistler 138). Lord Henry merges
Wilde's interpretations of James and Whistler.

Lord Henry takes sensuality to the extreme and in this respect he
is a radical aesthete-dandy within a typological continuum that

includes Morris Townsend, Louis Leverett, Rowland Mallett, Ralph Touchett and Gilbert Osmond. Osmond's character is closest to that of Lord Henry, especially in their shared fascination with watching 'life in its curious crucible of pain and pleasure' (W 53). Just as Osmond's attraction to Isabel conflates aesthetic, erotic and psychological drives, Lord Henry's desire is compartmentalised and rationalised by his needs. For him, Dorian's appeal resides in his beauty and in his interest as 'a wonderful study' (64). Under his influence, Dorian soon begins to look upon the world with 'almost scientific interest' (77). Jonathan Freedman persuasively argues that Lord Henry's remarks to Dorian echo James's advice to the aspiring novelist in *The Art of Fiction*, and that *The Picture of Dorian Gray* and *The Ambassadors* are interconnected through a complex chain of allusions and counterallusions.[50] According to Julia Prewitt Brown, the shadow of James's Gilbert Osmond hovers behind Lord Henry.[51] Just as Dorian develops under Lord Henry's influence, Wilde developed under the influence of James. There is in Wilde's vivid dissection of James, a strong element of admiration intermixed with his supposed disdain. By the same token, it is quite clear that Wilde's study of James's method was invaluable in helping him develop his own.

The extent of Wilde's interest in James and his attention to the subtleties of James's method reveal that Wilde was personally and professionally fascinated by James. And, by dint of studying, critiquing and paraphrasing James, Wilde began to look more and more like an over-the-top version of him: more sensual, more analytic and more strident. Wilde's blunt and deceptive anti-vivisectionist swagger against James became a convenient critical bluff for Wilde to conduct a little vivisecting of his own. There is, after all, no better way to formulate minute and merciless criticisms of one's opponent than by minutely and mercilessly studying him. Wilde's cutting analysis is made possible because of his quasi-obsessive study of James. In Wilde's repetition and modification of a lexicon of distinctly Jamesian allusions and tropes – from Balzac and 'the Realism of Paris filtered through the refining influence of Boston', to 'point of view', 'the air of reality' and vivisection – we can see that Wilde is essentially learning to speak James's language in order to elaborate a parallel idiom of his own. The repetition, alteration and distortion of Jamesian keywords is, in fact, a means of inflecting another's phrases with his native accent and, so doing, creating a new *lingua franca* of Aestheticism. Add to this linguistic hodge-podge that Wilde does much the same with Pater and Whistler (to mention but the two other figures that are the most relevant to us here), and we are well on the way to understanding how Wilde's aesthetic approach synthesizes Aestheticism's various discourses.

'In art as in life the law of heredity holds good. *On est toujours fils de quelqu'un*' (*SJW* 17), Wilde wrote in a review published just two weeks after 'Balzac in English'. Though he had accused James of plagiarism, he now declared the practice of 'literary petty larceny' inevitable, particularly in writers who studied others' works. Speaking with the authority derived from his own experience in the matter, Wilde explains that this type of studious writer 'is in no sense of the word a plagiarist' because his reinterpretation and revision of his precursor's ideas makes them new. We must read Wilde's rejection of the 'plagiarist' tag as deeply personal (he had, after all, often been branded one and wanted to remove all trace of this association), and as an explanation of his own review-as-revision method. If such a method was acceptable to Wilde, why had he not congratulated James, two weeks earlier, for his application of it in 'The Madonna of the Future'? Why did Wilde bridle against James's influence, when their kinship was becoming more and more apparent? It is very difficult 'to study a fine poet without stealing from him', Wilde explained; a writer achieves success when 'he is able to draw new music' from the reeds through which he blows, despite the fact that they 'have been touched by other lips' (*SJW* 17).

'The Decay of Lying':
'Mr Henry James writes fiction as if it were a painful duty'

Wilde's comments on James in the 1888 *Woman's World* were the semi-sweet casing to the bitter pill that would poison their relationship. In late 1888, at the same time as the epistolary debate between Whistler and Wilde was heating up, Wilde was meditating on realism and representationality. His reflections generated 'The Decay of Lying', a two-pronged offensive on James and Whistler that was published in *Nineteenth Century* in January 1889 and reprinted in *Intentions*. Wilde began to subvert Whistler by appropriating his comments to attack others. Realist novelists were his first target. In a letter to *The World* reprinted in *The Gentle Art*, Whistler had asked:

What has Oscar in common with Art? Except that he dines at our tables and picks from our platters the plums for the pudding he peddles in the provinces. Oscar – the amiable, irresponsible, esurient Oscar – with no more sense of a picture than of the fit of a coat, has the courage of the opinions . . . of others! (Whistler 164)

In 'The Decay of Lying', which Wilde was composing when Whistler's letter appeared in *The World*, Wilde seized upon Whistler's remarks and applied them to the 'modern novelist', guilty of the 'monstrous worship of facts' (W 1074) who 'has not even the courage of other people's ideas, but insists on going directly to life for everything' (1073). Wilde's appropriation did not escape Whistler, who bitterly complained in another public letter that Wilde, 'that arch-impostor and pest of the period – the all-pervading plagiarist!' (Whistler 236), had 'deliberately and incautiously incorporated' (237) his letter into 'The Decay of Lying'. As Nicholas Frankel observes, what was arresting about this was 'not that Wilde had plagiarised a phrase from Whistler, but that Wilde had plagiarised a phrase Whistler had used to describe Wilde's very tendency to plagiarism'.[52]

In 'The Decay of Lying', Wilde makes clear his distaste for what has become the 'modern vice': realism's 'monstrous worship of facts' (W 1074). Since Wilde reads James as a realist – which is perhaps not so difficult to do if one heeds only the catchiest of James's aphorisms, such as 'as the picture is reality, so the novel is history' (*LC1* 46) – it is not surprising that he makes James an anti-hero of his anti-realist aesthetic. After all, Wilde believes that 'the one duty we owe to history is to re-write it' (W 1121). By placing James among the offending camp of humourless, imagination-deficient fact-worship-pers (in which Robert Louis Stevenson and H. Rider Haggard were included), Wilde effectively makes James a prisoner of his misread-ing. By dint of reinterpreting and rewriting James's artistic philoso-phy, Wilde arrived at a version of it that justified the position in which he wanted to place James. As a result, Wilde could condemn James in one sentence: 'Mr Henry James writes fiction as if it were a painful duty, and wastes upon mean motives and imperceptible "points of view" his neat literary style, his felicitous phrases, his swift and caustic satire' (1074). By constantly interpreting James's aes-thetic at a remove, and returning always to his *impression* of James's writing rather than to the texts themselves, Wilde succeeds in recast-ing James's project as one that is wholly opposed to his own. Wilde's interpretation rests on a series of successive impressions which build upon each other and finally distort the picture. As is his wont, Wilde arrives at this iteration via another: in an article for the *Woman's World*, he attached one of the criticisms he would soon direct specifically at James ('mean motives') to contemporary fiction as a whole, of which 'meagreness of motive seem[s] to be becoming the dominant note' (*SJW* 160).

Though criticism has been attentive to the support in 'The Decay of Lying' for fiction over fact, and romance over realism, it is worth pointing out that Wilde's argument is framed by terms that resonate with James's 1879 study, *Hawthorne*. This constitutes another facet of Wilde's review-as-revision method since what we are dealing with here is not plagiarism or even paraphrase but a deployment of words and ideas that were current in general debates about realism but are employed in such a manner as to imply a more specific source. This is somewhat different from the re-visionary process I have been discussing thus far. I am not claiming that *Hawthorne* inspired Wilde in any direct way, but rather that the terms of Wilde's anti-realist aesthetic are heavily invested in opposing and misreading James's own set of terms and that, as a result, Wilde's aesthetic echoes the idiom and central dualism of James's study. This reverberation explains why the anti-realist stance of 'The Decay of Lying' sometimes sounds like a response to James's anti-romantic aesthetic. Significantly, Wilde's new aesthetic fixates on James's early criticism and thereby fixes James in time, deliberately disregarding the extent to which James's artistic philosophy had evolved since the late 1870s and early 1880s. Wilde's preoccupation with this period is not accidental: it roughly brackets the dates of his American lecture tour, the beginning of a more heightened awareness of contemporary American literature, and the beginning of his aesthetic apprenticeship with Whistler. This was in all probability the period of his most intense engagement with James's criticism and fiction, as we know from the dropped hints in his fiction such as his reformulation of *The Portrait of a Lady*'s claim that 'there is no more usual basis of matrimony than a mutual misunderstanding' (*N2* 340) into 'the proper basis for marriage is a mutual misunderstanding' (*W* 163) in 'Lord Arthur Savile's Crime'. There are also eyewitness accounts of him stepping into an American bookstore where he 'replenished his supply of novels by Howells and James', as a Cincinnati newspaper reported in 1882.[53] By referring his new aesthetic to this earlier one, Wilde underscores the end of his apprenticeship and the temporal and ideological difference between him and his previous masters. In adhering to this anachronistic view,

Wilde accentuates his role in this aesthetic dialogue. His essay becomes the triumphant opportunity of replying and having the *denier mot* of this debate, as well as being the *dernier cri* in Aestheticism.

Wilde had begun by criticising James's fitness to head a 'new school' of fiction in 'Literary and Other Notes'. In 'The Decay of Lying', he moved from critique to creative reinterpretation by making himself, rather than James, the exponent of a new aesthetic school. In response to the grim picture of literature's future painted by 'Literary and Other Notes', 'The Decay of Lying' draws the unsurprising conclusion that Wilde himself represents the movement's best prospect. Reiterating and extending the terms of Wilde's review, Vivian tells Cyril that he is not 'too despondent about the artistic future either of America or of our own country' (W 1081) because he is confident,

> That some change will take place before this century has drawn to its close . . . Bored by the tedious and improving conversation of *those who have neither the wit to exaggerate nor the genius to romance*, tired of the intelligent person whose reminiscences are always based upon memory, whose statements are invariably limited by probability, and who is at any time liable to be corroborated by the merest Philistine who happens to be present, *Society sooner or later must return to its lost leader, the cultured and fascinating liar* . . . Art, breaking from the prison-house of realism, will run to greet him, and will kiss his false, beautiful lips, knowing that he alone is in possession of the great secret of all her manifestations. (emphasis added)

In Wilde's scheme the liar usurps the position held by those writers who have neither enough imagination nor the inclination to romanticism. The nemesis of Wilde's 'fascinating liar' is America's 'lack of imagination', which is the result of the country 'having adopted for its national hero a man who, according to his own confession, was incapable of telling a lie . . . the story of George Washington and the cherry-tree has done more harm . . . than any other moral tale in the whole of literature'. Hawthorne is a notable exception to the pandemic Wilde diagnoses in American literature. In fact, Hawthorne was a close second to Poe as the American author Wilde most admired.[54]

By pairing imagination and romance together and opposing them to realism, Wilde builds his argument around the same terms as

James's *Hawthorne*, but Wilde arrives at very different conclusions. To James, Hawthorne 'was not in the least a realist – he was not to my mind enough of one' (*LC1* 369). To Wilde, James's fiction was deficient in 'Romance, picturesqueness, charm' (*SJW* 115), as he put it in his *Woman's World* review. James's position is anathema to the Hawthornian impulse in 'The Decay of Lying' towards imagination.[55] James had argued that Hawthorne's emphasis on imagination was the result of having lived in a time and place deficient in fact and history. America, after all, had 'no country gentlemen, no palaces, no castles, nor manors, nor old countryhouses, nor parsonages, nor thatched cottages nor ivied ruins', as James famously explained, noting that what remained was the American's 'secret' and 'joke' (*LC1* 351–2). Howells obliquely alluded to this in 'Henry James, Jr' where he wrote that James had 'indicated that we have, as a nation, as a people, our joke, and every one of us is in the joke more or less'.[56]

Whereas Hawthorne relied on imagination because, according to James, the soil of American history was too thin to allow his art to flower in any other way, Wilde believes that imagination is superior to the historical and factual '*documents humains*' the realists privilege. The moral of Hawthorne's simple life, James claimed, was that 'it takes a great deal of history to produce a little literature, that it needs a complex social machinery to set a writer in motion' (*LC1* 320). Despite being a cog-wheel unconnected to the machinery of history, Hawthorne's fiction succeeds because of its reliance on imagination. Nevertheless, James thinks that America's historical deficiencies – the absence of 'something for [writers] to write about' – proved detrimental to Hawthorne and that he would have achieved more had his fiction been able to feed on fact. 'There is in all of them [Hawthorne's writings] something cold and light and thin, something belonging to the imagination alone' (339). 'The Decay of Lying' turns James's case on its head by arguing that facts and history should be subordinate to fiction. Under the influence of realism, facts are 'not merely finding a footing-place in history, but they are usurping the domain of Fancy, and have invaded the kingdom of Romance. Their chilling touch is over everything' (*W* 1080). Arthur Symons called *Intentions* 'simply a plea for the dignity, an argument for the supremacy, of imaginative art'.[57] Agnes Repplier similarly commented that the essays 'clearly outlined a great truth that is slipping fast away from us – the absolute independence of art – art nourished by imagination and revealing beauty'.[58]

As a result of Wilde's anachronistic interpretation of James, the truth that always slips away from him – or that he voluntarily rejects – is just how similar his position is to that of James. In the Preface to *The American*, James connects reality and romance in a manner similar to Wilde's yoking in 'The Decay of Lying':

> The balloon of experience is in fact of course tied to the earth, and under that necessity we swing, thanks to a rope of remarkable length, in the more or less commodious car of the imagination; but it is by the rope we know where we are, and from the moment that cable is cut we are at large and unrelated: we only swing apart from the globe . . . The art of the romancer is, 'for the fun of it', insidiously to cut the cable. (*LC2* 1064)

Though realism and romance remain distinguishable, James indicates that they are irrevocably connected and that it is from their interplay that great art arises. And even in *Hawthorne*, there are signs of James's resistance to the realism Wilde ascribes to him. Elissa Greenwald argues that 'James's novelistic craft, sometimes seen as the ultimate extension of Realism, is deeply indebted to Hawthorne's Romance. The use of Romance to inform Realism enables James to use the novel to project imaginative views rather than imitate a pre-existent reality'.[59] John Carlos Rowe similarly suggests that James's ambivalence towards Hawthorne 'is the enabling ambiguity of James's transumption of his predecessor'.[60] James's 'Letter to the Deerfield Summer School', published in both the *New York Tribune* and *The Author* only seven months after the publication of 'The Decay of Lying', stated, 'There are no tendencies worth anything but to see the actual or the imaginative, which is just as visible, and to paint it. I have only two little words for the matter remotely approaching to rule or doctrine; one is life and the other freedom' (*LC1* 93).

'The Decay of Lying' enacts Wilde's 'new aesthetic' and artistic philosophy, the impressionistic process I have termed review-as-revision. Wilde idealises the liar because he is loyal to his impression and seeks to satisfy no one but himself. This is why the highest criticism is 'the purest form of personal impression' (*W* 1125). Just so, Wilde's personal impression of Whistler and James forms the basis of his criticism of them. 'The Decay of Lying' is constructed out of these very impressions and criticisms. The 'new aesthetic' Wilde outlines centres on three principles: art never expresses anything but itself; realism is a failure and all bad art stems from the idealisation of life and nature; life imitates art. Though the essay's purpose is ostensibly to propagate these doctrines, which Vivian repeats at the essay's close, the essay itself is its own subject insofar as it is a tissue of ideas woven out of Wilde's impressions. As such, Wilde's subjective tissue evokes Pater's 'strange, perpetual weaving and unweaving of ourselves'[61] as well as the common origin of all ideas. Ideas and language are finite and reinterpretation is the only method by which we can hope to achieve some originality. Just as the threads of a tapestry may be unwoven in order to weave another of a different pattern or figure in the carpet, so ideas and impressions must be reinterpreted in order to achieve new ways of thinking.

The temperament Wilde ascribes to the liar – the ability to make 'frank, fearless statements', 'superb irresponsibility', a 'healthy, natural disdain of proof of any kind' (W 1072) – is the character of someone who is confident about his personal impressions. Subjective impression announces that its own personal truth is truth enough, and is satisfied. It matters little that the threads which we weave and unweave are not our own, it suffices that what we make out of them is. Or, to use another metaphor, 'to arrive at what one really believes, one must speak through lips different from one's own' (1143). Wilde defines plagiarism as an extension of lying, a means to creating better and more beautiful art. The liar and the plagiarist seek only 'to catch by dainty mimicry' the mood and manner of a work, to win from its lips a faint echo of its music, 'and to add to it a music of one's own' (SJW 151).

One of the significant ways in which Wilde does this is by arguing, *contra* Whistler and James, that the writer and painter are not 'brothers of the brush', as James puts it in 'The Art of Fiction', nor is the painter superior to the writer. Rather, the writer is the superior artist. So doing, Wilde reinterprets his adversaries and asserts his own aesthetic. 'The arts are one, and with the artist the artist communicates', James wrote to Whistler in a 1897 letter echoing the sentiment he had expressed in 'The Art of Fiction'.[62] 'The Decay of Lying' challenges James's claim that 'the analogy between the art of the painter and the art of the novelist is, so far as I am able to see, complete' (LC1 46). In Wilde's early reviews of Whistler's 'Ten O'Clock' lecture, he argues that 'the poet is the supreme artist, for he is the master of colour and of form, and the real musician besides, and is lord over all life and all arts; and so to the poet beyond all others are these mysteries known; to Edgar Allan Poe and to Baudelaire, not to Benjamin West and Paul Delaroche' (RW 49). Wilde accuses the painter of being a plagiarist: 'as the painters are always pilfering from the poets, why should not the poet annex the domain of the painter?' (*SJW* 16) And finally, he rebukes those painters who spend 'their wicked and wasted lives in poaching upon the domain of the poets' (*SJW* 75). Gone is any expectation that the arts are one:

> The domain of the painter is, as I suggested before, widely different from that of the poet. To the latter belongs life in its full and absolute entirety; not merely the beauty that men look at, but the beauty that men listen to also; not merely the momentary grace of form or the transient gladness of colour, but the whole sphere of feeling, the perfect cycle of thought. The painter is so far limited that it is only through the mask of the body that he can show us the mystery of the soul; only through conventional images that he can handle ideas; only through its physical equivalents that he can deal with psychology. And how inadequately does he do it then, asking us to accept the torn turban of the Moor for the noble rage of Othello, or a dotard in a storm for the wild madness of Lear! (75–6)

Wilde applied this theory in *The Picture of Dorian Gray* and annexed the domain of the painter. In Wilde's novel, the painting realises Whistler's nightmare since the novel's emblematic use of art is, in Whistler's idiom, 'a method of bringing about a literary climax'. Basil Hallward's portrait of Dorian Gray brings Dorian to a climactic realisation that 'stir[s] him' (*W* 33) and 'flash[es] across him'. Viewing the painting is a turning point for Dorian. Foreshadowing the painting's destruction, the 'sharp pang of pain struck through him like a knife'.

The Picture of Dorian Gray

Despite Wilde's literary brag and patronizing descriptions of realists, *The Picture of Dorian Gray* manifests many of the characteristics of fiction that his criticism condemned. It is moralising, historically based and devoid of action but replete with descriptive catalogues.[63] But what *The Picture of Dorian Gray* also does, and more explicitly than one would expect, is dramatise Wilde's new aesthetic and to dramatise key scenes of his rivalry with Whistler and James. *The Picture of Dorian Gray* offers a total connection between art and life, between what happens to the painting, and what happens to Dorian. These alterations are not brought about by the painter, but by the critic, Lord Henry, the greatest agent of change in the novel. The picture Basil Hallward paints is static; to him it is always the same, because it always represents the encapsulation of one moment in time, when he realised the great truth of his life. Whereas the painter is allied with the topos of stillness – or, more appropriately, still-life – and with its complement, silence, the critic embodies creative polyphony and changeability. Dorian complains that Basil is silent while he paints, and part of Lord Henry's appeal is certainly his volubility, his orality, and the ease with which he can discourse on a subject at length. By contrast, Basil only really expresses one idea throughout the entire novel, namely that his painting is the perfect expression of the moment in which he came to know himself. The painting represents a shameful piece of autobiography and this is why he is reluctant to exhibit it. Because Basil's *ideas* about the painting never change, the painting itself never changes for him and stays stuck in the same interpretive moment. As a result, Basil's art is thin because it conveys only a single experience, not the richness of life's experiences. All that counts for Basil is Dorian's 'merely visible presence' (*W* 23). Though he claims the painting represents 'the lines of a fresh school, a school that is to have in it all the passion of the romantic spirit' (24), this school's vision is limited by Basil's infatuation and the fact that his passion is not quite platonic.

Lord Henry's forceful rhetoric alters both the picture and Dorian himself. His expressions give voice to the painting and imbue it with a depth and complexity that far exceed Basil's. Against the superficiality, stasis and silence of the painter, the critic offers depth, flux and the linguistic music of ideas. Lord Henry's rhetoric is emblematic of the critic's power over art, and exemplifies the way in which the critic reinterprets and recreates both life and art, and therefore surpasses his 'brother of the brush'. In the fraternity conjured by Wilde's novel, artistic expression is not the preserve of the artist only, but of all those who see life creatively and are able to reinterpret it at will. Lord Henry's criticism is, indeed, the highest form of creation, one that far surpasses Basil's limited pictorialism. 'The story is simply this', Basil tells Lord Henry, and proceeds to detail the first time he saw Dorian, a moment that is forever connected to 'a terrible crisis' in his life, 'a curious sensation of terror' (21). For Basil, Dorian and his painting always represent one moment, one story. As such, Lord Henry represents the Wildean response to Whistler's worry that a critic would read a painting as 'a hieroglyph or symbol of a story' (Whistler 146). The story that Lord Henry reads is the one the painting itself symbolises; it is precisely because he is able to see the painting as a cipher for itself that he is able to decipher it. The same can be said of his relation to Dorian, whose life-narrative is revealed to him by Lord

Henry. Because Dorian always enacts – makes real – Lord Henry's criticisms, he lends credence to the contention in 'The Decay of Lying' that art creates life. Lord Henry's method of criticising art and creating life is indebted to James since he relies on psychological analysis and vivisection – the very approach Wilde faults in his criticism of James. Following Wilde's interpretation of Pater, Lord Henry places his subjective, shifting impression at the centre of his aesthetic. In this respect, the novel affirms the essence of Wilde's 'new aesthetic' and confirms his achievement.

Lord Henry is the first person we see and hear in the novel, as well as the first to suggest what the picture of Dorian Gray looks like. Yet he does not actually describe the picture, but criticises and judges it, saying, 'It is your best work, Basil, the best thing you have ever done' (*W* 18). Wilde also makes clear that Lord Henry is a fixture in the painter's studio, one very comfortably ensconced in 'the corner of the divan of Persian saddle-bags on which he was lying, smoking, as was his custom'. This setting establishes Lord Henry's position with respect to the painter and it implies that the artist's studio is a natural setting for the critic.

Basil, however, feels artistically hampered by Lord Henry, whom he asks to leave. Dorian's reproach to Basil – 'You never open your lips while you are painting' (27) – safeguards the critic's position within the studio's creative confines. Seen and not heard, Basil works away at his painting of Dorian, while the voluble Lord Henry goes to work on Dorian himself. By the end of the sitting, Lord Henry's conversation has thoroughly transformed the boy, though the painter remains unaware of the fact that it is Lord Henry's persuasive analysis that has wrought this change. 'I have caught the effect I wanted – the half-parted lips, and the bright look in the eyes. I don't know what Harry has been saying to you, but he has certainly made you have the most wonderful expression', Basil indifferently tells Dorian (29). While the artist turns a deaf ear to life in order to translate it into art, the critic's effect is doubly perceptible for he transforms art and life. It is no accident that the topic on which Lord Henry lectures Dorian is 'influence' (28). The 'few words' that he speaks (which take up several paragraphs in the novel) transform Dorian physically as well as intellectually.

[Lord Henry's words] touched some secret chord that had never been touched before, but that he felt was now vibrating and throbbing to curious pulses. Music had stirred him like that . . . But music was not articulate . . . Words! Mere words! . . . One could not escape from them. And yet what a subtle magic there was in them! *They seemed to be able to give a plastic form to formless things, and to have a music of their own as sweet as that of viol or of lute.* Mere words! Was there anything so real as words? (29, emphasis added)[64]

Lord Henry's dialogue materialises, and is made real and palpable by the reaction it provokes in Dorian. Words have an effect on the physical world, just as an 'impression' defines both a material and a metaphorical experience. Though Dorian's physical and metaphysical alteration is perceptible to Dorian himself and to Lord Henry (who is 'amazed at the sudden impression that his words had produced'), it eludes the painter entirely. Indeed, Basil points out that Dorian has never sat better because he has been 'perfectly still'. What the painter registers as superficial and static is in fact in a profound change. This oversight is the central problem of the visible arts which, Wilde argues, can render only moments, not movement. In 'The Critic As Artist' Wilde explains that 'movement, that problem of the visible arts, can be truly realised by Literature alone. It is Literature that shows us the body in its swiftness and the soul in its unrest' (1124). Just so, Basil's picture is 'concentrated to one moment of perfection', and 'possesses no spiritual element of growth or change'.

The change in Dorian that Lord Henry provokes does not end with the completion of the painting. When Dorian looks at the picture of himself, his transformation registers as a succession of impressions that intensify the initial change. The succession of Dorian's impressions – from pleasure, to consciousness, pain, and anger – is transformative to the point that Basil is compelled to acknowledge the critic's creation in saying 'this is your doing, Harry' (34). When Dorian looks at the painting, he does not see its static surface, but the changing fate it represents. Dorian's impression is mediated by Lord Henry's criticism and his eye has been trained to read the painting as a narrative. Consequently, he does not see a painting of a beautiful young man but an allegory of youth's fleetingness and beauty's transience. The idiom used to describe the widening gyre of Dorian's impression resonates with Pater's Conclusion, whereby this same movement is a 'perpetual weaving and unweaving'[65] of the self. Every 'delicate fibre of his nature quiver[s]' (W 33) and as 'his eyes deepened into amethyst', he seems to embody Pater's gem-like flame.

Physically and intellectually responsive to Lord Henry's words, Dorian eventually becomes a cipher for Lord Henry's creativity. His body expresses the effect of Lord Henry's ideas upon him at every turn. Lord Henry notes this with satisfaction:

[Dorian's] startled eyes and lips parted in frightened pleasure, [as] he had sat opposite to him at the club, the red candleshades staining to a richer rose the wakening wonder of his face. Talking to him was like playing upon an exquisite violin. He answered to every touch and thrill of the bow . . . There was something terribly enthralling in the exercise of influence. (39)

By talking, Lord Henry creates a new awareness in Dorian, and Wilde's emphasis on orality here parallels the dialogue format of 'The Decay of Lying' but extends it by contending that 'it is simply expression . . . that gives reality to things' (W 85). Just as Wilde's new aesthetic responds to Whistler's aesthetic and combines elements of James's aesthetic, so Lord Henry also advocates a 'new manner in art' (40) that aims to surpass Basil's 'fresh school' of painting. The novel not only fictionalises the themes of the rivalry that contributed to its creation, it specifies the Jamesian influence on Lord Henry's 'psychological point of view'. Lord Henry's method is explained in realist terms analogous to those Wilde applies to James: his 'experimental method' (54) is, like vivisection, a means of arriving at a 'scientific analysis of the passions'. Soon enough, Dorian finds himself 'gazing at the portrait with a feeling of almost scientific interest' (77). Via his influence on Dorian and its physical manifestation, Lord Henry makes the young man a mouthpiece for his ideas. This device is perhaps most evident in chapter four, where Lord Henry's wife meets Dorian alone, recognises him from the many photographs of him her husband possesses, and listens to him speak her husband's thoughts. Dorian thus becomes a talking-picture, a creation that speaks its creator's thoughts. Dorian realises Lord Henry's ideas and becomes the public expression of them, much as a book would. Lord Henry indicates his awareness of this parallel by referring to Dorian as 'a wonderful study' (64). In his last conversation with Dorian before his death, Lord Henry tells him that he has made his life into an art as deep and expressive, as fine as music or literature: 'I am so glad that you have never done anything, never carved a statue, or painted a picture, or produced anything outside yourself! Life has been your art. You have set yourself to music. Your days are your sonnets' (155). With the publication of *Intentions* and *The Picture of Dorian Gray* in 1890–1 his apprenticeship was over. Like Dorian, Wilde had set himself to music and turned his days into sonnets.

The Picture of Dorian Gray enacts Wilde's personal drama of influence. Lord Henry's ability to charm 'listeners out of themselves' (43) is so great that he quickly gains new converts. One admiring listener asks Lord Henry: 'You talk books away, . . . why don't you write one?' (44). The answer to this question is that, were he to write one, Lord Henry's book would probably sound a lot like Wilde's novel. In fact, Lord Henry just about says so when he responds that he would like 'to write a novel certainly; a novel that would be as lovely as a Persian carpet, and as unreal'. This analogy between the novel and the carpet returns to an idea that was vital to Wilde's artistic transformation, namely Pater's 'strange, perpetual weaving and unweaving of ourselves'. Wilde develops this intratextual allusion still further by strewing Lord Henry's house with 'silk long-fringed Persian rugs' (45) and decorating Dorian Gray's home, symbolically, with a carpet 'in holes' (115) in the scene near the end of the novel where Dorian begins to unravel the mystery of his sinful nature. Significantly, this scene culminates in Dorian's wild stabbing of the painter Basil Hallward.

> There was a stifled groan, and the horrible sound of someone choking with blood. Three times the outstretched arms shot up convulsively, waving grotesque stiff-fingered hands in the air. He stabbed him twice more, but the man did not move. Something began to trickle on the floor . . . [Dorian] threw the knife on the table, and listened. *He could hear nothing but the drip, drip, drip on the threadbare carpet.* (117, emphasis added)

In a letter, Wilde said, 'Basil Hallward is what I think I am: Lord Henry what the world thinks me: Dorian what I would like to be' (LW 585). Wilde later said that Basil Hallward was libellously based on Whistler.[66] As to Wilde's relationship to Henry James, it may be encapsulated in the observation that Dorian is influenced by a man named Henry and almost murdered by another named James.

NOTES

1. Adams, *Letters*, 328.
2. Both were published in 1883. The collection became *Portraits of Places* and the short story appeared in *Century Magazine*.
3. Freedman, *Professions*, 169.
4. Ibid. 169–70.
5. Michael Davitt Bell, *The Problem of American Realism: Studies in the Cultural History of a Literary Idea* (Chicago: U of Chicago P, 1993) 1, 59.
6. On the hubbub occasioned by Howells's review, see Michael Anesko, *Letters, Fictions, Lives: Henry James and William Dean Howells* (New York: Oxford UP, 1997) 166–76.
7. Howells, 'Henry James, Jr', 26.
8. Anesko, *Friction*, 82.
9. Howells, 'Henry James, Jr', 27.
10. Ibid. 28, emphasis added.
11. Ibid. 27.
12. Ibid. 26.
13. Ibid. 25.
14. Ibid. 26.
15. Howells, 'Editor's Study'. *Harper's New Monthly Magazine* 73.436 (September 1886) 641.
16. Howells, 'Henry James, Jr', 25.
17. John Carlos Rowe, *The Theoretical Dimensions of Henry James* (Madison: U of Wisconsin P, 1984) 233.
18. Hazard Adams, *Critical Theory Since Plato* (New York: Harcourt Brace Jovanovich, 1971) 660. Terry Eagleton implies the same in *The English Novel: An Introduction* (Oxford: Blackwell, 2005) 10.
19. Freedman and Matz note that the emphasis in 'The Art of Fiction' on the autonomy of art sounds similar to Pater (Freedman, *Professions* 142–3; Matz, *Literary Impressionism*, 85–91).
20. Pater, *Renaissance* (1986), 151.
21. Douglas Mao, *Solid Objects: Modernism and the Test of Production* (Princeton, NJ: Princeton UP, 1998) 107.
22. This passage in 'The Art of Fiction' evokes Emily Dickinson's poem 'The spider as an artist' where the speaker takes the spider, whom she calls a 'neglected son of genius', by the hand (*The Complete Poems of Emily Dickinson*, ed. Thomas Herbert Johnson (Boston: Little Brown, 1961) 557). In the sentence after James's description of the mind-as-web, he describes a Dickinson-like 'young lady living in a village' (*LC1* 52) as a 'damsel on whom nothing is lost' who speaks the truth about gentlemen, just as 'a man of genius' might.
23. Pater, *Renaissance* (1986), 150, 152.

24. Freedman, *Professions*, 9, 18. Freedman's claims about Pater's perception of flux needlessly complicate the matter and lead him to overstate his case by claiming that 'aestheticist art, then, faces a temporal dilemma. It wishes to affirm two incompatible values: on the one hand, it seeks to celebrate the most transitory and exquisite of experiences . . . but on the other, it seeks to use this very means of celebration to escape time itself' (Freedman, *Professions*, 18). Such analysis flies in the face of Pater's repeated affirmation of the *complementarity* of stasis and flux. Moreover, it turns a blind eye to Pater's Heraclitean heritage, which offers a synthetic, harmonising view of the very elements Freedman claims are contradictory. To Pater and Heraclitus both, 'what appears most stable in our experience is in fact a state of incessant motion', as William Shuter notes (*Rereading Walter Pater* (Cambridge: Cambridge UP, 1997) 8).

25. Rowe, *Theoretical*, 229.

26. Ibid. 229.

27. Borelius, 'Oscar Wilde', 43.

28. Peter Collister, 'James's "The Madonna of the Future" and the Problem of Artistic Failure: Some French Models', *Journal of European Studies* (2002): 341–2. Though James wrote a number of essays on Balzac, he does not mention this story in any of them.

29. Henley, *Selected Letters* 105.

30. Honoré de Balzac, *Selected Short Stories/Contes Choisis: A Dual Language Book*, trans. Stanley Appelbaum (Mineola, NY: Dover, 2000) 129.

31. Ibid. 129.

32. Ibid. 127, my translation.

33. In a letter, James claimed, misleadingly, that Pater's *Renaissance* 'treats of several things I know nothing about' (*L1* 391).

34. Matz, *Literary Impressionism*, 93.

35. Ibid. 93; Ellmann, 'Henry James Among the Aesthetes', 219.

36. Hayes, *Henry James*, 70.

37. Edwin Sill Fussell, *The Catholic Side of Henry James* (Cambridge: Cambridge UP, 1993) 6. 'The Lesson of Balzac', the lecture James delivered during his 1905 tour of the United States, reconfirms Balzac's influence on James's development.

38. Danson, *Wilde's Intentions*, 57.

39. Howells, 'Henry James, Jr', 25.

40. Percy Lubbock, *The Craft of Fiction* (London: J. Cape, 1921) 251.

41. Gard, *Henry James*, 140.

42. The novel Wilde is referring to is probably *The Bostonians*, which was published in London by Macmillan on 16 February 1886.

43. Howells, 'Henry James, Jr', 27.

44. Danson, *Wilde's Intentions*, 57.

45. Wilde reuses this same quotation in 'The Decay of Lying' (W 1076).
46. In her edition of Wilde's *Selected Journalism*, Anya Clayworth misreads this allusion as a reference to Poe (*SJW* 204).
47. Anesko, *Letters*, 187.
48. Hayes, *Henry James*, xvii.
49. Andrew Lang formulated his aversion to realism in the same terms as Wilde in his 1886 essay on 'Realism and Romance'. 'Modern Realists', Lang writes, 'not only use the microscope, and ply experiments, but ply them, too often, *in corpore vili* [in matter of little value]' (quoted in Ledger and Luckhurst, *The Fin-de-Siède*, 101).
50. Freedman, *Professions*, 168–9, 192–6.
51. Brown, *Cosmopolitan Criticism*, 56.
52. Nicholas Frankel, *Oscar Wilde's Decorated Books* (Ann Arbor, MI: U of Michigan P, 2000) 89. Frankel offers a fascinating reading of *Intentions*'s materiality and the manner in which it echoed certain elements of *The Gentle Art*'s presentation in 'Wilde's *Intentions* and the Simulation of Meaning' (79–108).
53. Lewis and Smith, *Oscar Wilde*, 189.
54. See Kerry Powell, 'Tom, Dick, and Dorian Gray: Magic-Picture Mania in Late Victorian Fiction', *Philological Quarterly* 62.2 (1983), 149; O'Sullivan, *Aspects of Wilde*, 133. A reviewer commented that '[t]he central idea [of *The Picture of Dorian Gray*] is an excellent, if not exactly novel, one; and a finer art, say that of Nathaniel Hawthorne, would have made a striking and satisfying story of it' (Beckson, *Oscar Wilde: Critical Heritage* 77).
55. On the similarities between *The Picture of Dorian Gray* and Hawthorne's *The Prophetic Pictures*, see Kerry Powell, 'Hawthorne, Arlo Bates, and Dorian Gray', *Papers on Language and Literature* 16 (1980).
56. Howells, 'Henry James, Jr', 26.
57. Quoted in Beckson, *Oscar Wilde: Critical Heritage*, 94.
58. Ibid. 104.
59. Elissa Greenwald, *Realism and the Romance: Nathaniel Hawthorne, Henry James and American Fiction* (Ann Arbor, MI: UMI Research, 1989) 2.
60. Rowe, *Theoretical*, 49.
61. Pater, *Renaissance* (1986), 152.
62. Henry James, *Selected Letters*, ed. Leon Edel (Cambridge, MA: Harvard UP, 1987) 303–4.
63. Epifanio San Juan, Jr, *The Art of Oscar Wilde* (Princeton: Princeton UP, 1967) 62.
64. Wilde echoes this in 'The Critic As Artist': 'For the material that painter or sculptor uses is meagre in comparison with that of words. Words have not merely music as sweet as that of viol and lute, colour as rich

and vivid as any that makes lovely for us the canvas of the Venetian or the Spaniard, and plastic form no less sure and certain than that which reveals itself in marble or in bronze, but thought and passion and spirituality are theirs also, are theirs indeed alone' (W 1117).

65. Pater, *Renaissance* (1986), 152.
66. Quoted in Ellmann, *Oscar Wilde*, 261.

CHAPTER 4

'WILD THOUGHTS AND DESIRE! THINGS I CAN'T TELL YOU – WORDS I CAN'T SPEAK!': THE DRAMA OF IDENTITY IN *THE IMPORTANCE OF BEING EARNEST* AND *GUY DOMVILLE*

On 2 February 1895, Henry James wrote his brother William to describe the opening night of his play, *Guy Domville*. Too nervous to attend the performance, James had instead gone to the Haymarket to see Oscar Wilde's *An Ideal Husband*. He described his dramatic confrontation with Wilde as an awakening that had come too late:

> I sat through [*An Ideal Husband*] and saw it played with every appearance (so far as the crowded house was an appearance) of complete success, and *that* gave me the most fearful apprehension. The thing seemed to me so helpless, so crude, so bad, so clumsy, feeble and vulgar, that as I walked away across St James's Square to learn my own fate, the prosperity of what I had seen seemed to me to constitute a dreadful presumption of the shipwreck of *Guy Domville*; and I stopped in the middle of the Square, paralysed by the terror of this probability – afraid to go on and learn more. 'How can my piece do anything with the public with whom *that* is a success?' It couldn't – but even then the full truth was, 'mercifully,' not revealed to me; the truth that in a short month my piece would be whisked away to make room for the triumphant Oscar. (*L3* 514)

Guy Domville was replaced by *The Importance of Being Earnest* at the St James's Theatre on Valentine's Day, 1895. In March Wilde was arrested. In April he was tried. In May he was sentenced to two years' hard labour at Pentonville. Paradoxically, *The Importance of Being Earnest* has weathered the storm of personal history and the tides of public taste to become one of the few plays of the period still in theatrical repertoires.[1] James's play, on the other hand, has sunk into obscurity. But James's and Wilde's respective shipwrecks mark more than their simultaneous experience of private disaster and public shame. Although critics have focused on the plays' disparities,[2] the prominent identity and language debates that are at the core of both dramas reveal strong similarities which suggest James's and Wilde's shared investment in the ontology of modern selfhood. Both plays centre on emergent selves and attempt to find a language to express their nature. When James learned of Wilde's play, he told a friend that the subject of *The Importance of Being Earnest* 'is that the young hero's real name is Ernest, but he thinks it isn't! The pun halts for want of a letter – but the stern moral is scarcely less good.'[3] The message in both James's and Wilde's plays is that 'it isn't easy to be anything nowadays' (*PW* 259).

If the close of the nineteenth century saw the articulation of a discourse of male homosexuality because of the public dramatisation Wilde's trial entailed, then this new idiom of transgressive selfhood is latent in *Guy Domville*, *The Importance of Being Earnest* and 'The Modern Warning' where it is brought to bear upon identities in flux who lose their words as a result of their personal destabilisations. In *The Importance of Being Earnest*, Jack Worthing's realisation that he has unwittingly been leading a double-life causes temporary aphasia. In James's play, Guy Domville's surfacing desires prompt him to declare himself overcome by 'things I can't tell you – words I can't speak' (*Plays* 494). Why do their crises result in the loss of speech? What relationship do James and Wilde posit between desire, selfhood and language? The plays eloquently give voice to the unspeakable, to shame, and to the love that dare not speak its name – the very 'crime' that would put Wilde in prison. As such, both plays are uncanny preludes to Wilde's trial. Moreover, the typescript of *Guy Domville* contains a number of explicit homoerotic references that did not make it into the finished work, as I discuss in more detail later in this chapter. These plays expose the personal cost of transgression against normative masculinity, and their historical context inscribes this concern into a larger project, namely Wilde's and James's attempt to represent the effect of transgressive desires and behaviours on identity.[4] The unspeakable has been a particularly rich trope for queer theory and my intention here is to show that the unspeakable can also be applied productively to selfhood *tout court*, whether or not it explicitly involves same-sex desire. As Ed Cohen explains, the unspeakable is 'a nexus for language class, nationality, sexuality, and social status – if only through its ability to radically disrupt these connections'.[5] Indeed, the blank is an utterance that indicates that what is unexpressed may be threatening or terrible, but this terror need not be limited to sexuality.

At the start of the 1890s, James's and Wilde's plays began to target transgression by focusing on women with a past. James's *Tenants* (1890) and *The Reprobate* (1891), and Wilde's *Lady Windermere's Fan* (1892) and *A Woman of No Importance* (1893) developed a socially acceptable, censor-proof language for socially unaccepted women. Through verbal, visual and material signs the plays gave voice to these women's identities. So it is that the scheming heroine of *Tenants* claims not to be 'dangerous', but she conspires to have her illegitimate son marry her ex-lover's rich ward, and her French dresses and 'cosmopolitan air' repeat her *risqué* story for all to see (*Plays* 265). James's farce, *The Reprobate*, spotlights another woman with a past and a French pedigree in the form of Mrs Freshville who was once a singer in Paris and who returns to England to propose marriage to her ex-lover. In *Lady Windermere's Fan*, Mrs Erlynne's dress (which the audience hears of long before they set eyes on her) is a metonym for her dissipated character since she is a 'horrid woman. She dresses so well, too, which makes it much worse, sets such a dreadful example,' as the Duchess of Berwick opines (*W* 425). Mrs Erlynne's identity is as quickly altered as a dress because, though 'many a woman has a past . . . she has at least a dozen, and . . . they all fit' (426). When puritanical Lady Windermere prepares to run off with a lover, she appropriates Mrs Erlynne's fan, which is inscribed with 'Margaret', the name both women share. The fan is thus freed from fixed meaning: it is the ideal accessory for bad women as well as good women gone bad. The fan's shifting significance thus conveys the indeterminacy of the play's principal characters.[6] 'Women are pictures,' one man advises in *A Woman of No Importance*, 'if you want to know what a woman really means . . . look at her, don't listen to her' (*W* 493). Like Madame Merle in *The Portrait of a Lady*, these women believe that 'one's self – for other people – is one's expression of one's self; and one's house, one's clothes, the book one reads, the company one keeps – these things are all expressive' (*N2* 397–8) Fallen women wrap themselves up in shells of circumstance in order to cover their past and give themselves more acceptable social identities.

In the mid-1890s, James's and Wilde's plays shifted their attention to men behaving badly. In *The Importance of Being Earnest*, an eligible young man may have nothing but if 'he looks everything', Lady Bracknell reasons, 'what more can one desire?' (*PW* 300). Objects become increasingly important in *Guy Domville* and *The Importance of Being Earnest* because language fails to communicate. Here, too, visual and material signs are valuable, but their meaning becomes more and more unreliable. Because the characters' desires and behaviours are unspeakable, the characters resort to visual and material signs to articulate the words they cannot. *The Importance of Being Earnest* and *Guy Domville* are concerned with the struggle to establish a language – a visual, verbal, and material idiom – for the unspeakable.

The unspeakable and the unspoken are encoded within a matrix of linguistic and material signifiers that simultaneously define and destabilise normative language and, by extension, identity. What is at stake in these plays is not a certain *type* of late nineteenth-century identity, but *identity itself* because the very language by which it is constructed is destabilised. The fraught consciousnesses James and Wilde portray are powerfully modified by linguistic power dynamics. By understanding *Guy Domville* and *The Importance of Being Earnest* as articulations of a modern selfhood and the unspeakable as a potent signifier for linguistic and personal instabilities, these plays dramatise the emergence of an intricate and distinctly modern psychology. In other words, the characters in these plays are apostles of a psychosocial apocalypse. James's fiction had established his interest in interior, psychological action. Wilde said he wanted to test 'the capacity of the modern stage to represent, in any adequate measure or degree, works of introspective method and strange or sterile psychology' (*LW* 519). Now both James and Wilde translated a state of mind onto the stage, and into the language of external conflict.

Alan Sinfield, Joseph Bristow and Ed Cohen have cogently argued that a set of characteristics emerged at the tail end of the nineteenth century that fundamentally shaped our modern conception of homosexual identity. In his well known analysis of the *History of Sexuality*, Foucault explains that the late nineteenth century saw a shift in the meaning of sodomy: it became constitutive of a sexual being, and was no longer considered solely a sexual act.[7] The Wilde trial permanently altered the valence attached to the dandy and the lover of boys, the effeminate man and the aesthete. Therefore, it is not until after 1895 that one can begin to talk of the formal recognition of personal characteristics that we now associate with homosexuality. What I am arguing is that *Guy Domville* and *The Importance of Being Earnest*, which were both written and produced before Wilde's trial, express in elemental form a fluid and multi-faceted conception of modern identity that challenges the nineteenth-century model of a single, uniform identity. Neither play has a fully articulated homosexual subtext, nor does it limn what being homosexual might mean.[8] What both plays do, instead, is articulate identities in crisis, forms of emergent selfhood that are created by and through destabilisation.

The modern conception of identity, in the sense in which I use it throughout this chapter, dates back roughly to the first half of the twentieth century, and is deeply inflected by social features such as race, religion, gender and sexuality.[9] In *The Ethics of Identity*, Kwame Anthony Appiah traces the social component of identity from Max Weber's description of *Gemeinsamkeit* (commonality) as originating from a feeling of shared history, to Erik Erikson's explanation of a person's identity as the relation between his self-conception and 'his community's conception of him'.[10] Appiah also notes the importance of others' responses in shaping individuals' identities or, in Charles Taylor's words, 'love relationships . . . are crucial because they are crucibles of inwardly generated identity'.[11] These terms are helpful as ways of thinking of the ways in which sexuality, desire and love inform identity.

J. Hillis Miller has recently parsed James's various iterations of 'community' in *The Awkward Age* in order to suggest that there exists a 'hidden gay community that could only be referred to in the innuendoes' of the novel.[12] My own chapter makes a far more limited and historically contingent claim. If identity is partly created through interaction with a community and with others, then what happens when there is no community? What if the others one loves cannot be revealed – to themselves or to us? Where does this leave one's identity? If modern identity is dialogically constituted through the interaction of personal selfhood and community, then we can think of sexual identity as the combined result of a person's self-conception and his community's conception of him, as well as his investment in this community's past. But if we apply this idea to pre-Wilde-trial identities and attempt to derive the sexual identity of, say, Jack Worthing or Guy Domville, we run into an impasse: the community, one of the defining elements of modern identity, is absent. In terms of same-sex identity, the nineteenth century was neither a time of *Gemeinschaft* (community) nor of Weberian *Gemeinsamkeit* (commonality), but of *Einsamkeit* (solitude).

While there were certainly men who had sex with men, coteries with predilections for green carnations, and same-sex classifications generated by Karl Heinrich Ulrichs and Richard von Krafft-Ebing, these associations could not be considered a 'community'. Sodomy remained a sexual act, not a sexual identity. It is, therefore, ana- chronistic to speak of fully formed homosexual identities in *The Importance of Being Earnest* and *Guy Domville*. These are, rather, identities in crisis. The Wilde trial represented a very public coming together of people who would, in time, come to know themselves as a community.

'You look as if your name was Ernest'

In *The Importance of Being Earnest*, Wilde wanted to develop a verbal, visual and material language to describe emergent personali- ties. In the play, language is destabilised. Euphemism is pervasive, and nobody says quite what he or she means. Lane, the manservant, was married 'in consequence of a misunderstanding' (*PW* 253). Lady Bracknell thinks a railway station cloak-room is the locale for 'social indiscretion' (267). Even the weather is suspect since, whenever people talk about it, Gwendolen 'always feel[s] quite certain that they mean something else. And that makes me quite nervous' (262). Why is there so much misunderstanding, suspicion and nervousness among this set? Signs are not wholly independent entities; they depend on their contexts in order to generate a certain meaning. By the same token, identity relies in part on its social context or community. An individual's identity is premised on his expression of certain signs, which are made up of concepts and sound-images (which may be visual, verbal, material and so on). These concepts initially have no value in and of themselves; they only exist in relation to other similar signs. 'The self,' sociologist Erving Goffman explains, 'is not an organic thing that has a specific location, whose fundamental fate is to be born, to mature, and to die; it is a dramatic effect arising dif- fusely from a scene that is presented.'[13] Goffman's argument about the performative nature of selfhood anticipates and extends Judith Butler's assertion that:

> acts, gestures, enactments, generally construed are performative in the sense that the essence or identity that they otherwise purport to express are fabrications manufactured and sustained through corporeal signs and discursive means . . . In other words, acts and gestures, articulated and enacted desires create the illusion of an interior and organizing gender core, an illusion discursively maintained for the purposes of the

regulation of sexuality within the obligatory frame of reproductive heterosexuality.[14]

Goffman's theory is not limited to gender and sexuality as Butler's theory is, and therefore more effectively addresses the multiplicity of factors that generate the sense of self. An individual's identity is partially predicated on his ability to express signs that are intelligible to a certain community. Given another community, these signs might take on a very different meaning. But we must enter a caveat against misconception: these signs by no means express the essence and fullness of the individual's identity. All they can do is signify it. Identity, then, is a 'performed character' that is determined by its context or, in Goffman's words, 'in terms of the show that must go on'.[15]

The confrontation between Jack and Algernon at the beginning of act one dramatises this model. To Jack, having different names in the city and the country is motivated by his duty to maintain his health, happiness, and high moral tone; it is part of his identity as a guardian (PW 258). To Algernon, however, having different names in the city and the country signifies that Jack is 'a confirmed Bunburyist' (257). Left to his own devices, Jack can make his actions signify whatever he likes. But when confronted with Algernon's identification of him as a Bunburyist, Jack's actions take on a different meaning altogether, a meaning that threatens his sense of self. Consequently, the conflict between Jack and Algernon does not hinge on whether Jack is or is not, specifically, a Bunburyist. What is at stake is who Jack really is. Dramatised as Jack's quest for self-knowledge, it is this question that drives the play. By the end, Jack has realised for the first time in his 'life the vital Importance of Being Earnest' (307).

Jack's first conversation with Algernon confirms that he has been leading a double life, masquerading as 'Ernest' when he is in the city. Shocked by this revelation, Algernon attempts to prove his friend's identity through material evidence:

> You have always told me it was Ernest. I have introduced you to every one as Ernest. You answer to the name of Ernest. You look as if your name was Ernest. You are the most earnest looking person I ever saw in my life. It is perfectly absurd your saying that your name isn't Ernest. It's on your cards. Here is one of them. *(Taking it from case.)* 'Mr Ernest Worthing, B.4, The Albany.' I'll keep this as a proof that your name is Ernest if you ever attempt to deny it to me, or to Gwendolen, or to anyone else. (257)

Algernon's argument illustrates the process of identity-formation and linguistic signification discussed above. Jack has *verbally* signified that his name is Ernest and has been introduced to a community ('every one') as Ernest. He has *visually* signified that his name is Ernest. He has *materially* signified that his name is Ernest. Algernon's surprise is prompted by the realisation that none of these signs confirms his friend's identity.

'The truth,' Algernon concludes, 'is rarely pure and never simple. Modern life would be very tedious if it were either' (258). The pun on Jack's calling card confirms a complex truth: the card announces Jack as 'Mr Ernest Worthing, B.4, The Albany' and he is, indeed, Ernest when he is *before* the Albany, that is, when he is in the city. The calling card is doubly problematic: as a piece of evidence of his social identity, it is strictly true, but it is contradicted by another piece of evidence with an equal claim to truth: the cigarette case. Inscribed 'from little Cecily, with her fondest love to her dear Uncle Jack' (257), the cigarette case confirms Jack to be Cecily's guardian, which is how he likes to think of himself. The case attests to Jack's personal, private self, whereas the card attests to his social, public self. Jack's anxiety about the case, and particularly about the fact that Algernon has 'read what is written inside' (256), must be understood within this context. 'It is a very ungentlemanly thing to read a private cigarette case,' he chides Algernon, because it is an expression of his interior self. The cigarette case's private significance is satirised in act two when Cecily describes her diary as the private repository of her life's secrets that is 'consequently meant for publication' (282).

Everyone in this play seems to be someone else. Algernon's own disingenuousness is exposed when he admits that he has a double life and he reveals a set of 'Bunbury suits' (271) designed expressly for Bunburying. As a matter of fact, he takes the idea of clothing as a material language written on the body quite literally: he writes Ernest's address on his shirt-cuff before he impersonates him (270–1). This exercise in material signification develops to its absurd conclusion in act two, when Cecily produces the keepsakes of her engagement to Algernon, though they have never been engaged. The specificity of the objects she shows him – the tree where he supposedly proposed, the ring with his name, the lovers' bangle, and a box of letters (284) – gives comic emphasis to the scene. Wilde's method reveals that material signs, so prized by society as a means of classification, have only limited influence on an individual's identity.

Act one conveys who Jack is *to others* while eroding his own sense of his identity. So when Algernon exits and leaves Jack to enjoy a tête-à-tête with Gwendolen, this second encounter actually continues the operation of the first by undermining Jack's identity. The scenes build upon each other and their cumulative effect is to develop the idea that labels, names and signifiers do not inhere in a person's essence. 'For me you have always had an irresistible fascination. Even before I met you I was far from indifferent to you,' Gwendolen declares, much to Jack's amazement (262). What makes Gwendolen's love for Jack so absurd is not that she loves him before she meets him, but that a precondition of her love is that his name is Ernest. 'We live, as I hope you know, Mr Worthing, in an age of ideals . . . And my ideal has always been to love some one of the name of Ernest. There is something in that name that inspires absolute confidence,' she explains to her bewildered beloved. Wilde's argument builds to a comical climax as Gwendolen enumerates the name's improbable (yet supposedly intrinsic) merits: to be named 'Ernest' is to be safe, divine, vibration-producing and musical (263). A slip of the tongue soon exposes Jack's identity, and his need to become the Ernest she thinks him to be: 'Gwendolen, I must get christened at once – I mean we must get married at once.' With this, Wilde explodes the relationship between a name and what's in it, between Ernest and his character.

Up to this point in the play, the audience has learned that Jack is Ernest, a guardian, an uncle, a Bunburyist and Gwendolen's fiancé. But Wilde's drama of identity continues to gather momentum as it hurtles Jack towards his third and most devastating encounter. In calling Jack 'a parcel' (267), as Lady Bracknell does at the end of her interview with him, she revises Jack's identity for the third time in the play. Lady Bracknell's interrogation begins with a performative utterance: she annuls Gwendolen's engagement to Jack. The interview she conducts in order to assess if Jack can be included on her 'list of eligible young men' (265) replicates the identificatory process he has already undergone. Whereas Gwendolen focused on the verbal component of identity, her mother concerns herself with its social aspects. The scene proves that identity cannot be confirmed through social relations any more than it can be confirmed through language. Though Lady Bracknell asks about Jack's income and politics, her main concern is his lineage. Dismissing Jack as a potential suitor for her daughter, she concludes that his lack of social connections 'display[s] a contempt for the ordinary decencies of family life that reminds one of the worst excesses of the French Revolution'

(*PW* 267). As a self-appointed Cerberus of Society, Lady Bracknell's reference to 'that unfortunate movement' exposes the underlying social fears that prompt her line of inquiry. London Society of the 1890s was extremely concerned with rituals of access: according to Joel H. Kaplan and Sheila Stowell, 'London Society had by the '90s found its integrity threatened by new money, fresh claimants, and corresponding doubts about its own parameters.'[16] As a response to these external pressures and out of concern to maintain its 'rituals of access', Society responded by 'relying upon stifling subtleties of behaviour and dress to shut the door upon interlopers and parvenus'. Leonore Davidoff has noted that

> the emergence of a 'smart set' with a penchant for hedonistic consumption, and new roles for women as arbiters of taste and 'custodians of the turnstile' all contributed to . . . the 'theatricalization of society' itself, a phenomenon that shaded imperceptibly into the literal theatrics of the Social Season.[17]

By way of Lady Bracknell's futile interview, Wilde punctures Society's swollen sense of self-importance and mocks the ceremonies meant to ensure the protection of select social circles. Wilde deflates the value of these social displays while placing himself at the centre of Society through his ostentatious but knowing exhibition of its rules.

I have discussed the first act of *The Importance of Being Earnest* at some length in order to trace the pattern of the characters' interactions, and to demonstrate how they build up a dissonant identity for the play's central character. Act one thus crescendos to a paradoxical close with Gwendolen declaring her love to Jack because 'the simplicity of your character makes you exquisitely incomprehensible to me' (*PW* 270). Although we might expect that Jack, 'one of the most advanced Bunburyists' (258), would be able to maintain the different identities that Algernon, Gwendolen and Lady Bracknell have each confirmed for him, the high personal cost of maintaining so many secret selves is evident by the act's close. The exhaustion manifests by Jack reveals that he cannot hold these various guises together and still maintain his sense of self. Ernest and Bunbury – Jack and Algernon's vulnerable alter egos – also seem out of sorts: they are both ill, invalid and about to be murdered. Their invalidism and ill health caricature the degenerate language applied to reprobated sexualities and identities at the fin de siècle. Against the doctrine of moral purity and health, Jack explains that he has been forced to resort to

Bunburying because moralism (and repression) 'can hardly be said to conduce very much to either one's health or one's happiness'. His reference to 'a high moral tone' mocks the degenerationist discourse that construed the homosexual and 'degenerate' as a menace. As Arthur Symons notes in his article on 'The Decadent Movement in Literature', the movement could not be called 'healthy', nor did it wish to be considered so.[18]

The first act presents a systematic dismantling of traditional modes of selfhood. By the end of these invalidating encounters, Jack, too, abdicates by admitting, 'I don't actually know who I am' (*PW* 266). This admission rounds out the act's earlier revelation that Jack is a Bunburyist. Jack's successive encounters with Algernon, Gwendolen and Lady Bracknell serve to underscore the way in which none of their methods of appraisal encompasses him. Jack's encounters with these three methodically undermine material, verbal and social utterances as signs of identity. These dialogues essentially follow the same dialectical pattern by confronting Jack with a sign (material, verbal or social, depending on his interlocutor) that causes him to question his identity. By exposing the failure of signs to express modern social identity, Wilde underscores the fact that modern selfhood is determined by the multiple signs that surround it, as well as its context.

Jack's private identity crisis has consequences for the play's characters as a whole. Verbal, visual and material signs are destabilised for all. When Miss Prism mentions that she 'abandoned' her novel, she feels bound to specify that she 'use[s] the word in the sense of lost or mislaid' (273). Chasuble specifies the origins of the references and figures of speech he uses in order to avoid being misprized (274), a method Miss Prism soon begins to imitate (277). Wilde puts forward a modern articulation of selfhood – the idea that identity is constructed by both internal and external factors, which are made manifest by several signs. Unconvinced by verbal assurances about Cecily's lineage, Lady Bracknell requires proof of their authenticity. What ensues is an amusing but no more confirmatory presentation of 'certificates of Miss Cardew's birth, baptism, whooping cough, registration, vaccination, confirmation, and the measles; both the German and the English variety' (298). The play concludes that modern identity is woven of many signs. Wilde's method proves that single-sign assessments of identity may seem fixed, but are in fact subject to dialectical revision. The monological view of identity cannot hold because it calls for standards of homogeneity and consistency that are impossible to enact.

Guy Domville: *'Two souls, alas, are dwelling in my breast'*

Torn between his allegiances to his family and the Church, Guy Domville represents another instance of a fraught modern identity. According to Richard Salmon, Guy's inability to reconcile the attractions of monastic solitude with those of marriage also reflects James's own vacillating interpretation of private and public success. I agree that 'what is so fascinating about *Guy Domville* is precisely what contemporary critics perceived to be its weakness: namely the way in which Guy is seemingly propelled from one extreme to the other without the assistance of plausible mediation'.[19] By refusing his audience a smooth synthesis of the two opposites he presents them with, James does more than demonstrate that they are fundamentally irreconcilable. Instead, he offers his audience a privileged insight into a fraught consciousness representative of the dilemmas attendant upon modern selfhood. In this respect, Guy Domville resembles Jack Worthing far more than has been assumed. Indeed, I would suggest that, rather than 'having failed to make his hero's conduct comprehensible,'[20] as William Archer and other drama critics claimed, the play succeeds in portraying a state of being that is new and, in its very nature, incoherent. James's refusal to smooth out the contradictions inherent in Guy's dual identity results in a powerful rendering of the prominent contradictions that are part of what can be described as modern identity. What I am arguing is that Guy's ambivalent (and supposedly incomprehensible) behaviour is actually the result of a dilemma that forces him to revise his identity. In act one Guy is set to enter the priesthood and take a vow of chastity, but by the start of act two he is willing to marry Mary Brasier and make 'more little Domvilles . . . more good Catholics' (*Plays* 492). The mutually exclusive certainties in acts one and two work to move the drama closer to its crisis. Given this oppositional structure, the play's antitheses fairly propel it to an ambiguous and climactic representation of a split consciousness. Yet James further complicates this characterisation through the play's subtle but persistent troping of same-sex desire. Structurally, the play slides from certainty to uncertainty as Guy is torn between three possible versions of himself. So while James's play resembles Wilde's play in its depiction of the titular character's split self, *Guy Domville* also crucially inverts the dramatic structure of *The Importance of Being Earnest* because it travels from certainty about the self towards uncertainty.

Although the first act of *Guy Domville* solidly establishes Guy's credibility, the subsequent acts systematically undermine it. At the

outset, Guy's implicit but unspoken vow to join the priesthood is synonymous with his intention. His actions and words are fully concor-
dant. Frank Humber, who has known Guy since their schooldays in
France, illustrates this connection when he begs Guy to plead his suit
to the woman he loves, Mrs Peverel. 'Your thoughts are not as other
men's thoughts: your words are not as other men's words. It's to a
certain extent her [Mrs Peverel's] duty to act on them, so you're the
man of all men to plead my cause,' Frank tells Guy (*Plays* 489). Guy's
reliability is enhanced by his desire to be faithful to his vows. When
Mrs Peverel points out that he has not taken them yet, Guy responds
that the outward manifestation ('the form') and his inner purpose are
one and the same: 'I haven't burnt my ships. But the irrevocable
words are seated on my lips' (493). Guy seems resolved, but this
brazen conviction is soon tarnished by his confession that he is no
longer sure of his heart.

Guy initially defines himself by what he does not have. The
absence of material possessions supports his devotion to his unspoken vow to join the priesthood. He is 'one of those who *can*' (488)
give things up. However, Guy's identity shift is accompanied by a
substantial accretion of things. When he takes on the identity of 'the
last of the Domvilles', he inherits with it the style of the dandy and
the personality of a decadent, whereas all that he needs to signify his
duty to the church is 'black clothes and shy looks' (489). Lord
Devenish, himself a man of fashion, is instrumental in convincing
Guy to put on the vestments of a gentleman, rather than those of a
priest. 'Character's a treasure,' he tells Guy, 'pick it up, and brush it
off and wear it!' (492). Before Guy can do so, however, he must be
stripped of his previous identity. The card game he plays in the
second act initiates him to worldly amusements and, crucially, initiates his rebirth. Having lost 'almost all the clothes that covered'
(498) him, Guy comes to worldliness as naked as a new-born and
Devenish announces Guy's rebirth by christening him 'a born man
of pleasure' (497). Outfitted in a suit of white and gold, Guy is transformed from 'one of the Princes of the Church' into a marriageable
prince (487).[21] He describes his metamorphosis to his fiancée as
something 'arranged in the fairy-tales – only, you know, vastly
better!' (500). Yielding to the luxury and voluptuousness he had
once forsaken, Guy succumbs to every materialist impulse and
wears his new identity with pride. 'I like a fine anything! I can carry,
at any rate, what you put on my back,' he exclaims (*Plays* 498). His
alteration is so swift that by the middle of the second act he has

already become 'a monstrous fine gentleman in monstrous fine clothes' (504).

By the end of act one, Guy is faced with his altered identity and the loss of everything he once held dear. Troubled by this transformation, Guy's sea change is described in terms of a Manichean splitting of consciousness (493). He describes his state of mind to Mrs Peverel, who has long been his confidante and nurtures a secret love for him:

> *Guy.* If [my reasons] could only be good to *me*! But they're mixed with
>   wild thoughts and desire! Things I can't tell you – words I can't speak!
> *Mrs Peverel. (Soothing, encouraging.)* Be yourself, be your generous self,
>   and all will be straight and smooth to you!
> *Guy.* 'Myself' – the self of yesterday? I seem suddenly to have lost it
>   forever! (494)

That the arousal of 'images unsuitable, forbidden!' poses an irremediable challenge to his 'consecrated character' (491). Faced with new images and objects, Guy has no choice but to follow Devenish's advice to suppose his old self discontinued. 'The hour is too troubled' (*Plays* 492), Guy says, describing this passage in apocalyptic terms. 'Break with all the past, and break with it this minute? – turn back from the threshold, take my hand from the plough?' he asks, incredulous.

Guy's tone is *fin-du-monde*, but James's subtext is fin-de-siècle decadence. 'Scented like a duchess,' Devenish arrives 'on clouds of fragrance' (506) and holds out his gloves for Guy to smell. Guy identifies the odour as 'something French, you prodigal? To the fingertips!' The gloves are 'straight from Paris', and intended for Guy (507). The equation of France with decadence is apt, and Devenish's scented gloves are symbolic of the extravagances in dress that Anglo-American audiences associated with the French.[22] The disruption between past and present, between 'the self of yesterday' and the self he is becoming, is a threshold that Guy cannot keep himself from crossing. The anxiety created by the unfamiliarity of Guy's situation becomes the occasion for him to redefine himself by exploring the very spheres he had abjured. The threshold defines a space by what it keeps out. As a transition between restricted areas, the threshold's very nature suggests transgression. Guy finally gives in to sensual impulses, 'pick[s] up fresh feelings', and listens to the 'mysterious murmur of the world' (*Plays* 498). As if making up for lost time, he revels in feeling and lives all he can.

Guy makes a Faustian pact with Devenish: in exchange for sensuality, he gives up his spiritual values. In Goethe's tragedy, two competing spirits, the earthly and the spiritual, inhabit Faust – a situation that is echoed in Guy's own split soul. When Faust says, 'two souls, alas, are dwelling in my breast, and one is striving to forsake its brother',[23] we can easily imagine Guy speaking in similar terms. Dissatisfied with his existence, Faust succumbs to Mephistopheles's offer to be his servant in exchange for Faust's promise to serve the devil in hell. All this is, however, conditional on the devil being able to make Faust so content that he would ask that moment to last forever. 'If to the moment I should say: abide you are so fair – put me in fetters on that day, I *wish* to perish then, I swear,'[24] Faust vows. Before long he encounters Gretchen, a young, pious, highly idealised woman who represents an earthly version of *das Ewig-Weibliche* (the Eternal Feminine). Soon enough, Faust is speaking the dreaded words and condemning himself forever. There are individual elements of the Faust story within *Guy Domville*, especially in Guy's relation to Devenish, whose name barely conceals his devilish intentions. But who is Guy's Gretchen-figure? The young, submissive Mary Brasier to whom he is engaged by act two would seem a plausible candidate were it not for his noticeable indifference to her. Moreover, he surrenders her so quickly once he learns that the whole marriage has been contrived that it is impossible to see her as the sincere object of his affection. Though she is a rather mature candidate for the job of representing the Eternal Feminine, Mrs Peverel is the most feminine, maternal figure in the play. Yet here, too, James gives a further twist to the Faustian plot. He makes a significant change to the male-female gender valence of the love relationship upon which the Mephistophelean pact depends: indeed, it is Mrs Peverel who desires Guy, not vice-versa. Guy can only return her friendship, not her love. The last line of the play is a further echo of Goethe's tragedy, but once more with an inverted gender dynamic: it is Mrs Peverel who reveals her love for Guy and utters the play's poignant last word. 'Wait!' (*Plays* 516), she calls to Guy, who is already at the door. Mrs Peverel's futile imperative echoes Faust's 'Abide, you are so fair!',[25] his celebrated but fatal words begging the moment to stay. And like Gretchen, who ultimately gives herself up to God at the end of the first part of Goethe's tragedy, Guy surrenders to his calling: 'The Church *takes* me!'(*Plays* 516), he says by way of explanation.

Guy's relationship with Devenish redeploys a homoerotic leitmotiv prevalent in James's and Wilde's fiction: the theme of a younger man intellectually and aesthetically beguiled by an older mentor. Rooted in ancient Greek tradition, this pederastic model is described by Pater in *The Renaissance* and was familiar to both James and Wilde. Devenish seduces Guy with the lure of '*another possible life – the natural, the liberal, the agreeable, the life of the world of men – and of women*' (491). Much of the verbal interplay between Devenish and Guy relies on tacit understandings that are incomprehensible to women. Devenish's discussion of love is unintelligible to Mrs Domville, but Guy 'always know[s], now, what his lordship means' (498). Their affiliation is premised on shared knowledge that remains obscured even to Guy's closest friend, Mrs Peverel, to whom Guy haltingly says that there are things about his new self that he cannot say to her. To his fiancée, Guy also declines to speak Devenish's name, describing him instead as 'the wizard' (500). Devenish is the first to point out that Guy may not be as consistent as he appears. He 'smell[s] contradiction' (490) in Guy's reliance on Mrs Peverel as a 'confidant' and 'counsellor', as well as in the 'secret preference' (512) he has never addressed. Leon Edel suggests in his foreword to *Guy Domville* that Mrs Peverel is the object of Guy's affection and that she is 'a maternal image he does not even dare to admit to himself he loves' (*Plays* 472). While Guy's affection for her is visible, so are the play's strong images of same-sex desire.

Because Guy is not able to admit his desires to himself, James dramatised their effect on Guy's sense of self. To reinforce the subversive sexual valence of the play, James inverted the genders associated with the configuration he had borrowed from *Faust*. In Goethe's tragedy Faust and Gretchen represent, respectively, the active and the passive, but James up-ends this dynamic by making Mrs Peverel the active, worldly lover and Guy the passive, pious one. Inversion of this sort was part of James's plan for the drama from the first. In a letter to Edward Compton, the actor-manager who was considering the play for his Comedy Company in 1893, James insisted that Guy's failure to marry was essential to the drama. Compton tried to persuade James to change it, but James was adamant:

> The 'ending' that you express a dread of *is* the only ending I have ever dreamed of giving the play – it *is* the play, the very essence and meaning of the subject . . . To make him [Guy Domville] come out (of his old ideal) simply to *marry* Mrs Peverel is, for me, not only no subject at all, but a very ugly and displeasing (as well as flat and undramatic)

substitute for one . . . My *dénouement* is my very *starting-point* – and my subject is my subject, to take or to leave. If your conviction is that the piece won't *go* unless Guy marries Mrs Peverel (for he *doesn't* of course marry the other female), then it is a blessing (though mingled with bitterness) that the words of your letter have revealed it to me without a further prolongation of our illusion . . . My plan, such as it is, is an absolutely *final* one.[26]

The play's dramatic tension resides in the maintenance of a delicate gender balance. As James explained, Guy could only 'make himself happy at the *expense* of others – a woman [Mrs Peverel] in one case (act 2), a man [Frank Humber] in the other (act 3)'.[27] Guy's decision not to marry Mrs Peverel for Humber's sake is a magnanimous one, but as with his surrender of his fiancée, it is not convincing. For one thing, Guy's ambivalence towards Mrs Peverel hardly suggests undying affection. For another, Guy cannot admit to himself that he has any personal desires whatsoever – even his final decision to join the Church stems from his duty to his mother's vow to raise her son to be a priest.

Same-sex desire is part of the sensual life Devenish opens up for Guy, and it is for this reason that Guy thanks him *'with intensely controlled emotion'* (516), even as he shuns his affection:

You've been so good as to take a zealous interest in my future – and in that of my family: for which I owe you, and now ask you to accept, all *thanks*. But I beg you, still more solemnly, to let that prodigious zeal rest, from this moment, for ever! I listened to your accents for a day – I followed you where you led me. I looked at life as you showed it, and then I turned away my face.

Guy has looked, but he will touch neither women nor men. His choice of the monastery is a typically Jamesian method of avoiding desire, and of preferring repression over expression. In the novel of *The American*, for instance, Claire de Cintré absconds from the worldly by entering a Carmelite convent. Wilde poked fun at the idea of *fuga mundi* in *Lady Windermere's Fan* by having his adventuress reject the cloister as a possible escape: 'I suppose, Windermere, you would like me to retire into a convent . . . as people do in silly modern novels. That is stupid of you, Arthur; in real life we don't do such things – not as long as we have any good looks left, at any rate'(*W* 460).

James's typescript of *Guy Domville* reveals that Guy's homoerotic interests were far more overt in the drafts than they became in the final work. James excised Guy's suspicion that Devenish had come 'to seduce' him. In this earlier version, Guy addressed his doubts to Mrs Peverel. 'To seduce you?'[28] she responded incredulously. The final version, which appears in Edel's edition, uses a neutral, rather than a sexually suggestive, verb: 'Who *is* he, madam – *what* is he, that he comes here to draw me off?' (*Plays* 492). Guy's spectacular admission to Devenish – 'I fancy, my lord, that I'm *afraid* of the ladies!'[29] – was also expurgated, despite the fact that it makes Guy's final decision to become a priest more credible. In this respect, Guy resembles the sexually ambiguous men in James's earlier plays. In *The Album*, a comedy written in 1891 but never produced, Sir Ralph Damant has 'a terror of eminent women' (*Plays* 399) and he gives away his inheritance as a 'cheap' (358) solution to sidestep marriage. James considered *The Reprobate*, a farce he probably wrote in the same year as *The Album*, 'much the better' of the two comedies, yet *The Reprobate*'s central character, Mr Bonsor, is also a bachelor who 'is impervious to female charms' (413). 'There's no fear of his ever marrying,' Captain Chanter confirms. Chanter himself is a duplicitous paramour and an unmistakable prototype for Devenish in *Guy Domville*. Despite all these prefigurations of Guy's attitude to women and marriage, James nevertheless cut from *Guy Domville* the most overt discussion of same-sex desire – a double allusion to Devenish's scheme and Guy's sexuality:

> *Guy*. His interest in it [the plan] can *never* be!
> *Frank*. His interest in it is his interest in *you*!
> *Guy*. That's dark – that's false and falsest and darkest to have brought him back![30]

James also cut the description of Mrs Peverel's love for Guy as 'a raging passion.'[31] The setting for the final act was originally the 'Yellow Room'[32] – a colour that evokes *Yellow Book* culture and drawing-room decadence – but it became the innocuous-sounding 'White Parlour' (*Plays* 508). The significance of the decadent and homoerotic references intensifies in light of Guy's choice of monastic life which evidently offers him an environment where homosociality is the norm. The monastic brotherhood, then, is a way for him to deny the viability of same-sex desire while permitting a greater range and intensity of homosocial bonds.[33]

Bunburying as a modern condition

Discussions of *The Importance of Being Earnest* have been polarised by debates on its homosexual coding. What do we make of the exaggerated rivalries and ostentatiously catty verbal exchanges between Jack and Algernon? Are they just theatrical or are they camp? Did Wilde intend the Bunburyist to represent a homosexual? The answers to these questions have generally separated into two factions. From Christopher Craft's interpretation of *The Importance of Being Earnest* as a play that represents but 'cannot admit or acknowledge the erotic force of the gay male body'[34] to Russell Jackson's opposite contention that there is 'nothing of the overtly *Dorian* mode'[35] in the play, criticism is intensely divided on the significance of the behaviours the play's characters exhibit. While I agree with Alan Sinfield that there is no fully-fledged 'gay scenario lurking somewhere in the depths of *The Importance of Being Earnest*',[36] the pervasive homoerotics in both James's and Wilde's plays nevertheless merit our attention because they suggest both authors' shared investment in creating an idiom for same-sex desire. In addition to the homoerotic elements in *Guy Domville* that I have described above, there are, in *The Importance of Being Earnest*, also a number of 'in' jokes and allusions meant to delight a select set. The verb 'bunburying', for example, contains a fairly explicit pun on anal intercourse, and the multivalence of Earnest allows the word to stand for 'Jack's proper name, a patronym, an alias, and imaginary lover, and as a code-word for homosexual desire itself: since *Love in Earnest* [1892] titled a volume of Uranian poetry by John Gambril Nicholson',[37] as Bristow notes, and in 1896 Marc-André Raffalovich published a study of homosexuality titled *Uranisme et Unisexualité*. Likewise, Lady Bracknell's rejection of Jack on the grounds that he is a person 'whose origin was a Terminus' (W 408)[38] may be a subtle allusion to male-male intimacy (an erotic 'end game' that may also be a beginning), or to Sir Richard Burton's 'Terminal Essay' on pederasty, an appendix to his translation of *The Arabian Nights*. This type of 'end game' or anal pun is not as esoteric as it might seem. Louis Umfreville Wilkinson, one of Wilde's correspondents, used just such a pun in the title of his parody of James. Wilkinson's story 'The Better End: Conclusion of a Chapter from the Unpublished Novel, *What Percy Knew*, by H*nr* J*m*s' (1912) is an explicit account of intercourse between a James-figure and a young man 'stiffly' trying to satisfy 'their common intent'.[39]

The playful tension between Jack and Algernon peaks when Cecily asks, 'Uncle Jack, you are not going to refuse your own brother's hand?' (*PW* 280). Jack's response to Cecily's double-entendre-laden question – 'Nothing will induce me to take his hand' – is a flat refusal to be reconciled with Algernon and to seal their verbal relationship with action. Jack refuses the performative: he will not take Algernon's hand and, with it, all the conjugal implications of the verbal gesture. This brings full circle Algernon's opinion that marriage would be 'extremely problematic' (259) for Jack, and Jack's promise to give up Bunburying upon marriage.[40] Implicit in Jack's suggestion is the idea that marriage will cure him of his need for a double identity. By killing Ernest, his possibly Uranist namesake, Jack also seems to think he can eradicate his same-sex desire. In other words, his homoerotic, man-about-town brother will be obliterated through a heterosexual union:

> I'm not a Bunburyist at all. If Gwendolen accepts me, I am going to kill my brother, indeed I think I'll kill him in any case . . . So I am going to get rid of Ernest. And I strongly advise you to do the same with Mr . . . with your invalid friend who has the absurd name. (*PW* 259)

Killing the thing he loves is easier said than done, however. Jack hesitatingly confesses to his bride that 'it is very painful for me to be forced to speak the truth. It is the first time in my life that I have been reduced to such a painful position' (291). Indeed, speaking the truth about Ernest is as painful for Jack as killing his own brother.

Algernon's attempt to pin down Jack's identity as Ernest in act one correlates with the events of Wilde's trial. There too, a calling card and cigarette case were produced as evidence. It is not the articles themselves that interest us, but the identity debate they stimulated. During his trial, Wilde related a conversation in which Wilde had asked the Marquess of Queensberry if he accused Wilde of being a sodomite.

> WILDE: . . . I then said to him, 'Lord Queensberry do you seriously accuse your son and me of sodomy?' He said, 'I don't say that you are it, but you look it *(laughter)* –
> JUDGE: I shall have the Court cleared if I hear the slightest disturbance again.
> WILDE: – but you look it and you pose as it, which is just as bad.'[41]

What made the court audience laugh? Was it Wilde's use of the taboo word 'sodomy', or the idea that Wilde looked like a sodomite? If sodomy was such a menace, such an 'unspeakable vice' (as the euphemism of the day termed it), why did the audience laugh? Sometimes we laugh when we do not know what else to do: when words, actions and gestures fail us. We laugh in embarrassment and even in despair. But we also try to laugh off what threatens us. The audience's reaction reveals another, no less important aspect of the social perception of representations of same-sex desire: as a response to the sodomite's pose, laughter is the reverse of feeling threatened. Laughter turns fear on its head. Laughter and fear are different inter-linings of the same glove.[42] But laughter is also a velvet glove over an iron hand. Laughter is a *public* face for homosexual panic. Laughter is the free and open manifestation of what Eve Kosofsky Sedgwick has claimed is a private, psychologised form of vulnerability.[43]

Laughter, in the end, is what makes *The Importance of Being Earnest* a success, not *in spite of* its homoerotic subtext, but *because* of it. The fun of it is in the frisson it provokes. *The Importance of Being Earnest*'s characters do not say they are it, but they look it *(laughter)* and the play hinges on this dynamic interplay. For instance, the hilarity provoked by Algernon's 'very gay and debonair' entrance subverts the anxiety in Cecily's declaration that 'I have never met any really wicked person before. I feel rather frightened. I am so afraid he will look just like every one else' (*PW* 274). The play relies on the audience being able to identify the sodomite's pose enough to be tit-illated, but not threatened. While the play's verbal and visual languages talk transgression, its verbiage and artificiality mitigate any serious offence.

It is significant that one of the defining moments in the history of homosexuality hinges on a conversation in which the 'unspeakable vice' remains unmentioned and is, nevertheless, clearly identified. What does it mean to 'look it' and 'pose as it'? Unable to spell the word 'sodomite', Queensberry could not bring himself to speak it either. Like the identities of the characters in *Importance of Being Earnest* and *Guy Domville*, Queensberry's thoughts belong to the realm of the unspeak-able. The conversation between Wilde and Queensberry reminds us of the historically freighted nature of what we now understand as modern homosexual identity. Queensberry, it seems, had a definite idea of what a sodomite looked like. It is very possible that some members of the audience did, too. Nevertheless, it would be inaccurate to suppose that the precise look and pose of the sodomite was part of the general public's idiom in the way that it is today. Until this period, sodomy had been a practice; it had not been associated with a style of being, much less with the sexual identity we now call homosexuality. Queensberry's accusation conveniently (if tragically) pinpoints this emergent identity. It designates a transition from the practice of specific sexual acts, to the practice of specific social behaviours.

The concept of personality was the linchpin of Wilde's trial. The Marquess of Queensberry's barrister, Edward Carson, cross-examined Wilde and repeatedly tried to establish 'personality' as a synonym for a man with same-sex desires. In order to do so, he read out excerpts from *The Picture of Dorian Gray* and asked whether Wilde would say the passages described 'a natural feeling of a man towards another'.[44] Wilde resisted by responding that the passages described 'a beautiful personality', and Carson consequently tried to insinuate that 'a personality' was equivalent to a man with same-sex desires. Wilde rebuffed Carson's repeated questioning by variably describing 'a personality' as a friend, as someone with whom one's life would intersect, or as someone who could produce an influence on an artist or dominate his art.[45] Then Carson came around to the subject of Alfonso Conway, the newspaper boy of eighteen whom Wilde and Douglas had met on the beach at Worthing.[46] Wilde had given Conway a cigarette case (among other gifts) and, while he was still writing *The Importance of Being Earnest*, he took Conway to the Albion Hotel in Brighton, which Wilde had previously visited with Douglas. Wilde also gave Conway 'a suit of clothes, straw hat, flannels, a book to read'[47] – everything, in short, except a set of 'Bunbury suits'. Intent on finding a label that would define the precise nature of his relationship to Conway and confirm Wilde's identity, Carson again seized on the term 'personality'. Was Conway 'a nice personality'?[48] Carson asked. 'I would not say for him personality, no', Wilde responded, suggesting instead that Conway was a 'nature'. Wilde was, of course, fully aware of the terrible consequences that would follow if Carson succeeded in affixing a label to his behaviour, and Wilde's response to this last question stretches the truth too far. Wilde knew he was balancing precariously on the edge of falsehood; however, if we abstract from the legal implications of this, there is something fairly humorous in Wilde's responses. It is not surprising, then, that Wilde's own behaviour mirrors that of Jack in *The Importance of Being Earnest*, for both consistently resisted defining their identity by refusing to adhere to a single, stable sign. Jack is, after all, 'Mr Ernest Worthing, B.4, The Albany', as well as a guardian, an uncle, a Bunburyist and Gwendolen's fiancé. As for Wilde, he simply told Carson 'I will take any word you like.'[49]

Wilde's definition of 'personality' is a precursor for the concept we now refer to as selfhood. His trial was a seminal moment in the constitution of the same-sex desiring self and, consequently, homosexual identity. On the stand, Wilde insisted that what was at stake was personality, not feeling. The distinction between the two hinges on an important difference between ways of behaving (feeling), and a way of being (personality). To Carson, such subtleties seemed beside the point. As a result, he steadfastly clung to the idea that a man's feelings and behaviour would confirm his identity. When Carson tried to paint Wilde into a corner by asking him to judge as proper or improper 'the feeling of one man towards a youth'[50] in *The Picture of Dorian Gray*, Wilde refused the term 'feeling' and focused on 'personality', instead characterising the relationship as 'what an artist would feel on meeting a beautiful personality'. Feelings imply words and actions that are not necessarily coherent with one's identity. Personality, by contrast, implies being and therefore identity. The difference Wilde was asserting became crucial to the construction of what we consider modern homosexual identity, namely the shift away from the idea of same-sex desire as a feeling or behaviour, towards a conception of same-sex desire as a way of being, a constituent characteristic of one's identity.

Wilde's performance on the stand may be seen as a life-or-death exercise in semantics, as an attempt to keep his 'personality free from the reductive grip of realism's misreading'.[51] Such an interpretation would, however, risk seriously undervaluing Wilde's persistent efforts in creating a vocabulary for emergent identities, including (but not limited to) his own. I have argued in the foregoing pages that *The Importance of Being Earnest* emphatically focuses its energies in this direction, but such forces also operate elsewhere in his writings.[52] Wilde used 'personality' to describe a state of being, rather than a behaviour, in an open letter published in the *Daily Telegraph* in 1892. Wilde asserted that a superior theatre actor did not merely act, but that he could 'convert his own accidental personality into the real and essential personality of the character he is called upon to impersonate, whatever that character may be' (*LW* 519). Wilde assiduously distinguished acting from being; after all, he said, 'anybody can act. Most people in England do nothing else. To be conventional is to be a comedian.' An excellent dramatic performance, Wilde argued, relied on the actors *being* a certain way, not just *behaving* a certain way.

Much of what Wilde said on trial in 1895 was a repetition of assertions he had already made elsewhere. For example, his famous speech from the dock on 'the love that dare not speak its name' was a repetition of an extempore talk he had delivered at the Crabbet Club in 1891.[53]

The chronology traced here suggests the long-range ambitions of Wilde's classificatory idiom and encourages us to understand Wilde's play, legal performance and self-writing as part of a sophisticated and important project to make modern identity. In 1895, this project was not only fixed in Wilde's past, it also informed his future works. In *De Profundis*, the long letter-cum-autobiography that Wilde wrote from prison, he expanded upon his ideas about 'personality' by linking them to Christ. According to Wilde, Christ exemplified the type of person whose own personality revealed others to themselves. Through Christ, 'outcasts, those who are dumb under oppression and whose silence is heard only of God' (*LW* 742), as well as 'others who had been deaf to every voice' (743), recognise themselves for the first time:

> all who come in contact with his personality, even though they may neither bow to his altar nor kneel before his priest, in some way find that the ugliness of their sin is taken away and the beauty of their sorrow revealed to them'. (742)

Wilde's use of an explicitly verbal and visual vocabulary is significant for two reasons. First, it summarily displaces the standard idiom of religious revelation. The work of personality, Wilde implies, is akin to language triumphing over silence. This repeats the movement of *The Importance of Being Earnest*, where various sights and sounds are proffered in order to define identities that have traditionally been excluded from normative language. The second reason why *De Profundis*'s refusal of the language of revelation is important is that, in Wilde's articulation, the 'outcasts' who come into contact with Christ are not transfigured. In other words, they are not substantially changed and their nature remains the same, though their formal qualities ('ugliness' and 'beauty') are altered. Similarly, the behaviours that Carson insinuated were 'improper'[54] and unnatural were, Wilde insisted, 'beautiful'. So in Wilde's version, sin and sorrow are not removed, but revealed in a new light, as the building blocks of a modern identity.

Language and Silence: Shame and the Unspeakable

Considered historically, Wilde's and James's articulations can be interpreted as participating in the elaboration of forms of identity based on same-sex desire. Let me be clear: I am arguing that these plays are the premature and halting articulations of a modern identity, but I am not for a moment suggesting that they give voice to anything close to what we would now conceive of as Gay Pride. In fact, what *The Importance of Being Earnest* and *Guy Domville* give voice to is shame, which is the complete opposite of pride. As a result of the Wilde trial, 'shame', a euphemism for love between men current in homosexual subculture, became public knowledge.[55] More recently, Sedgwick has argued that shame is a foundational experience for queer identity because it

> floods into being as a moment, a disruptive moment, in a circuit of identity-constituting identificatory communication. Indeed, like a stigma, shame is itself a form of communication. Blazons of shame, the 'fallen face' with eyes down and head averted – and to a lesser extent, the blush – are semaphores of trouble . . . in interrupting identification, shame, too, makes identity. In fact, shame and identity remain in very dynamic relation to one another, at once deconstituting and foundational, because shame is both peculiarly contagious and peculiarly individuating.[56]

When the experience of shame is recuperated and put into the service of constituting identity – as successive generations of the queer community have successfully done – then acknowledging shame becomes a crucial stepping stone towards pride. As Canon Chasuble observes in *The Importance of Being Earnest*, 'what seem to us bitter trials are often blessings in disguise' (*PW* 279).

In order to illustrate the role of shame in both these plays, I want to examine the way James and Wilde twine the experience of shame with the loss of language. In both plays, acts that are generative of shame also generate an idiom for the experience: the unspeakable. Criticism has overlooked the fact that both Guy Domville and Jack Worthing experience temporary aphasia as a result of their fragmented identities, yet there is a strong case for arguing that James and Wilde posit a direct relationship between desire, selfhood and language. The experience of shame is intimately connected to the reformation of identity and the beginning of self-knowledge. The inability to speak is not the end of discourse, but the beginning of it: as Hugh Stevens observes, 'the inability to name . . . *creates* discourse'.[57] In order to explain how this works, let us return to a seminal moment in *The Importance of Being Earnest*: Jack's act-one admission that he does not know who he is. As a result of this personal crisis, his language becomes destabilised. The most basic elements of language seem to elude him and words are emptied of their meaning. As a result, he can say with certainty that Lady Bracknell is a Gorgon, but he does not know what a Gorgon is (*PW* 268); nor is he sure what cleverness is. Before long, verbal paralysis sets in and speech itself becomes difficult. His announcement – 'I loathe listening. . . . I hate talking' (*PW* 269) – signals a complete breakdown in communication. Jack's temporary aphasia is a by-product of his shame. In other words, he loses the power of speech as a result of his repeated and public experience of shame. Guy Domville's identity crisis also manifests itself through the loss of language. Troubled by 'the startling voice' (*Plays* 493) of change, he loses his own voice. In order to be able to speak the marriage vows that would cement his new identity, Guy must renounce his unspoken vow to the priesthood. 'To say the words I must say, I must forget the words I didn't' (499), he explains. Shamed by his renunciation of his holy vows, it is only by taking a vow of marriage that he might regain his voice, and so he tells his fiancée, 'I came here stammering and stumbling; but when I saw *you* it was as if I had caught the tune of my song!' (500).[58]

In James's private life, too, shame and the unspeakable went hand in hand. After *Guy Domville*'s failure, he refused to name the shameful experience that sealed his professional identity. Shame, Sedgwick reminds us, is 'the affect that mantles the threshold between introversion and extroversion, between absorption and theatricality'.[59] In the letter to William James quoted at the beginning of this chapter, James wrote that the imminent failure of *Guy Domville* was 'mercifully' not made known to him on the play's opening night (*L3* 514). He described as paralysing his slow realisation that Wilde's play was to be more successful, but he put a brave face on the situation, claiming the episode was already 'ancient history' to him. Publicly, James turned his shame into bravura, his embarrassment into quiet dignity. Edmund Gosse remembers James exuding 'a freedom which had hitherto been foreign to his nature' (quoted in Edel 4: 84). Privately, James admitted to himself that his preternatural calm was a mask for his disquiet:

To myself – today – I need say no more. Large and full and high the future still opens. It is now indeed that I may do the work of my life. And I will. x x x x x I have only to *face* my problems. x x x x x But all this is of the ineffable – too deep and pure for any utterance. Shrouded in sacred silence let it rest. x x x x x. (*Notebooks* 109)

By x-ing out the words that would describe his embarrassment, James privately acknowledges his experience and uses it as a catalyst for change. His loss of face galvanises him to '*face* my problems'. At the same time, shame produces silence. Even in his private notebook, his embarrassment manifests itself through erasure, excision, the unspoken. The crosses in this passage are markers of elision. Metaphorically, they may also be crosses marking the grave of a forsaken self – the part of James that would have been a successful dramatist. Wilde also used this obliterative process to reclaim his own experience of shame in 'The Ballad of Reading Gaol'. A loose superposition of his life on Christ's, Wilde's poem links the Cross to the crosses one bears when shamed. Like James's silent crosses, the unmarked grave in Wilde's poem conflates shame and the loss of face:

> In Reading gaol by Reading town
> > There is a pit of shame,
> And in it lies a wretched man
> > Eaten by teeth of flame,
> In a burning winding-sheet he lies,
> > And his grave has got no name.
> And there, till Christ call forth the dead,
> > In silence let him lie. (W 899)

As a memorial to a life of shame, the unmarked grave re-enacts the living effect of shame. The silence of the grave without a name replicates in death the silence life imposes on the 'wretched man' whose sin makes his name unspeakable. The face of shame – crestfallen, with downcast, averted eyes, and mute lips – is represented figuratively by the grave. In *De Profundis*, Wilde would take this idea further by presenting shame as transformative and positive.

A 'Modern Warning' about Modern Identity

Guy Domville and *The Importance of Being Earnest* make a strong case for the view that modern identity is constituted from many signs.

In other words, we are all Bunburyists. Modern identity is not woven with a solitary thread; it is a fabric formed by the intersection of several signs and selves.[60] James's and Wilde's plays are not only about homosexual coding, but about how modern identity is constituted from multiple features that need not necessarily be limited to gender or sexuality. In order to demonstrate the workings of this process within a conception of modern selfhood not restricted to the dynamics of desire, this final section turns to James's 'The Modern Warning' (1888), a short story that centres on the deep shame an American woman feels when she learns that her British husband abhors the United States. The story reveals that shame and the unspeakable are components of a modern selfhood that need not be conceived of as essentially sexual. According to Sedgwick, shame 'is the place where the *question* of identity arises most originarily, and most relationally',[61] and I would argue further that the value of the experience of shame as an identity-making moment can also be applied productively to a variety of identities. As a valuable, identity-making experience, shame need not be limited to homosexuality because it is also a powerful force in shaping ethnic, cultural and religious identity; it would be valuable for critics to examine more closely the ways in which this is manifest in literature.

'The Modern Warning' instances the double-dealing that the 'unspeakable' is associated with in *The Importance of Being Earnest* and *Guy Domville* by positioning an unspeakable domestic grievance at its centre. In this context, the domestic sphere is not synonymous with the woman's sphere; instead, it is the locus of male-female relations. There are two grievances at issue, one unspoken, the other unspeakable. The first originates when Agatha, the American wife of Sir Rufus Chasemore, realises that her British husband bears a deep antipathy towards her homeland. It emerges that, during their travels in America, Chasemore was exasperated by the country, that he 'disliked quite *unspeakably* things that she supposed he liked, . . . [and] suffered acutely on occasions when she thought he was really pleased' (CS3 419, emphasis added). When Chasemore reveals that his American encounters 'made him almost ill', Agatha retreats into silence. 'Unspeakably' acts here as a portmanteau word, a synonym for both 'unutterably' and 'awfully'. The unspeakable sits at the centre of Agatha's disillusionment: it underscores one character's fundamental misunderstanding of another. The second grievance occurs when the couple agree never to speak of the first. The unspoken (along with the secrecy implicit in it) is at the heart of this tale because it becomes the governing principle of the relationship. Agatha's omissions begin to echo those of her husband, and silence becomes the keynote of their marriage:

> It was agreed between them that neither of them would speak of the circumstance again, but she at least, in private, devoted an immense deal of meditation to it . . . Lady Chasemore began to feel at the end of a few months that their difficulties had after all not become the mere reminiscence of a flurry, making present security more deep. What if the flurry continued impalpably, insidiously, under the surface? She thought there had been no change, but now she suspected that there was at least a difference. She had read Tennyson and she knew the famous phrase about the little rift within the lute. It came back to her with a larger meaning. (426)

In Tennyson's poem 'Merlin and Vivien', 'the little rift within the lute' is a small mistrust that gradually causes a strangely unharmonious silence. Agatha realises that her husband's 'outward good manners misrepresented his real reaction' (427). She imagines 'that his cheek burned for this when it was turned away from her – that he ground his teeth with shame in the watches of the night'. Ultimately, her own embarrassment kills the things she loves. Unable to reclaim her negative experience and reinvent it for the better, her shame destroys her relationship and her identity. She chooses to commit suicide to escape from a relationship premised on words that 'made her bleed' (419) and unspeakable shame. 'Had she – a – had she some domestic grief?' the doctor asks, arriving too late to be of any use (433). The 'domestic grief' at the centre of it all is the unspeakable shame that hovers around Agatha's experience: it destabilises her relationship and undermines her identity. Had she been able to reinvent or revel in her shame, her fate might have been comparable to the one Lionel Johnson celebrates in his 1897 poem 'A Decadent's Lyric', in which the speaker explains that 'sometimes, in very joy of shame,/ Our flesh becomes one living flame:/ And she and I/ Are no more separate but the same.'[62]

Lady Agatha is not alone in being unable to enjoy her shame for she is closer kin to Guy Domville and Jack Worthing than any of them is to Johnson's speaker. In fact, Agatha's experience and self-annihilating actions inscribe her story among those described in *The Importance of Being Earnest* and *Guy Domville*. Her unmarked grave, so to speak, stands among those of Jack and Algernon's deceased alter egos, Ernest and Bunbury. Guy Domville's choice of the monastery also belongs to the realm of worldly self-denial.

As early as 1888, the year Lady Agatha's story was published, Wilde had stressed the need for the aesthetic Renaissance to 'have its linguistic side' (*CW* 99). If it was not accompanied by a new mode of expression, Wilde claimed, the Renaissance would be doomed. By 1895, the linguistic shift was a *fait accompli* and it had already achieved the dubious distinction of being attacked by Max Nordau. In a chapter in *Degeneration* devoted to decadents and aesthetes, Nordau described 'the "decadent" language' as symptomatic of 'the disposition of the mystically degenerate mind, with its shifting nebulous ideas, its fleeting formless shadowy thought, its perversions and aberrations'.[63] To express this degenerate state of mind, Nordau believed 'a new and unheard-of language must in fact be found, since there cannot be in any customary language designations corresponding to presentations which in reality do not exist'. He seems unaware that Guy Domville and Jack Worthing had, by this time, contributed to the creation of a language for selves that did indeed exist.

The Importance of Being Earnest and *Guy Domville* in particular are concerned with the struggle to establish a visual, verbal and material idiom for the unspeakable. The unspeakable and the unspoken are fixed within a matrix of linguistic and material signifiers that simultaneously define and destabilise normative language and, by extension, identity. To adapt to my own ends one of Emily Dickinson's well-known lines, Guy Domville and Jack Worthing 'dwell in possibility, a fairer house than prose'.[64] When faced with a new set of terms and experiences, their language shifts to such an extent that it covers their original identity.[65] The drama of *The Importance of Being Earnest* and *Guy Domville* revolves around the forging and refining of the modern self. Guy Domville and Jack Worthing are identities in crisis, selves at the white heat.

NOTES

1. Russell Jackson notes that *The Importance of Being Earnest* has enjoyed the most revivals of all Wilde's plays and that it has fared far better than the works of Wilde's contemporaries including W. S. Gilbert, Arthur Wing Pinero, Henry Arthur Jones, Haddon Chambers and Sydney Grundy ('*The Importance of Being Earnest*', *Cambridge Companion to Oscar Wilde*, ed. Raby, 165).

2. Susan Carlson notes that James's plays were not 'brilliant theatre pieces' but 'were better than average West End fare' though he would 'never rival' Wilde (*Women of Grace: James's Plays and the Comedy of Manners* (Ann Arbor, MI: UMI, 1985) xii–xiii). There exists relatively little criticism of James's plays, although notable contributions include Alan L. Ackerman, *The Portable Theater: American Literature and the Nineteenth-Century Stage* (Baltimore: Johns Hopkins UP, 1999) 181–220; Martha Banta, 'The James Family Theatricals: Behind the Scenes', *The Cambridge Companion to Henry James*, ed. Jonathan Freedman (Cambridge: Cambridge UP, 1998); Chris Greenwood, *Adapting to the Stage: Theatre and the Work of Henry James* (Aldershot: Ashgate, 2000).

3. George Monteiro, *Henry James and John Hay: The Record of a Friendship* (Providence: Brown UP, 1965) 683.

4. In his insightful examination of *Guy Domville*'s relation to eighteenth-century Catholic riots, Fred Bernard reminds us that James favoured broad interpretations, and that James went so far as to claim that a study of the 'history of religious intolerance . . . is, I really believe the history of humanity' (Bernard, 'Portents of Violence', 86).

5. Ed Cohen, *Talk on the Wilde Side: Towards a Genealogy of a Discourse on Male Sexualities* (New York: Routledge, 1993) 146.

6. Neil Sammells, *Wilde Style: The Plays and Prose of Oscar Wilde* (New York: Longman, 2000) 85–7; Kaplan and Stowell, *Theatre and Fashion*, 20.

7. Michel Foucault, *The History of Sexuality*, trans. Robert Hurley, vol. 1 (Harmondsworth: Penguin, 1981) 43.

8. My formulation here is indebted to Joseph Bristow, ' "A Complex and Multiform Creature": Wilde's Sexual Identities', in *The Cambridge Companion to Oscar Wilde*, ed. Raby, 197–8.

9. Kwame Anthony Appiah, *The Ethics of Identity* (Princeton: Princeton UP, 2005) 65.

10. Ibid. 296.

11. Ibid. 100–1.

12. J. Hillis Miller, *Literature as Conduct: Speech Acts in Henry James* (New York: Fordham UP, 2005) 140.

13. Erving Goffman, *The Presentation of Self in Everyday Life* (New York: Doubleday, 1959) 252–3. Jeff Nunokawa discusses the relationship between the physical body in Goffman and Wilde in *Tame Passions of Wilde: The Styles of Manageable Desire* (Princeton: Princeton UP, 2003) 54–71.

14. Judith Butler, *Gender Trouble: Feminism and the Subversion of Identity* (New York: Routledge, 1990) 136.

15. Goffman, *Presentation*, 252.

16. Kaplan and Stowell, *Theatre and Fashion*, 13.

17. Davidoff quoted in ibid. 13.
18. Quoted in Beckson (ed.), *Aesthetes*, 136.
19. Salmon, *Henry James*, 69.
20. William Archer, *The Theatrical World of 1895* (London: Walter Scott Ltd, 1896) 34.
21. Guy's suit is reminiscent of the 'white and gold doublet for Henry the Fifth' Wilde describes (in 'The Truth of Masks') as part of the 'the inventory, still in existence, of the costume-wardrobe of a London theatre in Shakespeare's time' (*W* 1161).
22. In his study of dandyism, Jules Barbey d'Aurevilly famously locates its ancestry in France because it was known to be more permissive than England (*Dandyism*, trans. Douglas Ainslie (New York: PAJ Publications, 1988) 40).
23. Johann Wolfgang von Goethe, *Faust: Part One and Sections from Part Two*, trans. Walter Kaufmann (New York: Random House, 1990) 145.
24. Ibid. 185.
25. Ibid. 184, 468.
26. Henry James, *Selected Letters*, ed. Leon Edel (Cambridge, MA: Harvard UP, 1987) 261–3.
27. Ibid. 261.
28. Henry James, *Guy Domville*, ts, fMS Am 1237.21, 22. Houghton Library, Harvard University.
29. Ibid. 21.
30. Ibid. 75.
31. Ibid. 79.
32. Ibid. 72.
33. James explored this subject in 'The Great Good Place' (1900), where a busy writer escapes his obligations by drifting away to an imaginary place resembling a monastery where he spends three restorative weeks with the 'Brothers'. In 'Collaboration' (1892), James converted a painter's studio into a church, among other places, in order to explore the intellectually and sexually charged notion of collaboration between male artists. George Bishop, Adeline Tintner and Adam Parkes have considered this story, though none deals with its peculiar sexual subtext: Bishop, *When the Master Relents: The Neglected Short Fictions of Henry James* (Ann Arbor, MI: UMI Research, 1988); Tintner, 'Rudyard Kipling and Wolcott Balestier's Literary Collaboration: A Possible Source for James's "Collaboration"', *Henry James Review* 4.2 (1983); Parkes, 'Collaborations: Henry James and the Poet-Critics', *Henry James Review* 23.3 (2002).
34. Christopher Craft, 'Alias Bunbury: Desire and Termination in *The Importance of Being Earnest*', *Representations* 31 (1990) 27. Bristow responds to Craft's argument in 'Complex' 196–7. On the homosexual subtext in *The Importance of Being Earnest*, see also chapter eight of

Beckson, *London in the 1890s: A Cultural History* (New York: Norton, 1992).

35. Jackson, 'Importance', 167.
36. Sinfield, *The Wilde Century*, vi.
37. Bristow, 'Complex', 197.
38. In light of this connection, the choice of *Terminations* as the title for James's collection of short stories published the same year as Wilde's trial seems less than felicitous.
39. Louis Umfreville Wilkinson, 'The Better End: Conclusion of a Chapter from the Unpublished Novel, *What Percy Knew*, by H*nr* J*m*s,' *Pages Passed from Hand to Hand: The Hidden Tradition of Homosexual Literature in English from 1748 to 1914*, ed. Mark Mitchell and David Leavitt (New York: Houghton, 1997) 390–1.
40. Note the similarity between the expressions 'confirmed bachelor' (a man who leads a single life and is bound not to marry) and 'confirmed Bunburyist', which Algernon uses when introducing the concept. Similarly, Chasuble calls himself 'a celibate', though his interest in Miss Prism is patent.
41. Merlin Holland, *The Real Trial of Oscar Wilde* (New York: HarperCollins, 2003) 58.
42. My formulation here is indebted to Eve Kosofsky Sedgwick, 'Shame and Performativity: Henry James's New York Edition Prefaces', in *Henry James's New York Edition: The Construction of Authorship*, ed. David McWhirter (Stanford, CA: Stanford UP, 1995) 211.
43. Sedgwick, *Between Men*, 89.
44. Holland, *Real Trial*, 89.
45. Ibid. 85, 86, 89, 90.
46. Ibid. 143–51.
47. Ibid. 149.
48. Ibid. 150.
49. Ibid. 86.
50. Ibid. 85.
51. Danson, *Wilde's Intentions*, 100.
52. In *The Renaissance* – the book Wilde described as having 'had such a strange influence over my life' (*LW* 735) – Pater argues that an aesthetic critic must be aware of what effect a person or a work of art produces on him in order to know his 'own impression as it really is, to discriminate it, to realise it distinctly' (*Renaissance* (1986) xxix). The aesthetic critic's guiding question must be, 'what is this song or picture, this engaging personality presented in life or in a book, to *me*?' (xxix). As Adam Phillips notices, this is also among 'the ordinary questions that initiate a sense of self' (x). Wilde takes up this idea in 'The Critic As Artist' (1890) where he describes the 'highest criticism' (*W* 1125) as 'the record of one's own soul'. A full analysis of Wilde's indebtedness to

Pater's 'personality' would be a rewarding subject for research, though even without exhaustively analysing this material, it is fairly clear that Wilde brings to fruition the aesthetic association between personality, sexuality and art.

53. Lucy McDiarmid, 'Oscar Wilde's Speech from the Dock', *Textual Practice* 15.3 (2001), 454.

54. Holland, *Real Trial*, 85, 89.

55. See, for instance, H. Montgomery Hyde (ed.), *The Three Trials of Oscar Wilde* (New York: University Books, 1956) 121. On the force of shame and pride in contemporary culture, see Douglas Crimp, 'Mario Montez, for Shame', in *Regarding Sedgwick: Essays on Queer Culture and Critical Theory*, ed. Stephen M. Barber and David L. Clark (New York: Routledge, 2002).

56. Sedgwick, 'Shame', 211–12.

57. Stevens, *Henry James*, 18.

58. Contrast this declaration to Guy's speech to Mrs Peverel, in act one, in which he says that he can only speak of marriage as a priest, 'the first law of whose profession, the rigid rule of whose life, is to abstain from' marriage (*Plays* 490).

59. Sedgwick, 'Shame', 211.

60. My thinking here is indebted to Lyotard's description of the social bond as being linguistic but 'not woven with a single thread. It is a fabric formed by the intersection of at least two (and in reality an indeterminate number) of language games, obeying different rules' (Jean-François Lyotard, *The Postmodern Condition: A Report on Knowledge* (Minneapolis: U of Minnesota P, 1984) 40).

61. Sedgwick, 'Shame', 211–12.

62. Beckson (ed.), *Aesthetes*, 121.

63. Nordau, *Degeneration* (1993), 300.

64. Dickinson, *Complete Poems*, 327.

65. Following Goffman in *Stigma: Notes on the Management of Spoiled Identity* (London: Penguin, 1968), I distinguish 'covering' an identity from 'passing'. Rather than trying to render a characteristic invisible, the person manages or mutes it by using a cover.

CHAPTER 5

DESPOILING *POYNTON*:
JAMES, THE WILDE TRIALS AND INTERIOR DECORATION

The Law has taken from me not merely all that I have, my books, furniture, pictures, my copyright in my published works, my copyright in my plays, everything in fact from *The Happy Prince* and *Lady Windermere's Fan* down to the staircarpets and door-scraper of my house, but also all that I am ever going to have.

De Profundis (LW 774)

'Oscar Wilde is the fashion. His catch and whimsicality of dialogue tickle the public. Just now the whole of society is engaged in inventing Oscar Wildeisms,'[1] the *Illustrated London News* reported in January 1895. A month later, the same newspaper announced that James's unfashionable, 'unhappily obscure comedy'[2] had failed. By March, it was Wilde's turn to be counted among the deeply unfashionable. His arrest, trials and imprisonment ensured the rapid decline of his popularity, even among the connoisseurs who had been his social allies and friends. James, who was neither an ally nor a friend, sought to wipe Wilde from his most public record – his fiction – in order to control and diminish any perceptible parallels between himself and 'his friend Oscar Wilde', as Marian Adams had acerbically put it in 1882.[3] James may have found Adams's teasing annoying but tolerable, but he now sensed that the time for witty, overt allusions to Wilde had passed.

Publicly, James did his utmost to disassociate himself from Wilde. In the spring of 1895, when Wilde had been at the epicentre of the most famous lawsuit in homosexual history, James became an avid, almost compulsive newspaper reader. While he had ardently denied that his personal interests intersected with those of the dull public and readers of yellow journalism, his letters testify to the fact that he was as spellbound by Wilde's trial as every other reader of halfpenny papers was.[4] Wilde's trial mesmerised the public, creating a real-life drama stimulated by the prurient and sensationalistic press. James closely followed the proceedings in the papers, dutifully alerting friends and family to changes in Wilde's outlook, and relating to his closest friends his fluctuating feelings about Wilde, and his ambivalent delight and disgust at the trial's events.

The sequence of three trials had begun in early April with Wilde's libel suit against the Marquess of Queensberry, who had accused him of being a 'posing Somdomite [sic]'.[5] By the end of April, the tables had turned and Wilde was being sued by Queensberry. Unable to pay his debts, Wilde declared bankruptcy and the entire contents of his home were auctioned (Figure 5.1). The highly publicised bankruptcy sale attracted voyeurs and buyers alike. The *Morning* reported that

> brokers were in great force, anxious to secure the books, prints, pictures and Moorish china to be disposed of; but there were also a large number of curiously-minded persons who made their way all over the premises with a morbid view of seeing something that belonged to a man on trial at the Old Bailey. Oscar Wilde's bedroom was the chief point of attraction.[6]

The article went on to give a detailed description of the bedroom's contents, as well as to relate that people had 'sported with' personal letters and a pornographic French novel until restrained. The *Illustrated Police News* ran a front-page illustration that synthesised Wilde's *curriculum vitae* for the public by collapsing his American lecture tour, the sale of his effects, and his trial (Figure 5.2). On 25 May 1895, Wilde was found guilty of gross indecency and sentenced to two years of hard labour. James, meanwhile, needed more than fascinating newspaper-reading to distract him from the disappointments of *Guy Domville*. Attempting to bounce back, James threw himself into new projects and vowed to rebuild his house of fiction by 'looking in a very different direction than in that of the sacrificed little play'[7] that had been 'whisked away to make room for the triumphant Oscar'. The works James produced over the next few years are fraught with terror and paranoia ('The Turn of the Screw', 1898), infanticide (*The Other House*, 1896), and stronger sexual themes ('In the Cage', 1898; *What Maisie Knew*, 1897; *The Awkward Age*, 1899).

BY ORDER OF THE SHERIFF.

A.D. 1895.　　　　　　　　　　　　No. 6907

16, Tite Street, Chelsea.

Catalogue of the Library of　　*1 . 2 . 6*

.4 . 0

Valuable Books,　*P*

.18 . 0

Pictures, Portraits of Celebrities, Arundel Society Prints, *2 . 7 . 6*

HOUSEHOLD FURNITURE

CARLYLE'S WRITING TABLE,

Chippendale and Italian Chairs, Old Persian Carpets
and Rugs, Brass Fenders,

Moorish and Oriental Curiosities,

Embroideries, Silver and Plated Articles,

OLD BLUE AND WHITE CHINA,

Moorish Pottery, Handsome Ormolu Clock,

and numerous Effects

The Property of Oscar Wilde,

Which will be Sold by Auction,

By Mr. BULLOCK,

ON THE PREMISES,

On Wednesday, April 24th, 1895,

AT ONE O'CLOCK.

May be Viewed the day prior, and Catalogues had of Messrs. CLARKE & Co.
16, Portugal Street, Lincoln's Inn; and of the Auctioneer,

211 HIGH HOLBORN. W.C,

5.1 Unable to pay his debts, Wilde declared bankruptcy and the entire contents of
his home were auctioned. ('Cover page of the Tite Street Sale Catalogue', Courtesy
of the Trustees of the National Library of Scotland.)

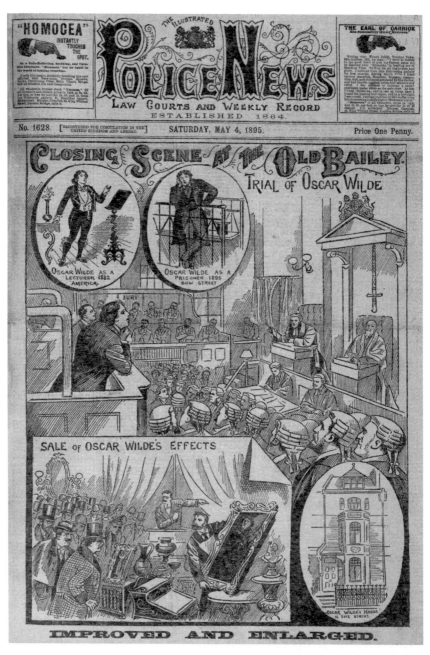

5.2 This front-page illustration synthesised Wilde's *curriculum vitae* by collapsing into one image his American lecture tour, the sale of his effects, and his trial. ('Closing Scene at the Old Bailey', The *Illustrated Police News* 4 May 1895, 1. Courtesy of the British Library.)

It was around this time that the germ of *The Spoils of Poynton*, which had been planted in 1893 but had lain dormant since then, began to develop. James's 'little tale' relating 'a small and ugly matter' was originally titled 'The House Beautiful' (*Notebooks* 79). On 13 May 1895, James saw 'the case vividly enough' yet felt it lacked 'the drama-quality' (121). Three months later, he decided on a suitable *dénouement*: 'What then is it that the rest of my little 2d act, as I call it, of *The House Beautiful* must do? Its climax is in the removal – *must absolutely and utterly be: voilà* – from the house, by Mrs Gereth, of her own treasures' (127). Four months after the liquidation of the contents of Wilde's 'beautiful' house, James decided that the crux of his story lay in the removal of personal possessions. Contracted to write a story by Horace Scudder, the editor of *The Atlantic Monthly*, the little tale blossomed into a novel and took almost a year to write. By 18 December 1895, the title had become problematic and James wrote to Scudder: 'I think the title of Clarence Cook's book is an objection to the retention of the "H. B." Therefore I will rechristen the thing on sending you the next copy. I *may* call it "The Great House" or something better' (*LL* 289). The story was serialised in 1896 as "The Old Things" and was published in 1897 as *The Spoils of Poynton*.

Given James's propensity for revision, it does not seem odd that he modified his story, making thousands of changes to the novel and revising it three times.[8] His avowed reasons for changing his title are, however, ambiguous: it hardly seems plausible that he would have done so merely to fend off associations between his tale and a popular guide to interior decoration first published nearly twenty years before. Though still in print in 1895, Cook's *The House Beautiful: Essays on Beds and Tables, Stools and Candlesticks* was a *succès de scandale* in America, yet its advice on interior decoration was hardly scandalous.[9] If, as Bill Brown observes, James's 'original title helps to situate the text within the decorating discourse of the era',[10] then we need to pay attention to James's reasons for wanting to remove his beautiful tale from this framework.

It is highly unlikely that James 'hoped to capture interest by invoking what had become a catch phrase for the aesthetically inclined'.[11] Quite the contrary, James was trying to fend off associations with the newly unfashionable Wilde who, in 1882, had titled one of his American lectures 'The House Beautiful' in order to take advantage of the popularity of Cook's book. Since Wilde continually revised his lectures, the other two lectures he delivered during his tour – 'The English Renaissance' and 'The Decorative Arts' – grew more and more similar to 'The House Beautiful', and entire passages are sometimes 'lifted' from one lecture to another.[12] 'The House Beautiful' was Wilde's 'walking tour of the typical bourgeois household'[13] which allowed Wilde to become a consummate guide by absorbing aesthetic decoration into an emerging 'system of values and attitudes, associated with a variety of movements in art and society, having in common their relation to an inchoate counterdiscourse of "homosexuality"'[14] which the Wilde trials eventually brought to the fore. James's title change indicates not only that he hesitated at being coupled with the conspicuous consumption advocated by Cook, but also with the infamy that had settled like a dark cloud over Wilde.

James was meticulous in his public associations and deeply preoccupied by his American image. Since 'The House Beautiful' was due to be published in an American magazine, James knew that he would do well to avoid traces of Wildeisms or linguistic *cartes de visite*. The story of James's title and of both authors' constructions of the 'House Beautiful' is an exemplary instance of their intricate relationship.

The 'germ' of *The Spoils of Poynton* was an anecdote that Vernon Lee's companion, Clementine Anstruther-Thompson, had regaled James with at an 1893 Christmas party. In the novel's Preface, James is quick to assert that what was of interest to him was the bare idea, not its factual trappings or the real-life drama surrounding it. His art lay in the exclusion of such details: 'Life being all inclusion and confusion, and art being all discrimination and selection, the latter, in search of the hard latent *value* with which alone it is concerned, sniffs round the mass as instinctively and unerringly as a dog suspicious of some buried bone' (*LC2* 1138). Confronted by *The Spoils of Poynton*'s allusiveness and impenetrability, or what David Lodge sees as 'hesitating between alternative meanings',[15] I have chosen to consider the connections between the novel's life and art.

Books, Letters and Newspapers

From 1894 to 1895, James published three stories in *The Yellow Book*, the short-lived but influential illustrated quarterly devoted to aesthetics, literature and art. The first issue was published in April 1894 with James's story 'The Death of the Lion' in the lead position.[16] Wilde read this issue and, though he did not comment on James's story, we can imagine that, in light of the mounting media frenzy regarding his private affairs, Wilde would have been inclined to sympathise with the retiring hero's distaste for publicity. Wilde was, however, explicit about his hostility towards the magazine: 'Have you seen *The Yellow Book*?' he asked his friends, 'it is horrid and not yellow at all . . . It is dull and loathsome, a great failure. I am so glad' (*LW* 588–9). The scorn Wilde poured on the magazine revealed his resentment at having been expressly barred from it. Though he never contributed to *The Yellow Book*, the public associated him with the magazine because of its yellow content,[17] as well as the fact that it was published by his publisher, Mathews & Lane at the Bodley Head. For instance, *Punch* ran a satirical article 'From the Queer and Yellow Book' (written by 'Max Mereboom') debating how the 'Decadent Sect' might be identified:

> What exactly this Title signified no two entomologists will agree. But we may learn from the Caricatures of the day what the *Decadents* were in outward semblance; from the Lampoons what was their mode of life. Nightly they gathered at any of the theatres where the plays of Mr WILDE were being given. Nightly, the stalls were fulfilled by Row upon Row of neatly-curled Fringes surmounting Button-holes of monstrous size.[18]

The accompanying picture, 'by our own Yellow-Booky Daubaway Weirdsley', showed Aubrey Beardsley in a flounced dress pulling a book-shaped car containing three inelegant male cross-dressers (Figure 5.3).

James was no more fond of the publication than Wilde. 'I hate too much the horrid aspect & company of the whole publication,' he said of *The Yellow Book*'s decadent coterie and implicit Wildean connection (*L3* 482). John Singer Sargent's portrait of James was nevertheless reproduced in the magazine in July 1894. The October 1895 issue included 'A Few Notes Upon Mr Henry James', an essay that judged him to be 'too analytical', 'a very apostle of form'.[19] James apologised for not sending his brother William 'The Death of the Lion', excused his association with the magazine by claiming it was merely 'for gold', and resigned himself to being 'intimately – conspicuously – associated with the 2d number' (*L3* 482).[20] Although he could keep the problematic publication from his family, Americans soon noticed his affiliation with what was perceived to be an organ of the Decadents. *Munsey's* commented that 'of late . . . Mr James has been in bad company . . . He has become one of *The Yellow Book* clique',[21] and it urged him to return to America's moral atmosphere. The *Atlantic*

5.3 Though Wilde never contributed to *The Yellow Book*, the public nevertheless associated him with the magazine because of its yellow content. *Punch* lampooned the magazine by depicting Aubrey Beardsley in a flounced dress pulling a book-shaped car containing three inelegant male cross-dressers. ('Picture by Our Own Yellow-Booky Daubaway Weirdsley, intended as a Puzzle Picture to preface of Juvenile Poems, or as nothing in particular', *Punch* 2 February 1895, 58. Courtesy of the Trustees of the National Library of Scotland.)

Monthly noted in 1897 that his 'super-subtlety of theme, for which no form of expression can be too carefully wrought . . . place[s] Mr James inextricably in the decadent ranks.'

The Yellow Book was effectively defunct by 1895, largely because of its implied connection with Wilde, an association that had also doomed Beardsley.[22] The headline of the *New York Times* of 4 April 1895 read 'Arrest of Oscar Wilde, *Yellow Book* under his arm'. Although the yellow-coloured volume was in fact a French novel, the false connection had severe repercussions for the Bodley Head. The firm's co-founder, John Lane, asserted that the implied association with Wilde had 'killed *The Yellow Book* and it nearly killed me'.[23] Outraged crowds swarmed into Vigo Street, the home of the Bodley Head, and manifested their censure by breaking a window. Public pressure forced the publisher to drop Wilde and Beardsley, even though Beardsley

> in no way subscribed to Wilde's philosophy of life. But the public in general did not know this. They took the esoteric quality of Beardsley's art as the outward manifestation of an inner debauchery like Wilde's. They thought the man who wrote *Salomé* and the man who illustrated it were kindred souls and that both represented *The Yellow Book*.[24]

Although an issue of *The Yellow Book* had been planned for 15 April 1895 – at the midpoint between Wilde's arrest (5 April) and the beginning of his first criminal trial (26 April) – the presses were stopped and Beardsley's designs removed.

James's response was not anomalous: this was neither the first nor the last time he would take pains to detach himself from a disgraced acquaintance or coterie. Both James and Wilde were acquaintances of Harold Frederic, the American writer and journalist best known for his novel *Illumination* (1896). As the London correspondent for *The New York Times*, Frederic had favourably reviewed *Guy Domville*; he reported that James 'received "ruffianly" treatment, [but] the play was drawing good houses, and "intelligent people who go speak highly of it." '[25] James was sent this clipping as an enclosure in a letter from William on 15 January 1895. At the close of the 1890s, Frederic had become an embarrassment in circles where he had once been welcomed.[26] Joseph Conrad called him 'a gross man who lived grossly and died abominably'.[27] Frederic's death in 1898 was fraught with scandal, and he left a number of illegitimate children whom Cora and Stephen Crane took in. According to Stephen Crane, James disappeared in order to avoid being linked to a man of disrepute: 'he professed to be er, er, er much attached to H[arold] and now he has shut up like a clam'.[28] James nevertheless gave the Cranes £50 for Frederic's orphans.

It was around this time, in the mid and late 1890s, that sexuality becomes more of a surface (rather than subterranean) theme in James's works. The cautious intimations of the early fiction, such as *Roderick Hudson*, gave way to what Edel claims was 'a new consciousness of humans as physical beings' and 'an intense wish to know what goes on in adult bedrooms' (*L4* xiii, xiv). Edmund Wilson remarks that, in James's post-1895 works, sex becomes 'a kind of obsession – in a queer and left-handed way'.[29] James's reading also became more sexually explicit: in January 1893 Gosse lent him Symonds's discussion of homosexual love, *A Problem in Modern Ethics* (1891), and James borrowed more of Symonds's writings after Wilde's arrest (*LL* 280). Obliquely referring to the inconsistencies between his own desires and their concealment, James judged Symonds

> a candid and consistent creature, and the exhibition [in *A Problem in Modern Ethics*] is infinitely remarkable. It's on the whole, I think, a queer place to plant the standard of duty, but he does it with extraordinary gallantry. If he has, or gathers, a band of the emulous, we may look for some capital sport . . . I will drop in with him and defy the *consigne*. (*L3* 398)

On 9 August 1895, James wrote to Gosse to recommend Huysmans's *En Route*, a thinly veiled autobiographical account of Huysmans's Catholic conversion after a licentious life. James thought it 'strange and vile and perverse, but of an extraordinary *facture* and an interesting sincerity'.[30]

If the failure of *Guy Domville* took James to the depths of depression, this did not inhibit him from deepening his interest in overtly sexual themes. The James we encounter in the mid-1890s is a noticeably freer and, at times, wittily bawdy man. The events of 1895 compounded the personal with the political: the Wilde case brought (homo)sexuality to the fore of Victorian society and of James's mind. James described the trial to the American physician William Wilberforce Baldwin, as earth-shattering explaining, 'our earthquake here, has been social – human – sexual (if that be the word when it's all one sex). You probably followed in some degree the Oscar Wilde horrors' (Edel 4: 139). Although the trial had the effect of increasing James's nervousness about being publicly associated with Wilde, it also seems to have increased his desire to discuss more overtly than before matters of a physical and sexual nature.

During *Guy Domville*'s run, James subjected himself to a news fast lest he should read any reproving reviews. He wrote to his siblings on 2 February 1895: 'The papers I have simply, in a single case, not read – & it was *impossible* for me to traffic in them – to gather them up and send them to you . . . *Please* don't send me anything out of newspapers.'[31] After the play's failure, James began to read the newspapers again. He avidly followed the Wilde trial and read of the fearful exposure it entailed with a mix of attraction and revulsion. When some newspapers suppressed the trial's insalubrious details, he read cheaper, halfpenny papers for enlightenment (*L4* 12).[32] William wrote to his brother eager for information – 'But does this finish him [Wilde] in London? In Paris I should think it would stamp him complete. I've seen no details'[33] – and James was happy to oblige:

> You ask of Oscar Wilde. His fall is hideously tragic – & the squalid violence of it gives him an interest (of misery) that he never had for me – in any degree – before. Strange to say I think he may have a 'future' – of a sort – by reaction – when he comes out of prison – if he survives the horrible sentence of hard labour that he will probably get. His trial begins today – however – & it is too soon to say. But there are depths in London, & a certain general shudder as to what, with regard to some other people, may possibly come to light.[34]

These letters show that James had been following newspaper accounts closely and had almost certainly discussed them with others. They also reveal his increasing interest in Wilde: as a tragic figure stripped of his status, James's rival became an object of fascination, pity and disgust.

Nervous newspaper reading figures strongly in *The Spoils of Poynton*. Fleda and Mrs Gereth rely on papers for the latest news, not of the world, but of Owen's marriage and their fates. The paper is the pivot around which their lives revolve. Its power is such that it is personified: 'As *The Morning Post* still held its peace she would be of course more confident'(*N4* 347). Newspaper idiom infiltrates Fleda's vocabulary and scouring the newspaper becomes an anxiety-filled routine for the pair (243, 308). Every morning Mrs Gereth 'looked publicly into *The Morning Post*, the only newspaper she received; and every morning she treated the blankness of that journal as fresh evidence that everything was "off." What did the *Post* exist for but to tell you your children were wretchedly married?' (306). When Owen's marriage to Mona Brigstock is announced, the paper describes the wedding in shamelessly voyeuristic detail: 'there were two ecclesiastics and six bridesmaids . . . as well as a special train from town . . . The happy pair . . . [took] their departure for Mr Gereth's own seat, famous for its unique collection of artistic curiosities' (382). Even after the *Post* tells Mrs Gereth her son is 'wretchedly married'(N4 387), she compulsively continues to read it, amassing reasons to dislike her new daughter-in-law.

James's Janus-faced letters regarding the trials demonstrate the emotional ambivalence Wilde aroused in him. The two principal correspondents with whom he discussed Wilde were his brother William and his close friend, Edmund Gosse. Henry was matter-of-fact with William, not wanting to give away how close he felt to the trial's events. However, in his correspondence with Gosse we witness James uncorseted and unbuttoned. Gosse, who was 'well known for his [homo]sexual preferences',[35] was worried that Robert Ross, Wilde's closest friend, would be dragged into the trial. This was what James guardedly referred to as the 'general shudder as to what, with regard to some other people, may possibly come to light'.[36] Gosse was peripheral to the trial insofar as he knew and cared for many of the men involved. James's proximity to these events (via Gosse) and the hideous yet tantalising press reports indicated that it would be wise to cover connections with Wilde and his circle. On 8 April 1895, three days after Wilde's arrest, James wrote to Gosse:

> Yes, too, it has been, it is, hideously, atrociously dramatic & really interesting – so far as one can say that of a thing of which the interest is qualified by such a sickening horribility. It is the squalid gratuitousness of it all – of the mere exposure – that blurs the spectacle. But the *fall* – from nearly 20 years of a really unique kind of 'brilliant' conspicuity (wit, 'art,' conversation – 'one of our 2 or 3 dramatists &c,') to that sordid prison-cell & this gulf of obscenity over which the ghoulish public hangs & gloats – it is beyond any utterance of irony or any pang of compassion! He was never in the smallest degree interesting to me – but this hideous human history has made him so – in a manner . . . Quel Dommage – mais quel Bonheur – que J. A. S. ne soit plus de ce monde! [on the flap of the envelope]. (*LL* 279)

Almost three weeks later, James wrote again:

> My dear Gosse,
> Thanks – of a troubled kind, for your defense of my modesty in the *Realm*.[37] The article is brilliantly clever – but I have almost the same anguish (that is my modesty has) when defended as when violated. You have, however, doubtless done it great good, which I hereby formally recognise. These are the days in which one's modesty is, in every direction, much exposed, and one should be thankful for every veil that one

can hastily snatch up or that a friendly hand precipitately muffles one withal. It is strictly congruous with these remarks that I should mention that there go to you tomorrow A.M. in two registered envelopes, at 1 Whitehall, the fond outpourings of poor J. A. S. . . . Did you see in last evening's 1/2d papers that the wretched O. W. seems to have a gleam of light before him (if it really counts for that), in the fearful exposure of his (of the prosecution's) little beasts of witnesses? What a nest of almost infant blackmailers! Yours ever Henry James. (*L4* 12)

The association of James's fragile modesty, Symonds's homosexual writings and Wilde's full-on exposure by the press is a curious one. These letters savour of insider trading in, for example, the knowing allusions to Symonds. Referring to a writer associated with same-sex desire creates an intriguing counterpoint (and countersign) to James's repeated denials that Wilde 'was never in the smallest degree interesting to' him (*LL* 279). Two years before the trial, James had told Gosse he was not surprised that some of Symonds's 'friends and relations are haunted with a vague malaise' (*L3* 398) because of the homosexual content of his works. When James's friend, Ariana Curtis, suggested he write an article on Symonds in March 1895, he politely declined by alluding to Symonds's pamphlets on homosexuality, *A Problem in Greek Ethics* and *A Problem in Modern Ethics*, and declaring them 'a Problem – a problem beyond me'.[38]

The Wilde trial proved that it was easy to expose and destroy any man, and particularly an artist whose works might be read as representative of his own thoughts and desires. James is explicit about his need for protection and his wish to conceal details that might prove unduly revelatory. His gratefulness for Gosse's ability to camouflage indicates the degree of his concern. He feels his modesty exposed by the contents of Symonds's writings; had its homosexual nature elicited a *prise de conscience*? It is clear that James was aware of the possible implications of being discovered in possession of such materials. It is 'strictly congruous with these remarks' about quiet concealment that the topic of Symonds's 'fond outpourings' is broached. It was with similar vigilance that, seven months later, as Wilde began to serve his sentence, James changed the title of his story from the Wilde-inflected (or perhaps Wilde-*infected*) 'The House Beautiful' to the more neutral 'The Old Things'. This was one of James's first post-*Guy Domville* publications and he was preoccupied that they should be redemptive, both financially and personally.

Although James had been privately fascinated with and sympathetic to Wilde, he was publicly undemonstrative. He refused to sign the petition for Wilde's release from prison that Jonathan Sturges brought him. Sturges visited James for ten days in late October 1895 while he was outlining *The Spoils of Poynton* (*Notebooks* 140).[39] On 27 November, Sturges reported that James

> feels sorry for Oscar . . . [but] James says that the petition would not have the slightest effect on the *authorities* here who have the matter in charge, and in whose nostrils the very name of Zola and even of Bourget is a stench, and that the document would only exist as a manifesto of personal loyalty to Oscar by his friends, of which he was never one. (*LW* 643)

The social stigma attached to Wilde's crime was so severe that it would have been almost unthinkable for anyone to defend it without attracting considerable negative attention. Privately, James discussed the case with a Member of Parliament who had visited Wilde in prison. This was likely R. B. Haldane, who had been part of the Commission for Penal Reform during the Rosebery government (Edel 4: 129–30). He told Alphonse Daudet on 10 November that 'le malheureux' Wilde had been found 'dans un état d'abattement complet, physique & moral . . . [sans] aucune faculté résistante ni récupérative. S'il l'avait, seulement, cette faculté, quel chef d'oeuvre il pourrait faire encore!' (*LL* 287). This marks a shift in James's public estimation of Wilde's talent; it is James's first open avowal of artistic respect for the man.

James's precaution was not unwarranted: the Wilde trials had revealed the public and the court's inability to distinguish the artist from his art. The narrative and the authorial voice were, for all intents and purposes, one. As Michael Foldy and Ed Cohen have shown, Wilde and his writings were put on trial and proofed for homosexual content.[40] The public and the courts conflated Wilde and his writing by assuming that one was the outcome of the other: a decadent lifestyle yielded decadent literature. Abandoned by almost all his friends and acquaintances, Wilde was also dropped from reminiscences, edited out of memoirs and, consequently, much of the social history of the 1880s and 1890s. Lord Ronald Sutherland Gower, a homosexual hedonist whom Wilde had known since his Oxford days and who was a possible inspiration for *The Picture of Dorian Gray*'s Lord Henry Wotton, re-edited his reminiscences and reduced the references to Wilde.[41] The MP George Wyndham (who had become friendly with Wilde through George Curzon and the Crabbet Club, as well as because of the family relationship with Lord Alfred Douglas) advised Wilde to leave for France before his arrest. Though Wilde mentions Wyndham's role in *De Profundis* (LW 763), none of this appears in Wyndham's *Life and Letters*, because the scandal of Wilde's conviction cut him off from this stratum of society.

By the time *The Spoils of Poynton* was published, the Wilde trials were over and they had been all over. At home and abroad, there had been an insatiable appetite for news and gossip. The *Daily Telegraph* and *The Star* had had the most comprehensive coverage, though most English papers, such as the *St James's Gazette*, declined 'to sully [their] pages by matter not fit to be printed' and adopted an 'attitude of reserve in regard to the malodorous evidence in the Wilde v. Queensberry trial at the Central Criminal Court'.[42] Americans were conversant with the key figures in the trial and had been avid for news and gossip about it.[43] In the United States, at least 900 sermons were preached against Wilde between 1895 and 1900.[44] The American public had been introduced to Wilde as the self-proclaimed prophet of 'the House Beautiful' in 1882. Upon returning to England, Wilde gave over 150 performances of aesthetically-themed lectures between 1883 and 1885. More than half of these were dedicated to 'The House Beautiful' and 'Personal Impressions of America' (*LW* 219–21).[45] When Wilde was engaged to Constance Lloyd in 1883, the press described her as 'the lady whom he has chosen to be the *châtelaine* of the House Beautiful'.[46] In 1888, Whistler published 'The Home of Taste; The Ideas of Mr Blankety Blank on House Decoration', a mock review of Wilde's lectures (Whistler 230). More than a decade after Wilde's first lectures on the subject, the connection between Wilde and interior decoration showed little sign of deteriorating. An 1894 article on 'Mrs Oscar Wilde at Home' told readers that 'like her husband . . . [Constance Wilde] may be truly called an apostle of the beautiful. She has . . . made everything that concerns the beautifying of the home a special study',[47] while an 1895 article offered guidance on 'How to Decorate a House' by 'Mrs Oscar Wilde'.[48] These examples illustrate the way in which American and English magazine publications kept the association between Wilde and decoration fresh in the public's mind. Vincent O'Sullivan, a friend of Wilde's later years, remembers

a man in London at the time of Wilde's trial speaking in his favour, and saying with a wave of his hand, 'We owe him this!' Now the room we were in was full of horrible bric-à-brac, false antiques, flimsy cane chairs, some kind of vegetation in 'aesthetic-blue' pots, and silk window curtains, pale green. Perhaps Wilde himself would have thought that room hideous; but I am not sure. Anyhow, he forced solid British families to put out of doors the beautiful heavy Victorian furniture and curtains, so comfortable, so secure . . . And to make their houses look like lawn tennis clubs on the Italian Riviera.[49]

Johnston Forbes-Robertson recounts that Whistler had refused to give Wilde any advice regarding the decoration of 16 Tite Street, telling him: 'Oscar, you have been lecturing to us on the House Beautiful; now is your chance to show us one.'[50]

The trope of the 'House Beautiful' has an extensive history that merges changes in interior design and the evolution of the transatlantic Aesthetic Movement. The expression may first have been used in John Bunyan's *Pilgrim's Progress*. Andrew Jackson Downing employed it in *The Architecture of Country Houses*, and the founder of the magazine *House Beautiful* was inspired by Stevenson's eponymous poem.[51] The American magazine's first issue declared its intentions to its readers: 'to help you to the house of your hopes and your ideals, to aid you in every step, and in every detail . . . to offer you the widest latitude your purse can buy, yet to narrow your choice to what is essentially the best . . . that is the purpose for which *The House Beautiful* exists'.[52] Reiterating the principles of Cook's and others' guidebooks, the magazine opposed both the perpetuation of vulgar display and the excess of ornament that had characterised most of the nineteenth century. The phrase was also used by writers including Eastlake (in *Hints on Household Taste*), Pater (in *The Renaissance* and *Appreciations*) and Twain (in *Life on the Mississippi*) and is now suffused with myriad cultural associations.[53]

To American fin-de-siècle readers the House Beautiful was an evocative phrase, primarily associated with domesticity and taste. An attractive house was said to further happiness, an idea Wilde used in his lecture on 'The English Renaissance of Art'. Associating the blissful with the beautiful home, he asked, 'in such dread moments of discord and despair where should we, of this torn and troubled age, turn our steps if not to that secure house of beauty where there is always a little forgetfulness, always a great joy' (RW 24). Like 'the House Beautiful', Aestheticism also summoned, for Americans, the image of a feminine and domestic world.[54] Yet by 1895, the House Beautiful had, because of the Wilde trial, become associated with broken homes and conditions unfavourable for domestic bliss. By the late 1890s, 'aesthetic' interior decoration had come to be associated with decadence and, consequently, the more neutral term 'artistic' was favoured. Domestic manuals also invoked the idea of 'taste' and argued that it was the result of individual artistic sensibilities.[55] Poynton is described as 'artistic' by the press (N4 382).

'The House Beautiful'

'The English Renaissance of Art', 'The Decorative Arts' and 'The House Beautiful' were staples of Wilde's North American lecture tour. Wilde's lectures on interior decoration are collations of partially plagiarised passages from Pater, Ruskin, Burne-Jones, Morris and others. 'The English Renaissance of Art' lecture had, according to the *Washington Post*, 'a good deal of Ruskin and Goethe flavoured with Burne-Jones and Swinburne, and largely diluted with Oscar Wilde'.[56] Delivered for the first time in New York on 9 January 1882 and revised extensively during the first month of his tour, this is also the lecture he gave in Washington on 23 and 25 January, around the time he met James. Although there are no records indicating that James attended the lecture, the newspaper coverage of Wilde's visit to Washington was extensive and in-depth. Long passages from the lectures were reprinted in newspapers and it would have been difficult for James to remain unaware of them. The New York *Daily Graphic* illustrated sentences from the lectures, while the *Washington Post* printed a long excerpt that quoted Wilde verbatim:

> Every object should be beautiful, and give delight to its maker as well as its user and lighten the burden of the toilers. For those, the lecturer said, with whom the end of life is not action but thought, 'who must burn always with one of the passions of this little, fiery, colored world, and to whom, valuing passion for its intensity and not for its permanence, over and over again in the progress of their culture find what was once precious has become indifferent – for those who find life interesting not for its secrets but for its situations, for its pulsations and not for its purpose, the passion of beauty engendered by the decorative arts will be more satisfying than any political or religious enthusiasm, any enthusiasm for humanity, any ecstasy or sorrow of love, for art comes to you professing frankly to give nothing but the highest qualities to your moments as they pass'.[57]

This excerpt reveals the extent of Wilde's borrowing, particularly from Ruskin and Pater. As well, it shows what was to become Wilde's standard practice, his habit of integrating and revising others' ideas, which I discussed in Chapters 2 and 3. Here, his use of both his Oxford mentors' ideas is more obvious than it later would be. When Wilde speaks of the passionate 'pulsations' that are the stuff of life, or the 'passions of this little, fiery, coloured world', we detect more than a hint of Pater's *Renaissance*. Wilde's lecture was deeply indebted to the corpus of the Aesthetic Movement and the handicrafts revival, from Ruskin through the Pre-Raphaelite Brotherhood and Morris. What Wilde was saying was neither his, nor was it new. 'The Renaissance in English Art' was old hat for Americans. The press had kept them abreast of British cultural innovations, and they had already contributed to the Movement to which Wilde mistakenly assumed he was introducing them for the first time.[58]

Unlike Wilde's other American lectures, 'The English Renaissance' contains little in the way of household hints. His comments on interior decoration are sparse, descriptive rather than prescriptive. Burne-Jones's 'marvel of design' (*RW* 23) and Morris's 'weaving of tapestry and staining of glass' are guarantees that 'in years to come there will be nothing in any man's house which has not given delight to its maker and does not give delight to its user.' Citing Plato (and omitting Ruskin and Morris, who had been the most recent champions of the idea), Wilde advances the none-too-novel notion that beautiful surroundings increase one's propensity for 'philosophy' and 'gracious existence', leading 'the boy naturally to look for that divine harmony of spiritual life of which art was to him the material symbol and warrant'.

'The House Beautiful' and 'The Decorative Arts' are the most prescriptive of Wilde's lectures and their suggestions for interior decoration are closely connected with those implicit in *The Spoils of Poynton*. American audiences received 'The English Renaissance of Art' with a yawn because of the lecture's excessive theoreticality, Wilde's unspectacular delivery, and the triteness of his message. As a result, he drafted 'The Decorative Arts', a more practical and exhortatory lecture, which became the basis of the remaining nine months of the tour. He generally saved 'the House Beautiful' for 'those occasions when he gave a second lecture in a city'.[59] First delivered on 11 February 1882 in Chicago (under the title 'Interior and Exterior House Decoration'), 'The House Beautiful' was delivered at least fifteen times in the United States and Canada and was subsequently delivered during Wilde's sporadic lectures in England, Scotland and Ireland from 1883 to 1885. Kevin O'Brien has traced some of the sources of the lecture to Ruskin's 'The Nature of Gothic' in *The Stones of Venice II*, Morris's *Hopes and Fears for Art*, Mary Haweis's *The Art of Dress*, and Rev. W. J. Loftie's *A Plea for Art in the House*.[60] His research is corroborated by the fact that Wilde explicitly sent for these guidebooks to aid him in writing his new lecture.

'The Decorative Arts' and 'The House Beautiful' are practical extensions of the principles articulated in 'The English Renaissance of Art'. The speeches are demotic and democratic in tone and suggest that taste and beauty be amenable to all. The House Beautiful is exclusively for everyone. As in 'The English Renaissance of Art', the lectures emphasise the correlation between beautiful homes and happy homes, and extoll art's ability to mould moral men. Against the tyranny of machine-made objects, they reiterate the need for 'democratic art', 'made by the hands of the people and for the benefit of the people' (W 926). The useful is beautiful, the beautiful is useful. Echoing Weber *avant la lettre* and Morris *après la lettre*, they counsel that good craftsmen are happy craftsmen and that they can only exist in a society that values their skills and work more than the financial bottom line. The lecture is, however, not anti-capitalist:

> I do not say anything against commercial people, for it is not commerce that destroys art; Genoa was built by its traders, Florence by its bankers, and Venice, loveliest of them all, by her noble and honest merchants. I do not regard the commercial spirit of the present age as being opposed to the development of art, and I look to our merchants to support the changes we seek to make. (930)

Wilde's 'The House Beautiful' was not directed at 'those millionaires who can pillage Europe for their pleasure, but those of moderate means' (913). He established house rules:

> Have nothing in your house that has not given pleasure to the man who made it and is not a pleasure to those who use it. Have nothing in your house that is not useful or beautiful; if such a rule were followed out, you would be astonished at the amount of rubbish you would get rid of. Let there be no sham imitation of one material in another, such as paper representing marble, or wood painted to resemble stone, and have no machine-made ornaments. (914)

Waterbath, the residence of the Brigstock clan in *The Spoils of Poynton*, breaks all these rules. Though the Brigstocks are not *sans le sou*, they are inclined to aesthetic nonsense, such as privileging simulacrum over substance. As a result, 'the house was bad in all conscience, but it might have passed if they had only let alone. This saving mercy was beyond them; they had smothered it with trumpery ornament and scrapbook art' (N4 215).

The Spoils of Poynton presents the reader with four very different houses: Mrs Gereth's Poynton, the Brigstocks' Waterbath, Ricks (left behind by the maiden aunt), and Mr Vetch's West Kensington lodgings. Mrs Gereth's notion of the correct constitution of a beautiful home is analogous to the views Wilde advocated in his lectures. This is not a case of influence but, rather, one of complex similarities that suggest the subtleties and intricacies of James's relationship to Wilde. The affinities between their Houses Beautiful can only be partly explained by the widespread circulation of the expression at the time. James's references reveal that he was reading from a specifically Wildean breviary of the Beautiful.

Poynton is the 'House Beautiful' of James's original title. Waterbath is Poynton's anti-type or, in Bernard Richards's words, the 'house ugly'.[61] Waterbath's

> was an ugliness fundamental and systematic, the result of the abnormal nature of the Brigstocks, from whose composition the principle of taste had been extravagantly omitted. In the arrangement of their home some other principle, remarkably active, but uncanny and obscure, had operated instead, with consequences depressing to behold, consequences that took the form of a universal futility. The house was bad in all conscience. (N4 215)

Despite their newly acquired money, the Brigstocks have not been able to acquire taste. The implication is not that they lack taste because they have not had the time to cultivate it, but that they are simply oblivious to it. James's is a more subtle point than that of William Dean Howells in *The Rise of Silas Lapham*, where the *nouveau riche* Laphams' house is a gimcrack-filled horror, in contrast to the Brahmanic Coreys' tasteful old residence. The Lapham-Corey relation is similar to the Brigstock-Gereth one in that two young lovers (one with old money, one with new) are to be married. A fire eventually destroys the Laphams' ugly house, leaving the family financially ruined but morally renewed. Whereas Howells reinforces the determinist credo that one should not aim to rise above one's station, James is not so conservative: the fact that he endows Fleda (who is of relatively low social standing) with exquisite taste shows that he regards taste as an indication of culture and morality, not breeding. Despite her father's bad taste, Fleda is sophisticated and moral, and this last quality is exacerbated to the point of becoming her tragic flaw.[62] In contrast, the Brigstocks are conniving, devoid of moral fibre and unrefined. There is, for James, a corollary between artistic taste and morality. Wilde argues for a similar relationship in his lectures:

> The most practical school of morals in the world, the best educator, is true art: it never lies, never misleads, and never corrupts, for all good art, all high art, is founded on honesty, sincerity and truth. Under its influence children learn to abhor the liar and cheat in art – the man who paints wood to represent marble, or iron to look like stone. (*W* 936)

James's text is a fictional enactment of Wilde's theorising on the decorative arts: Wilde's theory of the House Beautiful and, by extension, the house ugly is exemplified in James's tale.

The Brigstocks' drawing room is enough to cause Mrs Gereth's 'face to burn' and, privately, to reduce her to tears (215). What is it then that makes Waterbath so singularly 'bad'? Is it the 'strange excrescences and bunchy draperies, with gimcracks that might have been keepsakes for maid-servants and nondescript conveniences that might have been prizes for the blind'? Or the carpets and curtains 'gone wildly astray', the 'souvenirs of places even more ugly than itself', 'the acres of varnish' smeared over everything, 'the little brackets and pink vases, the sweepings of bazaars, the family photographs and illuminated texts, the "household art" ' (216, 223–4)? Fleda remembers Waterbath's conservatory containing 'a stuffed cockatoo fastened to a tropical bough and a waterless fountain composed of shells stuck into some hardened paste' (233). In 'The House Beautiful' lecture, Wilde explicitly advises not to have any 'of those gloomy horrors, stuffed animals or stuffed birds, in the hall, or anywhere else under glass cases' (*W* 915).

There is nothing specifically terrible about Waterbath; the whole thing is terrible. Ricks and Mr Vetch's lodgings do not conform to the canons of good taste, though there is nevertheless something human and touching about them. The degree to which the maiden aunt and Mr Vetch have invested themselves in their shabby possessions makes them more sympathetic than the objects in the Brigstock burlesque. Like Poynton's objects, the things at Ricks have been lovingly collected, though they are not quite beautiful. Although Mrs Gereth finds Ricks detestable, it is an intensely personal and harmoniously decorated place that exudes the pitiable sadness of a dream deferred. This is the melancholy note Fleda hears most poignantly and which indicates her heightened moral and aesthetic sense. Fleda 'instantly averted her eyes' (N4 247) from Ricks's 'ornaments', though James describes the rooms through her eyes:

> The room was practically a shallow box, with the junction of the walls and ceiling guiltless of curve or cornice and marked merely by the little band of crimson paper glued round the top of the other paper, a turbid grey sprigged with silver flowers. This decoration was rather new and quite fresh; and there was in the centre of the ceiling a big square beam papered over in white, as to which Fleda hesitated about venturing to remark that it was rather picturesque . . . It was all, none the less, not so bad as Fleda had feared; it was faded and melancholy, whereas there had been a danger that it would be contradictious and positive, cheerful and loud. The house was crowded with objects of which the aggregation somehow made a thinness and the futility a grace; things that told her they had been gathered as slowly and as lovingly as the golden flowers of Poynton.

Fleda's description echoes William Morris. He who joked in 'Making the Best of It' that 'it may be suggested that we should paper our ceilings like our walls, but I can't think that it will do . . . a room papered all over would be like a box to live in'[63] – a joke repeated by Wilde in 'The House Beautiful':

> About the ceiling: the ceiling is a great problem always – what to do with that great expanse of white plaster. Don't paper it; that gives one the sensation of living in a paper box, which is not pleasant. . . . Leave the main rafters of the ceiling exposed in outline; this conveys a sense of solidity and support . . . If you cannot have the cross-beams or woodwork, then have it painted in a colour which predominates in the room, but do not in any event paper it; on papered ceilings the light falls dull and lifeless and sodden. (W 917–18)

Ricks is the product of a life lived alone; the aunt never married. The doors symbolise the situation: Poynton is furnished exclusively with 'high double leaves' (N4 247) whereas 'at Ricks the entrances to the rooms were like the holes of rabbit-hutches'. Poynton's double doors represent good taste, money, elegance but, most of all, coupledom:

Mr and Mrs Gereth. This is important because its spoils are not only the result of Mrs Gereth's 'genius' (219) for collecting, but also of 'her husband's sympathy and generosity, his knowledge and love, their perfect accord and beautiful life together, twenty-six years of planning and seeking, a long, sunny harvest of taste and curiosity'. In contrast, Ricks is a modest, solitary space, a house of one's own. Fleda's sympathy for the space is perhaps the result of a fearful premonition that she will also end up alone.

Collectors and Collections: the Souls and Clouds House

A real house famous for its 'artistic' contents is the Wallace Collection in London, which James knew well. He reviewed 'The Wallace Collection in Bethnal Green' in 1873 for the *Atlantic Monthly*, focusing mainly on the picture collection, the main characteristic of which was 'its variety and magnificence . . . its genial, easy, unexclusive taste – the good-nature of well-bred opulence. It pretends as little as possible to be instructive or consistent, to illustrate schools or to establish principles.'[64] The collection's tasteful eclecticism is similar to Mrs Gereth's, but it bears no further similarity to Poynton. It was, however, photographed by A. L. Coburn in 1906 for the volume of the New York Edition which included *The Spoils of Poynton* (Figure 5.4).[65] James told Coburn to portray 'the beautiful Subject *obliquely* . . . and with as much of the damask on [the] wall as possible' (*L4* 431). Titled 'Some of the Spoils', the picture shows a firescreen with a panel of Gobelin tapestry, an eighteenth-century gilt and bronze musical clock on the mantelpiece along with two candelabra and two Louis XVI chairs flanking the maroon marble fireplace (Figure 5.5).

Drastically different from the other houses in the novel, Poynton stands as a monument to taste and a passion for collecting that could only be rivalled by a kleptomaniac. It is also remarkable insofar as it conforms to Wilde's conception of the House Beautiful. One of the commonplace comments on the novel is its fascinating allusiveness; much the same can be said of Poynton's contents. A nineteenth-century critic for the New York *Tribune* found Poynton's bric-à-brac 'mutely eloquent',[66] and scholarly comment on the objects has largely echoed this assessment. Adeline Tintner deems Poynton's specifications 'distinctly weak',[67] Millicent Bell suggests the objects were conceived 'abstractly',[68] and Bernard Richards declares them 'too shadowy to have an identifiable source'.[69] The descriptions James gives us are, however, sufficient to identify them as conforming to the

5.4 For the frontispiece to *The Portrait of a Lady*, Coburn took a view of Hardwicke, near Pangbourne, the house James had in mind when he wrote the novel's opening. Hardwicke is Jacobean, like Poynton. (Alvin Langdon Coburn, 'The English Home,' *The Novels and Tales of Henry James: The Portrait of a Lady*, vol. 1. New York: Charles Scribner's Sons, 1907, frontispiece. Courtesy of the Trustees of the National Library of Scotland.)

principles of the House Beautiful. Poynton contains all the accoutrements of a well-decorated, 'aesthetic' late nineteenth-century home, a fact that would have been readily recognised by contemporary readers. James's rendition of Poynton is masterful insofar as it subtly manages to imply that the house would have been held up as a superior specimen by any contemporary manual on interior decoration. According to Charlotte Gere and Lesley Hoskins,

> Wilde's most significant contribution to interior decoration was the notion that interior style should be a form of personal expression; rather than follow any closely defined rules, it was regarded as valuable to develop one's own ideas. The 'House Beautiful' could be created through an eclectic mix of antique and modern, with furniture, decorative arts and textiles perhaps imported from the East or made in Britain [or America, i.e. native to the country in which the householder lived],

5.5 Like Mrs Gereth's collection, the Wallace Collection was tastefully eclectic. Coburn photographed it for the New York Edition. (Alvin Langdon Coburn, 'Some of the Spoils', *The Novels and Tales of Henry James: The Spoils of Poynton, A London Life, The Chaperon*, vol. 10. New York: Charles Scribner's Sons, 1907, frontispiece. Courtesy of the Trustees of the National Library of Scotland.)

together with family heirlooms, souvenirs and personalia, selected and placed with an eye for colour and harmony to form a pleasing whole.[70]

Mrs Gereth, then, would typify the householder Wilde describes; the beauty and splendour of the spoils amassed at Poynton are a tribute to her own taste:

> she never denied, there had been her personal gift, the genius, the passion, the patience of the collector – a patience, an almost infernal cunning, that had enabled her to do it all with a limited command of money. There wouldn't have been money enough for any one else, she said with pride. (*N4* 220)

According to Wilde, a beautiful house is furnished with attractive, useful objects, and privileges simple elegance over gaudy styles.

Late nineteenth-century collectors chose pieces with a view to composing a harmonious whole by selecting from various styles. One might describe this method as synthetic eclecticism.[71] The vogue was to select broadly from a palette of styles and to bring them together harmoniously. A house should give the impression of containing not a collection of individual objects, but a harmonious arrangement of eclectic pieces. Unlike collectors of previous eras, the late nineteenth-century collector did not seek out a single style and then buy only from that one. Decorators introduced the custom of having a different style for each room: 'Gothic', 'Elizabethan', or 'Old English' for the dining room; 'Queen Anne', 'Chippendale', or 'Louis XVI' for the drawing room; with pseudo-Elizabethan furniture for the library. A fashion arose in the 1880s for Japanese fans and screens and blue and white porcelain, in conjunction with bamboo and lacquer furniture, a taste to some extent influenced by Whistler's paintings.[72]

Poynton's 'things' are eighteenth-century Louis Quinze brasses, 'Venetian velvets just held in a loving palm . . . cases of enamels . . . cabinets', 'old golds and brasses, old ivories and bronzes, and fresh old tapestries and deep old damasks', a 'great Italian cabinet', a brocaded sofa, a room 'all sweetest Louis Seize', an ivory Maltese Cross and a Venetian lamp in the form of Atlas hunching under his globe (*N4* 226, 250, 259, 261, 264). Poynton's style

> was written in great syllables of colour and form, the tongues of other countries and the hands of rare artists. It was all France and Italy, with their ages composed to rest. For England you looked out of old windows – it was England that was the wide embrace. (225)

The heterogeneous contents constitute a harmonious collection of tasteful and personal items: 'the quiet air of it was a harmony without a break' (264). James's description is reminiscent of Wilde's description of Lord Henry Wotton's house in Mayfair with its 'long-fringed Persian rugs', 'large blue china jars' and a 'Louis Quatorze clock' (W 45). Edouard Roditi believes Poynton's collections were 'very much of the same types and quality as those that decorated Dorian Gray's home'.[73] Millicent Bell has suggested that in presenting Poynton, James did not resort 'to exact particulars gathered from a gracious house he was familiar with. However specific his actual memory of one or another place, he preferred to suppress rather than exploit its details.'[74] This allusive and elusive style was, she argues, part of the development of James's technique and followed Balzac's example. If this is accurate, why did he not apply this technique evenly, that is, why is Waterbath described more specifically than Poynton? Further, why does James give us the key to the identity of the 'real' Waterbath in his notebooks? There, James compares Mrs Gereth's artistic anguish at Waterbath to his own experience while visiting Fox Warren, a large red-brick house in Surrey, built by Charles Buxton in the 1850s. James follows his critique of the distressingly 'Philistine', 'tasteless', 'hideous' Fox Warren with the self-conscious excuse, 'I didn't mean to write the name' (*Notebooks* 79–80). Why did James prefer to 'suppress' the details of the gracious house that inspired Poynton when he was so honest about Waterbath?

The spirit of the time at which *The Spoils of Poynton* was written was one of suppression, particularly with respect to things relating to Wilde. James's closeness to Gosse and Gosse's closeness to Ross are good reasons for being wary of attracting attention. The novel's very theme is the intricate web of the material and the personal, objects and subjects, and the manner in which even people with the best intentions may be entangled in this net. And this, too, is part of the story of *The Spoils of Poynton* and James's covert connection to Wilde and their shared social circles. Although not directly connected to the Wilde trial, an astounding number of James's friends and acquaintances were also friends of Wilde and Douglas. Their social worlds intersected like Venn diagrams. One of the places their circles met was at Clouds, a country house in Wiltshire owned by members of a select society called the Souls (Figure 5.6). Charlotte Gere's and Jane Abdy's identification of the house that may have inspired Poynton hints at a very valid reason for James's suppression and sheds light on James's supposedly innocuous title change.[75]

5.6 Clouds House from the south, c. 1885. (Photograph by William Weir. Courtesy of Mrs Helen Brandon-Jones.)

The Souls consolidated as a group around the mid-1880s, and their distinctiveness from other social circles such as the Marlborough House Set resided in their resolutely anti-philistine tone. The Souls had a civilising influence on English society: 'In their homes and at their country house parties writers, artists and poets conversed with aristocrats and politicians.'[76] Despite the clannish nature of English society, James, Wilde, H. G. Wells, Morris and Burne-Jones were guests. Until then, the division between the artistic and aristocratic social strata was 'thought too wide for society to risk. But the Souls bridged it.'[77] The group was largely composed of cultured, aristocratic politicians and their wives. Women dominated Souls society, yet the most famous members of the group were Arthur Balfour,[78] leader of the Tory Party and later Prime Minister, and George Curzon, his Viceroy of India. In 1894, Wilde wrote to Douglas that he had attended a play 'in the Royal Box with the Ribblesdales, the Harry Whites, and the Home Secretary' (*LW* 622),[79] other members of the Souls. In 1891, Wilde had dedicated 'The Star-Child' in *A House of*

Pomegranates to Margot Tennant, who later became the Home Secretary's wife; she was also a friend of James. Lady Elcho (née Mary Wyndham) introduced to the group a number of 'honorary Souls' including Edith Wharton, James and Wilde.

> James was the 'occasional Soul' whom every hostess delighted to entice to her house . . . but he remained determinedly an observer, not a participator. He was like Oscar Wilde, one of the few whom the Souls pursued but failed to ensnare – he preserved the cherished detachment of the creative artist.[80]

James repeatedly visited the Wyndham houses, Clouds (near Salisbury in Wiltshire) and Stanway (in Gloucestershire) (*L4* 506).[81]

'I spent 2 days, in the autumn, at a country house with B[alfour] & Wilfrid Blunt,' James told William on 20 February 1888 (*LL* 199). James omitted from his letter that Lord Alfred Douglas, a cousin of the Wyndhams, had also been there with his mother, the Marchioness of Queensberry.[82] Likewise, James passed over the fact that the locale in which he had visited this extraordinary collection of people was not just 'a country house', but Clouds House. James had been at Clouds at a crucial time, for it was on this weekend that Blunt and Balfour had discussed Irish nationalism and Balfour's vigorous enforcement of the Irish Crimes Bill. Balfour (then chief secretary for Ireland) was publicly taken to task for his views by Blunt, who supported the Irish cause. James later wrote that he had 'feared since that I shld. be called upon to testify in regard to that visit [to Clouds] – what passed between them – Blunt's allegations having since made it historical. . . . It all comes back to *race* . . .' (*LL* 199). A different debate involving Blunt had passed into Wilde's personal history. Blunt was the founder of the Crabbet Club, a bachelor set that met annually and defined itself as 'a convivial association which had for its object to discourage serious views of life by holding up a constant standard of its amusements'.[83] Wilde was present at the 1891 meeting, where he was attacked by George Curzon who, Blunt recalls, 'did not spare [Wilde], playing with astonishing audacity and skill upon his reputation for sodomy and his treatment of the subject in *Dorian Gray*'.[84] In response, Wilde delivered a version of the legendary speech on 'the love that dare not speak its name' that he would repeat in the dock in 1895. After Wilde's death, Blunt remembered him as the most brilliant talker he had ever encountered, a man much sought after by London's high society 'and especially the "Souls" . . . because they knew he could always amuse them, and the pretty women allowed him great familiarities, though there was no question of love-making.'[85]

Clouds resembles Poynton in four respects: its location, the style of its interior decoration, the devastating fire that destroyed it, and the remarkable similarities between the house's owners and the owners of Poynton. Like James's fictional house, Clouds is in 'the south of England' and is about 'eighty minutes' from London by train (N4 219, 390). Built in 1885 of green sandstone and red brick by Philip Webb, a partner in Morris & Co., Clouds was an £80,000 custom-built ancestral home. The architectural style – an amalgam of the local traditional style, Gothic Revival and monumental classicism – was contrived to suggest a dwelling adapted to the whims and rationales of successive generations. Clouds differs from Poynton externally insofar as it is not 'early Jacobean, supreme in every part' (N4 219).

Clouds was owned by Percy and Madeline Wyndham. In 1877, James reviewed G. F. Watts's portrait of *The Hon. Mrs Percy Wyndham* (Figure 5.7) at the Grosvenor Gallery and deemed it a 'portrait of an admirable model', a 'sumptuous picture' which made her look 'as if she had thirty thousand a year . . . she does; . . . dressed in a fashion which will never be wearisome; a simple yet splendid robe, in the taste of no particular period – of all periods.'[86] James and Wilde almost certainly met at this Grosvenor exhibition. As her painting suggests, Mrs Wyndham was a woman of exquisite taste with a 'captivating jumble of genius, beauty and charm'.[87] Gere and Abdy suggest her as a possible model for Mrs Gereth and James's review supports this claim, revealing that he appreciated Mrs Wyndham's timeless dress sense.

During his visit to Clouds in 1887, James toured the house with Mrs Wyndham and a local architect.[88] Clouds, like Mrs Wyndham, gave the impression of timeless taste. The Wyndhams spent the first half of their married life – twenty-five years – planning and building Clouds. Similarly, Poynton is the result of the Gereths' joint collecting effort, 'twenty-six years of planning and seeking' (N4 219). Although William Morris helped decorate Clouds, the house was unusual for the period, insofar as it made little use of colour in its decoration:

> the panelling was of unstained oak; the walls were mainly white, with here and there a Morris paper; the curtains were of Morris's silk and woolwoven 'tapestry' in shades of blue except in the drawing-room where they were plain white cloth. Morris carpets provided the only note of colour in the rooms.[89]

5.7 George Frederic Watts, *The Hon. Mrs Percy Wyndham* (Private Collection.)

Clouds wears its name well: the overall effect is luminous and light, unlike the traditional dim Victorian décor (Figure 5.8). Likewise at Poynton 'there were not many pictures – the panels and the stuffs were themselves the picture; and in all the great wainscoted house

5.8 Clouds House drawing room, c. 1892. (Photograph by Whitcomb & Son. Courtesy of Lord Max Egremont.)

there was not an inch of pasted paper.'[90] Wilde recommended wainscoting in his 'House Beautiful lecture' (*W* 915). The emphasis is on the creation of a harmonious yet eclectic whole, not on the specific value of individual pieces. The morning, drawing and dining rooms at Clouds were decorated with Oriental blue and white dishes and jars. Similarly, Poynton's things include 'rare French furniture and oriental china' (*N4* 227). In 1889, Clouds was gutted by a fire that had been prophesied by 'a mysterious old woman'.[91] By 1892, after the Wyndhams' restoration efforts, Clouds rose from the ashes.

The similarities between Poynton and Clouds are compounded by the events of 1895. Two members of the Souls, George Wyndham and Arthur Balfour, were implicated in the Wilde trial. George, an MP, was Madeline Wyndham's son and Lord Alfred Douglas's cousin. George's wife was Sibell Grosvenor, the belle who had been at the heart of the intrigue that was the germ for James's 'The Path of Duty' (1884).[92] Douglas went to see George Wyndham to ask whether Wilde's arrest was inevitable. Though many thought Douglas would also be arrested, George Wyndham wrote to his father, Percy Wyndham, that he knew on the authority of Arthur Balfour, who has been told the case by the lawyers who had all the papers, that Wilde is sure to be condemned, and that the case is in every way a very serious one, involving the systematic ruin of a number of young men. Public feeling is hostile to him, among all classes. There is no case against Bosie [Alfred Douglas] . . . Men like Arthur [Balfour] and Lord Houghton, who have spoken to me, speak in kind terms of him; but are unanimous in saying that he had better go abroad for a year or two . . . Whatever is proved, it is common knowledge in London that there was a sort of secret society around the man Taylor.[93]

Wyndham discussed the Wilde trial with Rosebery, Balfour and Lord Houghton, all of whom were James's close acquaintances. In March 1895, James visited Lord Houghton, also a friend of Wilde's, and wrote to Gosse about it.[94] In July, James dined with Rosebery and, separately, with Horatio Forbes Brown, J. A. Symonds's literary executor.[95] In a letter, he noted that Brown had been staying with Lord Ronald Gower, who was in James's opinion, 'a shady character'.[96] A year earlier, Drumlanrig, Rosebery's private secretary and Lord Alfred Douglas's eldest brother, had committed suicide, perhaps out of fear of 'blackmail over his relations with Lord Rosebery, of which his father had long been suspicious'.[97] 'Rosebery considered doing something to help Wilde . . . during his initial prosecution of Queensberry for libel, but was warned off by Arthur Balfour, the Chief Secretary, who claimed such interference would be a bad political decision which might cost the Liberals the election.'[98] As Michael Foldy concludes,

> the fact that Balfour, a very influential and respected MP, as well as a major player in the Conservative opposition to Rosebery's government, was at this early date closely following the developing situation surrounding the trial, indicates just how important and potentially explosive the case seemed to many in the highest government circles.[99]

Coincidentally, another trial involving homosexuality was playing itself out at the same time as the Wilde trial. Countess Russell had sued her husband, Lord John Francis Stanley Russell, for divorce on the grounds of cruelty in 1891 and was now suing for restitution of matrimonial rights. The Countess accused her husband of homosexual conduct with a 'Mr X'[100] who, she said, 'was visited in his bedroom in the small hours of the night and morning on four separate occasions by Lord Russell'.[101] The Wilde and Russell cases were reported side-by-side in the papers and thus appeared to rein-force each other. *The Morning Post* literally paralleled the cases (Figure 5.9).

Brother to Bertrand Russell, Lord Russell was sent down from Balliol in 1885 because of an obscene letter he had written.[102] The incident was alluded to in Russell's first matrimonial trial; the prose-cution attempted to connect the charge of homosexual conduct with Russell's actions at Oxford in order to show that Russell 'was a man who was addicted to such practices'.[103] Russell's third wife was Elizabeth von Arnim, a writer and social friend of James.[104] According to Douglass Shand-Tucci, George Santayana, who had studied at Harvard under William James, had 'an intensely physical affair' with Russell in 1894.[105] Bertrand Russell's *Autobiography* turns a blind eye to his brother's difficulties and the widespread interest in the Wilde trial: he claims that on a visit to America in 1896 no one seemed to know about the Wilde trial.[106] Countess Russell was advised to sue her husband by Sir Edward Clarke, Wilde's lawyer. Lord Russell's lawyer was Sir Henry James, QC.[107] As if it was not enough that his friends at Clouds were peripherally involved in the century's most scandalous trial, James had to bear the burden of seeing a name similar to his own appear daily in the press in connection with another trial involving aristocrats and homosexuality. *The Morning Post* and the *St James's Gazette* both printed Sir Henry James's comments in some detail, as did the legal reports.

Social relations and pressures converged upon James in 1895; as a result, sexual, personal, artistic and financial anxiety pervades *The Spoils of Poynton*. James's Preface to the novel invites a psychomate-rialist interpretation: 'a lively mark of our manners indeed the diffu-sion of this curiosity and this avidity [for collecting], and full of suggestion, clearly, as to their possible influence on other passions and other relations' (LC2 1142). Such a comment mirrors the creative *modus operandi* and opinions James describes in his Notebook com-mentaries on *The Spoils of Poynton*. Though the novel's narrative voice aligns itself with Mrs Gereth's tasteful aesthetic, it nevertheless questions her avarice and fixation on 'things' through Fleda. In the Preface, James symptomizes this as a common malady of the age. Irony, then, is a subtle tool skilfully applied to Poynton's *culte de l'objet* as much as to Waterbath's *kitsch*. James confides that materi-alism was, for him, the subject of the novel: 'one thing was "in it," in the sordid situation, on the first blush, and one thing only' and this

CENTRAL CRIMINAL COURT.—*Tuesday.*

(Before the RECORDER.)

Alfred Bellamy, 25, chemist, and *Lucie Bellamy,* 28, cook, were severally indicted for stealing a clock and other articles, value £40, the property of John Biddulph Martin. There were other charges of stealing the property of Louis Henry Moyse.—Mr. Hurrell prosecuted.—The prisoner Lucie Bellamy obtained a situation with Mr. Martin, who resided at Hyde-park, as cook, and within a few days disappeared with her employer's property, which her husband, the male prisoner, pledged. It was alleged that the woman had obtained other situations in the West-end, and had acted in a similar way.—The Jury found both the prisoners guilty.—It was stated that the male prisoner had been convicted previously.—The Recorder sentenced the man to three years' penal servitude, and the woman to nine months' hard labour.

(Before the COMMON SERJEANT.)

Frank Reid, labourer, pleaded guilty to burglary and to being in the possession of house-breaking implements by night.—Mr. De Michele prosecuted.—On the early morning of the 3rd inst. Police-constable Jackson, 186, P Division, who was wearing silent boots, came unexpectedly upon the prisoner in the act of forcing a window in the area of the house of the prosecutor with a "jemmy." The house was situate in Central-hill-road, Upper Norwood.—The prisoner, who had been several times convicted previously, was sentenced to three years' penal servitude.

In the case of *James Slater,* 42, labourer, indicted for publishing a libel of and concerning the Right Hon. Baron Henry de Worms, Mr. Percival Clarke, for the defence, applied for a postponement of the trial until the next Sessions, on the ground that the prisoner had not yet had time to prepare his defence, and had material witnesses to call who were not at present in London.—After arguments had been heard, the Common Serjeant said that the matter was a serious one, as an accusation was made against a gentleman occupying a public position, and it was in the interests of all parties that the case should be speedily disposed of. He would fix the case for Saturday next, and in the meantime the prisoner would have an opportunity of consulting with his legal advisers with respect to what course he should adopt.

The Grand Jury returned true bills against Oscar Wilde and Alfred Taylor for misdemeanour.—Sir Edward Clarke, Mr. Charles Mathews, and Mr. Travers Humphreys have been retained for the defence of Wilde ; and Mr. Grain and Mr. Paul Taylor for Taylor.

THE RUSSELL MATRIMONIAL SUIT.

Yesterday Baron Pollock and a Special Jury resumed in the Probate, Divorce, and Admiralty Division, the hearing of the case of "Russell v. Russell." The petition was that of Mabel Edith Countess Russell, of The Cottage, Bray, for restitution of conjugal rights. The respondent, Earl Russell, sought a judicial separation, alleging cruelty.

Mr. Murphy, Q.C., Mr. A. C. Gill, Mr. Barnard, and Mr. Graham Campbell appeared for the petitioner ; and Sir Henry James, Q.C., Mr. Robson, Q.C., and Mr. H. B. Deane for the respondent.

The petitioner and her mother, Lady Scott, occupied their usual seats at the solicitors' table, while Earl Russell sat at the opposite end.

On his Lordship taking his seat, he said he understood that one of the Jury had been seriously unwell. With the consent of counsel on both sides he was allowed to retire, and the case proceeded with a jury of 11.

Resuming his address to the Jury in this case (which was adjourned over the Easter vacation), Mr. Murphy submitted that Lady Russell was not responsible for what she said as a wife in that suit, though, of course, she was responsible for what she said as the Countess, the learned counsel contended that Lady Russell was perfectly entitled to write what she did when she demanded from her husband an explanation of certain passages referred to in some of the letters before she made the avowal of repentance which he insisted upon before he received her back. He insisted that Earl Russell was endeavouring to get out of paying for the support of his wife by raking up the charge of cruelty against her. He was, the learned counsel continued, making the present charge in order to avoid paying the money in discharge of his duty as a husband towards his wife, and he insisted that Lord Russell ought not now to be heard to say in this action that his wife was bringing the suit simply for an unworthy purpose, that of obtaining money from him. He thought it impossible to put the construction on the Countess's letters that she was making and adhering to the charge against her husband and Mr. Roberts. The husband had refused to see his wife, and she appealed to Mr. Lyulph Stanley to obtain an explanation from her husband of the "terrible things" she had been told, and these "terrible things," he insisted, did not refer to the Roberts incident, but to circumstances said to have occurred at Oxford. Dealing with the letters written by the Countess to the *Hawk* newspaper, the learned counsel said it was for the Jury to say whether a single statement of the sort, apart from other matters, was sufficient to justify a judicial separation. In this case there was nothing whatever suggested which could have caused danger to the health of Lord Russell. Referring to the fact that Lord Russell had employed detectives to obtain evidence against his wife, the learned counsel said the whole object of his Lordship in doing so was to find out something that would enable him to get rid of the expense of supporting a wife whom he otherwise was bound to do, and, in the result nothing could be discovered against her, and, notwithstanding all that had been done by the detectives, Earl Russell's suspicions were like those of Othello towards Desdemona, as the Countess had throughout her career led a perfectly virtuous life. It was admitted that Lady Russell had undoubtedly made some foolish statements, but she certainly had not repeated, as was alleged, the charge which was disproved at the trial. In conclusion, the learned counsel said it was absurd to hold that because a wife made a charge of infidelity against her husband, which was afterwards proved to be false, she was liable to an action for judicial separation. If every wife who made a false charge against her husband was to be treated as Countess Russell there would be plenty of work to do in the Courts of law ; but he expressed a firm opinion that, notwithstanding all that had been said on both sides, the Jury would, in the result, arrive at a satisfactory and an unprejudiced verdict.

Sir Henry James then replied on the whole case. He said if Lord Russell had not taken the steps he had done, and denounced those charges, they never would have been withdrawn, and he would never have been able to take part in any proceedings in this country, nor would he have been able to associate with any human being in this country. He believed the Jury would conclude that Lady Russell, acting under evil and pernicious advice, recklessly made atrocious charges against her husband, and so caused him the keenest pain. That was a matrimonial offence, and an answer to her action. He urged that Lady Russell was personally responsible for odious, foul, and disgraceful suggestions against her husband, and must not seek immunity on the ground of being ill-advised. He proceeded to review the incidents at the first trial, and commented on the action she afterwards took in publishing in a newspaper the statement that she had proof of the charges against her husband. As a fact, Lady Russell had no such proof either in the shape of letters from the Earl's relatives or from any other source. He severely condemned the conduct of Lady Russell in persisting with the charge she made against her husband after it had been proved to be untrue, and her refusing to make, until very late in the proceedings, any retractation of the charges she had made against Mr. Roberts, who, he said, had been made the victim in the case. He strongly insisted that there was no escape—there had been cruelty, and that of the worst description. His learned friend, Mr. Murphy, had endeavoured to tell them that Lady Russell was the person who had been injured, that her husband had inflicted that injury, and for that he ought to be condemned. He cared little whether the Jury would accept the evidence of Roe or not—all he desired was that the Jury should say whether the conduct of Lady Russell and her mother was not cruel conduct, and such as would justify Earl Russell in asking for the relief for which he prayed.

At the conclusion of Sir H. James's speech his Lordship postponed his summing up until to-day.

5.9 The Wilde and Russell cases were reported on side-by-side in the press. ('Central Criminal Court' and 'The Russell Matrimonial Suit', *Morning Post* [London] 24 April 1895, 2. Courtesy of the British Library.)

was that it might illuminate the contemporary compulsion to collect, 'that most modern of our current passions, the fierce appetite for the upholsterer's and joiner's and brazier's work, the chairs and tables, the cabinets and presses, the material odds and ends, of the more labouring ages' (1141–2). This enumeration of material 'passions' reproduces objects similar to those in the title of Cook's guidebook, *The House Beautiful: Essays on Beds and Tables, Stools and Candlesticks.*

Psychologised materialism was to be the cornerstone of the story, though James claims he did not come back to this idea until 'the year 1896', when he was asked to contribute three stories to *The Atlantic Monthly* (1142). James's notebooks and letters show that he had begun to think of the story in 1895 (around the time of the Wilde trial), not in 1896. This factual slip is magnified by his assertion that the artist's effort is the sum 'of so many lapses and compromises, simplifications and surrenders. Which is the work in which he hasn't surrendered, under dire difficulty, the best thing he meant to have kept?' (1144). The slip suggests the surrender of a detail, one of those real-life accretions he so scrupulously sought to divest his story of. James puts himself in Mrs Gereth's position, greedily hoarding his 'things' yet forced to 'surrender' them nevertheless. These 'things' – as much Mrs Gereth's as James's own – are 'the real centre', 'the citadel of the interest' and it is they that give the piece its drama. In language reminiscent of the theatre, James writes from 'my opera-box of a terrace' that the things were personified, 'their common consciousness of their great dramatic part established'. Of course, that James refers to his novel as 'my modest drama' (1145) will prick up the ear of any reader sensitive to the depths of despair to which James had been plunged by the failure of *Guy Domville*. Similarly, the notes for the novel reiterate James's obsessive desire to make the story dramatic, theatrical: he refers to 'act[s]', to 'the "Scene" at Ricks' and vows 'every thing of this kind I do must be a complete and perfect little drama' (*Notebooks* 127, 136, 121).

When James began to outline the novel in his notebooks, English and American society was saturated with the theatrics of the Wilde trial. James's connections to a social set involved not only in the trial, but also, via Clouds, in *The Spoils of Poynton*, were cause for concern. In an effort to dissociate himself from the Clouds set and the commodity culture that Cook's and Wilde's treatises on the House Beautiful advocated, James changed the title of his tale and portrayed the negative aspects of aesthetic materialism that Wilde had come to represent. The *Spoils of Poynton* shares one final similarity with Wilde's world. Mrs Gereth is extremely sensitive to wallpaper and feels a secret pain inflicted by ugliness. During the agonising last moments before his death, Wilde said 'my wallpaper and I are fighting a duel to the death. One or the other of us has to go.'[108] James did not feel an either/or dilemma in this respect. He therefore removed the wallpaper *and* Wilde from Poynton.

NOTES

1. Karl Beckson (ed.), *Oscar Wilde: The Critical Heritage* (London: Routledge, 1970) 178.
2. 'The Importance of Being Earnest', *Illustrated London News* 9 February 1895, 227.
3. Adams, *Letters* 328.
4. In a letter to Gosse on 28 April 1895, James refers to accounts of the Wilde trials in the evening's halfpenny papers (*L4* 12). Ed Cohen compares the coverage of the trials provided of morning and evening newspapers in *Talk* 251–2.
5. Ellmann, *Oscar Wilde*, 412.
6. 'The Wilde Case', *Morning* [London] 25 April 1895, 2.
7. W. James, *Correspondence* 8: 343.
8. Stanford Patrick Rosenbaum, '*The Spoils of Poynton*: Revisions and Editions', *Studies in Bibliography* 19 (1966), 162, 172. James's revisions have been analysed by Philip Horne, *Henry James and Revision: The New York Edition* (Oxford: Clarendon, 1990); David McWhirter (ed.), *Henry James's New York Edition: The Construction of Authorship* (Stanford, CA: Stanford UP, 1995).
9. Cook's book was second only to Charles Eastlake's *Hints on Household Taste. The House Beautiful* was reprinted in 1879, 1881 and 1895 (Burke (ed.), *In Pursuit of Beauty*, 413).
10. Brown, *Sense*, 145.
11. Thomas J. Otten, '*The Spoils of Poynton* and the Properties of Touch', *American Literature* 71.2 (1999), 269.
12. Carolyn Lesjak, 'Utopia, Use, and the Everyday: Oscar Wilde and a New Economy of Pleasure', *ELH* 67.1 (2000), 182–3.
13. Ibid. 182.
14. Linda Dowling, *Hellenism and Homosexuality in Victorian Oxford* (Ithaca, NY: Cornell UP, 1994) 132.
15. David Lodge, 'Introduction', *The Spoils of Poynton*, by Henry James (London: Penguin, 1987) 17.
16. James's other stories for *The Yellow Book* were 'The Coxon Fund' (which includes Frank Saltram, a curiously Wilde-like lecturer and

dresser), 'The Next Time,' and 'She and He: Recent Documents' in the magazine (Edel and Laurence, *Bibliography*, 340–1).

17. A number of Wilde's poems refer to the colour in relation to Aestheticism and Decadence; see, for instance, 'Symphony in Yellow', 'La Dame Jaune', 'Remorse (A Study in Saffron)' and 'In the Gold Room (a Harmony)'.

18. 'Picture by Our Own Yellow-Booky Daubaway Weirdsley, Intended as a Puzzle Picture to Preface of Juvenile Poems, or as Nothing in Particular', *Punch* 2 February 1895, 58.

19. Lena Milman, 'A Few Notes Upon Mr James', *The Yellow Book* October 1895, 72, 74.

20. It is worth noting that James's feelings towards *The Yellow Book* changed considerably in the years after the deaths of Wilde, Henry Harland and Beardsley. For James's rosy-coloured recollections of the quarterly, see *LC2* 1225–6.

21. Quoted in Freedman, *Professions*, 177.

22. Katherine Lyon Mix, *A Study in Yellow: The Yellow Book and Its Contributors* (Lawrence: U of Kansas P, 1960) 147.

23. Ibid. 143.

24. Ibid. 146.

25. W. James, *Correspondence* 8: 340.

26. Mix, *Study in Yellow*, 224.

27. Conrad quoted in Mix, *Study in Yellow*, 224.

28. Crane quoted in Mix, *Study in Yellow*, 224.

29. Edmund Wilson, *The Triple Thinkers and the Wound and the Bow* (Boston: Northeastern UP, 1976) 109.

30. Rayburn S. Moore (ed.), *Selected Letters of Henry James to Edmund Gosse, 1882–1915: A Literary Friendship* (Baton Rouge: Louisiana State UP, 1988) 130. In an 1897 letter, Wilde deemed *En Route* 'most over-rated. It is sheer journalism. It never makes one hear a note of the music it describes. The subject is delightful, but the style is of course worthless, slipshod, flaccid' (*LW* 682).

31. W. James, *Correspondence* 8: 343.

32. *The Morning Post* cost one penny in 1895. Lucy Brown notes that "the London evening papers had a less compelling range of news to offer [than the morning papers] . . . [but did offer] an account of the day's court hearings" (*Victorian News and Newspapers* (Oxford: Clarendon, 1985) 36).

33. W. James, *Correspondence* 8: 356.

34. Ibid. 359.

35. Freedman, *Professions*, 172.

36. W. James, *Correspondence* 8: 359.

37. This article dealt with Alphonse Daudet's impending visit.

38. Henry James, *Selected Letters*, ed. Leon Edel (Cambridge, MA: Harvard UP, 1987) 287.

39. James's notebooks record that it was during this visit that Sturges gave him the idea for the nouvelle that subsequently evolved into *The Ambassadors*. Possibly a model for Little Bilham in *The Ambassadors*, he was also a friend of Whistler, James and Wilde (*LW* 551).

40. Cohen, *Talk*; Michael S. Foldy, *The Trials of Oscar Wilde: Deviance, Morality and Late-Victorian Society* (New Haven, CT: Yale UP, 1997) 59.

41. Philippe Jullian, *Oscar Wilde* (London: Constable, 1969) 57, 59; Ronald Sutherland Gower, *My Reminiscences*, 2 vols (London: K. Paul Trench & Co., 1883). In the 1883 edition of *My Reminiscences*, Gower records several meetings with Wilde; in the 1895 edition there is but one record. In his *Old Diaries, 1881–1901* there is no mention of Wilde whatsoever.

42. *St James's Gazette* 5 April 1895, 3.

43. According to Jonathan Freedman, American journals overflowed with denunciations of Wilde until the end of the trial, when they dropped him altogether ('Aestheticism', 391).

44. Ellmann, *Oscar Wilde*, 515.

45. See also Geoff Dibb, 'Oscar Wilde's Lecture Tours of the United Kingdom, 1883–85', *The Wildean*, 29 (July 2006).

46. *World* 26 December 1883, quoted in Weintraub, *Whistler: A Biography*, 294.

47. 'Mrs Oscar Wilde at Home', *To-day* (24 November 1894), 93–4.

48. Constance Wilde, 'How to Decorate a House', *Young Woman: an Illustrated Monthly Magazine* (London, 1895), 132.

49. O'Sullivan, *Aspects of Wilde*, 155–6.

50. Charlotte Gere and Lesley Hoskins, *The House Beautiful: Oscar Wilde and the Aesthetic Interior* (Aldershot: Lund Humphries, 2000) 98.

51. David P. Handlin, *The American Home: Architecture and Society, 1815–1915* (Boston: Little Brown, 1979) 509.

52. *House Beautiful* September 1896, 1.

53. Pater uses the expression to refer to 'that *House Beautiful* which the creative minds of all generations – the artists and those who have treated life in the spirit of art – are always building together, for the refreshment of the human spirit' (*Appreciations, with an Essay on Style* (London: Macmillan, 1898) 253). Mark Twain's 'The House Beautiful' chapter in *Life on the Mississippi* deals with appalling tastelessness that outdoes even Waterbath's. The finest dwellings on the banks of the Mississippi are not beautiful but 'pathetic sham' containing, among other things, a 'large basket of peaches and other fruits, natural size, all done in plaster, rudely, or in wax, and painted to resemble the originals – which they don't' and a 'shell, with the Lord's Prayer carved on it' (*Mississippi Writings* (New York: Library of America, 1982) 457–61). Mario Praz gives ample illustration of the late nineteenth-century passion for overstuffed interiors in

   An Illustrated History of Interior Decoration: From Pompeii to Art Nouveau (London: Thames & Hudson, 1982) 368–79.

54. Blanchard, *Oscar Wilde's America*, xv.

55. Gere and Hoskins, *House Beautiful*, 110.

56. 'Aesthetic Syllabub', *Washington Post* 24 January 1882, 1.

57. Ibid. 1.

58. Freedman, 'Aestheticism', 385.

59. Kevin O'Brien, '*The House Beautiful*: A Reconstruction of Oscar Wilde's American Lecture', *Victorian Studies* 17.4 (1974), 395.

60. Ibid. 400.

61. Bernard Richards, 'Introduction', *The Spoils of Poynton*, by Henry James, ed. Bernard Richards (Oxford: Oxford UP, 1982) xix.

62. For a highly suggestive reading of Fleda's relation to her family and Mona Brigstock, see Stephanie Foote, 'Henry James and the Parvenus: Reading Taste in *The Spoils of Poynton*', *The Henry James Review*, 27 (2006).

63. Quoted in O'Brien, 'The House Beautiful', 400.

64. Henry James, *The Painter's Eye: Notes and Essays on the Pictorial Arts*, ed. John L. Sweeney (London: Rupert Hart-Davis, 1956) 68.

65. For the frontispiece to *The Portrait of a Lady*, James records that Coburn took a 'slightly nebulous view of the English country house (Hardwicke, near Pangbourne, on the Thames) which I had vaguely and approximately in mind, years ago, for the opening of the *Portrait* (the place belongs to Charles D. Rose, MP, with whom I had been staying there, and I can easily write to them about it)' (*L4* 410). The picture of the house bears a striking resemblance to Clouds. Hardwicke is Jacobean, like Poynton.

66. Hayes, *Henny James*, 263.

67. Adeline Tintner, ' "The Old Things": Balzac's *Le Curé de Tours* and James's *The Spoils of Poynton*', *Nineteenth-Century Fiction* 26 (1972): 440.

68. Millicent Bell, *Meaning in Henry James* (Cambridge, MA: Harvard UP, 1991) 208.

69. Richards, 'Introduction', xxv.

70. Gere and Hoskins, *House Beautiful*, 8.

71. Mario Praz notes that nineteenth-century eclecticism in interior decoration did not privilege objects from a particular period. By 'taking something from one style and something from another, in the end there was no style at all. Non-style was created from an excess of styles, just as all the colors of the rainbow, when mixed together, produce grey' (*An Illustrated History*, 368).

72. Madeline Wyndham – whom I, following Gere, Abdy and Dakers, suggest was a model for Mrs Gereth in terms of her tastes as a collector – owned Whistler's *Nocturne in Blue and Gold*. She loaned it to the

Grosvenor Gallery for its first exhibition in 1877, which James and Wilde both reviewed (E. R. Pennell and J. Pennell, *Whistler*, 154). James sent Whistler a copy of *The Spoils of Poynton* (*L4* 43).

73. Edouard Roditi, *Oscar Wilde* (Norfolk, CT: New Directions, 1947) 103.

74. Bell, *Meaning*, 207.

75. Charlotte Gere and Jane Abdy were the first to propose that Clouds might be Poynton's 'fictional equivalent' (Gere and Abdy, *The Souls* (London: Sidgwick & Jackson, 1984) 90–91). This suggestion was later taken up by Caroline Dakers in *Clouds: The Biography of a Country House* (New Haven, CT: Yale UP, 1993). Bernard Richards subsequently urged resistance to the temptation to consider Poynton the fictional equivalent of Clouds – despite having made a number of his own suggestions as to the 'real' house that inspired Poynton ('Clouds and Poynton', *Times Literary Supplement* December 17 1993, 15; 'James and His Sources: *The Spoils of Poynton*', *Essays in Criticism* 29.4 (1979)). Margaret Drabble suggests Mentmore as a possible Poynton (*A Writer's Britain: Landscape in Literature* (London: Thames & Hudson, 1984).

76. Angela Lambert, *Unquiet Souls: The Indian Summer of the British Aristocracy, 1880–1918* (London: Macmillan, 1984) 50.

77. Ibid. 50.

78. In 1891, Wilde suggested an 'entrancing and delightful' dinner with Balfour, Lady Elcho and Mrs Grenfell (*LW* 477).

79. 'The Ribblesdales' were Thomas Lister (Baron Ribblesdale) and Charlotte Monkton Tennant, the sister of Margot Asquith (née Emma Alice Margaret Tennant). The "Harry Whites" were the American ambassador to Italy and Paris, and his wife, Margaret Stuyvesant. James knew them both. The Home Secretary was Herbert Henry Asquith (Liberal Prime Minister 1908–16). In 1894, he married Margot Tennant.

80. Gere and Abdy, *Souls*, 160.

81. In December 1908, James reported that Wharton was having 'the Time of her Life' (*L4* 506) in London, that she had 'seen everyone and done everything', and that she attended 'some great houseparty away off in the Midlands (at Stanway – the Elchos')'. Wharton listed Balfour, Lord Ribblesdale, Lord and Lady Elcho, Gosse and 'Dear Henry J.' as guests at the Waldorf Astors's party at Cliveden a week before (Lyall H. Powers (ed.), *Henry James and Edith Wharton: Letters, 1900–1915* (New York: Scribner's, 1990) 11). Until the Waldorf Astors purchased Cliveden, it was owned by Lord Ronald Gower's family.

82. Lambert, *Unquiet Souls*, 60–1. James was a guest at one of the Wyndhams's first parties at Clouds, held during the first week of September 1887 (Dakers, *Clouds*, 124).

83. Gere and Abdy, *Souls*, 72. Wilde was present at the 1891 Crabbet meeting but was given his own room while the other men slept three to a room. Lambert surmises that James was not invited to join the Club because Blunt found his conversation boring (*Unquiet Souls*, 135; see also Dakers, *Clouds*, 125).

84. Blunt quoted in Ellmann, *Oscar Wilde*, 302.

85. Wilfrid Scawen Blunt, *My Diaries: Being a Personal Narrative of Events, 1888–1914* (London: M. Secker, 1922) 1: 375.

86. James, *Painter's Eye*, 142–3.

87. Gere and Abdy, *Souls*, 83.

88. Dakers, *Clouds*, 128.

89. Gere and Abdy, *Souls*, 88.

90. Henry James, *Novels, 1896–1899: The Other House, the Spoils of Poynton, What Maisie Knew, the Awkward Age*, ed. Myra Jehlen, vol. 4 (New York: Library of America, 2003) 226.

91. Gere and Abdy, *Souls*, 87.

92. In this story, Lady Vandeleur, who represented Sibell Grosvenor, discusses 'the question of how a London house whose appointments had the stamp of a debased period (it had been thought very handsome in 1850) could be "done up" without being made aesthetic' (*CS3* 151).

93. Quoted in Karl Beckson, *The Oscar Wilde Encyclopedia* (New York: AMS, 1998) 22.

94. Rayburn S. Moore (ed.), *Selected Letters of Henry James to Edmund Gosse, 1882–1915: A Literary Friendship* (Baton Rouge: Louisiana State UP, 1988) 125.

95. Henry James, letter to Mrs Daniel S. Curtis, 3 July [1895], ms unpublished, Dartmouth College Library.

96. Ibid.

97. Ellmann, *Oscar Wilde*, 402.

98. Foldy, *Trials*, 30.

99. Ibid. 58.

100. John Francis Stanley Russell, *My Life and Adventures* (London: Cassell, 1923) 169.

101. Ibid. 169.

102. Ibid. 107.

103. Ibid. 169.

104. See James's letter to Hugh Walpole, which mentions her as well as Wilde's friends Max Beerbohm and Robert Ross (James, *Dearly*, 224).

105. Douglass Shand-Tucci, *The Art of Scandal: The Life and Times of Isabella Stewart Gardner* (New York: Harper Collins, 1997) 87.

106. Bertrand Russell, *The Autobiography of Bertrand Russell*, 3 vols (London: Allen & Unwin, 1967) 1: 205–7.

107. Sir Henry James (1828–1911) was a lawyer, statesman and first Lord James of Hereford. He was a friend of Millais, Dickens and other artists (Leslie Stephen (ed.), *Dictionary of National Biography* (London: Oxford UP, 1885–1900) 359–61).
108. Ellmann, *Oscar Wilde*, 546.

CHAPTER 6

'A NEST OF ALMOST INFANT BLACKMAILERS': THE END OF INNOCENCE IN 'THE TURN OF THE SCREW' AND *DE PROFUNDIS*

> I was so typical a child of my age, that in my perversity, and for that perversity's sake, I turned the good things of my life to evil, and the evil things of my life to good.
>
> *De Profundis* (LW 732–3)

> Had I committed a crime against nature when my own nature found peace and happiness thereby? If I was thus, surely it was the fault of my blood, not myself. Who had planted nettles in my garden? Not I. They had grown there unawares from my very childhood.
>
> *Teleny: Or, the Reverse of the Medal, A Physiological Romance*[1]

In the preceding chapters, I have argued that artistically and professionally, James's and Wilde's careers resemble each other far more than has been thought. In the early 1880s, James made the transatlantic aesthete his own despite the figure's increasing association with Wilde. Though James privately dissociated himself from Wilde's artistic, sexual and identity politics, vestigial markers remain apparent in James's fiction and were remarked on by his critics. In the late 1880s and early 1890s, Wilde situated his art theory in reaction to that of James and Whistler, defining an oppositional aesthetic through a process of imaginative review-as-revision that aimed to mitigate Realism's vivisectionist tendencies. By the mid-1890s, James and Wilde's similarities came into focus through their plays' shared investment in the ontology of modern selfhood, and their desire to elaborate a language to describe this emergent identity. With Wilde's trial and imprisonment, the relationship between the two altered once again. As the previous chapter demonstrates, James was publicly unsupportive of Wilde and eager to shroud in narrative silence and equivocation the long-standing history of their common interest in English society, interior decoration and commodities. In this final chapter, I want to return to the fallout of Wilde's trial in order to examine its personal and psychological implications, and to argue further that these have specific and powerful implications for the narratives James and Wilde subsequently wrote. 'The Turn of the Screw' and *De Profundis* were both written in 1897, in the wake of the upheaval James called 'our earthquake' (Edel 4: 139). They dramatise the profound ambivalence each author felt towards the other and, ultimately, towards Aestheticism. The irrevocable pall Wilde's trial and imprisonment cast over the landscape of aesthetic culture caused a crisis in post-1895 Aestheticism that is manifest in both narratives' radical reassessment of the movement's central tenets, particularly its uncoupling of the aesthetic and the moral.

Long the seat of tantalising artistic and erotic ambiguities, Anglo-American Aestheticism of the 1870s and 1880s has often eluded definite recognition of its potentialities. With the advent of Wilde's trial, Aestheticism's playful and productive elusiveness was forced to account for itself, for what it represented and encouraged. Paterian impressions were cross-examined, fictions probed for facts, art interpreted as the transcript of life. By the end of May 1895, Aestheticism's fig-leaf, so to speak, had been removed and Wilde was in prison.[2] Thoroughly disgraced by a trial that linked it to tendencies of the most reprobated variety, Aestheticism was thrown into an unmitigated state of crisis. The movement had weathered crises before – most notably in the late 1880s, when Wilde had answered the pervasive call of *quo vadis* by reconfiguring aesthetic culture's creative mode, as I contend in Chapters 2 and 3. This time, however, no one stepped forward to assuage the movement's acute crisis of faith, and Wilde, who had not managed to save himself, seemed unlikely to be able to provide a salvational response for aesthetic culture's intense doubt and internal conflict. Instead of resisting Aestheticism's collapse, Wilde gave into it. In *De Profundis*, he relinquishes the idea that beauty devoid of morality can make life. On the stand, Wilde had been subjected to penetrating questions on the nature of the philosophy advocated in *The Picture of Dorian Gray*, and he had defended what the prosecution called 'the feeling of one man towards a youth, just grown up'[3] as inseparable from his artistic creed. A beautiful young man was, Wilde said, 'necessary to his art and life'. From inside

Reading Jail, Wilde began to see the situation very differently and, in *De Profundis*, he subjected his aesthetic ethos to some harsh questions of his own. This examination amounts not so much to 'a conscious renunciation of his transgressive aesthetic'[4] imposed by the brutality of carceral life, as an inquiry into the failed relationship between art and life, between beauty and ethics. It was in this context of crisis that James, too, returned to the figure of the child – a figure that had remained, until then, unproblematically pure and unalloyed with evil in his fiction – and projected upon it the dark anxieties about the decadent strain that had beset Aestheticism. James's narrative interrogation of Aestheticism radically undermines the premise that beauty is an end in itself and need not be troubled by moral concerns.

'The Turn of the Screw' and *De Profundis* reflect the problems of aesthetic values and moral responsibility which urgently pressed upon late nineteenth-century culture and society. As such, these narratives mark a turning point in James and Wilde's story, and in the story of Aestheticism, for which it is metonymic. These two narratives represent the beginning of the end of Aestheticism's innocence. By projecting the problematic questions Aestheticism was facing onto the child, James and Wilde could interrogate its moral quandaries. In *De Profundis*, Wilde persistently portrays Bosie (Lord Alfred Douglas) as a wanton boy who destroys for sport, or like a child who breaks 'a toy too wonderful for its little mind, or too beautiful for its but half-awakened eyes' (*LW* 773). By making 'little soul[s] . . . a battlefield of struggling forces, good and bad',[5] as one contemporary critic said of 'The Turn of the Screw,' James also engaged critically with the crisis in which Aestheticism was mired. The story's well known opening question – 'If the child gives the effect another turn of the screw, what do you say to *two* children – ?' (*CS4* 635) – thus becomes a manner of interrogating the fate of Aestheticism in the late 1890s.

The two children in this scenario are not only Miles and Flora, but James and Wilde as well, as there is a persistent idiom of puerility at work throughout the James-Wilde relationship. Criticism has long been interested in uncovering the power dynamics at the heart of the James-Wilde relationship,[6] yet the most pervasive expression of this dynamic has gone unnoticed: the child-adult configuration. This oppositional theme is *the* leitmotiv in the authors' association and it is deployed (to varying degrees) in virtually every document of their encounter, as this chapter will reveal. In this last stage of their relationship, James and Wilde manifest their similarities more than ever before and they do so by projecting the range of feelings they generate in each other – feelings that include sympathy, flirtatiousness, and *Schadenfreude* – onto the figure of the child. The child-figure thus becomes a screen for the psychological characteristics of their relationship, as well as the devastating realisations about Aestheticism prompted by Wilde's trial. In both stories, the child-figure's unusual and conspicuous lack of innocence and moral values generates a nightmarish situation for the adult characters, who struggle in vain to control the children. These narratives bring to a dramatic conclusion James's and Wilde's decades-long association and reveal their surprisingly similar final attitudes towards Aestheticism.

By the mid-1890s decadent Aestheticism was already well on its way to choking the movement's milder, more innocent forms and, by the late 1890s, a mouldy, overpowering scent of depravity had irrevocably infused itself into Aestheticism's delicately perfumed pages.[7] 'The bad smell has, as it were, to be accounted for,' James wrote in an 1904 essay that grappled with, among other things, Aestheticism's reputation for vulgarity. 'And yet where, amid the roses and lilies and pomegranates, the thousand essences and fragrances, can such a thing possibly be?' (*LC2* 935). Decadence and Aestheticism had grown up alongside each other like plants sharing the same soil. Over time, decadence's poor but hearty equivalent, immorality,[8] began to encroach until, in the mid-1890s, Aestheticism was choked by the tangle. James and Wilde's decadent turn is not coterminous with the turn of the century, but with 'The Turn of the Screw' and *De Profundis*, which were both written in 1897. James's tale was first published in 1898 and a heavily expurgated version of Wilde's narrative was published by his literary executor in 1905.[9] Together these narratives iterate a modern warning about the perils of amoral beauty. They are cautionary tales that effectively initiate the decline of aesthetic culture and its attendant forms of being. *De Profundis*, in particular, tragically enacts Wilde's prescient 1885 remark that 'artistic life is a long and lovely suicide' (*LW* 272). So it is that in their narratives James and Wilde challenge Aestheticism's central yet antithetical tenets: the belief in the life-affirming value of beauty without reference to its utility or morality, as well as the belief in the socially redemptive power of art and aesthetic contemplation (a principle best articulated by James's pithy formulation 'art makes life'). To notice that these two ideas are mutually exclusive is to take in one of the fundamental characteristics of Aestheticism, namely its essentially oppositional character and its artistic reliance on the tensions and instabilities provoked by the very oppositions on which it rests. There will be more to say about this, and about the crucial importance of this characteristic for James and Wilde, whose relationship, as I have been arguing throughout this book, exemplifies Aestheticism's most typical styles of artistic interaction. We will return to this idea in the conclusion of this chapter but we should begin by examining the way in which these tensions are first articulated thematically in James's and Wilde's responses to each other. These themes are subsequently played out in 'The Turn of the Screw' and *De Profundis* in order to drive narratives of aesthetic and cultural decline.

In the first instance, this chapter parses the authors' consistent deployment of a paradigm of maturity, immaturity and animality with regard to each other. In the second instance, the chapter argues that James and Wilde redeploy this range of impressions in order to criticise the relationship between aesthetic beauty and life. Both are, in the final analysis, critical of Aestheticism's central claim about the disjunction between aesthetic and moral beauty, and eager to dissect the gruesome implications of the end of that thought.

The child-adult paradigm that recurs throughout James's and Wilde's relationship may seem less surprising when we consider that late in life James took comfort in describing himself in the first twenty-nine chapters of his projected autobiography as essentially 'a small boy' accompanied by others. At forty, Wilde still held dear to the belief that 'the young know everything' (W 1245) and that 'to be premature is to be perfect'. The child-adult relationship is certainly one of the most fundamental and universal of human relationships – there is, after all, a great deal of truth in Wordsworth's adage that the child is the father of the man. However, by returning to this trope, James and Wilde deploy a potent signifier for the host of associations and emotions attendant upon childhood.

This begins to explain why Wilde, who was eleven years younger than James, delighted in slighting James for being a fastidious old boy who lacked youthful vigour. In 'The Child Philosopher' (1887), Wilde obliquely alluded to James as a novelist that 'the world has grown weary of' (*SJW* 80). In 'Balzac in English', Wilde reassured himself of his own position by classifying James as a recycler of second-hand themes and hence one of literature's exhausted old timers. Even when Wilde reluctantly acknowledged James's capacity for innovation by calling him the head 'of a school springing up among us' (115), his criticisms swiftly crushed the notion that there was much life in this incipient blossom by arguing that the Jamesian school would never flower. Its dispassion, Wilde asserted, was the worm in the bud: the niggling problem was James's tendency to write 'fiction as if it were a painful duty' (*W* 1074). Wilde thought James's dainty prose was squelched by its exacting attention to its own refinement. The school springing up was in the winter of its life because it 'waste[d]' itself 'upon mean motives and imperceptible "points of view"'. By dint of indulging the cerebral and suppressing the visceral, James had arrived at a literary style that had 'more psychology than passion' (*SJW* 115). By these standards, Wilde's praise for 'The Turn of the Screw' is generous. After reading it in 1899, he concluded, 'James is developing, but he will never arrive at passion, I fear' (*LW* 1118), a comment that has more than a hint of the condescension of world-wise precocity in it. Wilde implicitly presents himself as a clever youth whose vitality paradoxically affords him a position of mature superiority to James who is, after all, still 'developing', still unable to tap the passionate source of primal energy. According to Wilde, 'the young are always ready to give to those who are older than themselves the full benefit of their inexperience' (*W* 965).

We can detect the operation of a similar coping mechanism in James's restless 1893 letters about his play, *Mrs Vibert*. Written in 1890 and discussed in the theatrical press as a comedy of society soon to be performed at the Garrick Theatre, *Mrs Vibert* had been languishing in the limbo of promised but unfulfilled production for two years when the press began murmuring about Wilde's newest play, *A Woman of No Importance*. To James, who was in Paris at the time, the title implied a theme similar to his. The possibility caused him no little concern, as his frantic letters attest. 'Tell me 3 words about Oscar W's piece – when it is produced; and if in particular the *subject* seems to discount my poor three-year-older,'[10] he commanded the actress-producer Elizabeth Robins, visibly troubled by the thought that his more mature drama should be diminished by Wilde's. A few days later, he made another impassioned plea to the dramatist Mrs Hugh Bell. Framing his request in terms of childhood hierarchies, James described himself as a neglected starveling to Wilde's attention-worthy child, saying that 'any stray crust or two about Oscar's play . . . would be equally gobbled . . . And *don't* neglect Oscar! Neglect your children, rather, *for* him!'[11] James's growing anxiety reduced him to further similes of self-deprecation and self-consumption over 'Oscar W's tragedy', as he had begun to call *A Woman of No Importance*. 'I am consumed with curiosity . . . but I eat my heart out in silence.'[12] While all the theatrical world was in a 'strange rhapsody'[13] about 'the entrancing Oscar', as James put it yet another beseeching letter from Paris, James was condemned to sit in silence and beg for 'an echo of it'. James saw *A Woman of No Importance* as soon as he returned to London and was relieved that it was, after all, 'an *enfantillage* – a piece of helpless puerility' (*LL* 264). Returned to his position of lofty maturity, secure in his superior wisdom, James breathed a sigh of relief. He had not been overcome by the Wilde child.

These examples illustrate the puerile, ludic qualities to James's and Wilde's interaction and exemplify the ways in which both authors jostle for position in the adult-child hierarchy. To be child-like was not, however, to be powerless, as James and Wilde both recognised. There is no better example of the influence and authority exerted by the figure of the child than James's longest extant examination of Wilde: a letter he wrote to Mrs Bell on 23 February 1892, in response to the opening night of *Lady Windermere's Fan* three days earlier. James began by using his now usual method, saying 'Oscar's play . . . [is] infantine to my sense, both in subject and in form. As a drama it is of a candid and primitive simplicity' (*LL* 245). There was, he said, 'a perfectly reminiscential air about it – as of things *qui ont trainé*, that one has always seen in plays. In short it doesn't from that point of view, bear analysis or discussion.' James described the play as mixture of youthful verve and musty maturity; his account evokes a paradox of youthful decay similar to that embodied by Dorian Gray. The play's juvenile wit was but a mask for its fundamental staleness, but he thought these deficiencies would not hamper the play's success.

Two days after writing to Mrs Bell, James sent another letter about the opening night to the socialite Henrietta Reubell, who was also a friend of Wilde's. Here again he vigorously applied a paradigm of childhood to Wilde in order to give a manageable structure to his agitated response. Considered in dialogue with each other, these two letters indicate a key moment in James's association with Wilde for they compellingly demonstrate his appreciation for the power inherent in Wilde's child-like pose.[14] James's letters parse the manner in which Wilde embodies the characteristics of 'the child of power', a paradoxical figure James R. Kincaid describes as

somehow in contact with source of primal energy (not excluding sexual energy) adults would like both to deny and claim as our own. This child, then, strikes us as both valuable and dangerous, familiar and very

strange. We are never sure whether to worship this child or spank it . . .
This Romantic child has become central to the way we structure our
world of desire. He reappears throughout the nineteenth century and the
twentieth century as Bomba and Tarzan and a host of other savage children. He is also domesticated, in a variety of middle-class imps, leading
to a parade of mischief makers, recyclings of Kim and Buster Brown . . .
[This child manifests] a willingness to enter treacherous waters. This
child might offer an appealing image of innocence-in-need, a figure
crying out for our hugs and comfort; but he might also be asking for
money and offering in return some stinging social criticism. I'm thinking
of Huckleberry Finn here, of course . . . but ordinarily this child from
'the lower orders' is a little less threatening: think of Tom Sawyer and
Topsy or Hawthorne's Pearl, the Dead End Kids or the Little Rascals.
These children are sliding fast toward bourgeois accommodation, though
they carry some of the appeal of distance.[15]

In his letters, James attested to the child-like ease and dexterity with
which Wilde's drama played with the public. Kincaid's account of the
relationship between the child of power and his adult audience
cogently encapsulates the ambivalent reaction Wilde could elicit.
While James deemed his work powerfully innocent by virtue of its
'primitive simplicity' (*LL* 245), he nevertheless detected how swiftly
it moved to accommodate middle-class audiences' desires for titilla-
tion by performing what he called Wilde's 'usual trick of saying the
unusual' (246).

James keenly observed that Wilde's drama relied on the audience's
complicity in his power play. In fact the audience willingly took
Wilde's puerile repartee seriously so that it could arrogate to itself
something of Wilde's ambiguous decadence and erotic exoticism.
'There is so much drollery', James said of *Lady Windermere's Fan*,
'that is, "cheeky" paradoxical wit of dialogue, and the pit and gallery
are so pleased at finding themselves clever enough to "catch on" to
the ingenious – too ingenious – *mots* in the dozen, that it makes them
feel quite '*décadent*' and *raffiné* and they enjoy the sensation as a
change from the stodgy.'[16] Noting the disparity between the play and
the way in which the audience members perceived it, James further
explains that they 'think they are hearing the talk of the *grand monde*
(poor old *grand monde*), and altogether feel privileged and modern.'
By promising to fulfil the audience's deepest social and personal aspi-
rations (what they want to 'feel'), Wilde's drama encourages them
to imagine their way further into his witticisms, by dangling before

them the reward attendant upon insider knowledge. The discrepancy between real and perceived experience is thus elided by the play's manipulative wit and the audience's complicity. Wilde offers the audience a harmless frisson of decadence and thereby allows it to experience the vaguely dangerous but essentially harmless pleasure of associating with the decadent world he represents. The audience wants to be flattered that it is 'clever enough to "catch on" to' the airy *bon mots* floating by and thinks that these will lift them from their common, 'stodgy' existences to the realm of the *beau monde*'s light refinement. By lowering the level of the dialogue, Wilde lets the audience feel their superiority when, in matter of fact, his cool impishness is a contrivance. His ability to divine the public's inmost desires also allows him to manage them – a detail that does not escape James's shrewd perception that there is something suspect about Wilde's 'ingenious – too ingenious – *mots* in the dozen'.

To dangle enticements before an interested party, to promise but to withhold, to offer pleasure without consummation, to suggest the delightfully risqué while remaining chaste – this is the essence of flirtation. According to Freud, flirtation is in effect a form of risk-avoidance, a method of dodging real social or personal engagement 'in which it is understood from the first that nothing is to happen'.[17] Adam Phillips's *On Flirtation* takes up this idea to describe *Daisy Miller*'s dramatisation of a 'flirtation confusing the relationship between innocence and experience'.[18] As James observes in his letters about *Lady Windermere's Fan*, the strength of Wilde's presentation relies on just this sort of wilful confusion between the real and perceived experience he offers his audience. The play is an extended flirtation that sustains possibilities, rather than actually taking risks.[19] In his essay on flirtation, Georg Simmel describes it as a game 'because it does not take anything seriously'[20] and thus 'relieves the relationship . . . from every burden of a decision'. By deliberately playing on its ambiguities, Wilde's drama succeeds in maintaining a sense of innocence commingled with possibility. The play's relation to its audience is, at heart, a flirtation calculated to produce what James describes as the 'feel' of decadence (not decadence itself), and what Phillips calls 'a modest exposé of excitement as inextricable from tantalization'.[21]

On the opening night of *Lady Windermere's Fan*, Wilde stepped up his game. After the final curtain, he stood before the applauding audience with a green carnation in his buttonhole and a lighted cigarette between the fingers of his mauve-gloved hand. 'Ladies and gentlemen,' he said, 'I have enjoyed this evening *immensely*. The actors have given us a *charming* rendering of a *delightful* play, and your appreciation has been *most* intelligent. I congratulate you on the *great* success of your performance, which persuades me that you think *almost* as highly of the play as I do myself.'[22] Wilde's speech was a deliberate display of irony and self-satisfaction that prompted some members of the audience to respond with righteous indignation. Rather than taking Wilde's ironic detachment as an extension of the play, the conservative drama critic Clement Scott sharply criticised Wilde in the *Illustrated London News*.[23] James was also irritated by the curtain speech but his indignation was directed at the audience itself, not at Wilde, whose ruse he had divined from the first:

> The 'impudent' speech at the end was simply inevitable mechanical Oscar – I mean the usual trick of saying the unusual – complimenting himself & his play. It was what he was there for and I can't conceive the density of those who seriously reprobate it. The tone of virtuous journals makes me despair of our stupid humanity. Everything Oscar does is a deliberate trap for the literalist, & to see the literalist walk straight up to it, look straight at it & step straight into it, makes one freshly avert a discouraged gaze from this unspeakable animal. (*LL* 246)

In the first half of this passage, James reproaches the audience for its hypocrisy, its censure of a flirtatious relationship in which it is complicit. The 'stupid humanity' who succumbed to Wilde's 'usual trick of saying the unusual' were, after all, the same people who had been so quick to flatter themselves 'privileged and modern' for catching the play's decadent witticisms. What dismays James is the public's unflinching duplicity, its unwillingness to acknowledge the nature of its interest in Wilde. In the second half of the passage, James complicates his assessment of the curtain speech by adding to it the metaphor of an 'unspeakable' trapped beast. James further develops the metaphor by making it impossible to discern the identity of the 'unspeakable animal' – is it Wilde, or is it the 'literalist'? Freedman suggests that the latter is the animal because 'in the first half of the sentence, it is Wilde himself who sets the trap for his unwary adversaries.'[24] This clever observation neglects the very real possibility that the obfuscatory prose of James's metaphor is intentional and that he deliberately conflates Wilde and his audience in order to call attention to their mutual involvement. Such a reading is further supported by James's well-known preference for ambiguity – what William James called his brother's inveterate habit of preferring 'the complication of innuendo and associative reference'.[25] James's violent metaphor bundles Wilde and his audience together in a complicitous pact. Wilde and his audience are one: the 'unspeakable animal' is a two-headed creature caught in a trap of its own making. Any lingering doubts as to James's inclination to deploy such a grotesque image will be dispelled by the fact that he used the same metaphor to describe his own failed relationship with the average British theatregoer. Indeed, James explained *Guy Domville*'s failure by implying that it had not been able to attract the middlebrow audiences that flocked to Wilde's plays. 'Everyone who went to see it [*Guy Domville*] at all appears to have gone 3 or 4 times, but the many-headed monster stayed away,'[26] James explained.

Though James claimed that the off-putting events of *Lady Windermere's Fan*'s opening made him avert his 'discouraged gaze' from Wilde, his letters demonstrate that the proceedings actually made him focus his attention more intently. Five days after the opening night, James was still transfixed by, and ruminating over, Wilde's curtain speech. In the interim, his opinion of the night's events had altered completely. He now told Henrietta Reubell that Wilde alone was to blame for what he referred to as Wilde's 'stupid' speech (Edel 4: 45), a notable shift away from the earlier judgement that 'stupid humanity' was partly accountable.

> I was at the *première* on Saturday last and saw the unspeakable one make his speech to the audience, with a metallic blue carnation in his buttonhole and a cigarette in his fingers. The speech, which, alas, was stupid, was only to say that he judged the audience felt the play to be nearly as charming as he did. I expected something much more *imprévu*. (Edel 4: 45)

James reapplies the terms of his earlier letter to Bell but to opposite effect, inverting his original interpretation of Wilde's relationship to his public. The two-headed 'unspeakable animal' that James had previously evoked to describe Wilde's partnership with his audience now resolved itself into 'the unspeakable one' (Edel 4: 45), an unambiguous condemnation of Wilde alone.

The deliberately obfuscatory language of James's letters works to conceal the intensity of his attention to Wilde. While the letters claim that Wilde's 'trap' had sprung without catching James because he was so different from the average members of Wilde's audience, James's actions tell a different story. Indeed, his analytic gestures mimic those of the 'literalist' he so roundly condemns: James walked 'straight up to' Wilde's trap and looked 'straight at it' for five days; he may not have 'step[ped] straight into' it, but he certainly had not sidestepped it. 'I expected something much more *imprévu*,' James snappishly declared to Reubell, hinting at his overwrought feelings towards what he perceived to be dramatic claptrap. James's huffy summation – '*Ce monsieur* gives at last on one's nerves' (Edel 4: 45) – suggests the degree to which he had been figuratively ensnared by Wilde's tantalising performance. Regardless of James's protestations, we can discern a degree of pleasure in the nervous excitement that Wilde provokes in him.

Given the complexity of his response to Wilde, why does James consistently resort to a paradigm of adult-child relations to describe him? I have analysed James's response at some length in order to reveal the pleasure and play, flirtation and frustration inherent in it and to argue by implication that homosexual panic does not do justice to the intricacy and range of feelings that characterise James's reaction. It should be fairly apparent by now that James's and Wilde's use of a paradigm of adult-child relations is symptomatic of the fundamentally flirtatious nature of their relationship, and that the mixed pleasures of their intellectual association turn on a game of ambivalence fixed in childhood. Phillips explains that flirtation spins doubt and ambiguity into nervous tension, and in doing this it 'nurture[s] the child's sense of possible and future selves' and provides a 'mixture of pleasure, frustration and relief'.[27] Flirtation enables the child to find the limits of himself, and thus to define himself. The significance of these pleasant and frustrating encounters, for James and Wilde, is that they enable both of them to define themselves. And it is precisely this type of opposition that drives Aestheticism as a whole.

Until 1895 James always characterised Wilde in two ways: either in an idiom of underdevelopment and childhood – Wilde was 'infantine' (*LL* 245) and 'primitive' – or in terms of 'zoological sociability' (*LC2* 939) – Wilde was 'an unclean beast' (*LL* 135) and 'an unspeakable animal' (*LL* 246). During Wilde's trial, James mobilised the references to beasts and children he usually reserved for Wilde in order to describe his accusers, and thus implicitly sided with Wilde. 'Did you see,' he asked Edmund Gosse, '. . . the wretched O. W. seems to have a gleam of light before him (if it really counts for that!) in the fearful exposure of his (of the prosecution's) little beasts of witnesses? What a nest of almost infant blackmailers!'[28] James's recuperation of the idiom of childhood and animality to describe the Crown witnesses marks a turning point in his relationship to Wilde. This response differs markedly from those of the previous decade-plus, not least because James conflates the two sources of primal energy he regularly used to criticise Wilde in order to manifest his sympathy for him. James's *public* attitude to Wilde during his trial may have been one of 'no mercy'[29] that 'makes for painful reading',[30] but James's *private* stance was somewhat different and it was not one of 'extraordinary cold-bloodedness'.[31] He described the trial as a nightmare qualified by 'a sickening horribility' (*L4* 9), a communal experience of upheaval (Edel 4: 139). They were 'de trop tristes choses' (*L4* 26),[32] he said. In letters suffused with moments of sadness and compassion, James now admitted that Wilde had had 'a really unique kind of "brilliant" conspicuity (wit, "art", conversation – "one of our two or three dramatists, etc.")' (10), but that Wilde was at present 'pitoyable . . . dans un état d'abattement complet, physique et moral . . . [sans] aucune faculté résistante ni récuperative' (26).[33] James's letters to his closest friends attest to his shift towards an appreciation for Wilde that wavers between restrained praise ('I think he may have a "future" – of a sort')[34] and unparalleled enthusiasm ('Quel chef d'œuvre il pourrait faire encore!' (*L4* 26)).[35]

Amid this new-found refrain of sympathy and appreciation in James's letters, a dissonant and distinctive note of *Schadenfreude* can be heard. The sentiment is unmistakable in the comment to William that Wilde's 'fall is hideously tragic – & the squalid violence of it gives him an interest (of misery) that he never had for me – in any degree – before'.[36] And again in James's private indulgence in news about the trials despite his displeasure at their public nature: he breathlessly described the proceedings as 'hideously, atrociously dramatic and really interesting' (*LL* 279), while condemning them as a 'gulf of obscenity over which the ghoulish public hangs and gloats'.[37] This response, too, is a measure of the pervasiveness of the concept of childhood in the James-Wilde relationship since, as Freud explains, *Schadenfreude* originates in childhood, as the pleasurable feeling one derives from seeing someone else make a mistake one has avoided.[38] James undoubtedly derived pleasure from the 'spectacle of the mighty fallen'[39] offered by Wilde's 'hideous human history' (*LL* 279).[40] It is not difficult to see how this reduced, life-size version of Wilde (who had always seemed larger-than-life) held out a particular appeal. Given the depths to which James had fallen in 1895 as a result of his theatrical encounter with Wilde, it is not surprising that he derived some pleasure from seeing Wilde fall harder and lower than he himself had. 'Time has given you your revanche over poor Oscar Wilde,' William James wrote to his brother on 8 April 1895.[41] James responded indirectly to his brother's suggestion in a letter he wrote the same day to Edmund Gosse. There, he refused the idea that there was poetic justice in Wilde's fall by saying that what had happened to Wilde was 'beyond any utterance of irony' (L4 10).

James may have preferred the moral high road, but this was not incompatible with the opportunity that Wilde's compromised position offered him to play the rescuer, a figure prevalent in James's fiction from Roger Lawrence in *Watch and Ward* and Rowland Mallett in *Roderick Hudson* to its supreme figuration in *The Ambassadors'* Lambert Strether. Whether or not we take James at his word, the appeal of the 'wretched' Wilde is not far removed from the appeal of a helpless child, a figure Kincaid describes as offering an engaging picture of 'innocence-in-need'[42] pleading for consolation from sympathetic adults. James explained in the Preface to *What Maisie Knew* that 'no themes are so human as those that reflect for us, out of the confusion of life, the close connexion of bliss and bale, of the things that help with the things that hurt' (LC2 1158). Feelings of sympathy can coexist with *Schadenfreude*, and they did for Wilde and James.

Implicit in the sense of *Schadenfreude* is an uneasy acknowledgement of the precariousness of one's own position. *Schadenfreude* can activate two related responses in us: 'there but for the grace of God go I', or, less charitably, 'better him than me'. If James's response to Wilde tacitly admits his own human vulnerabilities and does so by deploying a wide range of emotional and psychological responses, then it seems needlessly restrictive to read these exclusively in sexual terms. I have indicated in the introduction to this book my reasons for resisting readings that reduce James and Wilde to a case of 'homosexual panic'[43] or 'homosexual self-loathing'.[44] I should add here that the dynamics examined in this chapter reinforce the validity of speaking about historically freighted sexual anxieties and, most importantly, they advocate the recognition of the multivalent nature of James's and Wilde's interaction. In this chapter in particular, I have endeavoured to draw attention to other patterns in the James-Wilde relationship and to the unexpected coexistence of flirtation, sympathy and *Schadenfreude* within these patterns. In doing do, I have been activated by several aims: to reveal the involutions in the authors' figurations of each other, to demonstrate how this complex response is symptomatic of patterns in their narratives and, finally, in Aestheticism itself. In short, there is not a single figure in the carpet, but several.

'Nothing to whack!': Aesthetic Innocence and the Child of Power

I want to turn here to an instance of this patterning in 'The Turn of the Screw'. In this story, as in his relationship to Wilde, James conjoins flirtation, care and discipline and inscribes them within a paradigm of childhood. By placing these startling oppositions at the centre of the adult's caring relationship to the child, 'The Turn of the Screw' dramatically enacts aspects of James's response to Wilde. James's letters depict Wilde as a captivating child-figure who is both manipulative and vulnerable, powerful yet exposed. These characteristics arouse an antithetical response in James, and they prompt an equally mixed reaction from his governess-narrator. 'I remember the whole beginning as a succession of flights and drops, a little see-saw of the right throbs and the wrong' (CS4 642), she writes in the opening lines of her account. Fascinated from the first by her beautiful little charges, she displays her affection for them largely in terms of aesthetic approval – in descriptions of Flora as 'the most beautiful child I had ever seen', and her of Miles as 'incredibly beautiful' (650). Her affection for the children takes the form of an intense desire to defend them from harm. 'I saw my service so strongly and so simply,' she declares. 'I was there to protect and defend the little creatures in the world the most bereaved and the most lovable, the appeal of whose helplessness had suddenly become only too explicit. . . . They had nothing but me' (667). Despite this, her thoughts move seamlessly from the children's perfection ('I was dazzled by their loveliness' (657)) to a violent articulation of the punishment she might impose on them in the name of love and protection:

> Both the children had a gentleness (it was their only fault, and it never made Miles a muff) that kept them – how shall I express it? – almost impersonal and certainly quite unpunishable. They were like the cherubs of the anecdote, who had – morally, at any rate – nothing to whack!

The governess's meditation on punishment turns on a biblical pun about two angels made of beaten gold 'in the two ends of the mercy seat'.[45] Her concern about 'the children's lack of punishable bottoms'[46] (as T. J. Lustig aptly puts it) may be interpreted as an extreme enactment of the Old Testament precept that 'the care of discipline is love'.[47] However, the severity of her concern as well as its brutally graphic language and striking onomatopoeia should give us pause. Can we reconcile affection, protection and *whacking*? Is this loving discipline or masochistic punishment? Is there pleasure in this infliction of hurt, that is, *Freude am Schaden*? 'The Turn of the Screw' consistently makes punishment an ally of care in the same manner that James makes his experience of *Schadenfreude* ancillary to his concern for Wilde. Like James's five-day wonder at Wilde's performance at the opening of *Lady Windermere's Fan* and his circumlocutions about Wilde's 'trap', the more the governess falls 'under the spell' (CS4 657) of the children, the more she becomes wary of their power and willing to enforce what she eerily refers to as 'my discipline' (695). James's personal experience and his narrative both attest to the conflicting response the powerful child elicits in the adult; as Kincaid notes, when it comes to the powerful child, 'we are never sure whether to worship this child or spank it'.[48]

In response to Flora's quasi-confession, the governess enacts her premeditated discipline, but surprisingly enough this punishment does not involve spanking. Instead Flora is isolated and 'locked in safe' (CS4 725) as soon as she reveals her knowledge of the adults' sexual relations. The course of action the governess selects – solitary confinement over spanking – neatly parallels James's personal belief that Wilde should have been put in isolation rather than being sentenced to hard labour (Edel 4: 129). While the governess's relish of her punitive task is palpable, the reader also gets a clear sense of the care that activates her disciplinary impulse. Flora's incarceration is a means of ensuring that what is left of the little girl's innocence remains intact, and the governess's decision to enforce innocence reflects a view prevalent among nineteenth-century protectors of children, that 'the innocence needing protection is so feeble and is beset by foes so numerous and wily that any measures are justified, including putting innocence into protective custody or solitary confinement'.[49] Miles, the governess's other charge, is not incarcerated, but James's narrative nevertheless achieves a tidy symmetry in the penalties it imposes on naughty children through a strategic displacement: the boy may go free so long as the truth about his offence is contained and, as the governess says, 'the horrible letter locked up in my room, in a drawer' (*CS4* 650).

. . .

In 'The Turn of the Screw', Douglas prepares his audience for the governess's narrative by saying that 'the little boy, at so tender an age, adds a particular touch. But it's not the first occurrence of its charming kind that I know to have involved a child' (*CS4* 635). The figure of the child was often invoked in James's and Wilde's pre-1890 stories to represent a *tabula rasa* waiting to be inscribed with meaning, a happy blank blotched by the sins of his fathers, mothers, or those of society writ large. In *Daisy Miller* (1878), the fate of the eponymous heroine is determined by a society that would rather see her dead than defiled.[50] In *The Portrait of a Lady* (1881), Pansy Osmond embodies her father's morbid aesthetic preoccupations and her name, too, reminds us of her flower-like beauty and fragility. In 'The Point of View' (1882), an American goes on at length '*à propos* of the young people' (*CS2* 536), describing them emphatically as 'our other danger.' 'They are often very pretty . . .,' she concedes, 'But the little boys kick your shins, and the little girls offer to slap your face!' (537). In 'The Author of Beltraffio' (1884), Dolcino Ambient (whose name again underscores the air of sweetness he emanates) is the innocent victim of parents too preoccupied with their own aesthetico-moral problems to see the immorality at the heart of their actions. Wilde, for his part, also preferred to depict the child as an innocent. In 'The Canterville Ghost' (1887), order can only be restored to a haunted house if 'a golden girl can win prayer from the lips of sin' (*W* 198). In 'The Young King' (1888), the titular character is mocked and threatened by his adult subjects when he begins to assert his moral values. In 'The Happy Prince' (1888), the eponymous hero gradually sacrifices his body for the sake of the citizens of his town. There are ominous forebodings in these stories of escalating levels of intolerance towards the child.

A conspicuous change takes place in James's and Wilde's fiction after 1890: they begin to invest the figure of the child with ideas of power, nightmare and illicit knowledge, making him a problematic font of primitive drives and desires. Previously an innocent, the child was reconfigured as a threat, and this gloomy figure was further darkened by Wilde's trial. In 'The Pupil' (1891), a precocious lad develops a strong attachment to his tutor but dies of excitement when his neglectful parents propose the tutor take him away. Whether the lad wants 'the care and attention of his parents',[51] as John Carlos Rowe suggests, and finds a surrogate in his tutor, or whether his alliance with his tutor makes them 'like a pair of neglected children, like the brother outcasts they really are',[52] as Millicent Bell believes, the boy's seductiveness eerily foreshadows Miles's in 'The Turn of the Screw'. Moreover, the 'visual and erotic captures and struggles'[53] in 'The Pupil' foreshadow the similarly unsettling dynamics of 'The Turn of the Screw'. In *The Other House* (1896), a little girl is drowned by her father's admirer. In *What Maisie Knew* (1897), bitterly divorced parents use their daughter as a cipher whose value increases or decreases inasmuch as she allows them to provoke each other.[54]

Published a year after *What Maisie Knew*, 'The Turn of the Screw' was, as the reviewer for *Literature* put it, another 'remarkable study of abnormal childhood; but *What Maisie Knew* was a trifle compared to the weird knowledge of little Miles and Flora'.[55] *The Bookman* agreed that 'The Turn of the Screw' was yet 'another study of the same unpleasant kind of fact, but so much more horrible, that it surely marks the climax of this darker mood, out of which Mr James may emerge with a profounder, or perhaps only a bitterer strain.'[56] *The Awkward Age* (1899) realised the reviewer's prediction by thickly enmeshing its children within adult power dynamics and systems of sexual and economic exchange.[57] The peculiar mother-daughter dynamic played out by Mrs Brookenham and little Nanda may owe something to Herodias and Salomé in Wilde's *Salomé* (1893–4), and to the manner in which the child asserts her sexuality and ultimately relegates the parent to a subordinate role.[58] It is significant in this connection that *Salomé* was the only book by Wilde that James still owned when his library came to be catalogued in the 1930s.[59] Salomé is possibly the most iconic embodiment of the paradox of the child of power. In the play's opening scene, before the audience even glimpses her, she is described by other characters in a succession of similes – 'like a dead woman', 'like a little princess' and 'like a dove that has strayed' (W 583, 586). These suggest a precocious, weird eroticism confirmed by her first utterance: 'it is strange that the husband of my mother looks at me like that. I know not what it means. In truth, yes, I know it (586).'

What does this knowing child know? A great deal for someone so little. Likewise, the child-figures in 'The Turn of the Screw' and *De Profundis* are much too old for their age. Symptomatically, Flora's knowledge transfigures her, making 'every inch of her, quite old' (CS4 723) – a physical fulfilment of the preternatural psychological maturity she evinces. In the 1890s, the child is no longer the locus of all that is good and pure, but becomes an ambiguous signifier, an 'erotic enigma'[60] who embodies 'a paradox of innocence and licentiousness in the same character', as Ellis Hanson argues. James R. Kincaid and Kevin Ohi note the dangerous consequences of insisting that the child can be 'both sexual and pure'[61] because the child's 'erotic innocence provides erotic pleasure that can deny itself as such'.[62] The narrative repercussions of 'The Turn of the Screw' and *De Profundis* are several and acute, not least insofar as the child-figure's ostensible wholesomeness almost always results in the adult being accused (as Wilde was and the governess often is, too) of 'a revolting and insidious attempt to corrupt Innocence' (*LW* 702). These consequences are meaningful to us insofar as they intricately interweave the problems of Aestheticism with the same social, cultural and moral dilemmas it had attempted to transcend.

James's and Wilde's narratives are keenly attentive to the wider implications of the naughty-but-nice paradox the child incarnates, and these narratives tie the child's perilous ontology to the hazards associated with post-1895 aesthetic culture. When it comes to children in James's writings, Rowe is correct in observing that criticism is often 'unwilling to engage the ugly truth they reveal'.[63] This ugly truth need not be limited to what the adult does to the child, but must also encompass the reality that, in James's and Wilde's works, children themselves can be malicious actors who, like Miles and Flora, '*play a part* of innocence and consistency' (*CS4* 710, emphasis added).[64] In the following section, I want to explore the idea that the children in 'The Turn of the Screw' are, in fact, aware of their actions and that they consciously manipulate the governess. This assumes, of course, that the governess's record is reliable – a premise that James's story neither nor confirms nor denies. Indeed, 'The Turn of the Screw' famously offers the reader as much backing for the view that the governess is sane and the ghosts are real, as for the view that the governess is a repressed neurotic and the tale is the product of her overheated brain (this is basically the argument put forward by Edmund Wilson's 1924 account, 'The Ambiguity of Henry James').[65] Despite these ambiguities, it has become *de rigueur* to point out the story's conflation of narrative and adult psychosexual uncertainties. However, James's tale offers just as few psychosexual certainties when it comes to the children. What is the child's cathexis? And why is it directed so strongly at the governess? If we go on the assumption that the governess's record is trustworthy, then the children's behaviour seems, at best, weird and, at worst, sexually perverse. Their conduct seems all the more strange given that Miles and Flora are orphans and that they direct their peculiar energies squarely at the governess, the person who has clearly been designated as their ersatz-parent, their caregiver. In *Henry James and the Art of Power*, Mark Seltzer helpfully suggests that the story's 'advertised ambiguities . . . – the undecidable 'choice' between ghost and madness narratives, however taken up – have worked to displace by repeating in another register, this inside – or perhaps too-evident – story of desire, knowledge and power.'[66] By reading 'The Turn of the Screw' and *De Profundis* as stories of *aesthetic* desire, knowledge and power, I argue for a return to the tale's 'inside' ambiguity that reveals the unexpected parallels between the plight of children and the plight of Aestheticism at the fin-de-siècle. The Gothic horror of 'The Turn of the Screw' and *De Profundis* counterpoints moral and aesthetic concerns in order to question their validity. The narratives' shared investment in the interrogation of highly specific cultural dilemmas suggests a powerful and critically unexplored connection between them.[67]

'Bosie wakes up at night and cries like a child for the best haschish' (*LW* 629), Wilde told Robert Ross in early 1895. In *De Profundis*, Alfred 'Bosie' Douglas, who was twenty-one when Wilde met him, combines the physical attractions of a winsome child with an intimate knowledge of adult dissipations. This vivid scene encapsulates the heady mix of immaturity and sophistication Douglas offered Wilde, who referred to him as 'my child' (651), 'sweetest of all boys' (652), and his ideal 'in all the worlds of pain and pleasure'. The pubescent child-figure is thus constructed as partaking of a heightened aesthetic awareness. Wilde explains how he detected this sense within himself 'at the very dawn of my manhood' (729) when he realised that he 'stood in symbolic relations to the art and culture of [his] age'. Just as Flora's name evokes her flower-patterned charm, so Douglas is renamed to evoke his sweet nature: he is Hyacinth, Jonquil, Narcise and Prince Fleur-de-Lys (702, 716). Wilde, following Christ's injunction to consider the lilies of the field ('they toil not, neither do they spin'), thinks the child's 'flower-like life' makes it an ideal to be emulated (750). However, there is a portentous note in Wilde's asseveration that 'for me, . . . flowers are part of desire' (777). The child-figure embodies Aestheticism's moral underdevelopment and stunted growth. Marshalled to represent both darkness and light, blight and bliss, the beautiful child-figures in *De Profundis* and 'The Turn of the Screw' exemplify and extend two central values attributed to aesthetes. The first fundamental value attributed to Aestheticism, especially in its decadent manifestations, is a tendency to live outside the moral realm and to prefer what James calls 'beauty at any price' (*LC2* 908). This is the position taken up by Gilbert Osmond, Mark Ambient and Maggie Verver, as well as Henry Wotton, Dorian Gray and Thomas Griffiths Wainewright in 'Pen, Pencil and Poison', and recuperated by the beautiful child-figures who are associated with innocence despite their cloudy morality. James articulates the second of Aestheticism's central values as that of the hypocritical and manipulative 'modern aesthete, who poses for artistic feelings, but is very hollow' (*L2* 414). His early figurations of the transatlantic aesthete – from Louis Leverett to Morris Townsend and Gilbert Osmond – and the Anglo-American public's perception of Wilde from the late 1870s to the early 1890s indicate that Aestheticism and manipulation were closely twined. The child-figures in 'The Turn of the Screw' and *De Profundis* amplify this characteristic and bring it closer to its tragic climax by revealing the moral vacuity inherent in their handling.

This final chapter thus marks a return to some of the themes that preoccupied us in the first chapter, but they are reconfigured in terms of James's and Wilde's exploitation of the figure of the child. The continuities between the aesthetic young men of the 1870s and 1880s, discussed in Chapter 1, and the beautiful but morally ambiguous children of the 1890s, which are examined here, confirm continuities in Aestheticism's approach. It brings James's and Wilde's association with each other and aesthetic culture to an end by returning them to Aestheticism's beginnings: the authors' initial investment in aesthetic culture was predicated on their shared ability to create narratives for aesthetic young men; returning to this type, they both invest their narratives with darker figurations of youth. Whereas their early narratives ambiguously suggest the aesthetic young man's subversive, dissipated tendencies, in their later fictions it is the figure of the child who is fully invested with the most decadent inclinations.

Both 'The Turn of the Screw' and *De Profundis* seriously question the moral validity of the adults' persistent conflation of the child's physical beauty and moral perfection. On her first encounter with Miles, the governess feels she has looked into his soul by gazing upon his beauty: 'I had seen him, on the instant, without and within' (*CS4* 651), she claims, describing his physical attractions as permeated by an aura of goodness, a 'positive fragrance of purity'. Flora's beauty is 'beatific' (643) and has 'the deep sweet serenity indeed of one of Raphael's holy infants' (644). When the governess and Mrs Grose discuss Miles's misdemeanour at school, Mrs Grose encourages the idea that it would be impossible for beautiful little Miles to be 'an injury' (647) to others: 'See him, Miss, first. *Then* believe it! . . . You might as well believe it of the little lady. Bless her, . . . *look* at her!' Mrs Grose misses the point that morality bears no visual proof, and that seeing is not a means to confirming a child's innocence. Yet the governess also falls prey to this idea, declaring it 'monstrous' (650) that Miles, who 'was incredibly beautiful', 'should be under an interdict'. Although the governess takes him for 'something divine', she is nevertheless rankled by the persistent feeling that 'his indescribable little air of knowing nothing in the world but love' is too studied to be true.[68] Though she soon finds herself repeating Mrs Grose's own incitement – 'My dear woman, *look* at him!' – her account nevertheless registers the fallibility inherent in yoking aesthetic and moral beauty.

'The faith that others give to what is unseen, I give to what one can touch, and look at', Wilde explains in *De Profundis* (LW 732). Like the governess and Mrs Grose, Wilde locates truth in the visual and tangible and he explicitly links this tendency to Aestheticism by invoking one of the movement's earliest proponents. 'Like Gautier I have always been one of those *pour qui le monde visible existe*' (777), he says, in an explanation that forcefully suggests that his artistic worldview and his personal fate are the result of his adherence to the credo of art for art's sake. Even as he unpacks the layers of Douglas's depravity, Wilde (like the governess) shields himself from full acknowledgement of the child-figure's wickedness, holding out the hope that 'so young a life . . . amidst all its ugly faults had still promise of beauty in it' (*LW* 696).

'A burnt child loves the fire': The Child as Aesthetic Topos

In *De Profundis* and in 'The Turn of the Screw', the tropes of Aestheticism – the flame, manipulation and amorality – are persistently evoked and these references function as reminders and warnings of the increasingly problematic nature of the movement's ethical and social qualities. The movement's association with the child is implicit in the sheer quantity of aesthetic allusions, particularly to its most famous formulation, Pater's flame. If, as the Conclusion to *The Renaissance* advocates, 'to burn always with this hard, gem-like flame, to maintain this ecstasy is success in life',[69] then the 'The Turn of the Screw' virtually self-immolates in its own success. As such, James's story vividly enacts Wilde's aphorism 'that a burnt child loves the fire' (*W* 142). This theme is announced in the story's opening frame, in which the rapt audience is held 'round the fire, sufficiently breathless' (*CS4* 635), in imitation of Pater's deathless 'hard, gem-like flame'. Flames, fires and candles accompany the tale's moments of ecstasy, emblematising its passionate sentiment. When Mrs Grose clasps Flora to her breast to protect her from the sight of Miss Jessel, Flora's face has a 'flicker' (718) that prefigures Miss Jessel's appearance, moments later, as a raging emblem of depraved passion. 'She's as big as a blazing fire!' (721), the governess cries. By attaching a distinctly aestheticist topos to the child, Flora becomes a miniature symbol of decadent Aestheticism's corrosive power. The vision of Miss Jessel climaxes with Flora's repudiation of the governess. When Miles appears, the governess takes on Miss Jessel's role as adult keeper of the flame. The governess replicates the topos incarnated by her predecessor by extinguishing the candle (associated with Flora who, despite being 'so markedly feverish that an illness was perhaps at hand' (723), has been put in solitary confinement) and drawing closer to the hearth to 'sit in the glow with my thoughts'. The governess tries to find solace in Miles, who consents to sit with her 'by the schoolroom fire'. As Miles joins the governess by the fire, she feels certain that he 'wanted . . . to be with me', an assertion which, following the day's events, can almost certainly be read in an erotic light. So intricate is James's symmetry of pain and pleasure that when Flora is isolated, Miles is granted the fullest of freedoms (describing his experience self-referentially as one of being 'miles and miles away' (733)). The final appearance of Quint's ghost replicates the terms of Flora's encounter with Miss Jessel but it is the governess, this time, who holds Miles to her breast and feels 'in the sudden fever of his little body the tremendous pulse of his little heart' (736). Although she attempts 'to shade, as it were, my flame' (737) and 'let[s] the impulse flame up to convert the climax' (740), the scene culminates in the fatal fulfilment of Pater's warning that 'a counted number of pulses only is given to us of this variegated, dramatic life.'[70] Miles's pulsing 'little heart, dispossessed, had stopped' (*CS4* 740). The story ends with a dramatic enactment of the perils of moral disengagement by making Miles the victim of an aesthetic passion. Shoshana Felman cogently reads the violence of the governess's grip on Miles as an attempt on her part to recover meaning and power, a purpose that is not far

removed from her desire to give meaning to her life through the aes-
theticisation of her charges.[71] Disengaged from morality, beauty and
pleasure for their own sake take on a distinctly sinister air. 'The Turn
of the Screw' thus brings to a heart-rending conclusion the governess's
aesthetic adventure with her charges.

Wilde also invokes the flame topos in *De Profundis* to represent
the reckless passions of youth as well as suffering alloyed with juvenile intemperance. Wilde called *The Renaissance* 'that book which
has had such a strange influence over my life' (*LW* 735), and he
steadily returns to its most famous image in order to describe
Douglas. In 'Two Loves', Douglas personified same-sex desire as
Shame cloaked in a robe of 'fiery flame' that contrasts the 'mutual
flame'[72] of heterosexual love. *De Profundis* returns to this image and
personifies it: Douglas's face 'flush[ed] easily with wine or pleasure
. . . scorched, as though by a furnace-blast, with shame' (*LW* 710).
Whereas James's children symbolise passionate potential, Wilde portrays Douglas as foul precisely because he fails to live up to the
promise inherent in youth. Douglas perverts the flame-like life he represents by casting it away in favour of lesser enchantments. 'With very
swift and running feet' (*LW* 684), he passes from 'the morning dawn
of boyhood with . . . its clear pure light, its joy of innocence', preferring instead 'the gutter and the things that live in it'. By preferring sensuality to the moments of 'highest quality'[73] Pater describes as
yielding 'a quickened, multiplied consciousness',[74] Douglas distorts
Pater's vision of the fulfilled, aesthetic life as one in which one aims
to 'pass most swiftly from point to point, and be present always at the
focus where the greatest number of vital forces unite in their purest
energy'.[75] Moreover, Douglas's violation is distinctly represented as
an aesthetic infraction against the normal order of things since 'the
war every child of light has to wage' (*LW* 751) is 'against the
Philistines'.

The child-figure's aesthetic violation is endowed with a definite
moral dimension through its explicit failure to defend its beautiful life
from Philistinism. *De Profundis* intensifies this point by comparing
Douglas's childish transgression to *Marius the Epicurean*, a novel in
which, Wilde says, 'Marius is little more than a spectator . . . and
perhaps a little too much occupied with the comeliness of the vessels
of the Sanctuary to notice that it is the Sanctuary of Sorrow that he is
gazing at' (740). For the child, sense experience and sensuality are all
one, and his inability to distinguish the superficial from the vital poses
a threat to those around him. In 'The Turn of the Screw' and *De*

Profundis, the child's inability to distinguish the quality of the pleasures put before it makes him a danger. 'If one gives a child a toy too
wonderful for its little mind, or too beautiful for its but half-awakened
eyes, it breaks the toy, if it is wilful; . . . so it was with you' (773),
Wilde explained to Douglas, further arguing that his being '*very
young*' meant not that he 'knew so little about life, but that [he] knew
so much' (684). Wilde develops this idea of the child as threat by artic-
ulating it as an artistic and ethical menace that endangers the artist's
'flamelike imagination' (741) and menaces the adult's 'natural superiority' (690). *De Profundis* is a retaliation of sorts, a letter that
promises to heal and hurt. Its every word, Wilde tells the child-like
Douglas, will chastise him 'as the fire or the knife of the surgeon that
makes the delicate flesh burn and bleed' (685).

Social sleight of hand was one of the most commented-upon characteristics of the aesthetic *poseur*, a feature that stimulated the sense
that Aestheticism was, in some incarnations, a manner of wheedling
one's way into society, and a means of influencing people to one's own
ends, as I discussed in Chapter 1. In a 1904 essay, James remembered
Aestheticism's inception as being interconnected to the rise of nebulous artistic opportunism. 'The conception of the "esthetic" law of
life . . . had begun to receive the honours of a lively appetite and an
eager curiosity, but was at the same time surrounded and manipulated
by as many different kinds of inexpertness as probably ever huddled
together on a single pretext' (*LC2* 908). The detachment in James's
description of Aestheticism's unsettling association conveniently
omits his own role in fostering this association, particularly through
his depictions of 'artistic' young men in his stories and novels of the
late 1870s and 1880s. 'The Turn of the Screw' recuperates this theme
and reformulates it in terms of a sinister immorality that pursues to
its logical end James's concern about Wilde's flirtatious and manipulative relationship to his audience. On the opening night of *Lady
Windermere's Fan*, James noted that the power of Wilde's performance lay in his ability to manipulate the audience without it discov-
ering it was being lured and, further, in his skill for making the
audience complicit in the process. Just as James was reluctantly
beguiled by what he referred to as Wilde's 'trap' and 'trick', the children take in their governess with their 'trick of premature cunning'
(*CS4* 675) and she realises too late that 'it was I who fell into the trap!'
(691). *De Profundis* demonstrates the power of the child's pose via
Douglas's repeated enactment of it to cajole Wilde to return to him.
Wilde tells Douglas he was swayed by 'the unfeigned joy you evinced

at seeing me, holding my hand whenever you could, as though you were a gentle and penitent child: your contrition, so simple and sincere, at the moment' (*LW* 696). This sort of 'innocent' hand-holding amounts to manipulation because it is a pose that can be assumed for effect, as when Douglas seeks 'consolation and help, as a child might seek it' (701) and Miles and Flora 'act their pretty parts of innocent babes to perfection.'[76]

In 'The Turn of the Screw' and *De Profundis* the children are literary figures for the displacement of Aestheticism's ambiguities: Bosie, Miles and Flora become willing and wilful participants in the adults' aesthetic game and their refined manipulations offer a compelling consummation of the aesthetic agenda of life-making art.[77] The power of the child's pose resides in the manner in which it controls the adult through its aesthetic appeal. Wilde explains his aesthetically-motivated desire to be with youthful males by saying that 'they, from the point of view through which I, as an artist in life, approached them, were delightfully suggestive and stimulating' (*LW* 758), though he concedes, however, that 'the danger was half the excitement'. The allure and lure of the child are one: 'their poison was part of their perfection' (759), he writes of the cobra-like youths who made him feel like a snake-charmer before they strangled him.

Likewise, Flora is initially responsive to the governess, but she also inverts the terms of her tutelage. The most precious gift she offers the governess is not only the sight of her 'angelic beauty' (*CS4* 643), but the opportunity to make a life out of caring for 'the radiant image of my little girl', as the governess puts it, in fulfilment of Aestheticism's belief that beauty makes life worthwhile. 'To watch, teach, "form" little Flora would too evidently be the making of a happy and useful life,' she asserts, in a statement of a life directive that foreshadows James's belief that 'it is art that *makes* life . . . and I know of no substitute whatever for the force and beauty of its process' (*L4* 770). The language of artistic connoisseurship and creation the governess invokes in her emphasis on the aesthetic training she intends to impart on her little charge underscores her status as an artist in life. Flora inverts the terms of her tutelage by usurping the role of the governess 'with her confidence and courage', 'her disposition to tell me so many more things than she asked' and, as a result, the governess feels as if Flora 'led me on' (*CS4* 645). This inverted and beguiling form of tutelage soon becomes the keynote of the governess's relationship to both children, as she succumbs to the satisfying vision of the pretty plays they make for her aestheticising gaze. She realises that even their solitary amusement was 'a spectacle they seemed actively to prepare and that engaged me as an active admirer. I walked in a world of their invention' (668). So adept are the children at playing to the governess's need to feel herself the figure of authority that their play becomes work. She is made to think 'I was something very important' while the children play 'very hard' for her benefit and go about 'their little tasks as if they loved them' (680). The governess thus becomes complicit in the children's play – a situation reminiscent of Wilde's relationship to his theatre-audience and what James called his 'deliberate trap for the literalist'.[78] The governess, like James, cannot avert her gaze and she finds that 'the immediate charm of my companions was a beguilement still effective even under the possibility that it was studied' (CS4 681).

While both James's and Wilde's narratives play on the idea of the child as innocent victim, they also use figurative language that vigorously counteracts this impression. The youths with whom Wilde associated are described at many turns as predatory animals whose menace far outweighs Wilde's. Being with them, Wilde writes, 'was like feasting with panthers' (LW 758). Was Douglas, then, like an 'ominous infant panther smuggled into a great gaudy hotel', to borrow a phrase from James?[79] Wilde also associates these youths with snakes, wasps and lions (758, 692). Miles and Flora pounce on the governess 'as animals' (CS4 680) and tigers. The child's marginal status – innocent and knowing, beautiful and ethically untried – makes it a surprisingly talented manipulator of adults. In this, the aesthetic child is a precocious version of the aesthete who influences others to act according to his own artistic vision of things. History, Wilde explains, ascribes Douglas's behaviour to 'the Infant Samuel theory' (LW 765), according to which Douglas represents the quintessence of godliness in a child, like Samuel who was dedicated as a servant of God before his conception. Yet this pure image could not be further from the truth. 'The world looks on you like a good young man who was very nearly tempted into wrong-doing by the wicked and immoral artist,' Wilde tells Douglas, 'it sounds all right. And yet, you know you have not escaped' (765).

In *De Profundis* the child-figure is a victimiser who makes human sacrifices on the altar of 'art'.[80] Willing to publish Wilde's private letters 'for the jaded *décadent* to wonder at, . . . for the little lions of the Quartier Latin to gape and mouth at' (LW 717), and to write telegrams 'of which the commonest street-boy would have been ashamed' (708), Douglas's only guide is his appetite for 'unlimited pleasure' (704). 'This unreflectingly ferocious young man',[81] as Linda Dowling calls him, is anomalous in the extremes to which he carries his passions, yet the cacoethes that motivate him are unequivocally those of a child smilingly leading the adult to his own doom (726). 'Prince-fleur-de-lys' lures Wilde, from the 'world of Art where once I was King' to 'the imperfect world of coarse uncompleted passions, of appetite without distinction, desire without limit'. Indiscriminate in his selections, this powerful child will destroy even the adults who have tried to protect him, a fact that puts Wilde in mind of Aeschylus's story of a lord who brings up a lion-cub 'and loves it because it comes bright-eyed to his call and fawns on him for its food . . . And the thing grows up and shows the nature of its race . . . and destroys the lord and his house and all that he possesses' (691). Wilde concludes, 'I feel that I was such a one as he.'

The End of Aestheticism's Innocence

By the late 1890s, aesthetic culture seems overwrought with energies that simultaneously threaten it with implosion and explosion. Whereas the crisis of originality Aestheticism faced in the 1880s had been resolved through Wilde's dazzling redefinition of creative modes, and the crisis of identity had been resolved through the formulation of an idiom of modern selfhood, the crisis of morality it now faced could not be settled so neatly. And just as Aestheticism's first crisis had reinvigorated and developed it, this second crisis now offered new, if terrifying, avenues for self-indulgence and moral decay in the name of aesthetic culture.

Aestheticism's decadent phase marks a turning point, one which I contend marks the end of Aestheticism's innocence. As I have been arguing, it indicates the end of a certain kind of knowing innocence not unlike that of children, and begins the reign of the child of power. While this knowing innocence enables Aestheticism to flirt with decadent topoi, 'The Turn of the Screw' and *De Profundis* precariously are positioned atop a moral precipice, one which many of James's and Wilde's contemporary critics believed them to have already plummeted into. Although Daisy Miller and her sisters already might have passed through the world with their 'clear quiet eyes wide open; skirting the edge of obscene abysses without suspecting them' (CS2 499), the suspicions of immorality that had been held at bay had, with Aestheticism's more and more decadent manifestations in the 1890s and the earth-shattering effects of the Wilde trial, irrevocably altered the landscape. 'Obscene abysses' were opening up everywhere – from the 'gulf of obscenity over which the ghoulish public' (*LL* 279) gloated over Wilde and his 'cry from the depths'[82] (as one reviewer would call *De Profundis*) to contemporary reviews of 'The Turn of the Screw' that considered it the climax of James's 'darker mood', and noted that 'nearly all his later stories have been tending to the horrible, have been stories of evil, beneath the surface mostly, and of corruption.'[83]

I have been pursuing the argument that the narrative uncoupling of aesthetics and ethics fosters a radical interrogation of Aestheticism's values. While 'The Turn of the Screw' and *De Profundis* offer James's and Wilde's darkest and bleakest assessments of aesthetic culture to this point, both narratives pull back from the gaping void they expose in order to save Aestheticism from being sacrificed entirely to this abysmal vision. Nevertheless, these stories mark the end of certain types of innocence – aesthetic, moral and personal – for both James and Wilde. Crucially, they also indicate the beginning of certain types of dark knowledge that later bear fruit in James's most successful articulations of aesthetic culture, namely *The Ambassadors*, *The Wings of the Dove* and *The Golden Bowl*. Under the dual historical impulses of Wilde's trial and James's failure to succeed as a dramatist, Aestheticism was forced into a state of crisis that achieved its first articulation in 'The Turn of the Screw' and *De Profundis*, both of which offer a vision of post-lapsarian innocence that is alarming and vivifying. If James and Wilde cast their aesthetic child-figures from Eden, both authors are nevertheless keenly aware of the rich and varied rewards attendant upon the worldliness before them, although both deliberately elude definition of the precise nature of this new world.

In suggesting that this end is in fact a beginning, Aestheticism's argumentative nature reveals itself more fully. The fact that both narratives boldly face the possibility that there may be no moral resolution to the problem they anatomise indicates the authors' commitment to an aesthetic vision that foregoes closure and finds its strength in ambiguities rather than monolithic certainties. Indeed, the bleakness of these narratives reinforces James's determination to rework them to other ends, and we can infer that Wilde would have done the same were it not for his untimely death three years after his release from prison. This is why Wilde's vow to make good on the promise of art's redemptive power sits, quite literally, at the very centre of *De Profundis*. Midway between the beginning and the end,

Wilde vows that 'if I can produce only one beautiful work of art I shall be able to rob malice of its venom, and cowardice of its sneer, and to pluck out the tongue of scorn by the roots' (*LW* 734). And while the death scene with which 'The Turn of the Screw' seems to close would seem to be an ill omen for the personally and socially redemptive forms of aesthetic culture the story parses, the story's explicit and repeated refusal of narrative closure (what exactly has happened to Miles in that last scene? Are the ghosts real or is the governess insane?) effectively defers resolution so that similar questions can be exercised and reworked in James's later fiction.

Both James's and Wilde's narrative interrogations propel us towards a reassessment of Aestheticism's fundamental question, namely the relation between art and morality, and by extension, art and life. It is explicitly as an interrogation of this question that these narratives offer themselves to the reader. In the opening of 'The Turn of the Screw', Douglas frames the story as an exercise in discernment, enjoining the narrator in the most personal terms. 'You'll easily judge why when you hear', he says, 'You'll easily judge . . . *You* will' (*CS4* 637). *De Profundis* adopts a similar approach, making delicate discrimination the reader's imperative. 'People must adopt some attitude towards me, and so pass judgment, both on themselves and me' (*LW* 734), Wilde advises. Rather than answers, James and Wilde compel the reader to evaluate, analyse and judge for herself – to become, in other words, an aesthete sensitive to her own impressions and able to evaluate for herself the aesthetic and moral claims the text evokes. The dark, deviant and degenerate Aestheticism that is the keynote of the fin-de-siècle is built upon this opposition, this idea that the true aesthete must always maintain a critical, amoral stance, come what may. The process of self-creation and self-destruction are therefore one. The entanglements engendered by this paradoxical process are exemplified by Dorian Gray's destruction of his portrait and himself, Guy Domville's drunken bid for social acceptance, and *The Importance of Being Earnest*'s naughty-but-nice Bunburyists, among others.

In the preceding chapters, I have argued that Wilde and James's relationship was mediated by the very aesthetic culture they participated in creating. I have also been arguing that this relationship exemplifies a mode of interaction particular to Aestheticism. Aestheticism's process, like the James-Wilde relationship itself, is premised on a paradox: it constructs itself by the same process that deconstructs it. Aestheticism constitutes itself by critiquing itself, which is to say that the same dialectical process that is responsible for its genesis – the process I have been arguing James and Wilde exemplify – is also responsible for its degeneration. To criticise Aestheticism is to be a participant in it and thus, to be partly responsible for its flourishing as well as its demise.

. . .

Under the force of the critical energies both texts direct at themselves and at the reader, 'The Turn of the Screw' and *De Profundis* fairly hum with the air of impending crisis. This crisis is neither localised nor is it short-lived, though it does mark the end of my own study. Indeed, the richly ambiguous and antagonistic air that overhangs both narratives has serious and wide-ranging implications for Aestheticism, which finds in it the impetus for its darker, more deca-dent iterations at the turn of the century and beyond. The narrative interrogations this chapter parses can be read as symptomatic of Aestheticism's pervasive critical tendencies as well as a highly specific response to the weight of the pressures applied on it at a historically contingent moment in time. Of course, the dual historical impulses that inform James's and Wilde's narratives are not the only reasons for Aestheticism's decadent turn – one might also cite socio-economic transformations, the rise of the New Woman, the emergence of a sci-entific discourse of sexology, psychology and of 'degeneration', urban change and individual alienation, imperialist fears and disputes, among others – but I have focused on these stories because they are, I think, among the most significant ones for James and Wilde and their engagement with aesthetic culture. What I hope this chapter has shown is that their ever-darkening representations of the child allow them to develop and criticise their perceptions of each other and aes-thetic culture.

The crisis this chapter has examined does not mark the end of James's and Wilde's relationship. Quite the contrary. In the years fol-lowing Wilde's death in 1900, James's compassion extended to Wilde's family and closest friends. Another chapter might be written on the afterlife of the James-Wilde relationship, and how it subsisted (one-sidedly) after Wilde's death – a phenomenon that might be adumbrated by noting that in 1907 James was one of only eleven guests at a twenty-first birthday dinner for Wilde's youngest son, Vyvyan Holland.[84] In his book, *Son of Oscar Wilde*, Holland remem-bered James among the people with whom he 'formed friendships'.[85] Indeed, the intensification of James's engagement with Wilde's family, his circle and his work after 1900 is a sure indicator of the strength of their interaction. If interest in aesthetic culture continues to increase, as it has over the past decades, then the terrain I have left untilled may yet prove of interest to others.

Throughout this book, I have been proposing that Aestheticism was an *argument* about art and life. In putting forward this thesis I have sought to underscore Aestheticism's aims and processes, as well as to draw attention to complexities and powerful ambiguities. From aesthetic parodies and caricatures to painting and criticism, from theatre to interior decoration, aesthetic culture is predicated on a tension between irreconcilable oppositions, each of which makes competing claims for legitimacy. James's and Wilde's relationship exemplified the paradoxes and ambivalences of Aestheticism, a culture fundamentally at odds with itself. This dialectic – between the outsider's exultant independence verging on solipsism and his simultaneous yearning for another, or for community – is the paradox of Aestheticism, and this pattern is discernible in every manifestation of aesthetic culture.

The story of Aestheticism is fundamentally a dialectical one. The oppositions between James and Wilde are symptomatic of the cultural oppositions of Aestheticism itself, antagonisms between American and British culture, elite and mass culture, plagiarism and originality, hetero- and homosexuality, social inclusivity and exclusivity. In enumerating such a diverse set of oppositions, I have intentionally chosen, in this final section, to gesture to Aestheticism's wider scope, to reveal just how much its arc encompasses. Aestheticism's apparent inconsistencies and oppositions should not diminish the fact that it was a movement to which many in late nineteenth-century Britain and America felt drawn, because it would cradle them yet offer them room to grow. The inconsistencies that frustrated some were, I argue, at the heart of Aestheticism's project.

There is good reason to see the tension between Wilde and James as a parable about two cultures in conflict that externalised their concerns about one another while silently internalising each others' values. But there is equally good reason for seeing the James-Wilde relationship as a parable about *opposition*, and about what *oppositions* – in particular and in general – do in artistic contexts, which is to say the way in which these oppositions allow individuals and groups to externalise their concerns about one another while silently internalising each others' values. The best reason for seeing the James-Wilde relationship in the most catholic sense – as an example of so many other conflicts and tensions – is that it partakes of them equally. A number of critics have pointed to Aestheticism's social strands and missionary tendencies, to its ability to engage women as much as men, Americans as much as Britons, elite literary culture as well as more democratic artistic outlets. Because it participates in all these conflicts, I have resisted the temptation to fine Aestheticism down to a fundamental point but have gestured instead towards the common characteristics underwriting its various manifestations.

'It brought with it no repose, brought with it only agitation,' James wrote of Aestheticism four years after Wilde's death, in an essay for the *Quarterly Review* (LC2 908). Referring to the series of crises that had been the hallmark of Aestheticism and its attendant sense of unhoming, James concluded that 'esthetic consciousness' always held out the tantalising but unfulfilled promise of a 'reign of peace, the supreme beatitude; but stability continued to elude us'. Be this as it may, one of the movement's most striking and fascinating features is its ability to encompass so much and so many. Indeed, what impresses one again and again is Aestheticism's ability to reach a mass audience while claiming to speak to each member of this audience as an individual. It offered its adherents – from Oxford tutors to Leadville miners, from Mrs Ponsonby de Tompkins to Vernon Lee, from James to Wilde – the opportunity to be part of an artistic movement larger than themselves, while allowing them to define for themselves the exact form their aesthetic allegiance would take. This says as much about aesthetic culture's capacity to encompass as it does about the sense of purpose it imbued its adherents with. 'To encompass' is, of course, to include, but the word itself contains the idea of a compass, a guide that one can rely on to take one boldly in the direction of one's ideals. When it comes to Aestheticism, then, the journey is the destination. It was this sense, rather than the promise of a peaceful, definite end, that made Aestheticism a vehicle for the growth, development and transformation of Anglo-American culture.

NOTES

1. Oscar Wilde, *Teleny: Or, the Reverse of the Medal, a Physiological Romance; a Novel Attributed to Oscar Wilde*, ed. Winston Leyland (San Francisco: Gay Sunshine Press, 1984) 119.
2. Gagnier concurs that 'British Aestheticism as a movement ended in 1897, when Wilde left prison for Paris. Then the struggle between art and life was over' (*Idylls*, 11).

3. Holland, *Real Trial*, 85.

4. Dollimore, *Sexual Dissidence*, 95.

5. Hayes (ed.), *Henry James*, 309.

6. Freedman reads the relationship as premised on the power of professionalisation, whereas Ellmann, Sedgwick and others have read it in terms of sexual power.

7. My argument modifies Freedman's suggestion in *Professions of Taste* that James's turn towards decadent Aestheticism was contemporaneous with his so-called Major Phase and that both movements achieve their apotheosis in *The Wings of the Dove* (1902) and *The Golden Bowl* (1904). Although Freedman's argument is highly persuasive, there is strong evidence that the dark Aestheticism he relegates to the twentieth century was already pervasive at the end of the nineteenth.

8. See Weir, *Decadence*, 109.

9. 'The Turn of the Screw' ran in *Collier's Weekly* from 27 January to 16 April 1898 before being revised and reprinted in *The Two Magics* in October 1898. *De Profundis* has an intricate publication history, the details of which are too complex to render here but which Ian Small thoughtfully traces in his introduction to Oscar Wilde, *De Profundis*, '*Epistola; in Carcere et in Vinculis*', *The Complete Works of Oscar Wilde*, ed. Ian Small, vol. 2 (Oxford: Oxford UP, 2005) 1–31.

10. Henry James and Elizabeth Robins, *Theatre and Friendship: Some Henry James Letters* (London: J. Cape, 1932) 113.

11. Ibid. 115.

12. Ibid. 121.

13. Ibid. 125.

14. My reading differs from those offered by Freedman and Stevens, although my position is not incompatible with theirs. Freedman reads these two letters as instances of James's professional envy of Wilde, while Stevens interprets them in terms of James's dismay at Wilde's queerness (Freedman, *Professions* 73–5; Stevens, *Henry James*, 130–2).

15. James R. Kincaid, *Erotic Innocence: The Culture of Child Molesting* (Durham, NC: Duke UP, 1998) 63–4.

16. Henry James, *Selected Letters*, ed. Leon Edel (Cambridge, MA: Harvard UP, 1987) 252.

17. Freud, 'Thoughts', 290.

18. Adam Phillips, *On Flirtation* (London: Faber & Faber, 1994) xxi.

19. My formulation here is indebted to Phillips, *On Flirtation*, xxi.

20. Georg Simmel, 'Flirtation', *Georg Simmel on Women, Sexuality and Love*, ed. Guy Oakes (New Haven: Yale UP, 1984) 147.

21. Phillips, *On Flirtation*, xvii.

22. Ellmann, *Oscar Wilde*, 346.

23. As Joseph Bristow justly observes, Scott's judgement was somewhat anomalous, and those audience members who reacted negatively to Wilde's speech were, in fact, echoing general social and moral anxieties about the late nineteenth-century theatre world (*Effeminate* 29–30). Ever eager to lampoon Wilde, *Punch* caricatured him as the 'quite too-too-puffickly precious!! . . . new dramatic author Shakespeare Sheridan Oscar Puff, Esq.', and included an explanatory excerpt from the *Daily Telegraph* ('Fancy Portrait', *Punch* 5 March 1892, 113). The actors in the caricature are pictured as puppets, an allusion to Wilde's provocative address to the Playgoers' Club in which he had claimed that 'the stage is only "a frame furnished with a set of puppets" ' (*LW* 518). Capitalising on the caricature and Wilde's comments, Charles Brookfield and J. M. Glover staged a satire of Wilde entitled *The Poet and the Puppets* in 1892. It included a solo that alluded to Wilde's curtain speech at the opening of *Lady Windermere's Fan*. The Wilde-figure sings: 'the piece came out and it stood the test, for he'd borrowed only the very best; And those who came to scoff at the play had to hammer applause 'ere they drove away . . . While this magnetic, peripatetic author remains to say, he was much delighted that those invited enjoyed his four-act play' (Brookfield et al., *The Poet and the Puppets: A Travestie on Lady Windermere's Fan* (New York: Garland, 1978) 19).
24. Freedman, *Professions*, 174.
25. Roger Gard, ed. *Henry James: The Critical Heritage* (London: Routledge, 1968) 430.
26. Monteiro, *Henry James and John Hay*, 683.
27. Phillips, *On Flirtation*, xxiii, xxiv.
28. Rayburn S. Moore (ed.), *Selected Letters of Henry James to Edmund Gosse, 1882–1915: A Literary Friendship* (Baton Rouge: Louisiana State UP, 1988) 127.
29. Ellmann, *Oscar Wilde*, 474.
30. Stevens, *Henry James*, 130–1.
31. Kaye, *The Flirt's Tragedy*, 177.
32. Horne translates this letter in *LL* 288.
33. Nicola Nixon suggests that this letter is 'ostensibly earnest in its sympathy and enthusiasm for Wilde's potential', but that it borders on 'mild disingenuousness' ('The Reading Gaol', 179).
34. W. James, *Correspondence* 8: 359.
35. I disagree with Ellmann's claim that 'this seems *pro forma* sympathy, as if for the record' ('Henry James Among the Aesthetes', 42).
36. W. James, *Correspondence* 8: 359.
37. By resurrecting the image of a gulf over which the hypocritical public could gloat over Wilde, James reversed the scene of Wilde's curtain speech at the opening night of *Lady Windermere's Fan*. Standing over

the audience, Wilde had gloated on his success but now the public stood over Wilde and gloated. This was, like the trial, a Wildean 'spectacle' for which James was a member of the audience.

38. Sigmund Freud, 'Jokes and Their Relation to the Unconscious', in *The Standard Edition of the Complete Psychological Works of Sigmund Freud*, ed. James Strachey, vol. 8 (London: Hogarth, 1960) 224.

39. Joseph Epstein, *Envy: The Seven Deadly Sins* (Oxford: Oxford UP, 2003) 70.

40. Matheson judiciously observes that James's description of Wilde's trial as a piece of 'hideous human history' argues against 'the potentially demonizing effects of the letter's Gothic language by implying that Wilde's personal tragedy involves the suffering of a person imagined as kindred rather than other' (Neil Matheson, 'Talking Horrors: Henry James, Euphemism, and the Specter of Wilde', *American Literature* 71.4 (1999), 727). Moreover, the shock James manifests 'is associated not with Wilde's alleged transgressions,' but with the public's reactions to them (726).

41. William James, *The Correspondence of William James*, ed. Ignas K. Skrupskelis and Elizabeth M. Berkeley, 10 vols (Charlottesville: U of Virginia P, 1993) 2: 356.

42. Kincaid, *Erotic Innocence*, 64.

43. Sedgwick, *Epistemology*, 185.

44. Stevens, *Henry James*, 131.

45. See Exodus. 25: 18–20.

46. Henry James, *The Turn of the Screw and Other Stories*, ed. T. J. Lustig (Oxford: Oxford UP, 1998) 253.

47. See Song of Solomon 6: 17

48. Kincaid, *Erotic Innocence*, 63–4.

49. James R. Kincaid, *Child-Loving: The Erotic Child and Victorian Culture* (New York: Routledge, 1992) 73. Ohi analyses the parallels between protection and endangerment in *Innocence*, 123–54.

50. *Daisy Miller* is also receptive to a reverse reading to the one I suggest. Such an interpretation would, however, hinge on Daisy's complicity in her dishonour. Her case seems to me exemplary of Freud's 'American flirtation' – a flirtation that, as Phillips puts it, confuses 'the relationship between innocence and experience, between the Old World and the New World' (*On Flirtation*, xxi). Much rests on our interpretations of situations that James intentionally blurs, such as Winterbourne's observation: 'Miss Daisy Miller looked extremely innocent. Some people had told him that, after all, American girls were exceedingly innocent; and others had told him that, after all, they were not' (*CS2* 247). James's depiction of childhood in this novella is further complicated by his depiction of Daisy's brother, Randolph, as a wild and undisciplined child.

51. Rowe, *Other*, 22.
52. Millicent Bell, 'The Unmentionable Subject in "The Pupil"', *The Cambridge Companion to Henry James*, ed. Jonathan Freedman (Cambridge: Cambridge UP, 1998) 144.
53. Michael Moon, *A Small Boy and Others: Imitation and Initiation in American Culture from Henry James to Andy Warhol* (Durham: Duke UP, 1998) 24. On the story's homosexual theme, see also Philip Horne, 'The Master and the "Queer Affair" of "The Pupil"', *Critical Quarterly* 37.3 (1995).
54. As Rowe suggests, this novel also raises the spectre of the incest taboo when Sir Claude realises that his relationship with Maisie would hopelessly entangle romantic and parent-child loves (*Other*, 133).
55. Quoted in Hayes (ed.), *Henry James*, 301.
56. Ibid. 304.
57. This is a point I argue in '"I'm Not a Bit Expensive": Henry James and the Sexualization of the Victorian Girl', in *Small Change: Nineteenth-Century Childhood and the Rise of Consumer Culture*, ed. Dennis Denisoff (Aldershot: Ashgate, forthcoming).
58. On Salomé's refusal to be 'a mere innocent manipulated by her mother', see William Tydeman and Steven Price, *Wilde: Salome*, Plays in Production (Cambridge: Cambridge UP, 1996) 19. In a similar vein, Miles, who is ten years old and therefore stands on the cusp of puberty, can already be seen to have taken on adult responsibilities such as being his uncle's representative at Bly. John Fletcher considers this aspect in 'The Haunted Closet', 65.
59. Leon Edel gives a detailed account of the history of James's collection in his introduction to *The Library of Henry James* (Ann Arbor, MI: UMI Research, 1987). Despite my best efforts, I have not been able to trace the copy of *Salomé* that James once owned.
60. Ellis Hanson, 'Knowing Children: Desire and Interpretation in *The Exorcist*', in *Curiouser: On the Queerness of Children*, ed. Steven Bruhm and Natasha Hurley (Minneapolis: U of Minnesota P, 2004) 109–10.
61. Kincaid, *Erotic Innocence*, 16.
62. Ohi, *Innocence*, 124.
63. Rowe, *Other*, 22.
64. The critical tendency to view children as always *acted upon*, rather than *actors* in their own right hinges on limiting interpretations of authority, as well as oppositions of activity and passivity similar to those that Hélène Cixous and others have revealed to be reductive to conceptualisations of gender (Cixous and Catherine Clément, *The Newly Born Woman*, Theory and History of Literature 24 (Minneapolis: U of Minnesota P, 1986). Much as Jamesian criticism has been resistant to inversions of the parent-child hierarchy, James's narratives make a

strong case for such readings through the agency with which they empower the child.

65. Edmund Wilson, *The Triple Thinkers and The Wound and the Bow* (Boston: Northeastern UP, 1976).

66. Mark Seltzer, *Henry James and the Art of Power* (Ithaca: Cornell UP, 1984) 157.

67. A full analysis of aesthetic culture's relation to the child-figure would be daunting at this point, but it is worth indicating the prevalence of this trope in aesthetic texts as diverse as Pater's parable of impression-building, 'The Child in the House' (1878); Gabriele D'Annunzio's depiction of the decadent hero as a 'Child of Pleasure' in his novel *Il Piacere* (1889); Aubrey Beardsley's illustration of 'A Child at Its Mother's Bed' (1895); John Barlas's eroticised poem about 'The Dancing Girl'; the 'boyish noise, grace, pliancy' of J. A. Symonds's young man fresh from the wrestling-ground in the second volume of *Studies of the Greek Poets* (1873); and Max Beerbohm's '*credo junioribus*' and his recollection of London's fascinating society children in 'Diminuendo' (Beckson (ed.), *Aesthetes* 69, 73). In James's and Wilde's invocation, the child-figure stands for a problematic combination of Aestheticism's moral and social qualities.

68. Ellis Hanson has noted that 'to know or to display innocence is to be corrupted; the category is available only retrospectively, and its constitution leads ahead to its ruin' (Hanson, 'Screwing with Children in Henry James', *GLQ: A Journal of Lesbian and Gay Studies* 9.3 (2003), 374); see also Ohi, *Innocence*, 131.

69. Pater, *Renaissance* (1986), 152.

70. Ibid. 152.

71. Shoshana Felman, 'Turning the Screw of Interpretation', in *Literature and Psychoanalysis: The Question of Reading – Otherwise*, ed. Shoshana Felman (Baltimore: Johns Hopkins UP, 1977) 162–77.

72. Beckson (ed.), *Aesthetes*, 81–2.

73. Pater, *Renaissance* (1986), 153.

74. Ibid. 153.

75. Ibid. 152.

76. Hayes (ed.), *Henry James*, 308.

77. James further developed the idea of the beautiful child as a satisfaction of the aesthete's desire for a life-making art in his incomplete short story 'Hugh Merrow' which he began to outline in 1898, a month after 'The Turn of the Screw' finished its serial run. The story revolves around a couple that commissions an artist to paint a picture of their unborn child in order to provide what Cynthia Ozick calls 'an aesthetic birth' that is an explicit substitution of art for life (*Metaphor & Memory: Essays* (New York: Knopf, 1989) 63). In 'Maud-Evelyn' (1900), James portrayed a family who builds their life around the memory of their

beautiful, deceased daughter who continues to grow, thrive and eventually marry – in their fond imaginations.

78. Setting himself up as a hunter of bigger game than would be caught by
Wilde's 'trap', James claimed in the Preface to 'The Turn of the Screw'
that he did not want to the story to appeal to literal-minded audiences
such as Wilde's, but to a reader like James himself, someone 'not easily
caught (the "fun" of the capture of the merely witless being ever but
small)' (*LC2* 1184–5).

79. This phrase appears in the story 'A Round of Visits'; see Stevens, *Henry
James*, 154.

80. This offers a sharp contrast to Wilde's earlier stories, where youth is the
victim. In an 1888 story titled 'The Young King', Wilde made a tame,
animal-like youth the prey of adults because he was 'wild-eyed and
open-mouthed, like a brown woodland Faun, or some young animal of
the forest newly snared by the hunters' (*W* 213). 'The Star-Child' (1891)
punished a once-beautiful child by giving him the face of a toad and the
body of an adder.

81. Linda Dowling, *Hellenism and Homosexuality in Victorian Oxford*
(Ithaca, NY: Cornell UP, 1994) 123.

82. Beckson (ed.), *Oscar Wilde: Critical Heritage*, 245.

83. Hayes (ed.), *Henry James*, 304.

84. Jonathan Fryer, *Robbie Ross: Oscar Wilde's Devoted Friend* (New
York: Carroll & Graf, 2000) 198. The other guests were Wilde's son
Cyril Holland, Robert Ross, Reggie Turner, More Adey, William
Rothenstein, Charles Ricketts, Charles Shannon, Ronald Firbank, Sir
Coleridge Kennard and Sir William Richmond.

85. Vyvyan Holland, *Son of Oscar Wilde*, ed. Merlin Holland (Oxford:
Oxford UP, 1988) 191.

BIBLIOGRAPHY

Ackerman, Alan L. *The Portable Theater: American Literature and the Nineteenth-Century Stage*. Baltimore: Johns Hopkins UP, 1999.

Adams, Hazard. *Critical Theory Since Plato*. New York: Harcourt Brace Jovanovich, 1971.

Adams, Marian. *The Letters of Mrs. Henry Adams, 1865–1883*, ed. Ward Thoron. Boston: Little, Brown, & Co., 1936.

'Aestheticism as Oscar Understands It', *The Daily Graphic: An Illustrated Evening Newspaper* [New York] 11 January 1882, 1.

'Aesthetic Love in a Cottage', *Punch* 19 February 1881, 78.

'Aesthetic Syllabub', *Washington Post* 24 January 1882, 1.

'Affiliating an Aesthete', *Punch* 19 June 1880, 14.

Albery, James. 'Where's the Cat?' in *The Dramatic Works of James Albery*, ed. Wyndham Albery, vol. 2. London: Peter Davies, 1939, 473–570.

Albright, Daniel. *Quantum Poetics: Yeats, Pound, Eliot, and the Science of Modernism*. Cambridge: Cambridge UP, 1997.

'American Appreciation (From the London Saturday Review)', *Life* 7 June 1883, 272.

'An Aesthetic Midday Meal', *Punch* 17 July 1880, 23.

Anesko, Michael. *'Friction with the Market': Henry James and the Profession of Authorship*. New York: Oxford UP, 1986.

Anesko, Michael. *Letters, Fictions, Lives: Henry James and William Dean Howells*. New York: Oxford UP, 1997.

Appiah, Kwame Anthony. *The Ethics of Identity*. Princeton: Princeton UP, 2005.

Archer, William. *The Theatrical World of 1895*. London: Walter Scott Ltd, 1896.

'Artistic Amenities', *Punch* 26 July 1879, 14.

Balzac, Honoré de. *Selected Short Stories/ Contes Choisis: A Dual Language Book*, trans. Stanley Appelbaum. Mineola, NY: Dover, 2000.

Banta, Martha. *Barbaric Intercourse: Caricature and the Culture of Conduct, 1841–1936*. Chicago: U of Chicago P, 2003.

Banta, Martha. 'From "Harry Jim" to "St. James" in *Life Magazine* (1883–1916): Twitting the Author; Prompting the Public', *Henry James Review* 14 (1993), 237–56.

Banta, Martha. 'The James Family Theatricals: Behind the Scenes', in *The Cambridge Companion to Henry James*, ed. Jonathan Freedman. Cambridge: Cambridge UP, 1998, 40–62.

Barbey d'Aurevilly, Jules. *Dandyism*, trans. Douglas Ainslie. New York: PAJ Publications, 1988.

Baxandall, Michael. *Patterns of Intention: On the Historical Explanation of Pictures*. New Haven, CT: Yale UP, 1985.

Beardsley, Aubrey. *Best Works of Aubrey Beardsley*. New York: Dover, 1990.

Beckson, Karl (ed.). *Aesthetes and Decadents of the 1890's: An Anthology of British Poetry and Prose*. Chicago: Academy, 1981.

Beckson, Karl. *London in the 1890s: A Cultural History*. New York: Norton, 1992.

Beckson, Karl. *The Oscar Wilde Encyclopedia*. New York: AMS, 1998.

Beckson, Karl (ed.). *Oscar Wilde: The Critical Heritage*. London: Routledge, 1970.

Bell, Ian. *Washington Square: Styles of Money*. New York: Twayne, 1993.

Bell, Millicent. 'From *Washington Square* to *The Spoils of Poynton*: Jamesian Metamorphosis', in *Henry James: The Shorter Fiction: Reassessments*, ed. N. H. Reeve. Basingstoke: Macmillan, 1997, 95–113.

Bell, Millicent. *Meaning in Henry James*. Cambridge, MA: Harvard UP, 1991.

Bell, Millicent. 'The Unmentionable Subject in "The Pupil"', in *The Cambridge Companion to Henry James*, ed. Jonathan Freedman. Cambridge: Cambridge UP, 1998, 139–50.

Bell-Villada, Gene H. *Art for Art's Sake and Literary Life: How Politics and Markets Helped Shape the Ideology and Culture of Aestheticism, 1790–1990*. Lincoln: U of Nebraska P, 1996.

Bernard, Fred V. 'Portents of Violence: Jamesian Realism in *Guy Domville*', *Henry James Review* 17.1 (1996), 85–94.

Binghamton, NY. 24 August 2006. http://www.cityofbinghamton.com/history.asp.

Bishop, George. *When the Master Relents: The Neglected Short Fictions of Henry James*. Ann Arbor, MI: UMI Research, 1988.

Blanchard, Mary Warner. *Oscar Wilde's America: Counterculture in the Gilded Age*. New Haven, CT: Yale UP, 1998.

Bloom, Harold. *The Anxiety of Influence: A Theory of Poetry*, 2nd edn. New York: Oxford UP, 1997.

Blunt, Wilfrid Scawen. *My Diaries: Being a Personal Narrative of Events, 1888–1914.* London: M. Secker, 1922.

Bogardus, Ralph F. *Pictures and Texts: Henry James, A. L. Coburn, and New Ways of Seeing in Literary Culture.* Ann Arbor, MI: UMI Research, 1984.

'Bookishness', *Life* 8 March 1883, 128.

Borelius, Birgit. 'Oscar Wilde, Whistler and Colours', *Scripta Minora* 3 (1966–7), 3–62.

'Born So', *Life* 3 May 1883, 213.

Bray, Alan. *Homosexuality in Renaissance England.* London: Gay Men's Press, 1982.

Bristow, Joseph. ' "A Complex and Multiform Creature": Wilde's Sexual Identities', in *The Cambridge Companion to Oscar Wilde*, ed. Peter Raby. New York: Cambridge UP, 1997, 195–218.

Bristow, Joseph. *Effeminate England: Homoerotic Writing after 1885.* Buckingham: Open UP, 1995.

Brookfield, Charles, Jimmy Glover, and L. S. Amery. *The Poet and the Puppets: A Travestie on Lady Windermere's Fan.* New York: Garland, 1978 [1892].

Brown, Bill. *A Sense of Things: The Object Matter of American Literature.* Chicago: U of Chicago P, 2003.

Brown, Julia Prewitt. *Cosmopolitan Criticism: Oscar Wilde's Philosophy of Art.* Charlottesville: U of Virginia P, 1997.

Brown, Lucy. *Victorian News and Newspapers.* Oxford: Clarendon, 1985.

Bruder, Anne. 'Constructing Artist and Critic between J. M. Whistler and Oscar Wilde: "In the Best Days of Art There Were No Art-Critics",' *ELT* 47.2 (2004),161–80.

Burke, Doreen Bolger (ed). *In Pursuit of Beauty: Americans and the Aesthetic Movement.* New York: Rizzoli, 1986.

Butler, Judith. *Gender Trouble: Feminism and the Subversion of Identity.* New York: Routledge, 1990.

Butler, Judith. 'Values of Difficulty', in *Just Being Difficult?: Academic Writing in the Public Arena*, ed. Jonathan Culler and Kevin Lamb. Stanford: Stanford UP, 2003, 199–215.

Byerly, Alison. *Realism, Representation, and the Arts in Nineteenth-Century Literature.* Cambridge: Cambridge UP, 1997.

Cargill, Oscar. 'Gabriel Nash – Somewhat Less Than Angel?', *Nineteenth-Century Fiction* 14.3 (1959), 231–9.

Cargill, Oscar. 'Mr James's Aesthetic Mr Nash', *Nineteenth-Century Fiction* 12.3 (1957), 177–87.

Cargill, Oscar. *The Novels of Henry James.* New York: Macmillan, 1961.

Carlson, Susan. *Women of Grace: James's Plays and the Comedy of Manners.* Ann Arbor, MI: UMI, 1985.

Cave, Richard Allen. 'Wilde's Plays: Some Lines of Influence', in *The*

Cambridge Companion to Oscar Wilde, ed. Peter Raby. Cambridge: Cambridge UP, 1988, 219–48.

Chai, Leon. *Aestheticism: The Religion of Art in Post-Romantic Literature*. New York: Columbia UP, 1990.

Charteris, Evan (ed.). *The Life and Letters of Edmund Gosse*. London: Heinemann, 1931.

Cixous, Hélène, and Catherine Clément. *The Newly Born Woman*. Theory and History of Literature 24. Minneapolis: U of Minnesota P, 1986.

Clements, Patricia. *Baudelaire and the English Tradition*. Princeton, NJ: Princeton UP, 1985.

'Closing Scene at the Old Bailey', *Illustrated Police News* 4 May 1895, 1.

'A Code for Anglomaniacs', *Life* 26 April 1883, 201.

Cohen, Ed. (ed.). *Talk on the Wilde Side: Towards a Genealogy of a Discourse on Male Sexualities*. New York: Routledge, 1993.

Cohen, Ed. 'Writing Gone Wilde: Homoerotic Desire in the Closet of Representation', in *Critical Essays on Oscar Wilde*, ed. Regenia Gagnier. New York: G. K. Hall, 1991, 68–88.

Cohen, William A. *Sex Scandal: The Private Parts of Victorian Fiction*. Durham: Duke UP, 1996.

Collister, Peter. 'James's "The Madonna of the Future" and the Problem of Artistic Failure: Some French Models', *Journal of European Studies* 32 (2002), 339–50.

'A Consideration', *Punch* 13 September 1879, 110.

Constable, Liz, Dennis Denisoff, and Matthew Potolsky. *Perennial Decay: On the Aesthetics and Politics of Decadence*. Philadelphia: U of Pennsylvania P, 1999.

Cook, Matt. *London and the Culture of Homosexuality, 1885–1914*. Cambridge: Cambridge UP, 2003.

Craft, Christopher. 'Alias Bunbury: Desire and Termination in *The Importance of Being Earnest*', *Representations* 31 (1990), 19–46.

Crimp, Douglas. 'Mario Montez, for Shame', in *Regarding Sedgwick: Essays on Queer Culture and Critical Theory*, ed. Stephen M. Barber and David L. Clark. New York: Routledge, 2002, 57–70.

Dakers, Caroline. *Clouds: The Biography of a Country House*. New Haven, CT: Yale UP, 1993.

Dalziel, Davison and Harry W. McVickar. *A Parody on Patience (Respectfully Dedicated to the Conductors of the Chicago & Alton Railroad)*. New York: Wemple & Co., 1882.

Danson, Lawrence. *Wilde's Intentions: The Artist in His Criticism*. Oxford: Clarendon, 1997.

Davitt Bell, Michael. *The Problem of American Realism: Studies in the Cultural History of a Literary Idea*. Chicago: U of Chicago P, 1993.

De Monfort, Patricia. 'The Gentle Art – An Artistic Autobiography?' *Whistler Review* 1 (1999), 37–44.

Dellamora, Richard. *Masculine Desire: The Sexual Politics of Victorian Aestheticism*. Chapel Hill: U of North Carolina P, 1990.

Denisoff, Dennis. *Aestheticism and Sexual Parody, 1840–1940*. Cambridge: Cambridge UP, 2001.

Denney, Colleen. *At the Temple of Art: The Grosvenor Gallery, 1877–1890*. London: Associated UP, 2000.

Dibb, Geoff. 'Oscar Wilde's Lecture Tours of the United Kingdom, 1883–85', *The Wildean* 29 (July 2006), 2–11.

Dickinson, Emily. *The Complete Poems of Emily Dickinson*, ed. Thomas Herbert Johnson. Boston: Little Brown, 1961.

'Distinguished Amateurs – The Art-Critic', *Punch* 13 March 1880.

'Distinguished Amateurs – The Way to Please Them', *Punch* 11 June 1881, 267.

Dollimore, Jonathan. *Sexual Dissidence: Augustine to Wilde, Freud to Foucault*. Oxford: Oxford UP, 1991.

Dowling, Linda. *Hellenism and Homosexuality in Victorian Oxford*. Ithaca, NY: Cornell UP, 1994.

Drabble, Margaret. *A Writer's Britain: Landscape in Literature*. London: Thames & Hudson, 1984.

'Du Maurier. Condensed from a Review by H-nry J-mes, Jr., in the last "Century" ', *Life* 3 May 1883, 209.

Dupee, F. W. *Henry James*. New York: Doubleday, 1956.

Eagleton, Terry. *The English Novel: An Introduction*. Oxford: Blackwell, 2005.

Edel, Leon. *Henry James*, 5 vols. Philadelphia: J. B. Lippincott, 1953–72.

Edel, Leon, and Dan H. Laurence. *A Bibliography of Henry James*, 3rd edn. New Castle, DE: Oak Knoll, 1999.

Edel, Leon, and Adeline Tintner. *The Library of Henry James*. Ann Arbor, MI: UMI Research, 1987.

Elliott, Maude Howe. *This Was My Newport*. Cambridge, MA: A. Marshall Jones, 1944.

Elliott, Maude Howe. *Uncle Sam Ward and His Circle*. New York: Macmillan, 1938.

Ellmann, Richard. 'The Critic as Artist as Wilde', in *The Artist as Critic: Critical Writings of Oscar Wilde*, ed. Richard Ellmann. New York: Random House, 1969, ix–xxviii.

Ellmann, Richard. 'Henry James Among the Aesthetes', in *Henry James and Homo-Erotic Desire*, ed. John R. Bradley. New York: St Martin's, 1999, 25–44.

Ellmann, Richard. *Oscar Wilde*. London: Hamish Hamilton, 1987.

Epstein, Joseph. *Envy: The Seven Deadly Sins*. Oxford: Oxford UP, 2003.

Erikson, Erik H. *Childhood and Society*. New York: Norton, 1963.

'Fancy Portrait', *Punch* 5 March 182, 113.

Felman, Shoshana. 'Turning the Screw of Interpretation', in *Literature and*

Psychoanalysis: The Question of Reading – Otherwise, ed. Shoshana Felman. Baltimore: Johns Hopkins UP, 1977, 94–208.

Fletcher, John. 'The Haunted Closet: Henry James's Queer Spectrality', *Textual Practice* 14.1 (2000), 53–80.

'Fleur des Alpes; or Postlethwaite's Last Love', *Punch* 25 December 1880, 293–4.

Flint, Kate. *The Victorians and the Visual Imagination*. Cambridge: Cambridge UP, 2000.

Foldy, Michael S. *The Trials of Oscar Wilde: Deviance, Morality and Late-Victorian Society*. New Haven, CT: Yale UP, 1997.

Foote, Stephanie. 'Henry James and the Parvenus: Reading Taste in *The Spoils of Poynton*', *The Henry James Review* 27 (2006), 42–60.

Forbes, Archibald. 'Letter to Oscar Wilde', 26 January 1882, ms. William Andrews Clark Memorial Library.

Foucault, Michel. *The History of Sexuality*, trans. Robert Hurley, vol. 1. Harmondsworth: Penguin, 1981.

Frankel, Nicholas. *Oscar Wilde's Decorated Books*. Ann Arbor, MI: U of Michigan P, 2000.

Freedman, Jonathan. 'An Aestheticism of Our Own: American Writers and the Aesthetic Movement', in *In Pursuit of Beauty: Americans and the Aesthetic Movement*, ed. Doreen Bolger Burke. New York: Rizzoli, 1986, 385–99.

Freedman, Jonathan (ed.). *The Cambridge Companion to Henry James*. Cambridge: Cambridge UP, 1998.

Freedman, Jonathan. *Professions of Taste: Henry James, British Aestheticism, and Commodity Culture*. Stanford: Stanford UP, 1990.

Freud, Sigmund. 'Jokes and Their Relation to the Unconscious', in *The Standard Edition of the Complete Psychological Works of Sigmund Freud*, ed. James Strachey, vol. 8. London: Hogarth, 1960.

Freud, Sigmund. 'Thoughts for the Times on War and Death', in *The Standard Edition of the Complete Psychological Works of Sigmund Freud*, ed. James Strachey, vol. 14. London: Hogarth, 1953, 275–300.

Frith, William Powell. *My Autobiography and Reminiscences*, 2 vols. London: Richard Bentley & Son, 1887.

'Frustrated Social Ambition', *Punch* 21 May 1881, 229.

Fryer, Jonathan. *Robbie Ross: Oscar Wilde's Devoted Friend*. New York: Carroll & Graf, 2000.

Fussell, Edwin Sill. *The Catholic Side of Henry James*. Cambridge: Cambridge UP, 1993.

Fussell, Edwin Sill. *The French Side of Henry James*. New York: Columbia UP, 1990.

Gagnier, Regenia. *Idylls of the Marketplace: Oscar Wilde and the Victorian Public*. Stanford, CA: Stanford UP, 1986.

Gard, Roger (ed.). *Henry James: the Critical Heritage*. London: Routledge, 1968.

Gere, Charlotte, and Jane Abdy. *The Souls*. London: Sidgwick and Jackson, 1984.

Gere, Charlotte, and Lesley Hoskins. *The House Beautiful: Oscar Wilde and the Aesthetic Interior*. Aldershot: Lund Humphries, 2000.

Gilbert, William, and Arthur Sullivan. 'Patience', in *The Annotated Gilbert and Sullivan*, ed. Ian Bradley, vol. 2. Harmondsworth: Penguin, 1984, 121–209.

Goethe, Johann Wolfgang von. *Faust: Part One and Sections from Part Two*, trans. Walter Kaufmann. New York: Random House, 1990.

Goffman, Erving. *The Presentation of Self in Everyday Life*. New York: Doubleday, 1959.

Goffman, Erving. *Stigma: Notes on the Management of Spoiled Identity*. London: Penguin, 1968.

Golahny, Amy. *Rembrandt's Reading: The Artist's Bookshelf of Ancient Poetry and History*. Amsterdam: Amsterdam UP, 2003.

Gordon, D. J., and John Stokes. 'The Reference of *The Tragic Muse*', in *The Air of Reality: New Essays on James*, ed. John Goode. London: Methuen, 1972, 81–167.

Gower, Ronald Sutherland. *My Reminiscences*, 2 vols. London: K. Paul Trench & Co., 1883.

Gower, Ronald Sutherland. *My Reminiscences*, London: Kegan Paul, 1895.

Gower, Ronald Sutherland. *Old Diaries, 1881–1901*. London: John Murray, 1902.

Graham, Wendy. *Henry James's Thwarted Love*. Stanford, CA: Stanford UP, 1999.

Greenwald, Elissa. *Realism and the Romance: Nathaniel Hawthorne, Henry James and American Fiction*. Ann Arbor, MI: UMI Research, 1989.

Greenwood, Chris. *Adapting to the Stage: Theatre and the Work of Henry James*. Aldershot: Ashgate, 2000.

'The Grosvenor Gallery: A Lay of the Private View', *Punch* 14 May 1881, 218.

Guy, Josephine M. 'Oscar Wilde's "Self-Plagiarism": Some New Manuscript Evidence', *Notes and Queries* 52.4 (2005), 485–8.

Guy, Josephine M. and Ian Small. *Oscar Wilde's Profession: Writing and the Culture Industry in the Late Nineteenth Century*. Oxford: Oxford UP, 2000.

Hadley, Tessa. *Henry James and the Imagination of Pleasure*. Cambridge: Cambridge UP, 2002.

Hamilton, Lisa. 'Oscar Wilde, New Women, and the Rhetoric of Effeminacy', in *Wilde Writings: Contextual Conditions*, ed. Joseph Bristow. Toronto: U of Toronto P, 2003, 230–53.

Hamilton, Walter. *The Aesthetic Movement in England*, 3rd edn. Folcroft, PA: Folcroft Library Editions, 1973 [1882].

Handlin, David P. *The American Home: Architecture and Society, 1815–1915*. Boston: Little, Brown, 1979.

Hanson, Ellis. 'Knowing Children: Desire and Interpretation in *the Exorcist*', in *Curiouser: On the Queerness of Children*, ed. Steven Bruhm and Natasha Hurley. Minneapolis: U of Minnesota P, 2004, 107–36.

Hanson, Ellis. 'Screwing with Children in Henry James', *GLQ: A Journal of Lesbian and Gay Studies* 9.3 (2003), 367–91.

Haralson, Eric. 'The Elusive Queerness of Henry James's "Queer Comrade": Reading Gabriel Nash of *The Tragic Muse*', in *Victorian Sexual Dissidence*, ed. Richard Dellamora. Chicago: U of Chicago P, 1999, 191–210.

Haralson, Eric. *Henry James and Queer Modernity*. Cambridge: Cambridge UP, 2003.

Haralson, Eric. ' "His Little Heart Dispossessed": Ritual Sexorcism in *The Turn of the Screw*', in *Questioning the Master: Gender and Sexuality in Henry James's Writings*, ed. Peggy McCormack. Newark: U of Delaware P, 2000, 133–48.

Harris, Wendell V. 'Arnold, Pater, Wilde, and the Object as in Themselves They See It', *SEL* 11.4 (1971), 733–47.

Hart-Davis, Rupert (ed.). *Letters to Reggie Turner*. London: Rupert Hart-Davis, 1964.

Hawthorne, Nathaniel. *The Marble Faun*. Everyman's Library. London: J. M. Dent, 1995.

Hayes, Kevin J. (ed.). *Henry James: The Contemporary Reviews*. Cambridge: Cambridge UP, 1996.

The Health Exhibition Literature, vol. 1. London: W. Clowes & Sons, 1884.

Henley, William Ernest. *The Selected Letters of W. E. Henley*, ed. Damian Atkinson. Aldershot: Ashgate, 2000.

Hocks, Richard A. *Henry James: A Study of the Short Fiction*. Boston: Twayne, 1990.

Holland, Merlin. *The Real Trial of Oscar Wilde*. New York: HarperCollins, 2003.

Holland, Merlin. *The Wilde Album*. London: Fourth Estate, 1997.

Holland, Vyvyan. *Son of Oscar Wilde*, ed. Merlin Holland. Oxford: Oxford UP, 1988.

Horne, Philip. *Henry James and Revision: The New York Edition*. Oxford: Clarendon, 1990.

Horne, Philip. 'The Master and the "Queer Affair" of "The Pupil" ', *Critical Quarterly* 37.3 (1995), 75–92.

House Beautiful (December 1896).

Howells, William Dean. 'Editor's Study', *Harper's New Monthly Magazine* 73.436 (September 1886), 639–44.

Howells, William Dean. 'Henry James, Jr', *Century Illustrated Monthly Magazine* 3 (November 1882), 25–29.

Howells, William Dean. 'Introduction', *Daisy Miller*, by Henry James. New York: Harper and Brothers, 1906, vii–xv.

Howells, William Dean. *The Rise of Silas Lapham*. Boston: Houghton, Mifflin, 1884.

Hrebenar, Ronald J. *Interest Group Politics in America*. London: M. E. Sharpe, 1997.

Hughes, Clair. *Henry James and the Art of Dress*. London: Palgrave, 2001.

Hughes, Linda. 'A Female Aesthete at the Helm: *Sylvia's Journal* and "Graham R. Tomson," 1893–1894', *Victorian Periodicals Review* 29.2 (1996), 173–92.

Hyde, H. Montgomery (ed.). *The Three Trials of Oscar Wilde*. New York: University Books, 1956.

'The Importance of Being Earnest', *Illustrated London News* 9 February 1895, 227.

Jackson, Russell. '*The Importance of Being Earnest*', in *The Cambridge Companion to Oscar Wilde*, ed. Peter Raby. Cambridge: Cambridge UP, 1988.

James, Henry. *The Ambassadors*, ed. S. P. Rosenbaum, 1909 edn. New York: Norton, 1964.

James, Henry. *The Art of Criticism: Henry James on the Theory and the Practice of Fiction*, ed. William Veered and Susan M. Griffin. Chicago: U of Chicago P, 1986.

James, Henry. *Collected Travel Writings*, 2 vols. New York: Library of America, 1993.

James, Henry. *The Complete Notebooks of Henry James*, ed. Leon Edel and Lyall H. Powers. Oxford: Oxford UP, 1987.

James, Henry. *The Complete Plays of Henry James*, ed. Leon Edel. London: Rupert Hart-Davis, 1949.

James, Henry. *Complete Stories, 1864–1874*, ed. Jean Strouse, vol. 1. New York: Library of America, 1999.

James, Henry. *Complete Stories, 1874–1884*, ed. William Vance, vol. 2. New York: Library of America, 1999.

James, Henry. *Complete Stories, 1884–1891*, ed. Edward Said, vol. 3. New York: Library of America, 1999.

James, Henry. *Complete Stories, 1892–1898*, ed. John Hollander, David Bromwich and Denis Donoghue, vol. 4. New York: Library of America, 1996.

James, Henry. *Complete Stories, 1898–1910*, ed. John Hollander, David Bromwich and Denis Donoghue, vol. 5. New York: Library of America, 1996.

James, Henry. *Dearly Beloved Friends: Henry James's Letters to Younger

Men, ed. Susan E. Gunter and Steven H. Jobe. Ann Arbor, MI: U of Michigan P, 2001.

James, Henry. 'Du Maurier and London Society', *Century Illustrated Monthly Magazine* May 1883, 48–65.

James, Henry. 'George Du Maurier', *Harper's New Monthly Magazine* September 1897, 594–609.

James, Henry. *Guy Domville*, ts, fMS Am 1237.21. Houghton Library, Harvard University.

James, Henry. *Henry James: A Life in Letters*, ed. Philip Horne. London: Allen Lane, 1999.

James, Henry. *Letters, 1843–1875*, ed. Leon Edel, vol. 1. Cambridge, MA: Harvard UP, 1974.

James, Henry. *Letters, 1875–1883*, ed. Leon Edel, vol. 2. Cambridge, MA: Harvard UP, 1975.

James, Henry. *Letters, 1883–1895*, ed. Leon Edel, vol. 3. Cambridge, MA: Harvard UP, 1980.

James, Henry. *Letters, 1895–1916*, ed. Leon Edel, vol. 4. Cambridge, MA: Harvard UP, 1984.

James, Henry. 'Letter to Mrs Daniel S. Curtis', 3 July [1895]. Ms. Darmouth College Library.

James, Henry. 'Letter to Robert Ross', 18 April 1913. Ts. Leon Edel Papers. McGill University, Montréal.

James, Henry. 'Letter to Robert Ross', 6 August 1912. Ts. Leon Edel Papers. McGill University, Montréal.

James, Henry. 'Letter to T. S. Perry', 7 January [1882]. Microfilm. Duke University.

James, Henry. *Literary Criticism: Essays on Literature, American Writers, English Writers*, ed. Leon Edel and Mark Wilson, vol. 1. New York: Library of America, 1984.

James, Henry. *Literary Criticism: French Writers, Other European Writers, the Prefaces to the New York Edition*, vol. 2. New York: Library of America, 1984.

James, Henry. *Novels, 1871–1880: Watch and Ward, Roderick Hudson, The American, The Europeans, Confidence*, ed. William T. Stafford, vol. 1. New York: Library of America, 1983.

James, Henry. *Novels, 1881–1886: Washington Square, The Portrait of a Lady, The Bostonians*, ed. William T. Stafford, vol. 2. New York: Library of America, 1985.

James, Henry. *Novels, 1886–1890: The Princess Casamassima, The Reverberator, The Tragic Muse*, ed. Daniel Mark Fogel, vol. 3. New York: Library of America, 1989.

James, Henry. *Novels, 1896–1899: The Other House, The Spoils of Poynton, What Maisie Knew, The Awkward Age*, ed. Myra Jehlen, vol. 4. New York: Library of America, 2003.

James, Henry. *The Painter's Eye: Notes and Essays on the Pictorial Arts*, ed. John L. Sweeney. London: Rupert Hart-Davis, 1956.

James, Henry. *Picture and Text*. New York: Harper and Brothers, 1893.

James, Henry. *Selected Letters*, ed. Leon Edel. Cambridge, MA: Harvard UP, 1987.

James, Henry. *Selected Letters of Henry James to Edmund Gosse, 1882–1915: A Literary Friendship*, ed. Rayburn S. Moore. Baton Rouge: Louisiana State UP, 1988.

James, Henry. *The Tragic Muse*, ed. Philip Horne. London: Penguin, 1995.

James, Henry. *The Turn of the Screw and Other Stories*, ed. T. J. Lustig. Oxford: Oxford UP, 1998.

James, Henry, and Elizabeth Robins. *Theatre and Friendship: Some Henry James Letters*. London: J. Cape, 1932.

James, William. *The Correspondence of William James*, ed. Ignas K. Skrupskelis and Elizabeth M. Berkeley, 10 vols. Charlottesville: U of Virginia P, 1993.

Jullian, Philippe. *Oscar Wilde*. London: Constable, 1969.

Kaplan, Fred. *Henry James: The Imagination of Genius*. New York: William Morrow, 1992.

Kaplan, Joel H., and Sheila Stowell. *Theatre and Fashion: Oscar Wilde to the Suffragettes*. Cambridge: Cambridge UP, 1994.

Kaye, Richard A. *The Flirt's Tragedy: Desire Without End in Victorian and Edwardian Fiction*. Charlottesville: U of Virginia P, 2002.

Kelly, Richard. *The Art of George Du Maurier*. Aldershot, Hampshire: Scolar Press, 1996.

Kincaid, James R. *Child-Loving: The Erotic Child and Victorian Culture*. New York: Routledge, 1992.

Kincaid, James R. *Erotic Innocence: The Culture of Child Molesting*. Durham, NC: Duke UP, 1998.

Knowles, Ronald. ' "The Hideous Obscure": "The Turn of the Screw" and Oscar Wilde', in *The Turn of the Screw and What Maisie Knew*, ed. Neill Cornwell and Maggie Malone. Basingstoke: Macmillan, 1998, 164–78.

Laird, J. T. 'Cracks in Precious Objects: Aestheticism and Humanity in *The Portrait of a Lady*', *American Literature* 52.4 (1981), 643–8.

Lambert, Angela. *Unquiet Souls: The Indian Summer of the British Aristocracy, 1880–1918*. London: Macmillan, 1984.

Lambourne, Lionel. *The Aesthetic Movement*. London: Phaidon, 1996.

Landau, John. *'A Thing Divided': Representation in the Late Novels of Henry James*. Madison, NJ: Fairleigh Dickinson UP, 1996.

Landow, George P. 'Ruskin's Version of Ut Pictura Poesis', *Journal of Aesthetics and Art Criticism* 26 (1968), 521–8.

Lane, Christopher. *The Burdens of Intimacy: Psychoanalysis and Victorian Masculinity*. Chicago: U of Chicago P, 1999.

Lane, Christopher. 'Framing Fears, Reading Designs: The Homosexual Art of Painting in James, Wilde and Beerbohm', *ELH* 61.4 (1994), 923–54.

Lane, Christopher. 'Jamesian Inscrutability', *Henry James Review* 20.3 (1999), 244–54.

Larminie, William. *Fand and Other Poems*. Dublin: Hodges, Figgis & Co., 1892.

Ledger, Sally, and Roger Luckhurst (eds). *The Fin-De-Siècle: A Reader in Cultural History, C. 1880–1900*. Oxford: Oxford UP, 2000.

Lee, Rensselaer W. *Ut Pictura Poesis: The Humanistic Theory of Painting*. New York: Norton, 1967.

Lee, Vernon (Violet Paget). *Vanitas: Polite Stories*. Lovell's International Series. New York: Lovell, Coryell & Co, 1892.

Lesjak, Carolyn. 'Utopia, Use, and the Everyday: Oscar Wilde and a New Economy of Pleasure', *ELH* 67.1 (2000), 179–204.

Lewis, Lloyd, and Henry Justin Smith. *Oscar Wilde Discovers America, 1882*. New York: Harcourt, Brace and Company, 1936.

Lillie, Lucy. *Prudence: A Story of Aesthetic London*. New York: Harper & Brothers, 1882.

Litvak, Joseph. *Caught in the Act: Theatricality in the Nineteenth-Century English Novel*. Berkeley: U of California P, 1992.

Lodge, David. 'Introduction', *The Spoils of Poynton*, by Henry James. London: Penguin, 1987, 1–18.

Lubbock, Percy. *The Craft of Fiction*. London: J. Cape, 1921.

Lucas, John. 'Washington Square', in *The Air of Reality: New Essays on Henry James*, ed. John Goode. London: Methuen, 1972, 36–59.

Lyotard, Jean-François. *The Postmodern Condition: A Report on Knowledge*. Minneapolis: U of Minnesota P, 1984.

'The Macaulayflower Papers', *Life* 4 January 1883, 16.

Maltz, Diana. *British Aestheticism and the Urban Working Classes, 1870–1900: Beauty for the People*. Basingstoke: Palgrave, 2006.

Mao, Douglas. *Solid Objects: Modernism and the Test of Production*. Princeton, NJ: Princeton UP, 1998.

Marez, Curtis. 'The Other Addict: Reflections on Colonialism and Oscar Wilde's Opium Smoke Screen', *ELH* 64.1 (1997), 257–87.

Matheson, Neil. 'Talking Horrors: Henry James, Euphemism, and the Specter of Wilde', *American Literature* 71.4 (1999), 709–50.

Matz, Jesse. *Literary Impressionism and Modernist Aesthetics*. Cambridge: Cambridge UP, 2001.

'Maudle on the Choice of a Profession', *Punch* 12 February 1881, 62.

McDiarmid, Lucy. 'Oscar Wilde's Speech from the Dock', *Textual Practice* 15.3 (2001), 447–66.

McWhirter, David (ed.). *Henry James's New York Edition: The Construction of Authorship*. Stanford, CA: Stanford UP, 1995.

Mendelssohn, Michèle. 'Homosociality and the Aesthetic in Henry

James's *Roderick Hudson'*, *Nineteenth-Century Literature* 57.4 (2003), 512–41.

Mendelssohn, Michèle. ' "I'm Not a Bit Expensive": Henry James and the Sexualization of the Victorian Girl', in *Small Change: Nineteenth-Century Childhood and the Rise of Consumer Culture*, ed. Dennis Denisoff. Aldershot: Ashgate, forthcoming.

Merrill, Linda. *A Pot of Paint: Aesthetics on Trial in Whistler v. Ruskin*. Washington: Smithsonian Inst., 1992.

Mikhail, E. H. *Oscar Wilde: An Annotated Bibliography of Criticism*. Totowa, NJ: Rowman and Littlefield, 1978.

Mikhail, E. H. *Oscar Wilde: Interviews and Recollections*, 2 vols. London: Routledge, 1970.

Millard, Christopher (Stuart Mason). *Oscar Wilde and the Aesthetic Movement*. Dublin: Townley Searle, 1920.

Miller, J. Hillis. *Literature as Conduct: Speech Acts in Henry James*. New York: Fordham UP, 2005.

Milman, Lena. 'A Few Notes Upon Mr James', *The Yellow Book* October 1895, 71–83.

Mitchell, W. J. T., 'Ekphrasis and the Other', *South Atlantic Quarterly* 91.3 (1992).

'Mrs Oscar Wilde at Home', *To-day* 24 November 1894, 93–4.

Mix, Katherine Lyon. *A Study in Yellow: The Yellow Book and Its Contributors*. Lawrence: U of Kansas P, 1960.

'Modern Aesthetics', *Punch* 10 February 1877, 77.

Monk, Leland. 'A Terrible Beauty Is Born: Henry James, Aestheticism, and Homosexual Panic', *Genders* 23 (1996), 247–65.

Monteiro, George. 'A Contemporary View of Henry James and Oscar Wilde, 1882', *American Literature* 35.4 (1964), 528–30.

Monteiro, George. *Henry James and John Hay: The Record of a Friendship*. Providence: Brown UP, 1965.

Moon, Michael. *A Small Boy and Others: Imitation and Initiation in American Culture from Henry James to Andy Warhol*. Durham: Duke UP, 1998.

Moore, Rayburn S. (ed.). *Selected Letters of Henry James to Edmund Gosse, 1882–1915: A Literary Friendship*. Baton Rouge: Louisiana State UP, 1988.

Munby, A. N. L. 'Oscar Wilde', *Sale Catalogues of Libraries of Eminent Persons*, vol. 1. London: Mansell Publishing, 1971, 371–88.

Munhall, Edgar. *Whistler and Montesquiou: The Butterfly and the Bat*. Paris: Flammarion, 1995.

'The Mutual Admirationists', *Punch* 22 May 1880, 234.

'Nincompoopiana', *Punch* 27 November 1880, 243.

'Nincompoopiana', *Punch* 13 December 1880, 147.

'Nincompoopiana – the Mutual Admiration Society', *Punch* 14 February 1880, 66.

Nixon, Nicola. 'The "Reading Gaol" of Henry James's "In the Cage" ', *ELH* 66.1 (1999), 179–201.

Nordau, Max. *Degeneration*, trans. from 2nd edn. New York: D. Appleton and Co., 1895.

Nordau, Max. *Degeneration*, intro. George L. Mosse. Lincoln: U of Nebraska P, 1993.

Norton, Rictor. *Mother Clap's Molly House: The Gay Subculture in England 1700–1830*. London: Gay Men's Press, 1992.

Nunokawa, Jeff. *Tame Passions of Wilde: The Styles of Manageable Desire*. Princeton: Princeton UP, 2003.

O'Brien, Kevin. '*The House Beautiful*: A Reconstruction of Oscar Wilde's American Lecture', *Victorian Studies* 17.4 (1974), 395–418.

Ohi, Kevin. 'The Author of "Beltraffio": The Exquisite Boy and Henry James's Equivocal Aestheticism', *ELH* 72.3 (2005), 747–67.

Ohi, Kevin. *Innocence and Rapture: The Erotic Child in Pater, Wilde, James, and Nabokov*. New York: Palgrave, 2005.

Ojala, Aatos. *Aestheticism and Oscar Wilde*. Helsinki: Finnish Academy of Sciences and Letters, 1954.

Ormond, Leonée. *George Du Maurier*. Pittsburgh: U of Pittsburgh P, 1969.

Orvell, Miles. *The Real Thing: Imitation and Authenticity in American Culture, 1880–1940*. Chapel Hill: U of North Carolina P, 1989.

O'Sullivan, Vincent. *Aspects of Wilde*. London: Constable, 1936.

Otten, Thomas J. '*The Spoils of Poynton* and the Properties of Touch', *American Literature* 71.2 (1999), 263–90.

Ozick, Cynthia. *Metaphor & Memory: Essays*. New York: Knopf, 1989.

Painter, Nell Irvin. 'Ut Pictura Poesis; or the Sisterhood of the Verbal and Visual Arts', in *Writing Biography: Historians and Their Craft*, ed. Lloyd E. Ambrosius. Lincoln: U of Nebraska P, 2004, 103–32.

Parkes, Adam. 'Collaborations: Henry James and the Poet-Critics', *Henry James Review* 23.3 (2002), 283–93.

Pater, Walter. *Appreciations, with an Essay on Style*. London: Macmillan, 1898.

Pater, Walter. *The Renaissance*. ed. Adam Phillips, 4th edn. New York: Oxford UP, 1986.

Pater, Walter. *The Renaissance: Studies in Art and Poetry: The 1893 Text*, ed. Donald L. Hill. Berkeley: U of California P, 1980.

Pennell, Elizabeth and Joseph Pennell. *The Life of James McNeill Whistler*, 5th edn. Philadelphia: J. B. Lippincott, 1911.

Phillips, Adam. *On Flirtation*. London: Faber & Faber, 1994.

'Picture by Our Own Yellow-Booky Daubaway Weirdsley, Intended as a Puzzle Picture to Preface of Juvenile Poems, or as Nothing in Particular', *Punch* 2 February 1895, 58.

Poole, Adrian. *Henry James*. London: Harvester, 1991.

'Postlethwaite on Refraction', *Punch* 15 January 1881, 14.

Powell, Kerry. 'Hawthorne, Arlo Bates, and Dorian Gray', *Papers on Language and Literature* 16 (1980), 403–16.

Powell, Kerry. 'Tom, Dick, and Dorian Gray: Magic-Picture Mania in Late Victorian Fiction', *Philological Quarterly* 62.2 (1983), 147–70.

Powers, Lyall H. (ed.). *Henry James and Edith Wharton: Letters, 1900–1915.* New York: Scribner's, 1990.

Powers, Lyall H. 'James's *The Tragic Muse* – Ave Atque Vale', in *Henry James: Modern Judgements*, ed. Tony Tanner. London: Macmillan, 1968, 194–203.

Powers, Lyall H. 'Mr. James's Aesthetic Mr. Nash–Again', *Nineteenth-Century Fiction* 13.4 (1959), 341–49.

Praz, Mario. *An Illustrated History of Interior Decoration: From Pompeii to Art Nouveau.* London: Thames and Hudson, 1982.

'The Private View', *World* Christmas Issue 1882.

Psomiades, Kathy Alexis. *Beauty's Body: Femininity and Representation in British Aestheticism.* Stanford: Stanford UP, 1997.

Raby, Peter (ed.). *The Cambridge Companion to Oscar Wilde.* New York: Cambridge UP, 1997.

Rawlings, Peter. 'Pater, Wilde, and James: "The Reader's Share of the Task"', *Studies in English Language & Literature* 48 (1998), 45–64.

Reed, John Robert. *Decadent Style.* Athens, Ohio: Ohio UP, 1985.

Richards, Bernard. 'Clouds and Poynton', *Times Literary Supplement* December 17 1993, 15.

Richards, Bernard. 'Introduction', *The Spoils of Poynton*, by Henry James, ed. Bernard Richards. Oxford: Oxford UP, 1982, vii–xxvi.

Richards, Bernard. 'James and His Sources: *The Spoils of Poynton*', *Essays in Criticism* 29.4 (1979), 302–23.

Richardson, William King. 'Letter to Roland Lincoln', 18 July 1880. Ts. Houghton Library, Harvard University.

Riquelme, John Paul. 'Oscar Wilde's Aesthetic Gothic: Walter Pater, Dark Enlightenment, and *The Picture of Dorian Gray*', *Modern Fiction Studies* 46.3 (2000), 609–31.

Rodd, Rennell. *Rose-Leaf and Apple-Leaf: L'envoi*, intro. Oscar Wilde. Philadephia: Stoddart, 1882.

Roditi, Edouard. *Oscar Wilde.* Norfolk, CT: New Directions, 1947.

Roosevelt, Theodore. *American Ideals: And Other Essays, Social and Political.* New York: Putnam, 1897.

Rosenbaum, Stanford Patrick. '*The Spoils of Poynton*: Revisions and Editions', *Studies in Bibliography* 19 (1966), 161–74.

Rothenstein, William. *Men and Memories: A History of the Arts 1872 to 1922 Being the Recollections of William Rothenstein.* 1931. Whitefish, MT: Kessinger, 2005.

Rowe, John Carlos. *The Other Henry James.* Durham, NC: Duke UP, 1998.

Rowe, John Carlos. *The Theoretical Dimensions of Henry James*. Madison: U of Wisconsin P, 1984.

Ruskin, John. *The Genius of John Ruskin: Selections from His Writings*, ed. John D. Rosenberg. Charlottesville: U of Virginia P, 1998.

Russell, Bertrand. *The Autobiography of Bertrand Russell*, 3 vols. London: Allen & Unwin, 1967.

Russell, John Francis Stanley. *My Life and Adventures*. London: Cassell, 1923.

'The Russell Matrimonial Suit', *Morning Post* [London] 24 April 1895, 2.

Saint-Amour, Paul K. *The Copywrights: Intellectual Property and the Literary Imagination*. Ithaca: Cornell UP, 2003.

Saint-Amour, Paul K. 'Oscar Wilde: Orality, Literary Property, and Crimes of Writing', *Nineteenth-Century Literature* 55.1 (2000), 59–91.

Salamensky, Shelley. 'Henry James, Oscar Wilde and "Fin-De-Siècle Talk": A Brief Reading', *Henry James Review* 20.3 (1999), 275–81.

Salmon, Richard. *Henry James and the Culture of Publicity*. Cambridge: Cambridge UP, 1997.

Sammells, Neil. *Wilde Style: The Plays and Prose of Oscar Wilde*. New York: Longman, 2000.

Samuels, Ernest. *Henry Adams: The Middle Years*. Cambridge, MA: Harvard UP, 1958.

San Juan, Epifanio, Jr. *The Art of Oscar Wilde*. Princeton: Princeton UP, 1967.

Savoy, Eric. ' "In the Cage" and the Queer Effects of Gay History', *Novel* 28.3 (1995), 284–307.

Savoy, Eric. 'The Jamesian Thing', *Henry James Review* 22 (2001), 268–77.

Schaffer, Talia. *The Forgotten Female Aesthetes: Literary Culture in Later-Victorian England*. Charlottesville: U of Virginia P, 2000.

Schaffer, Talia, and Kathy Alexis Psomiades. *Women and British Aestheticism*. Charlottesville: U of Virginia P, 1999.

Sedgwick, Eve Kosofsky. *Between Men: English Literature and Male Homosocial Desire*. New York: Columbia UP, 1985.

Sedgwick, Eve Kosofsky. *Epistemology of the Closet*. Berkeley: U of California P, 1990.

Sedgwick, Eve Kosofsky. 'Shame and Performativity: Henry James's New York Edition Prefaces', in *Henry James's New York Edition: The Construction of Authorship*, ed. David McWhirter. Stanford, CA: Stanford UP, 1995, 206–39.

Sedgwick, Eve Kosofsky. *Touching Feeling: Affect, Pedagogy, Performativity*. Durham, NC: Duke UP, 2004.

Seltzer, Mark. *Henry James and the Art of Power*. Ithaca: Cornell UP, 1984.

Shand-Tucci, Douglass. *The Art of Scandal: The Life and Times of Isabella Stewart Gardner*. New York: Harper Collins, 1997.

Sherard, Robert Harborough. *The Life of Oscar Wilde*. New York: Mitchell Kennerley, 1906.

Shewan, Rodney. *Oscar Wilde: Art and Egotism*. London: Macmillan, 1977.

Shuter, William. *Rereading Walter Pater*. Cambridge: Cambridge UP, 1997.

Siegel, Sandra. 'Caricature, Wilde, "Cartomania" ', *The Center and Clark Newsletter* 32 (1998), 4–5.

Simmel, Georg. 'Flirtation', in *Georg Simmel on Women, Sexuality, and Love*, ed. Guy Oakes. New Haven: Yale UP, 1984, 133–52.

Sinfield, Alan. *The Wilde Century: Effeminacy, Oscar Wilde and the Queer Moment*. New York: Columbia UP, 1994.

The Sins of the Cities of the Plain, or Confessions of a Mary-Ann. New York: Masquerade, 1881.

Sontag, Susan. *Against Interpretation and Other Essays*. New York: Farrar, Straus & Giroux, 1966.

Spielmann, M. H. *The History of 'Punch'*. London: Cassell & Co., 1895.

St James's Gazette 5 April 1895, 3.

'Staircase Scenes. – No. 1. The Private View, Royal Academy', *Punch* 30 April 1892, 215.

Stambaugh, Sara. 'The Aesthetic Movement and *The Portrait of a Lady*', *Nineteenth-Century Fiction* 30.4 (1976), 495–510.

Stein, Roger B. 'Artifact as Ideology: The Aesthetic Movement in Its American Cultural Context', in *In Pursuit of Beauty: Americans and the Aesthetic Movement*, ed. Doreen Bolger Burke. New York: Rizzoli, 1986, 23–51.

Stephen, Leslie (ed.). *Dictionary of National Biography*. London: Oxford UP, 1885–1900.

Stevens, Hugh. *Henry James and Sexuality*. New York: Cambridge UP, 1998.

Stewart, Garrett. 'Reading Figures: The Legible Image of Victorian Textuality', in *Victorian Literature and the Victorian Visual Imagination*, ed. Carol T. Christ. Berkeley: U of California P, 1995, 345–68.

Sutton, Denys. *Nocturne: The Art of James McNeill Whistler*. Philadelphia: J. B. Lippincott, 1964.

Taylor, Andrew. *Henry James and the Father Question*. Cambridge: Cambridge UP, 2002.

Thomas, Lately. *Sam Ward: 'King of the Lobby'*. Boston: Houghton, Mifflin Co., 1965.

Tintner, Adeline. *Henry James's Legacy: The Afterlife of His Figure and Fiction*. Baton Rouge: Louisiana State UP, 1998.

Tintner, Adeline. ' "The Old Things": Balzac's *Le Curé De Tours* and James's *The Spoils of Poynton*', *Nineteenth-Century Fiction* 26 (1972), 436–55.

Tintner, Adeline. 'Rudyard Kipling and Wolcott Balestier's Literary Collaboration: A Possible Source for James's "Collaboration" ', *Henry James Review* 4.2 (1983), 140–3.

Tóibín, Colm. 'Love in a Dark Time (Review of *The Complete Letters of Oscar Wilde*)', *London Review of Books* (19 April 2001), 11–17.

Tóibín, Colm. *Love in a Dark Time: Gay Lives from Wilde to Almodovar*. London: Picador, 2002.

Trask, Michael. 'Getting into It with James: Substitution and Erotic Reversal in *The Awkward Age*', *American Literature* 69 (1997), 105–38.

Trilling, Lionel. *Sincerity and Authenticity*. Cambridge, MA: Harvard UP, 1972.

Twain, Mark. 'Life on the Mississippi', in *Mississippi Writings*. New York: Library of America, 1982, 217–617.

Tydeman, William, and Steven Price. *Wilde: Salome*. Plays in Production. Cambridge: Cambridge UP, 1996.

Veeder, William R. *Henry James: The Lessons of the Master: Popular Fiction and Personal Style in the Nineteenth Century*. Chicago: U of Chicago P, 1975.

Vicinus, Martha. 'The Adolescent Boy: Fin-De-Siècle Femme Fatale?', in *Victorian Sexual Dissidence*, ed. Richard Dellamora. Chicago: U of Chicago P, 1999, 83–108.

Wadsworth, Sarah A. 'Innocence Abroad: Henry James and the Re-Inventions of the American Woman Abroad', *Henry James Review* 22.2 (2001), 107–27.

Waldrep, Shelton. 'The Uses and Misuses of Oscar Wilde', in *Victorian Afterlife: Postmodern Culture Rewrites the Nineteenth Century*, ed. John Kucich and Dianne F. Sadoff. Minneapolis: U of Minnesota P, 2000, 49–63.

Walker, Pierre A. *Reading Henry James in French Cultural Contexts*. DeKalb: North Illinois UP, 1995.

Ward, Samuel. 'Letter to Oscar Wilde', 9 January 1882. Ms. William Andrews Clark Memorial Library.

Weeks, Jeffrey. 'Inverts, Perverts, and Mary-Annes: Male Prostitution and the Regulation of Homosexuality in England in the Nineteenth and Early Twentieth Centuries', in *Hidden from History: Reclaiming the Gay and Lesbian Past*, ed. Martin Duberman. New York: Meridian, 1989, 195–211.

Weintraub, Stanley. *Whistler: A Biography*. New York: Weybright and Talley, 1974.

Weir, David. *Decadence and the Making of Modernism*. Amherst: U of Massachusetts P, 1995.

Weisbuch, Robert. 'Henry James and the Idea of Evil', in *The Cambridge Companion to Henry James*, ed. Jonathan Freedman. Cambridge: Cambridge UP, 1998, 102–19.

Whistler, James McNeill. *The Gentle Art of Making Enemies*, intro. by Alfred Werner. New York: Dover, 1967.

Wilde, Constance. 'How to Decorate a House', *Young Woman: an Illustrated Monthly Magazine* (London) 1895, 132.

Wilde, Oscar. *Aristotle at Afternoon Tea: The Rare Oscar Wilde*, ed. John Wyse Jackson. London: Fourth Estate, 1991.

Wilde, Oscar. *The Artist as Critic: Critical Writings of Oscar Wilde*, ed. Richard Ellmann. Chicago: U of Chicago P, 1982.

Wilde, Oscar. *Collins Complete Works of Oscar Wilde*. Glasgow: HarperCollins, 1999.

Wilde, Oscar. *The Complete Letters of Oscar Wilde*, ed. Merlin Holland and Rupert Hart-Davis. London: Fourth Estate, 2000.

Wilde, Oscar. *De Profundis, 'Epistola; in Carcere Et in Vinculis'*, in *The Complete Works of Oscar Wilde*, ed. Ian Small, vol. 2. Oxford: Oxford UP, 2005.

Wilde, Oscar. 'The Grosvenor Gallery', *Dublin University Magazine* July 1877, 118–26.

Wilde, Oscar. *The Importance of Being Earnest and Other Plays*, ed. Peter Raby. Oxford: Oxford UP, 1995.

Wilde, Oscar. *The Picture of Dorian Gray: The 1890 and 1891 Texts*, ed. Joseph Bristow. Oxford: Oxford UP, 2005.

Wilde, Oscar. *Selected Journalism*, ed. Anya Clayworth. Oxford: Oxford UP, 2004.

Wilde, Oscar. *Teleny: Or, the Reverse of the Medal, a Physiological Romance; a Novel Attributed to Oscar Wilde*, ed. Winston Leyland. San Francisco: Gay Sunshine Press, 1984.

'The Wilde Case', *Morning* [London] 25 April 1895, 2.

Wilkinson, Louis Umfreville. 'The Better End: Conclusion of a Chapter from the Unpublished Novel, *What Percy Knew*, by H*nr* J*m*s', in *Pages Passed from Hand to Hand: The Hidden Tradition of Homosexual Literature in English from 1748 to 1914*, ed. Mark Mitchell and David Leavitt. New York: Houghton, 1997, 389–91.

Wilson, Edmund. *The Triple Thinkers & the Wound and the Bow*. Boston: Northeastern UP, 1976.

INDEX